Software Development with C++:
Maximizing Reuse with Object Technology

Kjell Nielsen

AP Professional

Boston San Diego New York
London Sydney Tokyo Toronto

This book is printed on acid-free paper. ∞

Copyright © 1995 by Academic Press, Inc.
All rights reserved.
No part of this publication may be reproduced or
transmitted in any form or by any means, electronic
or mechanical, including photocopy, recording, or
any information storage and retrieval system, without
permission in writing from the publisher.

All brand names and product names mentioned in this book
are trademarks or registered trademarks of their respective companies.

AP PROFESSIONAL
955 Massachusetts Avenue, Cambridge, MA 02139

An Imprint of ACADEMIC PRESS, INC.
A Division of HARCOURT BRACE & COMPANY

United Kingdom Edition published by
ACADEMIC PRESS LIMITED
24–28 Oval Road, London NW1 7DX

ISBN 0-12-518420-4

Printed in the United States of America
94 95 96 97 IP 9 8 7 6 5 4 3 2 1

Software Development with C++:
Maximizing Reuse with Object Technology

To Vicki

Contents

Preface xxi

Part I The Software Development Process 1

1 Introduction 3

1.1 Why Do We Need a Development Process? 3
1.2 Why Switch to Object-Oriented Techniques? 6
1.3 Current Practices 7

2 Steps in the Development Process 11

2.1 Overview of the Development Process 12
2.2 Domain Analysis 14
2.3 System Requirements Analysis 14
2.4 System Design 15
2.5 Software Requirements Analysis 16
2.6 Software Design 16
    2.6.1 Process Structuring 18
    2.6.2 Object-Oriented Design 19
    2.6.3 Software Design Evaluation 19
2.7 Implementation 20
2.8 Summary 20

3 Development Process versus Methods 23

- 3.1 Methods That Support the Development Steps 23
- 3.2 Traditional Methods versus Object-Oriented Methods 28
  - 3.2.1 Why Introduce Object-Oriented Methods? 28
  - 3.2.2 Comparing Structured and Object-Oriented Methods 29
  - 3.2.3 Comparing Structured and Object-Oriented Programming 30
  - 3.2.4 Effect of OT Methods on the Steps of the Process 32
- 3.3 Notation 33
- 3.4 Language Dependence 34
- 3.5 Summary 34

Part II Object Technology 37

4 Object-Oriented Paradigms 39

- 4.1 Classes and Objects 40
- 4.2 Encapsulation and Information Hiding 41
- 4.3 Data Abstraction 43
- 4.4 Responsibilities 45
- 4.5 Collaborations and Message Passing 45
- 4.6 Inheritance 46
- 4.7 Polymorphism 48
- 4.8 Binding 50
- 4.9 Modularity 51
- 4.10 Genericity 52

5 Classes and Objects 55

- 5.1 Definitions 55
  - 5.1.1 Objects 55
  - 5.1.2 Classes 59
  - 5.1.3 Roles of Classes and Objects in OOA and OOD 60

Contents ix

    5.2   Creating Classes   60
             5.2.1   Class Categories   61
             5.2.2   Operations Categories   62
    5.3   Inheritance and Class Hierarchies   63
    5.4   Aggregation   64
    5.5   Association   67
    5.6   Using   69
    5.7   Mixin Classes   70
    5.8   Container Classes   70
    5.9   Metaclasses   70
    5.10   Reusability Issues   71

6   Object-Oriented Analysis and Design Models   73
    6.1   Object-Oriented Models   74
    6.2   Static Models   75
    6.3   Dynamic Models   78
    6.4   System Design Models   82
    6.5   Concurrency Models   83
    6.6   Functional Models   85
    6.7   Summary   85

7   Object-Oriented Methods   87
    7.1 Object Modeling Technique (OMT)   87
             7.1.1   OOA   89
             7.1.2   System Design   90
             7.1.3   OOD   92
             7.1.4   Real-Time Aspects and Concurrency   93
             7.1.5   CASE Tools   93
    7.2   Object-Oriented Software Engineering (OOSE)   93
             7.2.1   OOA   94
             7.2.2   System Design   98
             7.2.3   OOD   99
             7.2.4   Real-Time Aspects and Concurrency   102

        7.2.5   CASE Tools   103
  7.3   Booch'93   104
        7.3.1   OOA/OOD   104
        7.3.2   System Design   108
        7.3.3   Real-Time Aspects and Concurrency   109
        7.3.4   CASE Tools   110
  7.4   Shlaer-Mellor   110
        7.4.1   OOA   111
        7.4.2   System Design   113
        7.4.3   OOD   113
        7.4.4   Recursive Design   118
        7.4.5   Real-Time Aspects and Concurrency   119
        7.4.6   CASE Tools   119
  7.5   RDD and CRCs   119
        7.5.1   OOA   119
        7.5.2   OOD   121
        7.5.3   System Design   121
  7.6   Coad-Yourdon   122
        7.6.1   OOA   122
        7.6.2   System Design   126
        7.6.3   OOD   126
        7.6.4   Real-Time Aspects and Concurrency   128
        7.6.5   CASE Tools   129
  7.7   Other Methods   129
  7.8   Summary   129

8 **Using Object-Oriented Methods**   131
  8.1   Benefits of Object-Oriented Methods   132
  8.2   Potential Problems with Object-Oriented Methods   132
        8.2.1   Problem Areas   133
        8.2.2   Risk Areas   134
  8.3   When to Use Object-Oriented Methods   135
  8.4   Mixing Object-Oriented and Structured Methods   136

Contents

- 8.5 Selecting the "Right" Method   137
  - 8.5.1 Evaluation Criteria   138
  - 8.5.2 Picking OT Methods   139
  - 8.5.3 Rule-Based Development   140
- 8.6 Recommended Modeling Approach   141
  - 8.6.1 System Model   141
  - 8.6.2 Scenario-Driven Approach   141
  - 8.6.3 Static Models   144
  - 8.6.4 Dynamic Models   146
  - 8.6.5 Subsystem Model   150
  - 8.6.6 Concurrency Model   151
  - 8.6.7 Functional Models   153
  - 8.6.8 Notation   154
- 8.7 Identifying Real-World Classes and Objects   156
  - 8.7.1 Classes and Objects Based on Functionality   156
  - 8.7.2 Classes and Objects Based on Scenarios   157
- 8.8 Transitioning from Structured to OT Methods   158
- 8.9 Effect on Steps in the Development Process   159
  - 8.9.1 Large Systems   159
  - 8.9.2 Medium-Size Systems   159
  - 8.9.3 Small Systems   160
- 8.10 Summary   161

Part III Using OT in the Software Development Process   163

9 Domain Analysis   165

- 9.1 Understanding the Problem Domain   167
- 9.2 Capturing Existing Expertise and Software   168
- 9.3 Creating Real-World Classes and Objects   170
  - 9.3.1 Classification   170
  - 9.3.2 Finding Classes and Objects   171
  - 9.3.3 Class/Object Descriptions   172

	9.4	Evaluation of Objects 173
	9.5	Work Products 174
	9.6	Risk Areas 176
10	**System Requirements Analysis 179**	
	10.1	Using Scenarios 180
		10.1.1 What Is a Scenario? 180
		10.1.2 Properties of Scenarios 181
		10.1.3 Finding Scenarios 183
		10.1.4 Documenting Scenarios 185
		10.1.5 Scenario-Driven Design 188
	10.2	Object-Oriented Analysis 190
		10.2.1 Object Classification 191
		10.2.2 Object-Oriented Analysis Methods 192
	10.3	The Analysis Model 193
		10.3.1 Interface Objects 194
		10.3.2 Entity Objects 195
		10.3.3 Control Objects 196
		10.3.4 Combining the Analysis Objects 197
		10.3.5 Stopping Criteria 198
		10.3.6 Subsystems 198
	10.4	Heuristics for Creating Analysis Objects 199
		10.4.1 Identifying Analysis Objects 200
		10.4.2 Selecting Classes 201
		10.4.3 Evaluation of Analysis Objects 202
	10.5	Refinements of Builds and Prototypes 202
	10.6	Risk Areas 204
		10.6.1 OOA Methods versus a Development Process 204
		10.6.2 Training 204
		10.6.3 Notation 205
		10.6.4 Analysis versus Design 206
		10.6.5 First Large Project Using OOA 206
	10.7	Work Products 207

11 System Design 209

- 11.1 Partitioning 210
  - 11.1.1 Views 210
  - 11.1.2 Partitions 211
  - 11.1.3 Partitioning Guidelines 211
    - 11.1.3.1 Subsystem View 212
    - 11.1.3.2 Configuration Item View 215
    - 11.1.3.3 Product Line View 216
  - 11.1.4 Work Products of Partitioning 216
    - 11.1.4.1 Architecture Interconnect Specification 218
    - 11.1.4.2 Architecture Module Specification 218
    - 11.1.4.3 Architecture Dictionary 218
    - 11.1.4.4 System Design Document 219
    - 11.1.4.5 Message Description Document 220
- 11.2 Configuring 221
  - 11.2.1 Functional Allocation 221
  - 11.2.2 Using Structured Methods 222
  - 11.2.3 Hardware Architecture 227
  - 11.2.4 Work Products of Configuring 229
  - 11.2.5 Subsystems and Object-Oriented Methods 229
  - 11.2.6 Subsystems and the Scenario Driven Approach 230
- 11.3 Summary 231

12 Software Requirements Analysis 233

- 12.1 Models 234
- 12.2 Object-Oriented Analysis 239
- 12.3 Creating Scenarios 239
- 12.4 Identifying Classes and Objects 240
- 12.5 Identifying Attributes and Operations 242
- 12.6 Preparing Object Views 243
- 12.7 Data Modeling 244
- 12.8 Class/Object Evaluation 245

12.9	Work Products 245	
12.10	Summary 248	

13 Software Design 249

- 13.1 Transitioning from the Analysis Phase 250
- 13.2 Process Structuring 251
  - 13.2.1 Concurrent Elements 255
  - 13.2.2 Process Selection 256
  - 13.2.3 Message Passing 258
  - 13.2.4 Distributed Systems Issues 259
  - 13.2.5 Interprocess Communication (IPC) Mechanisms 260
- 13.3 Object-Oriented Design 262
- 13.4 OOD Products 262
- 13.5 Exception Handling 264
  - 13.5.1 Exception Handling Categories 265
  - 13.5.2 Design Strategy 265
- 13.6 Design Evaluation 266
  - 13.6.1 Design Reviews 266
  - 13.6.2 Process Structure 267
  - 13.6.3 Class Structure 268
  - 13.6.4 Class Interfaces 268
  - 13.6.5 Use of Inheritance 269
  - 13.6.6 Use of Exceptions 270
- 13.7 Summary 271

14 Implementation 273

- 14.1 Transitioning from Design 273
- 14.2 Programming 274
- 14.3 Exception Handling 275
- 14.4 Testing 275
- 14.5 Debugging 276
- 14.6 Summary 277

Contents

Part	IV	Object-Oriented Design for C++ 279

15 Why Use C++? 281
- 15.1 Object-Oriented Languages 281
  - 15.1.1 Object-Orientedness 282
  - 15.1.2 Desired Programming Language Features 282
- 15.2 Benefits of C++ 284
- 15.3 Potential Problems with C++ 285
- 15.4 Summary 286

16 Transitioning from Analysis to Design 287
- 16.1 Design Goals 287
- 16.2 OOA Products 288
- 16.3 OOD Modeling Views 289
- 16.4 Transitioning Rules 289
- 16.5 Reusability Issues 291

17 Designing Classes 293
- 17.1 Class Design 294
  - 17.1.1 Design Decisions 294
  - 17.1.2 Class Construction 296
- 17.2 Class Interfaces 297
- 17.3 Class Architecture 299
  - 17.3.1 Inheritance 299
  - 17.3.2 Aggregation 300
  - 17.3.3 Using 301
- 17.4 Exception Handling 302
  - 17.4.1 Exception Handling Categories 302
  - 17.4.2 Design Strategy 302
  - 17.4.3 Implementation and Performance Issues 303
- 17.5 Class Libraries 303
  - 17.5.1 Design Trade-Offs 304

		17.5.2	Language Features 305
	17.6	Frameworks 306	
	17.7	Evaluation of Class Design 306	
	17.8	Class Management 307	
	17.9	Real-Time Issues 309	

18 C++ Concurrency Support 311

- 18.1 Programming Languages 311
- 18.2 C++ Libraries 314
- 18.3 Summary 315

Part V Object-Oriented Programming with C++ 317

19 Implementing Object-Oriented Features in C++ 319

- 19.1 Transitioning from Design to Programming 319
- 19.2 Types and Classes in C++ 321
- 19.3 Using structs versus Classes 323
- 19.4 Inheritance 326
- 19.5 Aggregation 329
- 19.6 Using Relationship 330
- 19.7 Constructors 331
  - 19.7.1 Ordinary Constructor 332
  - 19.7.2 Default Constructor 333
  - 19.7.3 Initialization Constructor 333
  - 19.7.4 Copy Constructor 335
  - 19.7.5 Assignment Operator 338
  - 19.7.6 Constructor Invocation 340
- 19.8 Destructors 343
- 19.9 Polymorphism 345
- 19.10 Exception Handling 348
- 19.11 Templates 349
- 19.12 Performance Issues 351

Contents

- 19.13 Reusability Issues 351
- 19.14 Summary 352

20 Class Construction in C++ 355
- 20.1 Public 355
- 20.2 Private 357
- 20.3 Protected 357
- 20.4 Friend Functions 359
- 20.5 Friend Classes 361
- 20.6 Virtual Member Functions 363
- 20.7 Abstract Base Classes 365
- 20.8 Static Members 366
- 20.9 Program Organization 368
- 20.10 Summary 370

21 Exception Handling in C++ 371
- 21.1 Declaring Exceptions 372
- 21.2 Raising Exceptions 373
- 21.3 Handling Exceptions 376
- 21.4 Propagation of Exceptions 378
- 21.5 Exception Categories 378
- 21.6 Exception Handling in C++ Libraries 381
- 21.7 Summary 382

22 Developing a Windows C++ Library 383
- 22.1 Domain Analysis 383
- 22.2 System Design 385
- 22.3 Software Requirement Analysis (OOA) 385
  - 22.3.1 Creating Real-World Classes and Objects 386
  - 22.3.2 Client/Server Class Model Using CRC Cards 392
- 22.4 Designing the Interfaces (OOD) 394
- 22.5 Implementing the Classes (OOP) 396
  - 22.5.1 Encapsulations 397

		22.5.2	User Interfaces 399

        22.5.2   User Interfaces   399
        22.5.3   Inheritance Interfaces   400
        22.5.4   File Structure   400

22.6   Summary   401

Appendix A   **Moving from C to C++**   **403**

   A.1   ANSI C and C++   404
        A.1.1   New Keywords   404
        A.1.2   Declaration of Variables   404
        A.1.3   Type Checking   405
   A.2   Function Prototypes   406
   A.3   Function Parameters   406
   A.4   Call-by-Reference Parameters   406
   A.5   Variable Number of Parameters   408
   A.6   Function Overloading and Type Safe Linkage   408
   A.7   The *const* Type Modifier   409
   A.8   Classes and Structs   409
   A.9   I/O Libraries   410
   A.10   Inline Functions   411
   A.11   Functions *new* and *delete*   412
   A.12   Organizational Issues   412
   A.13   Strategy for Adopting C++   413

Appendix B   **C++ Coding Guidelines**   **415**

   B.1   Design of ADTs   415
   B.2   Use of Classes and Structs   416
   B.3   Class Interfaces   417
   B.4   Virtual Functions   418
   B.5   Inheritance   419
   B.6   Public versus Private Derivation   419
   B.7   Dynamic Allocation   419
   B.8   Use of Friends   420
   B.9   Inline Functions   420

Contents

B.10	Mixing C and C++ Functions	420
B.11	Parameter Passing	421
B.12	Use of Macros	422
B.13	Exception Handling	422

Appendix C   Object Technology Glossary   425

References   431

Index   439

Preface

This book is about software development and object-oriented technology (OT for short), with applications implemented in C++. The basis for any software development project of complex systems is the *process*, rather than an individual *method*, which simply supports the overall process. This book is not intended as a general, all-encompassing treatise on OT. The intent is to provide practical information that is directly applicable to a development project. Explicit guidelines are offered for the infusion of OT into the various development phases. This is not a cookbook with a number of recipes ready for all projects. The process steps and methods to be used will differ depending on the size of the project, and a software manager or project leader will adapt the suggested techniques for his or her small, medium, or large development project.

One of the major problems with understanding software development paradigms is that there are a number of methods that differ in their basic approach and appear to reach similar results. Which method do we choose? A related problem is that different paradigms and models may be used in a sequence of development steps or in parallel for a given step. What are the relationships between the paradigms? How do we transition from one phase to the next? Throughout this book we will attempt to provide a rationale for each development step, and explain how the different models, views, and phases relate to each other.

Some of the steps described for the development process, e.g., domain analysis, requirements analysis, and the first parts of the design phase, are language independent and can be used for projects implementing software in C, C++, Ada, Fortran, etc. The emphasis of the software design steps in this book is on an implementation in C++, to take advantage of the potential reuse benefits of an object-oriented programming language. We are not only considering the reuse of C++ code; reusability in-the-large is discussed extensively as it applies to the reuse of the entire process, methods, documentation, class libraries, and, finally, individual coding segments.

The goals of this book are to provide OT background material and specific guidelines for designing and implementing C++ applications:

- describe the overall software development process for complex applications
- describe the fundamental concepts of OT
- discuss and compare OOA/OOD methods
- provide hints for picking the "right" OOA/OOD method(s)
- describe the use of OT in the software development process
- provide guidelines for transitioning from structured to OT methods, and discuss the potential risk
- describe object-oriented design concepts for C++ implementations
- provide guidelines for transitioning from analysis to design
- describe object-oriented programming with C++
- describe C++ class library structures for Microsoft Windows applications
- provide guidelines for moving software development projects from a C environment to C++
- provide a summary of C++ design guidelines

This book is divided into five major parts. Part I describes why we need a development process, the phases and steps of the software process, and how we use individual methods to support this process.

In Part II, we lay the foundation for the concepts included in OT. Some of these concepts, e.g., encapsulation, data hiding, and data abstraction, are not strictly object-oriented paradigms, and may be familiar to developers who have used advanced structured techniques. The object-oriented paradigms of classes and objects are discussed in detail, with particular emphasis on some of the features that may be confusing to OT novices, such as the differences between inheritance hierarchies, aggregation, and association. A description of object-oriented analysis (OOA) and object-oriented design (OOD) is provided, and includes a comparison of the most popular OOA and OOD methods. The number of these methods has escalated over the last few years and poses a major problem for developers who are starting their first project using OT. Part II concludes with a comparison of OT methods and structured methods, and offers guidelines for picking the "right" method(s) for a project using OT.

Part III describes how OT is used in the various phases of the software development process, including the domain analysis, system requirements analysis, system design, software requirements analysis, software design, and implementation. Recommendations are included for an orderly transitioning from structured to OT methods, and for using OT in small, medium, and large projects. This part also includes design evaluations for how OT is implemented on a particular project.

Part IV deals exclusively with design issues for an anticipated C++ implementation. This is the part of the book that is strictly programming language dependent, although examples in the earlier parts use the C++ syntax to illustrate object-oriented concepts. After a short discussion of why we want to use C++ to implement our design, we describe the transitioning phase from the analysis phase to the design phase. Class/object structuring is discussed, with an emphasis on building frameworks and class libraries. Many real-time systems are dependent on parallel processing features for efficient execution, and an outline is provided for the structuring of parallel processes within an application.

Part V is devoted to object-oriented programming with C++. This part starts with a description of how we transition from the design phase to the programming phase. C++ object-oriented features are discussed in detail, and include the use of exception handling and templates. An entire chapter is devoted to the implementation of C++ class interfaces; the most important issue in determining the degree of reusability of C++ code. The concept of exception handling is new to many C/C++ programmers, and details of this topic are included in a separate chapter. Part V concludes with an overview of C++ programming for Microsoft Windows applications. The emphasis here is on the construction of class libraries for Windows domain applications.

Appendix A includes guidelines for moving from projects now using the C programming language to C++ implementations. Appendix B contains a summary of C++ design guidelines. Appendix C provides concise definitions of various OT concepts used throughout the book. A comprehensive list of OT, design, and C++ programming texts is included in the References section.

This book is intended for practicing software developers, software managers, and computer science and software engineering students. Sufficient guidelines are included to aid project leaders in establishing an overall development process for small, medium, and large system applications. For example, a software technical director may decide to pick Jacobson's Object-Oriented Software Engineering (OOSE) approach for the overall process, and augment this with the Object Modeling Technique (OMT) or Booch's method (see Chapter 7). It is especially important to grasp the significance of having an overall process, and the steps included in this process. Equally important is the understanding that an OT method is just a tool that supports the process. Software managers will benefit from understanding the OT process and, in particular, what is different from the traditional structured approach. They will also be able to participate in the decision making of picking a process and the supporting OT methods. C++ developers will benefit greatly by establishing an understanding of the, sometimes subtle, differences between various design decisions, such as when not to use inheritance, and the proper use of *friends* and exception handling.

It is recommended that all readers become familiar with the material in both Parts I and II. Chapter 8 should be of interest to anyone moving from structured design to using an OT approach. The material in Part III assumes a knowledge of the OT methods described in Chapter 7 and expands on the use of OT in the development process. Project leaders should make their adapted approach for a small, medium, or large project from this material; especially from Chapter 8. Parts IV and V should be read by anyone designing and implementing C++ applications. Managers and project leaders planning to move their projects from C to C++ implementations will get a feel for the expected differences by reading Appendix A. Appendix B can be used by project leaders to implement specific design guidelines for their projects. Appendix C can be used by all readers for a quick lookup of OT concepts.

PART I

The Software Development Process

In Part I, we first present a rationale for why we need a development process for producing high quality software products. The term "object-oriented" is used today almost as a synonym for "good" software development. The ramifications of switching from traditional structured methods to object-oriented techniques are discussed in terms of the benefits and risks associated with using the new techniques.

An overview of the individual steps of the development process is provided. The initial step in the system development process is usually the system requirements analysis. We have added another step to the process: domain analysis. The primary purpose of domain analysis is to assess the potential for substantial reuse for the development of large systems, and this analysis should be performed very early in the project life cycle, even during proposal time. The focus of this effort is to determine reusable hardware and software components as well as the potential for reusing entire subsystems.

An unfortunate trend in the use of methods to support a software development process is that the method itself may get such a prominent emphasis that it becomes the process. This is a case of the tail wagging the dog and may prevent an orderly progression of the phases that are required for the creation of high quality software products. The relation between methods and the development process is described. The emphasis is on how the various methods can support the overall process.

The development approach described here is a generalized process that applies to system development, including the allocation of system requirements to hardware and software. We only provide guidelines for software development, however, guidelines for hardware design are not included in this book.

The approach presented applies to the development of small, medium, and large systems. The suggested process is not intended as a "cookbook" approach. The development process should be tailored to fit an individual project, and some of the steps in the process can be omitted for small and medium systems. Specific recommendations for tailoring will be included later in Chapter 8.

1

Introduction

This chapter includes the rationale for why we need a development process, based on the inherent complexity of even small software products. The emphasis throughout this discussion is on the creation of high quality software, and on teams of developers working on separate phases of the development process.

The differences between structured and object-oriented approaches are described, with an emphasis on the advantages of an object-orientation. Current development practices are described with an eye toward organizations that are on the verge of, or are agonizing over whether they should be switching to object-oriented approaches.

1.1 WHY DO WE NEED A DEVELOPMENT PROCESS?

The code segment shown in Figure 1-1 is a portion of a final software product. But what does it represent, and where did it come from? The code segment is a C++ implementation of an abstraction of a "window" entity [DIL92], and can be used in various Microsoft Windows applications. It is highly unlikely that even the brightest programmer could create this code segment in isolation without the benefit of prior analysis and design. A sequence of development steps necessarily preceded the programming task for this code segment. This sequence represents a development process.

```
class WPWin {
private:
  static WPWin* NewWin;  // window being created
  FARPROC oldProc;       // original window proc
  HWND hwnd;             // handle to window
  BOOL deletable;        // FALSE if stack object

  void linkHwnd (HWND newhwnd);
  void unLinkHwnd ();

  friend LRESULT _export FAR PASCAL WPWndProc
                   (HWND, UINT, WPARAM, LPARAM);

protected:
  virtual LONG msgProc (WPEvent &e);

public:
  WPWin (CSTR classnm);  // constructor
  virtual ~WPWin ();     // destructor

  static WINCREATEARGS createArgs;
                  // creation/registration args

  void *operator new (size_t size);
  void operator delete (void *ptr);
  ...
};
```

Figure 1-1. Windows abstraction

The development of software products is an inherently complex task. The complexity manifests itself in the understanding of detailed customer requirements, as well as specific analysis, design, and programming techniques that are necessary to produce a high quality software product.

A software product is approached with completely different viewpoints by its ultimate users and the software developers. The users are interested in desired features and how easy the product will be to use. The developers look at a software product with regard to design and programming techniques, and how efficient the product will be in terms of execution time and the amount of storage required.

Because of the limited capabilities of humans (even the most gifted!) to comprehend a large number of new and complex concepts, an immediate problem arises at the communication level between users and developers. Neither of these two groups fully understands the domain of the other, and some means of communication has to be created to bridge the gap of understanding.

Every software product is created to satisfy the needs of actual or perceived customers. These needs are specified in a system requirements document if a real customer is contracting to have the work done. This document represents the requirements for the new product. If a new software product line is being planned, there are a number of perceived customers who are the potential buyers of the product. In this case, the requirements may be less formally stated, but they exist nevertheless, and should be documented in a system requirements specification just as for a real customer.

Software products can be created by programming directly from loosely formulated requirements specifications. This is referred to as "hacking," and rarely results in high quality software that can form the basis for a product line with reusable components. An extensive analysis of the system requirements and a subsequent design effort should be performed prior to the start of the actual programming effort. The analysis effort will ensure that the product we are about to create will satisfy our customers' needs. The design effort will help in the construction of reusable software entities.

The discussion above implies that any software development effort should consist of at least three steps: analysis, design, and implementation. These three steps represent a development process. This does not imply that the steps are necessarily performed in a strict sequential order. For a large system, there are usually parallel activities happening simultaneously for several smaller portions of the system. The different development teams are dependent on the work produced by the other teams from other phases of the development.

We will note in later chapters that the three suggested steps of analysis, design, and implementation are not sufficient, and other steps that can improve the process will be added, in particular, a domain analysis step (see Chapter 2).

To summarize the discussion above, we need a development process to manage the inherent complexity of producing software. This process is repeatable (i.e., reusable!) and scales up to large projects. Some of the steps included for large systems may be omitted for small and medium systems.

Each phase of the process includes a number of intermediate analysis and design products that ease the communication barrier between users and developers, and between various development teams working on different portions of a large system. The intermediate products include important analysis and design documentation that is used in design reviews.

The steps in the process are also used in tracking the progress and achievement of intermediate goals for large projects.

1.2 WHY SWITCH TO OBJECT-ORIENTED TECHNIQUES?

It used to be that "modular" and "structured" design (we will lump this into "structured techniques" henceforth) and programming techniques were considered "good" and necessary for developing a high quality software product. Over the last few years, however, the term "object-oriented" is being associated with "good" software products, and is used profusely about anything remotely connected to software development. The structured techniques are becoming associated with old-fashioned and less quality-oriented approaches. Many software vendors are marketing their products with the object-oriented label attached, and methods and tools vendors are fiercely competing for our attention with CASE tools supporting specific object-oriented methods.

Many of the claims made for object-oriented products do not satisfy the paradigms and concepts defined in the later chapters. The old cliché of buyer beware still prevails: Even if a product sounds like "object-oriented," it may very well not live up to these claims.

Why is it that so much attention has been focused on object-oriented techniques in the last few years? Are there definite advantages to using these new techniques over the older, well-proven structured approaches? Any time we move to new development techniques there are significant initial costs associated with training, acquisition and licensing of new development tools, and potential organizational changes. These costs must be offset by future benefits of using the new techniques and tools. We would also like to have some measure of the risks associated with the switch regarding potential higher costs and longer schedules.

Some of the benefits of using object-oriented techniques can be summarized as follows:

- *High Degree of Reusability.* Object-oriented entities can be structured with interfaces that permit several applications within the same domain to use the same entities, e.g., C++ class libraries.

- *Better Communication with Our Customers.* "Objects" can describe real-world entities that our customers can readily relate to.
- *Shorter Development Time.* Object-oriented approaches lend themselves to rapid prototyping with concept development that a customer can inspect and approve before the development team heads down a wrong and subsequently expensive track.
- *Ease of Maintenance.* With a close correspondence between user concepts and implemented software entities, requirements changes and extensions can be isolated to a few objects, resulting in reduced coding and testing efforts.

It should be understood at the outset that the benefits of using object-oriented techniques are not automatic. Significant planning, training, and support must be committed to make the perceived benefits come to fruition. This is especially important for the reusability issue, and will be discussed throughout the book.

1.3 CURRENT PRACTICES

Since no one single person can comprehend and create large, complex systems, the total set of requirements defining a system must be broken down into smaller parts. This is usually referred to as *decomposition*. Generally speaking, there are two primary methods used to decompose large systems: functional decomposition and object-oriented decomposition.

Functional decomposition is also referred to as procedural or algorithmic decomposition. The primary objective of this type of decomposition is to create hierarchical layers of functions that can be broken down to a "primitive" level. The hierarchy shown in the data flow diagram (DFD) in Figure 1-2 represents a functional decomposition of the interpretation of user inputs coming from a control panel, for example, in the manipulation of a robot with multiple joints.

An object-oriented decomposition attempts to identify real-world objects and their interfaces that, together, will make up the system. The rectangles shown in Figure 1-3 represent entities that are used to describe components of the system rather than how the system will function. These components are referred to as "objects" and can be thought of as building blocks of a system, just like the hardware components that make up a computer. An obvious difference between these two approaches is the naming conventions used.

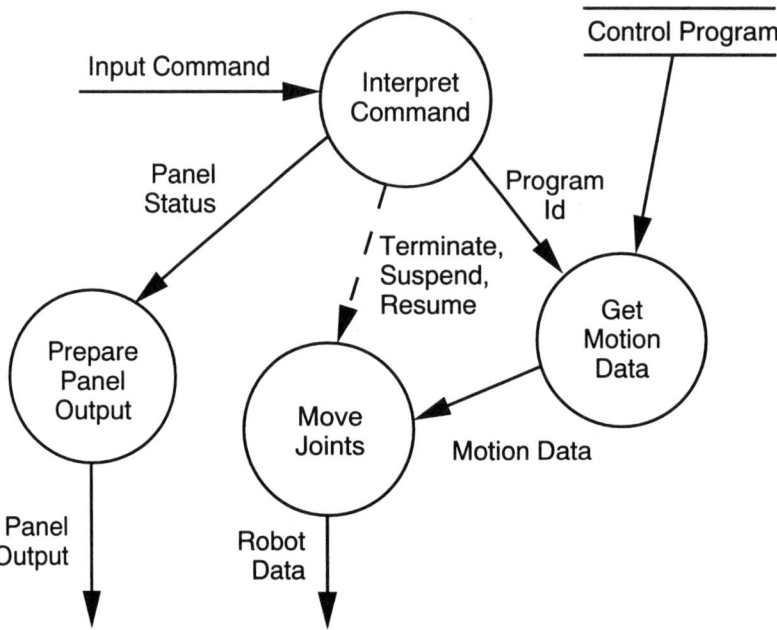

Figure 1-2. Functional decomposition

The circles in the functional approach are labeled with a verb phrase to signify the actions of the function. The rectangles for the object-oriented decomposition are named with a noun phrase to indicate an analysis entity, rather than a function, and represent a higher level of abstraction. The description and characteristics of an "object" will be covered in great detail in later chapters.

The successful implementation of any development process is highly dependent on the availability of methods and tools that support the process. Current practices for employing a system development process can be classified roughly into two approaches that apply to both structured and object-oriented techniques:

1. Pick one or more methods that can support the various development phases, and try to find Computer Aided Software Engineering (CASE) tools that implement these methods.
2. Pick a CASE tool and let this tool dictate which methods are used to support the process.

Chapter 1 • Introduction 9

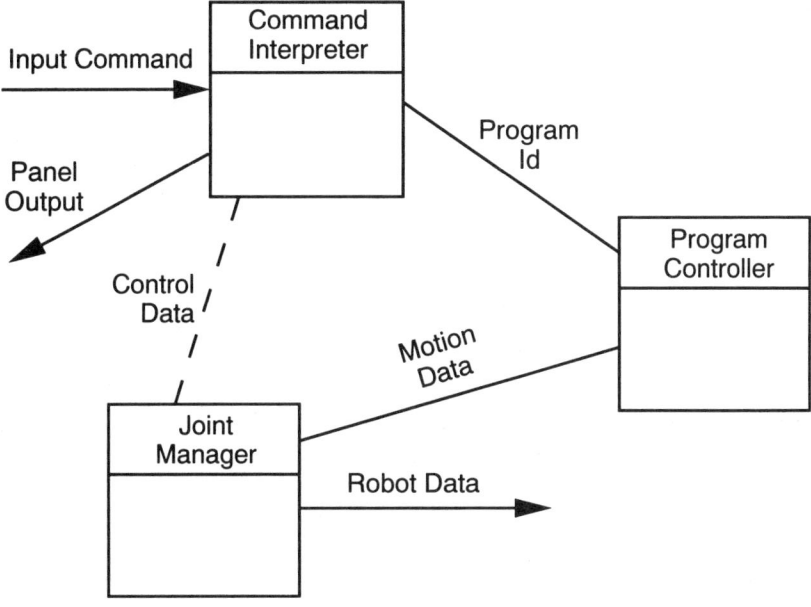

Figure 1-3. Object-oriented decomposition

Neither of these two approaches is ideal, since there is no CASE tool in existence that can support a wide variety of methods. The first approach usually leads to the acquisition and use of a number of tools that employ different notations for similar analysis and design concepts. The second approach limits the use of methods to those embedded within the CASE tool.

Most of the current CASE tools available for the development of large systems were based on structured methods, such as DeMarco [DEM79], Hatley-Pirbhai [HAT87], Ward-Mellor [WAR85], and Yourdon-Constantine [YOU79]. Almost all of the vendors that market these CASE tools are attempting to include object-oriented methods. Most of the object-oriented methods (see Chapter 7) are associated with vendors who have tools that support their particular method, but not an overall system development process.

There are no exact figures available to estimate the relative use of structured techniques versus object-oriented techniques by software development organizations. A general agreement among developers seems to be that most organizations are still using structured techniques. Judging from the number of OT seminars offered and software conferences dealing exclusively with OT, it is safe to say that most software development organizations are at least aware of the potential benefits of using OT, and are considering employing these techniques.

The theme of this book will be to encourage the use of OT techniques, especially for applications implemented with C++. Potential risk areas of switching to these techniques from structured methods are discussed in Chapter 8.

2

Steps in the Development Process

In this chapter, we describe each phase of an idealized system development process as a series of distinct steps. It must be realized that in practice, there is rarely that a large project is developed in a serialized fashion; nor is every step described here performed for every software product created. The rationale for having a development process to produce high quality software was discussed in Chapter 1.

Explanations are provided for the relations between steps that are performed in sequence, in parallel, via an iterative procedure, or are optional.

Particular emphasis is placed on real-time aspects with expectations of having to design systems that handle interrupts and are both data and control driven, rather than strictly data driven.

Strictly sequential systems can also use this approach by simply tailoring out the steps that are not needed, e.g., process structuring.

Only a cursory discussion is included here for the implementation steps of programming and testing. Several chapters in Part V discuss C++ programming in detail.

The process described here is independent of operating systems and particular development platforms. Most of the early development steps are independent of a particular programming language, and can be used for language implementations other than C++, which is assumed throughout this book.

2.1 OVERVIEW OF THE DEVELOPMENT PROCESS

The development process is based on a number of different models that are used in the various steps. Models are used to create abstractions (e.g., an object model showing the interfaces between objects) that hide unnecessary details and thus helps to reduce the complexity of the system we are analyzing and designing. The same models are used in different steps, wherever possible, to provide a consistent set of methods with a unified notation. An example of this is the use of an object model for both the system requirements analysis and the software requirements analysis.

An overview of the complete development process is shown in Figure 2-1. The development phases proceed, in general, from top to bottom and follow the direction of the arrows. Each rectangle represents a major development step and may include substeps, e.g., Software Design is composed of the following substeps:

- transitioning from OOA
- process structuring for run-time scheduling entities
- object-oriented design
- design evaluation

It is important to realize that a real development will not happen strictly top to bottom with all the steps implemented in sequential order. When system requirements change, we may have to retreat back to a previous step to affect these changes. Drawing arrows in both directions and linking all the rectangles will make the illustration complicated and obfuscate the general flow of the process.

The following design paradigms and modeling approaches can be included in a development approach:

- real-world entities as key abstractions for a given application domain
- layered abstractions including inheritance and aggregation relations
- classes as collections of related objects
- encapsulation and information hiding
- static models showing relationships between key abstractions, and static design structures
- dynamic models showing event flows and message passing between key abstractions

Chapter 2 • Steps in the Development Process

- concurrency models showing control and concurrency primitives of schedulable entities

These paradigms and models will be described in Part II when we discuss the general features of object technology.

The sections that follow present an overview and rationale for each of the major development steps. A detailed description of how we apply OT to these same steps is included in Part III.

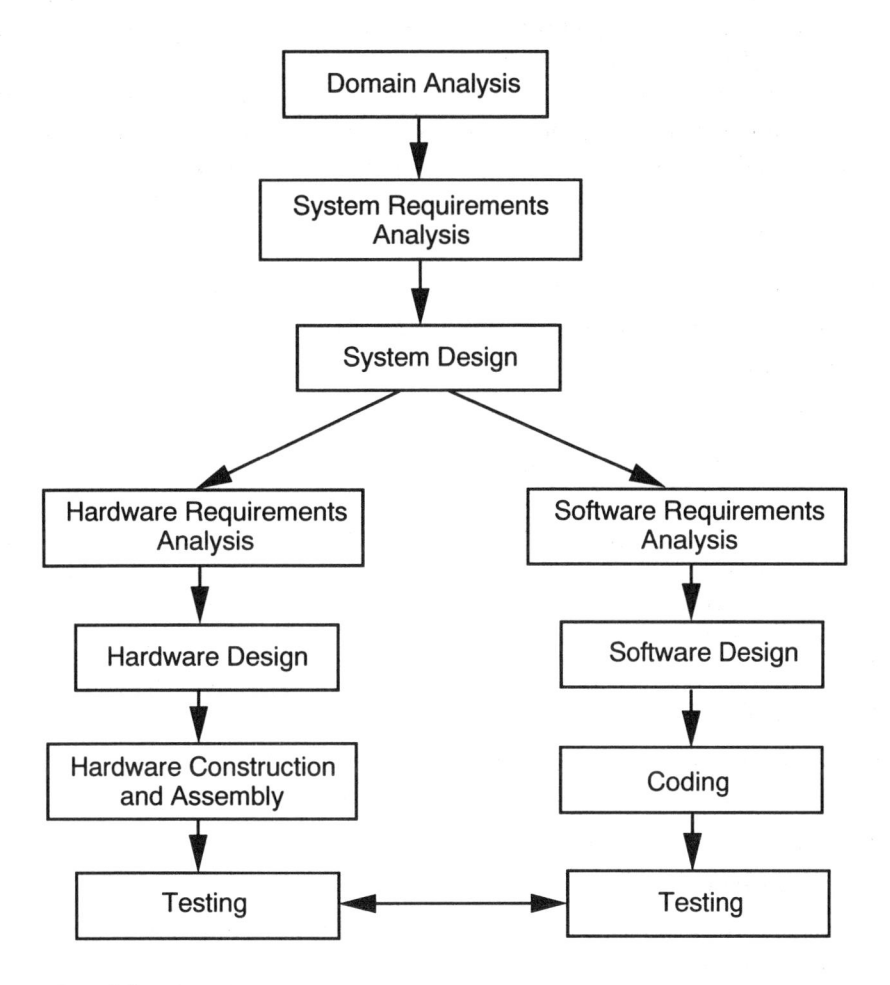

Figure 2-1. The development process

2.2 DOMAIN ANALYSIS

A domain analysis should be performed very early in the development process, even as early as the proposal phase. The primary purpose of this activity is to identify reusable hardware and software components, as well as complete subsystems.

We refer to a problem domain as a general description of a problem area for which we will develop similar or related applications. Examples of problem domains include Windows applications, robotics, banking systems, and air traffic control systems.

A product line is represented by a series of applications within a given domain. These applications may represent different software tools such as Word, Quicken, or FoxPro, all running under Windows. The applications will then take advantage of reusable Windows entities that apply to each application. A product line may also be represented with a narrower focus such as small, medium, and large configurations of the same application, e.g., air traffic control systems for different customers. The amount of reuse for the latter type of product line can be significant if we are careful about planning the development process.

We refer to reusability in-the-large in this context, since we are looking for a repeatable development process, reusable software and hardware entities, associated documentation, and in-house experts who understand the problem domain and its implementation.

A risk reduction plan should be prepared during this phase, and will usually include prototyping efforts and an initial "build" plan for an incremental development approach.

The primary documentation items for this step include a system functional specification (this may already be available), descriptions of reusable components, risk reduction plan, and a "build" plan for an incremental implementation.

2.3 SYSTEM REQUIREMENTS ANALYSIS

The purpose of this step is to gain an understanding of the requirements for the total system. We are assuming we have a system that needs to be decomposed into smaller entities for configuration management and design.

It is important that this analysis be performed to understand the *customer's views and expectations* of what the system is supposed to accomplish when it is delivered. This will usually entail the operational concepts and a set of performance requirements. We may decide that these requirements are unrealistic, and we can then attempt to negotiate or tailor the system for less severe performance restrictions.

This step forms the basis for system design and is closely coupled to the partitioning and configuring functions of the next step.

We can perform the system requirements analysis without having first done a domain analysis. This is not recommended, however, as the domain analysis is the most important step of a major, new development.

The most important document for this phase is a System Requirements Specification. A specific customer has, hopefully, prepared one before we start the analysis. If the requirements for the system are not properly stated, we must prepare such a document with the customer's concurrence. For a new product line, we must develop this document, and it should be based on the functional requirements determined during the domain analysis.

2.4 SYSTEM DESIGN

This step is closely linked to the system requirements analysis and should not be started until the prior analysis is completed. The purpose of system design is to decompose a large system into smaller entities, usually referred to as *subsystems*. The total system is usually too complex to be managed and understood by a single development team. The partitioning effort will allow several teams of hardware and software engineers to analyze and implement well-defined pieces of the total system that can be integrated as a whole.

The entities determined during the decomposition phase will be configurable components that form the basis for hardware and software design. They may also be complete subsystems in the form of existing "black boxes" that can be reused with, hopefully, only minor modifications. Major system upgrades may include additional memory, a bigger or additional hard drive, or a faster processor. System "ports" may also be considered in this phase, such as moving an entire system from a Pentium-based machine to an Alpha or RISC machine.

The primary activity of this step is the allocation of system requirements to hardware and software and to identify the interfaces between the chosen components. The final design is the result of carefully evaluating a number of possible solutions based on certain design criteria. These criteria will usually include the potential for reusability in future products and ease of maintenance.

The primary documentation for this step is a System Design Document, describing hardware and software components and potential subsystems. Supporting documentation will include graphical and textual descriptions of the interfaces between the various components.

After the system design is completed, separate teams will usually be formed for the hardware and software development, as shown by the fork in Figure 2-1. As mentioned earlier, we will only consider software development in this book and will ignore the hardware development steps. Some hardware elements will be discussed in a later chapter for distributed systems issues.

2.5 SOFTWARE REQUIREMENTS ANALYSIS

This step is performed after the system design is completed. The system requirements have been allocated to hardware and software components or subsystems, and we can now focus on the subsets of requirements assigned to each software configuration item. A configuration item is a software entity that shows up on planning time-lines and which requires a certain amount of documentation. It is also used for tracking development progress. Examples of software configuration items include a console display module for an air traffic control system, and an accounts receivable module for an accounting system.

The starting point for this activity is the set of system requirements associated with a particular software configuration item. These requirements were established during the system design phase.

The requirements analysis for the various components can be done in parallel by several development teams. The teams can be made up of developers within the same software organization or among a number of different contractors for very large systems. It is very important that the same methodologies and documentation standards be employed by all the different teams. Without this kind of discipline, the required integration effort can turn into a nightmare of extended schedules and cost overruns.

2.6 SOFTWARE DESIGN

The software design step involves a difficult transitioning from analysis to design. For large real-time systems, this includes the determination of a suitable process architecture as a model for the concurrent elements representing the parallel execution entities. The remainder of this step is the creation of a set of software modules (to be implemented in a particular programming language) that can affect the behavior of the concurrency model, or the modules that make up a sequential program. The software design step shown in Figure 2-1 can be expanded to include the substeps illustrated in Figure 2-2.

The software design phase is preceded by an analysis phase. We are assuming the use of OOA here, which has created certain analysis products, e.g., lists of key abstractions for the particular application domain in the form of classes and objects. The transitioning phase provides guidelines for moving from a requirements analysis to the creation of design structures. In particular, the transitioning includes rules for how high-level classes and objects become design-level classes and objects.

Process structuring is important in determining concurrency relations. This can be done with *apparent* concurrency, where several schedulable entities (i.e., tasks) compete for the use of the same CPU; or *true* concurrency, where one or more CPUs will constitute nodes in a distributed architecture.

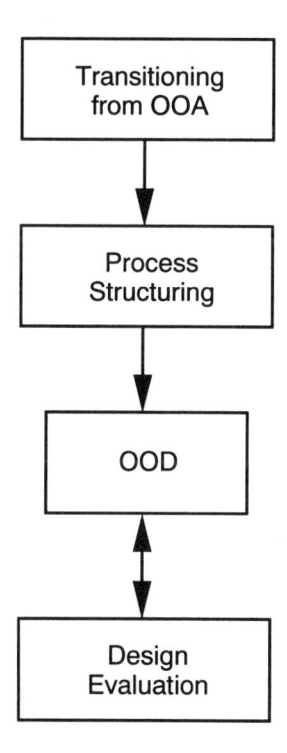

Figure 2-2. Substeps of the design phase

The OOD subphase creates the actual software architecture, and includes the formation of software modules using the design-level classes and objects.

The most important part of the design phase is the design evaluation. Even though it is depicted as the last substep in Figure 2-2 (for the purpose of illustration), it should be performed throughout the design phase. In the same figure we have indicated a feedback between only the last two substeps to keep the diagram simple. Feedback and iteration are likely to occur between any of these substeps

2.6.1 Process Structuring

There is an extremely important transitioning phase from analysis to design for real-time systems. This transitioning involves the creation of a process abstraction model of concurrent elements that can be implemented as independent, schedulable entities. This step is performed before the programming language dependent software design starts. It is important to note that we are using the term "process" in two entirely different contexts:

- the set of steps shown in Figure 2-1, which represents the overall development approach
- concurrent element that can be implemented to execute as an independent schedulable entity on the target machine

Which of the two meanings are applicable in a particular instance can usually be deduced from the context, and doesn't normally present a problem. If the meaning is ever ambiguous, we will point out the intended interpretation.

The starting point for this phase is a set of software requirements specifications with a graphical representation of an object model. A set of Process Selection Rules is used to combine a set of objects (sometimes referred to as a cluster [MEL93]) into a set of concurrent, schedulable entities. The primary concerns for this step include concurrency issues, such as producer/consumer pairs and their interfaces, asynchronous and synchronous processes, and protection of shared data [NIE90, NIE92]. The process abstraction model represents a logical view of the dynamic behavior for this portion of the real-time system.

This part of the design phase is programming language independent. The independent processes represent a logical model that must later be implemented using the features of a particular operating system, such as the Unix or DEC VMS process model. An alternative implementation would be to use a built-in tasking model, e.g., for the Ada programming language. C++ does not have such a built-in tasking mechanism, and we will have to rely on operating system features or tasking libraries for the implementation. This will be discussed further in Chapter 18.

2.6.2 Object-Oriented Design

The OOD phase starts after the process structuring is completed. The process abstraction model is transformed into an object view that can be implemented with C++ (physical view). An important part of this activity is the determination of the proper interfaces between the objects.

The objects include functionality that can be traced to the requirements determined during the software requirements phase. They are also architectural implementations of the real-world objects created during domain analysis or OOA.

As we mentioned earlier, the emphasis of the class/object structuring is on the creation of objects and not classes. We will elaborate on this further during the detailed description of this step.

It is expected that a significant amount of iteration will take place between the process structuring and the object structuring to obtain a good, robust design. The process structuring is used in the transitioning from analysis to design, but is usually no longer required once the initial object structure is obtained. The process abstraction model is always kept with the other design decision documents for historical purposes or for formal audit procedures.

The primary document produced at the completion of this step is a Software Design Document. This will include the object architecture and interfaces to other software components and devices.

2.6.3 Software Design Evaluation

Design reviews are scheduled at various times during the design phase. These reviews may include formal meetings with the customer, as well as informal internal reviews. The formal reviews are important for making the customer feel comfortable that we understand how we are going implement the requirements we have agreed upon. The completion of the formal review may be used as a partial payment milestone by the customer, and a positive result is, of course, of the utmost importance to the development organization.

The informal reviews are also extremely important for obtaining the best possible design. The reviewers are usually peers and experts in certain areas and can evaluate the design with regard to feasibility and performance.

This activity is highly iterative with the OOD step and is used to obtain an acceptable architecture. The evaluation phase is performed in parallel with all of the substeps of the design phase.

Particular areas of evaluation for an object-oriented real-time design include the process structure, including the number of processes, process interfaces, distributed issues, potential for deadlock or starvation, and the level of complexity.

The object structure will be evaluated closely with regard to reusability and portability. Other evaluations include object encapsulations, object relationships, and the use of exception handling.

The primary documentation of this step is an accumulation of the rationale for the design decisions made during formal and informal evaluations.

2.7 IMPLEMENTATION

The implementation phase includes the programming module testing and integration required for a large system implementation. An early implementation phase may include rapid prototyping to validate operational concepts. The early versions can be used as demonstration projects to validate the entire development process, as well as to demonstrate a partial implementation of the customer's requirements. A potential risk with this approach is that a customer may decide to accept the system as-is, and not pay for any further developments. Another risk is that the customer will continue to make system changes because he or she never fully understood the product they wanted as users.

The implementation phase for large systems was planned with a series of "builds" back in the domain analysis phase. This provides for an incremental development with a shell that displays the user interfaces in the first build. This will, typically, include a number of stubs for the internal modules. Subsequent builds implement the hidden details of the internal modules. Software drivers and "canned" scenarios may be used to simulate the modules that have not yet been implemented.

2.8 SUMMARY

We have completed an overview of the various steps included in the overall development process. The details of these steps will be furnished in Part III

Chapter 2 • Steps in the Development Process

when we describe how we employ OT in connection with these steps. It is important to realize that separate development teams may be working in parallel and using different phases of the development process. Careful planning is required to ensure that the various teams receive the required products in time from the other teams.

Even though some iteration between the different steps is expected, it is highly recommended that the domain analysis be completed before any detailed requirements analysis is started. For each development team, the analysis phase should be completed before the design phase is started, and the design should be completed before the programming starts. An exception to this recommendation is the creation of prototypes for defining system requirements. Portions of the requirements that deal with user interfaces or difficult algorithms can be analyzed, designed, and implemented during the early development phases.

The portion of the requirements implemented is determined by the build structure. The builds must be carefully planned during the early development phases to ensure a proper incremental development, and that the required hardware is available for the implementation of each build.

3

Development Process versus Methods

The successful implementation of any development process is highly dependent on the availability of methods and tools that support the process. This chapter describes some of the tools used to support the traditional structured analysis and design (SA/SD), and the alternate tools used with the object-oriented approach. The potential benefits of using OT methods are also described

3.1 METHODS THAT SUPPORT THE DEVELOPMENT STEPS

In the previous chapter, we noted that the development process consists of a number of steps that are usually performed in a suggested sequence to create a software product. It was also noted that a certain amount of iteration between the various steps should be anticipated when system requirements change. Several different methods have traditionally been used to support these steps for a structured approach, and a new set of methods has evolved in support of an object-oriented approach.

The use of the term "method" connotes the meaning of a tool, representation, or model to help us understand the complexities of a software development for large systems. An example of a method used to support the analysis phase for a structured approach is a functional decomposition, and is illustrated with a data flow diagram (DFD) in Figure 3-1 for a small part of the requirements for an air traffic control system. The circles represent functions, the parallel lines a data store, and the arrows the direction of data flows. The DFDs provide one of the major tools used in decomposing large sequential and real-time systems for structured analysis. The focus of this tool is on how transient data (contrasted with persistent data) is flowing between the various functional entities.

Another method is derived from information modeling and depicts the relationships between major data structures within a system. This is illustrated in Figure 3-2 with an entity relationship diagram (ERD) attributed to Chen [CHE76]. The rectangles represent the data structures, and the diamonds depict the relations between the data structures. ERDs have been used extensively in the analysis and design of large, data-intensive applications.

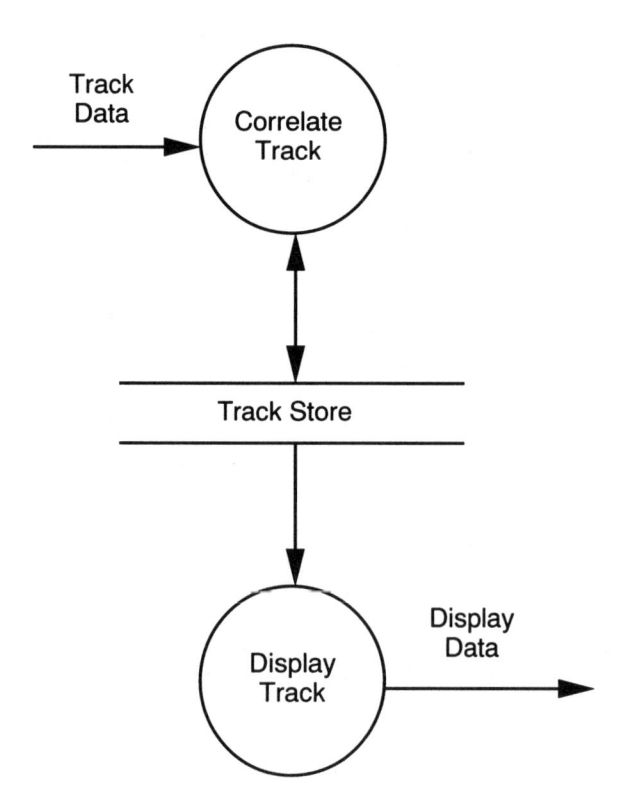

Figure 3-1. Data flow diagram

Chapter 3 • Development Process versus Methods

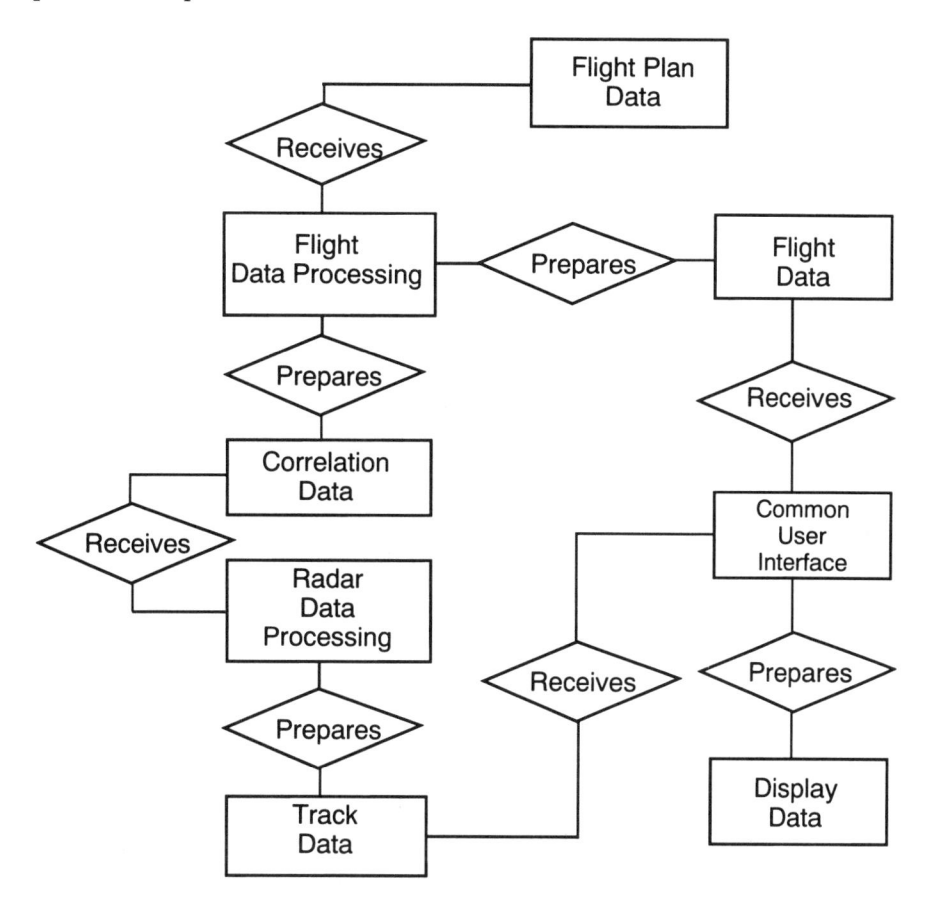

Figure 3-2. Entity relationship diagram

The primary tool used to support the design phase of the structured approach is the structure chart as shown in Figure 3-3. This is also a representation of a functional decomposition, now using design entities, rather than the analysis entities used in the DFDs. The rectangles in Figure 3-3 will be implemented as procedures and functions for a particular programming language such as Ada, Fortran, or C. The connecting lines show the direction of data flows. The focus of this tool is on the calling hierarchies of procedures and functions, data passed between procedures and functions, and the use of shared data, if any.

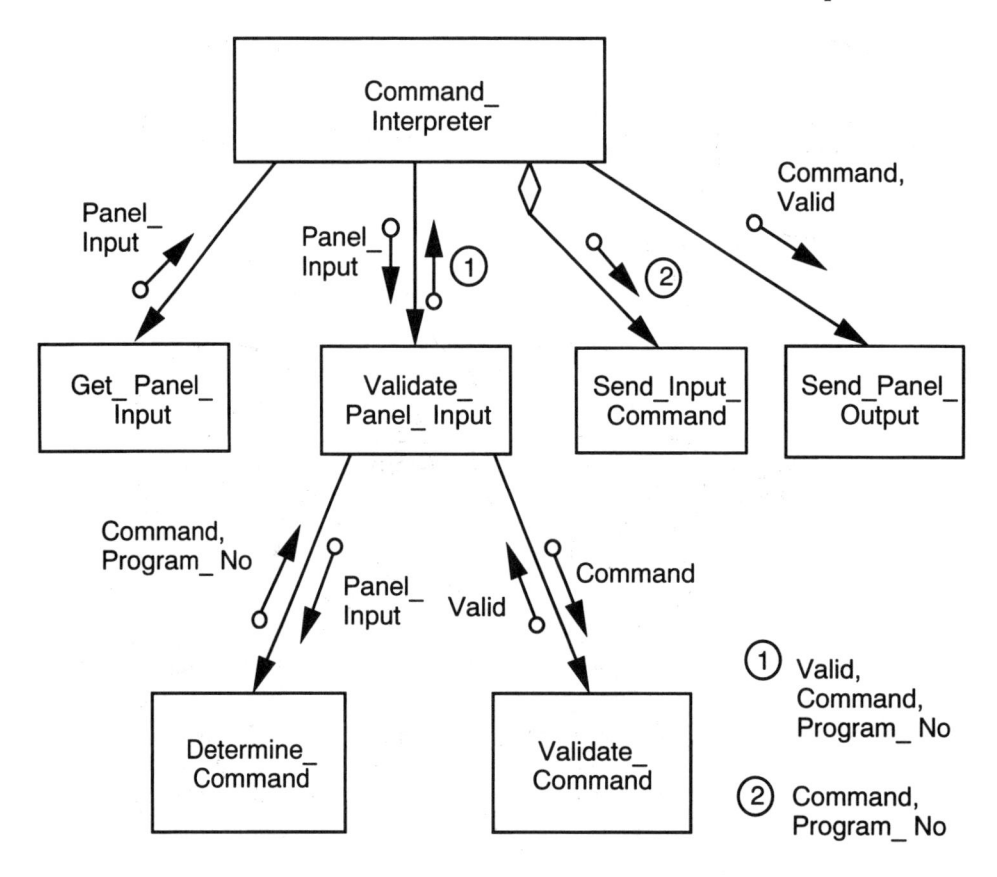

Figure 3-3. Structure chart

The primary structured tool used to understand the dynamic behavior of a system is the state transition diagram (STD) as illustrated in Figure 3-4. Each circle (sometimes illustrated with rectangles) represents one of a set of mutually exclusive states the system can attain while it is running. The annotated directed graphs indicate the actions required for making the system transition from one state to another. STDs are especially useful in analyzing and designing control-driven real-time systems.

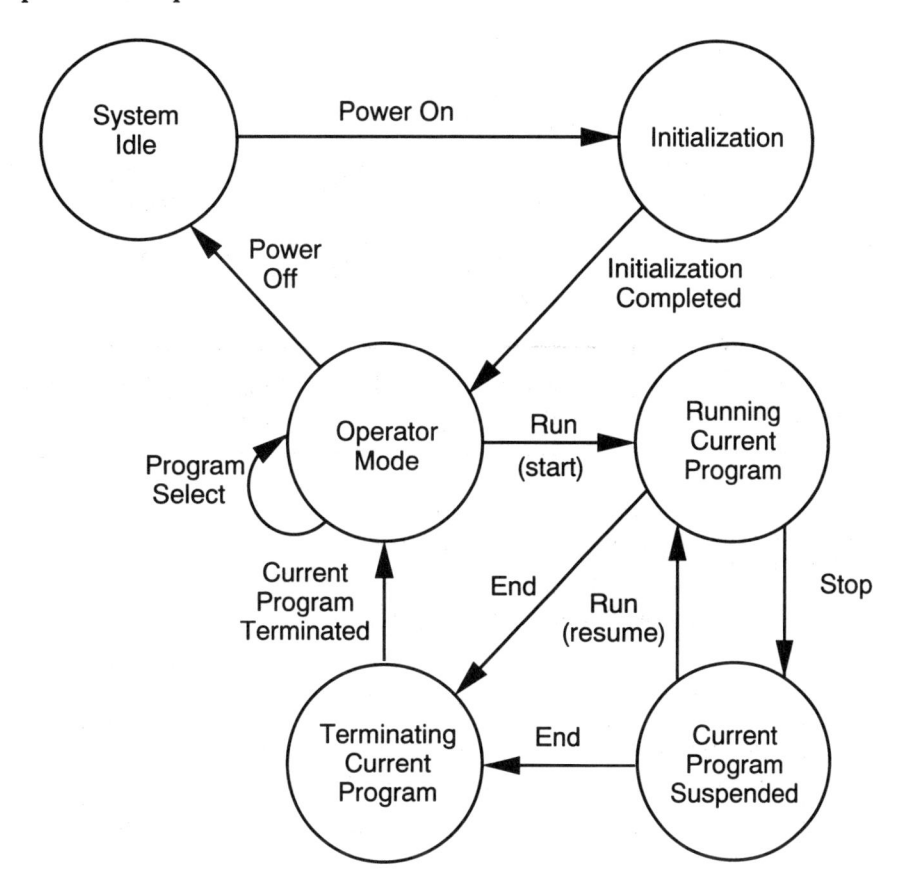

Figure 3-4. State transition diagram

This short exposé is not intended to be an exhaustive list of methods and tools used to support the traditional SA/SD approach. We are merely setting the stage for showing the alternate methods that are used to support an object-oriented approach. A complete treatment of structured methods, including extensions for real-time systems, can be found in [HAT87, WAR85, and SHU92].

3.2 TRADITIONAL METHODS VERSUS OBJECT-ORIENTED METHODS

Object-oriented methods used in OT approaches are replacing or augmenting the SA/SD methods described above for the equivalent development phases. The overall process should remain the same, although some tendencies to shorten the process are evident in some OT techniques. Some of the attempts to shorten the process are manifested by a blurring of the distinction between the analysis and design phases. Other attempts include the combination of the domain analysis and the requirements analysis into one phase. The most drastic effort to shorten the development process is to skip the domain analysis, perform a requirements analysis, and then jump directly to the programming phase without any design phase.

The infusion of OT methods to support the development process should not alter the development phases outlined in the previous chapters. Some of the attempts to shorten the cycle are simply ways of justifying hacking under the guise of object-oriented development.

3.2.1 Why Introduce Object-Oriented Methods?

Why should we introduce OT methods into our development process? This can, perhaps, best be answered by first creating a wish-list for what we would like to improve about the development process and our development environment:

- shorten the development process
- improve the quality of the finished software product
- simplify the development and configuration efforts required for a software product line
- improve customer relations
- improve employee morale and productivity by introducing leading-edge technology

The first item on our wish list is accomplished with the potentially higher level of reuse than when using structured methods.

The interfaces to the encapsulated entities utilized in OT methods must be carefully designed with a client/server view. The implementation of these entities tends to produce more robust software than structured methods that employ open data structures.

The higher level of potential reuse can make it easier to plan and manage a number of similar products within an application domain, as well as to produce expected product upgrades.

Discussions and design reviews with our customers can be made in terms of real-world entities that they can readily relate to, rather than obscure and confusing design artifacts. A related customer issue is that the customer may simply demand that we use OT in our development approach.

In the current business world of constant reorganization and downsizing, it is now common that employees are asked to work longer hours with reduced pay, and the employee morale is very likely to be at an all-time low. Providing in-house OT training and implementing new, promising development approaches may ease some of the tension and improve productivity.

Having made a strong case for introducing OT methods, let us now move on to provide an overview of how they differ from structured methods.

3.2.2 Comparing Structured and Object-Oriented Methods

The major difference between structured and OT methods is that the former is function-driven and treats data entities separately from the functions. The latter is entity-driven and deals with higher levels of abstractions that include encapsulated entities with hidden data structures. These entities can readily be isolated when requirements change, and minimizes redesign efforts. The structured approach has open (visible) data structures that can freely be accessed by any number of operations. This creates a tighter coupling among the software modules, and may result in rippling effects of redesign when system requirements change.

A graphical representation of the differences at the design level is illustrated with Figures 3-5 and 3-6. The structured architecture in Figure 3-5 shows two routines with direct access to a visible data element (shaded area) in Common_1. This could be a design for a Fortran or C implementation. The C version would have Common_1 as a *struct* and Sub_1 and Sub_2 as functions accessing an element within the struct. If any data element within Common_1 is changed or moved, coding changes will have to be made to both of the two routines for proper access.

The object-oriented architecture shown in Figure 3-6 includes two encapsulated objects that hide data structures A and B, respectively. Any access to a data element in either of these two objects can only be made via the operations shown on the left boundary, which provide the object interfaces. Changes can be made to the data elements A and B without changing the client code that accesses the two objects (provided the interfaces don't change, of course).

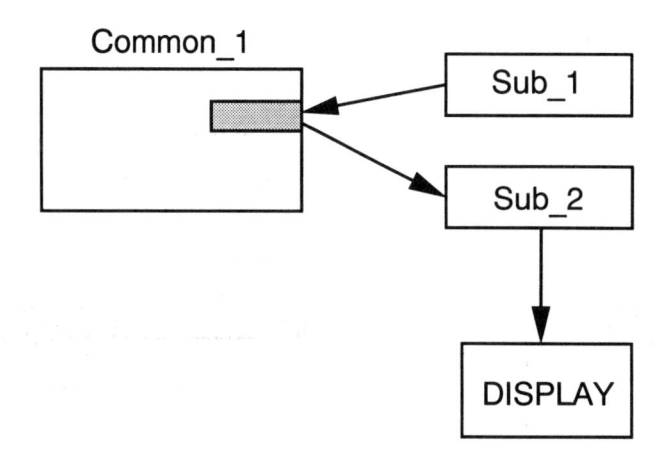

Figure 3-5. Structured design

The comparison between the structured approach and the object-oriented approach can be viewed as a paradigm shift from a functional (procedural, algorithmic) focus to a higher level of abstraction that includes encapsulated entities. The primary design entities for structured design are functions, procedures, and shared data. The fundamental design entities for an object-oriented approach are encapsulated objects and collections of common objects into classes.

3.2.3 Comparing Structured and Object-Oriented Programming

Object-oriented programming differs from structured programming primarily by the available features of inheritance and polymorphism (multiple versions of functions with the same name available for automatic invocation at run-time). Stroustrup discusses various programming paradigms [STR91, pp. 15–32] and characterizes Procedural Programming (using functional decomposition) as:

> "Decide which procedures you want;
> use the best algorithm you can find."

This was illustrated with the structure chart shown in Figure 3-3, and is the capstone of structured design.

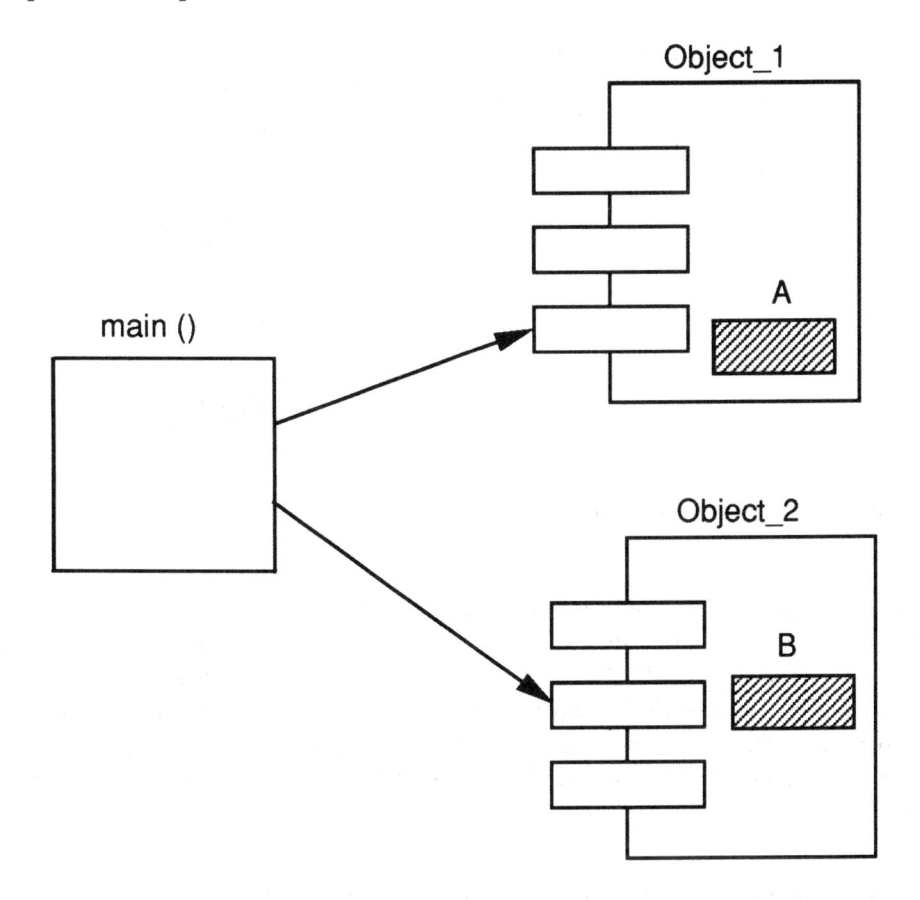

Chapter 3 • Development Process versus Methods 31

Figure 3-6. Object-oriented design

Stroustrup describes Modular Programming as:

> "Decide which modules you want;
> partition the program so that data is hidden in modules."

Data hiding and encapsulation was championed by Parnas [PAR72a, PAR72b] and was a significant extension to structured design. Associated with modular programming are the old structured design paradigms of high cohesion within a module, and loose coupling between modules.

Data Abstraction is described by Stroustrup as:

> "Decide which types you want;
> provide a full set of operations for each type."

This has been discussed extensively by Liskov and Guttag [LIS86] before object-oriented techniques became popular. Data abstraction represents one of the important paradigms for supporting information hiding and loose coupling.

Stroustrup describes Object-Oriented Programming as:

> "Decide which classes you want;
> provide a full set of operations for each class;
> make commonality explicit by using inheritance."

All of these programming paradigms are used in the programming phase with an OT approach. Only the use of inheritance (and availability of polymorphism) is unique for object-oriented programming. The primary advantages of employing OT methods are the encapsulation and information hiding that lead to a more robust software product, and the potential reuse with inheritance.

3.2.4 Effect of OT Methods on the Steps of the Process

The same OT models and techniques that are used for OOP can be elevated to support analysis and design as well. The encapsulation mechanism, for example, can be used to represent higher levels of abstractions during the analysis and design phases.

The use of OT methods should not alter the development steps of domain analysis, requirements analysis, design, and implementation. We are simply employing OT methods to support these steps.

Some OT methods may tend to blur the boundary between analysis and design by using identical models and notations for the two phases, e.g., analysis objects and classes that represent real-world entities can't be distinguished from design entities. Stopping criteria can be used to determine when we are finished with one phase. Rule-based transitioning between phases can help to prevent this blurring. Lack of guidelines may promote hacking and create tightly coupled designs.

Using distinct notations for OOA and OOD models may also help alleviate the blending of requirements with designs, but this may require a CASE tool to support the different model notations or two separate CASE tools.

3.3 NOTATION

Important analysis results and design decisions are captured using certain graphical and textual representations. These diagrams and documents are used to discuss system requirements with a customer, to ease the transitioning between the development steps, to describe a software architecture during design reviews, and to create user manuals for final delivery of a product. These documents must be clearly written and well illustrated for them to be of any use. Hopefully, they will also contain a uniform notation from project to project.

The evolution of SA/SD did not include a standardization of the notation for the graphical or textual representations. There were very few major different structured methods, however, and the lack of standard notation has not created a major problem. The notations used in DFDs and ERDs are similar and are fairly easy to comprehend. They both depict a static model of the system requirements with a focus on transient and persistent data, respectively. The STD is a little more involved and models the dynamic behavior of the changes in the system states during execution. The structure chart is a static model of the calling hierarchies of procedures and functions within a module or program.

The use of structure charts represents a sharp delineation between analysis and design, since the DFDs, STDs, and ERDs used during the analysis phase are completely different from the structure charts used during the design phase.

Object-oriented methods also do not have any standard notation, and the differences cause major problems for the novice who gets exposed to different OT methods. Although most of the methods are based on a similar object model, their graphical representations are significantly different. This will be discussed in detail in Chapter 7 when we compare the various OT methods.

The object model is used both during the analysis phase and during the design phase. This means that, for a given OT method, it is sometimes difficult to distinguish between the two phases. Some observers consider this to be an advantage, with an automatic transitioning from analysis to design. This can become a trap, however, and it is highly recommended that a dividing line be kept between the two phases. If these two phases become blurred, it becomes difficult to evaluate the required user concepts before we are suddenly in the middle of the design phase. Architecture diagrams, such as was shown above in Figure 3-6, should augment the object models for the design phase.

3.4 LANGUAGE DEPENDENCE

The introduction of OT methods should not alter the language dependence of the various development phases. The domain analysis, requirements analysis, and the first part of the design phase, including process structuring, are all language independent, and should be kept free of implementation technology.

The part of the design phase that considers the use of inheritance, exception handling, and genericity is very much dependent on the features of the implementation language. It does not make sense, for example, to have design entities structured in inheritance hierarchies if inheritance is not supported by the programming language. This will become more evident when we get into OOD for C++. In general, we do not recommend the creation of object-oriented artifacts for their own sake. The whole purpose of transitioning between design and programming is to be able to implement design entities directly using the appropriate language constructs.

3.5 SUMMARY

In Part I, we have discussed the importance of having a development process, and have illustrated the steps of the software development process for large systems: domain analysis, system requirements analysis, system design, software requirements analysis, software design, and implementation.

A cursory comparison was made between structured methods and OT methods, and we noted that the primary difference between them can be viewed as a paradigm shift from considering a procedural decomposition to the creation of higher level abstractions that can be implemented as encapsulated entities. The primary potential benefits of using an OT approach can be summarized as follows:

- shorter development process
- improved quality of the finished software product
- simplified development and configuration efforts required for a software product line
- improved customer relations
- improved employee morale and productivity by introducing leading-edge technology

It is important to realize that simply employing OT methods in the software development process does not guarantee success. Significant training efforts and management support are necessary for attaining the potential benefits of using an OT approach.

In the next few chapters we will describe object-oriented paradigms in general, with an emphasis on the various relations between classes and objects. We will also discuss and compare some of the most promising OT methods that can support the steps of our development process.

PART II

Object Technology

Paraphrasing *Open Computing Magazine* [UNI94]: Object Technology (OT) is somewhat mythical and overrated:

1. It is on everyone's mind all the time.
2. Everyone talks about it all the time.
3. Everyone thinks everyone else is doing it.
4. Almost no one is doing it.
5. The few who are doing it are
    a. doing it poorly.
    b. sure it will be better next time.
    c. not practicing it safely.

The referenced magazine article was discussing client/server technology. But the article snippet fits equally well to object technology. Certainly, everyone is talking about it, very few are doing it, or they are possibly doing it poorly. There are numerous benefits to using OT, and an understanding of the underlying concepts can help alleviate the fears of the risk associated with this technology.

In Part II, we present the definitions of object-oriented paradigms that make up the global concept of object technology. Classes and objects form the basis for all object-oriented techniques, and are covered in Chapter 5.

A plethora of object-oriented analysis and design techniques have emerged during the last few years, and one of the difficult problems facing an analyst or designer is to know which method to pick for his or her project. The most promising of these techniques are described, and we include a recommended modeling approach.

Part II concludes with a discussion of the impact of switching from structured to OT methods, and recommendations for how to pick the "right" OT method(s) for a particular project.

4
Object-Oriented Paradigms

Object-oriented computing is considered the most important software development tool since the advent of Structured Design [DEM79, PAG80, YOU79]. Object-oriented *programming* (OOP) was introduced as the initial OT concept, and have been advanced with programming languages like Simula [DAH70], Smalltalk-80 [GOL83], C++ [STR91, LIP91], and Eiffel [MEY88].

Object-oriented *design* (OOD) has been promoted with the approaches suggested by Abbott [ABB83], Booch [BOO86, BOO91, BOO93], and Liskov [LIS86]. The major benefits promised with the use of OOD include a high level of modularity to support loose coupling, an encapsulation mechanism to support information hiding, data abstraction to support the creation of objects that refer to a single data type and associated operations, and a classification and inheritance mechanism that provide reusability and extendibility.

Object-oriented concepts have been elevated from the design phase to also include the *analysis* phase (OOA) [BOO93, JAC92, SHL92, COA91], and, thus, object-oriented techniques can be used for the entire software development process.

The objective of this chapter is to provide an insight into the various object-oriented concepts, and, thus, create a consistent vocabulary for the remainder of the book. Some of the concepts discussed here are not unique to object-oriented approaches, they apply equally well to structured analysis and design. The cornerstone of object technology, classes and objects, is only given a cursory treatment in this chapter; they are discussed in great detail in Chapter 5.

4.1 CLASSES AND OBJECTS

The terms *class* and *object* are used extensively to describe object-oriented concepts in OOA, OOD, and OOP. Numerous variations exist for their definitions, with many gradations in the levels of abstraction or abstruseness. In this chapter, we will only provide a cursory discussion of classes and objects that is sufficient to understand the other OT concepts.

Loosely speaking, an object is a "thing," or a concept that is used to describe specific entities related to the system we are constructing. Examples of objects within a banking system, for example, include customers who are identified by account numbers, and automated teller machines (ATMs) in certain physical locations. Associated with each object is a set of attributes (data valued characteristics) and operations that define the behavior of each object.

A class is a template or prototype describing common attributes and operations that apply to a set of related objects that belong to that class. A specific object is considered an *instance* of a class, and is identified by a name or numeric identifier. For example, a general class within a banking system can be described as Customer, and an instance (object) of that class can be John Smith with a unique identification number. Another class can be ATM, with an instance of ATM_4 located at the corner of First Street and Main.

When an object is created, it is associated with a set of attributes and operations. Attributes for the banking system may include CustomerName, AccountNumber, and Personal Identification Number (PIN) for use with the ATM machine. Operations for a Customer object may include OpenNewAccount, DeleteAccount, AddToCheckingAccount, and CalculateBalance. Operations for ATM objects may include ReadATMCard, VerifyPIN, DeliverCash, and PrintReceipt.

Why are the concepts of classes and objects so vital for object-oriented analysis, design, and programming? Here are some of the most important reasons:

1. **Decomposition.** We can use classification as a means of decomposing a large system into a number of abstract classes. These classes and their associated objects have direct relations to real-world entities, and can be used to manage the complexity of large systems.

2. **Communication and Documentation.** Since the abstract classes and objects are directly related to real-world entities, they can be used in discussions with the customer and end-users to increase our understanding of the system requirements.

3. **Reusability.** The classification strategy implies a hierarchy and a potential for inheritance, i.e., a superclass/subclass relationship. The sub-

classes can inherit attributes and operations from the superclass, and we simply add unique attributes and operations for the subclass.

4. **Ease of Maintenance.** The potential for reusability supports extendibility, ease of reconfiguration for future systems, and reduced maintenance efforts.

With this rather informal discussion of classes and objects, we can now describe the other object-oriented concepts that are closely related to and based on the class/object notion.

4.2 ENCAPSULATION AND INFORMATION HIDING

The common characteristic of object-oriented analysis, design, and programming is the extensive use of abstractions. An abstraction is a high-level description or model of a detailed or complex concept. Abstractions are not unique to OT. We have been using abstractions extensively with structured analysis, design, and programming. A BankAccount software module could, for example, contain an operation called CalculateInterest(...) as a callable procedure. This procedure represents a functional or procedural abstraction. The details of how interest is calculated (based on a given time period and compounding model) have been abstracted away by a single procedure call. Higher level forms of program abstractions include processes and tasks as schedulable entities (process abstraction), and dynamic link libraries (DLLs) that contain callable Graphical User Interface (GUI) implementations.

An abstraction that represents a software entity must somehow be described with a uniform notation that is recognizable to a software developer, and, possibly, to a compiler or other software processing tool. The embodiment of the abstraction is referred to as an *encapsulation*. Associated with the encapsulation is the notion that this is the only way to access the desired information for the given abstraction. The encapsulation of the procedure referred to above, for example, is accomplished with a procedure name CalculateInterest and suitable parameters, e.g., AccountNumber and TimePeriod. For the remainder of this section, we will focus on the encapsulation of classes and objects.

A well designed object encapsulates a single real-world entity that has a set of attributes and operations. The proper encapsulation of a software module has several important design characteristics:

1. The implementation details of the data structure and the algorithms used in the operations are hidden from the user. This provides a loose coupling between the various application modules using the object, and changes to the object implementation can be made without design modifications rippling through the entire system.
2. The visible part of the module provides an unambiguous and unique interface to the encapsulated object. This interface is the only way to access the data structures representing the abstraction. This provides a high degree of reusability where the encapsulated objects can be used in different systems without changing the interfaces.

An example of an encapsulation at the programming level is the following C++ Stack class (constructor/destructor operations have been omitted for the sake of simplicity):

```
class Stack {
public:
   void stackInit();
   long topOfStack();
   long pop();
   void push(long);
private:
   long stackItems[50];
   int stackPtr;
};
```

A graphical representation of this class as an encapsulated object is shown in Figure 4-1. The encapsulation consists of the name of the abstraction, a visible interface which provides access to the operations, an impenetrable boundary, and hidden (private) data objects. Everything concerning the Stack class is embodied within the encapsulation. How the actual stack is implemented is hidden from the clients using this abstraction.

We thus see that an encapsulation implies information hiding, and sometimes these two concepts are used as synonyms. With a programming language, such as C++, which provides direct support for information hiding, a large part of our design effort is directed towards providing the appropriate level of information hiding.

Chapter 4 • Object-Oriented Paradigms

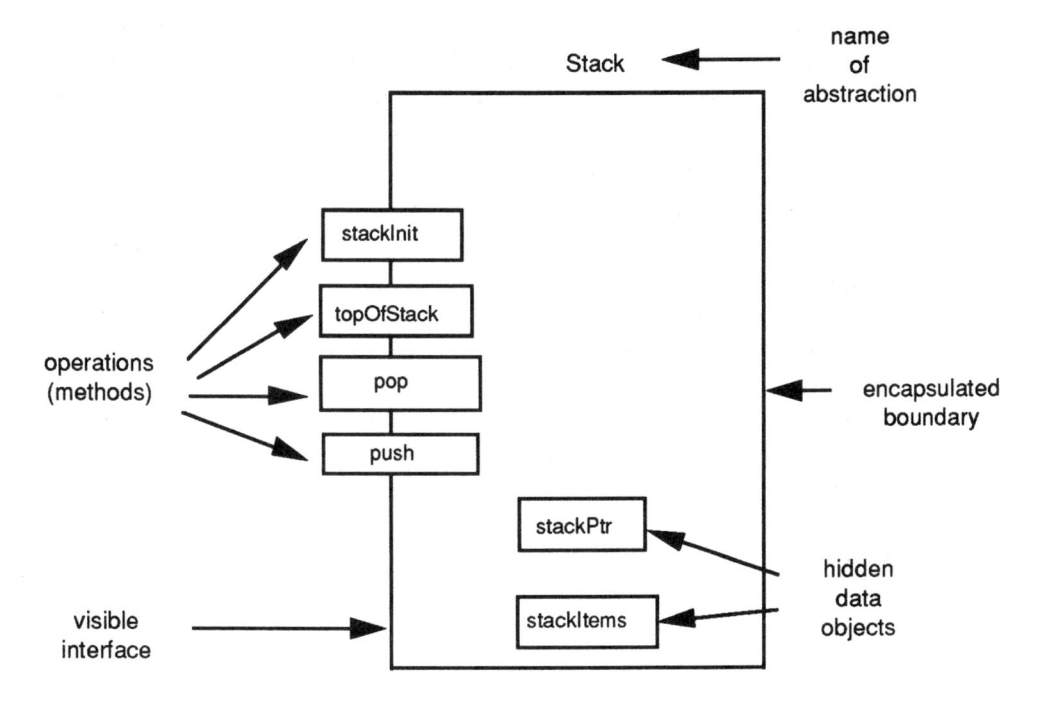

Figure 4-1. Encapsulated object

4.3 DATA ABSTRACTION

Data abstraction is related to how we implement encapsulation and information hiding at the design and programming level. This can be described as the process of creating user-defined types to implement the real-world classes and objects that make up the system design. These new types represent an extension to the built-in types that are normally available with a given programming language, such as integer, floating point, and character types.

The concept of data abstraction is based on the combination of procedural abstraction (e.g., calling CalculateInterest with AccountNumber and TimePeriod as parameters) and abstraction by specification [LIS86]. A data structure, declared as a type, and the operations required to manipulate objects of the type are specified together and collected as a program module. The operations become a part of the new type. The module represents an encapsulation of the type and the operations, and the operations are considered an interface for affecting the behavior of objects of the type.

Here is another look at the C++ Stack class used above to demonstrate encapsulation and information hiding:

```
class Stack {
public:
   void stackInit();
   long topOfStack();
   long pop();
   void push(long);
private:
   long stackItems[50];
   int stackPtr;
};
```

We now consider the class Stack an abstract data type (ADT). This is a user-defined type that will be recognized by a C++ compilation system, in addition to the built-in types of long, int, char, etc. The ADT is specified using C++ constructs that implement the Stack abstraction. The keyword *private* is used to implement the hidden data structures, and *public* is used to define the operations that allow access to the data structures. This *specification* of the Stack class defines the structure of the ADT as well as the interface (contract) in the client/server relation.

A characteristic of an ADT is that it should only encapsulate a single abstraction. We would not create a combination ADT called StackQueue, for example, that could handle both stacks and queues. The interface to such an ADT would increase the coupling between the clients and the server, and result in additional reprogramming when changes had to be made.

Direct programming language support for the creation of ADTs is of the utmost importance for the implementation of an object-oriented design. This language feature can be a significant factor in the creation of large software systems that exhibit the desired characteristics of strong cohesion within modules, and loose coupling between modules. (We'll say more about modularity later in this chapter.)

4.4 RESPONSIBILITIES

We can think of a C++ class as a specification with a client/server view. The visible class interface includes a number of operations that represent a server to a number of clients who will use the operations associated with specific instances (objects) of the class. Some of the class operations may be hidden from the clients and will only be used by the object itself. The operations (member functions in C++) associated with the object determine the behavior of that object, and are referred to as the *responsibilities* of the object.

A slightly different view of the client/server mechanism is presented by Booch [BOO93, p. 43] where the visible class interface provides a *contract* to the clients. This contract contains the responsibilities of the object, i.e., the behavior for which it is held responsible.

It may, at first, appear that the term *responsibility* is simply a fancy term for an operation. We will return to this concept in Chapter 7, however, when we discuss an object-oriented design technique which involves the use of Class Responsibility Collaboration (CRC) cards.

4.5 COLLABORATIONS AND MESSAGE PASSING

A collaboration can be defined as a service provided by one object for use by other objects. Collectively, the objects define the expected behavior at the system level.

Collaborations are closely related to the concept of message passing, which is a description of how software modules communicate. Communication between modules can also be accomplished with shared data, but that is not of interest here.

The concept of an object sending a "message" to another object is usually implemented with a combination of parameter passing and returning value results. In C++, for example, parameters are passed by value or reference via function calls. Values are returned via *return* statements or by modifying reference variables.

Passing messages in C++ is, thus, nothing more than making function calls on the visible member functions declared in the class specification. Sending a "message" to get the value of a square root declared in a Math class library, for example, could be accomplished with the function call

```
Y = Math::Sqrt (X); // message
```

The direction of message passing can be indicated with a directed graph, as shown in Figure 4-2. Data passed as parameters can flow in both directions, as shown with the small arrows with open circles. Exactly how a data element is returned, is dependent on the programming language we are using for the implementation. A closed circle can be used to show the passing of a flag rather than a data element.

So far we have only mentioned message passing in connection with the calling of operations on objects that are assumed to execute sequentially. For real-time systems, however, we also need to consider collaboration and message passing in a multiprocessing environment. Message passing between concurrent objects will be covered in Chapter 8 and 18.

4.6 INHERITANCE

The concept of inheritance is used to describe the creation of subclasses from one or more superclasses. Each subclass inherits the structure and behavior of its superclass, including the attributes and operations specified. If a subclass is allowed to inherit from more than one superclass, the particular programming language supports *multiple* inheritance.

The inheritance relation is shown graphically in Figure 4-3, where the arrow is pointing to the ancestor. The superclass is Window and the subclasses at the first level are Main Window, Control, and Dialog. The subclass Control has lower level subclasses of Edit, List Box, and Scroll Bar.

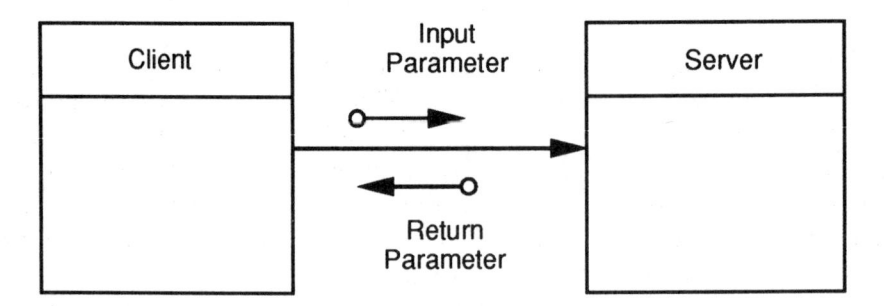

Figure 4-2. Message passing direction

Chapter 4 • Object-Oriented Paradigms

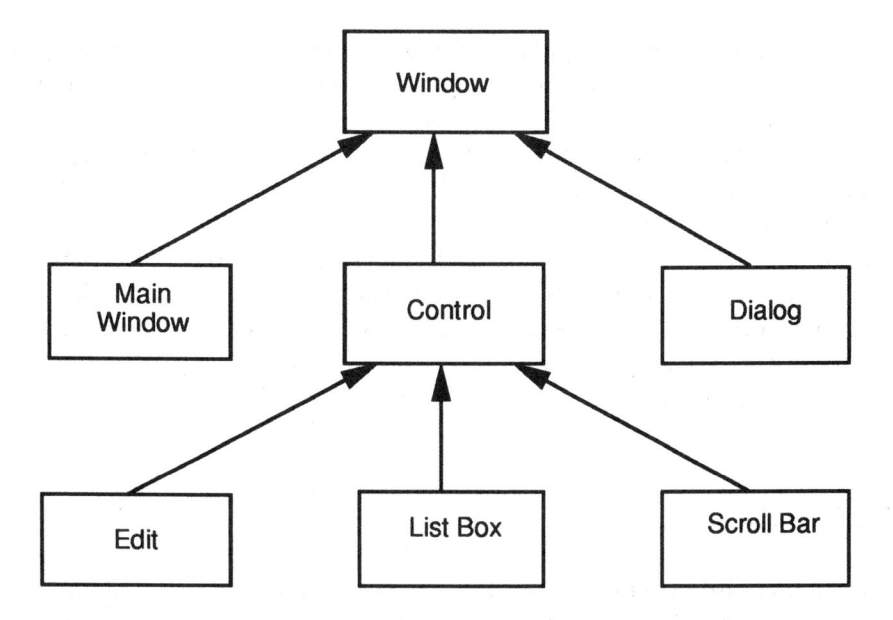

Figure 4-3. Inheritance relations

The applicable attributes (characteristics) and operations of superclasses are inherited by each subclass as a subset. Additional operations that are unique to a given subclass can then be added as extensions. The attributes of a Window class, for example, could include starting point, height, width, background color, and title bar. The operations could be to register a class, update a class, and repaint a damaged area (when another object is moved on top of the window).

The arrows in Figure 4-3 point from a subclass to a superclass to denote the concept of "is–a," e.g., a Control is a Window. The relation of "kind-of" [BOO93] is also expressed by the arrow, e.g., a Dialog is a kind of Window.

The inheritance feature allows a redefinition of (child) classes based on parent classes. This provides a tool for organizing and building reusable classes based on existing modules. If any of the operations in the higher level class structures are modified, the changes are automatically inherited by the lower level classes (after recompilation). Without the inheritance feature, every class must be developed as an independent entity in a bottom-up fashion. Any consistency required across the classes will then be based on a programming discipline, rather than type and interface checking performed by a compiler that supports the inheritance feature.

The net effect of inheritance should be a reduction of code to be developed through reusability. One problem to anticipate is a more complicated debugging phase, unless a sophisticated program browser is available to navigate through the various hierarchical class levels.

4.7 POLYMORPHISM

Polymorphism refers to the characteristic that an object can exist as an instance of different classes at run-time. In a programming language that implements polymorphism, operations have both static and dynamic types associated with them, and the dynamic type reference may change during execution.

A class hierarchy to illustrate the concept of polymorphism is shown in Figure 4-4, where a Polygon is the superclass, and Triangle, Rectangle, and Parallelogram are the subclasses.

A C++ code skeleton for the superclass Polygon and subclass Rectangle can be sketched out as follows (the significance of the *virtual* keyword will be explained later in Chapter 19):

```
class Polygon { // superclass
public:
  float Perimeter ();
  points Translate ();
  virtual float Area ();
  virtual boolean pointInside ();
protected:
  void Display ();
};

class Rectangle: public Polygon { // subclass
public:
  virtual float Area ();
  virtual boolean pointInside ();
  void setRectangle ();
private:
  float Top;
  float Bottom;
  float Left;
  float Right;
};
```

Chapter 4 • Object-Oriented Paradigms

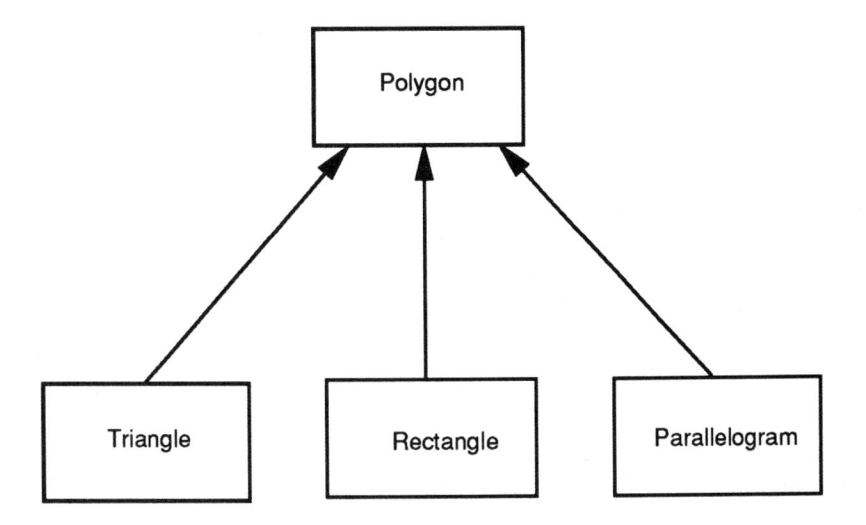

Figure 4-4. Class inheritance

An implementation of a member function to calculate the area of a rectangle can be specified as follows:

```
float Rectangle::Area () {
  return ((Bottom - Top) * (Right - Left));
};
```

Different implementations of Area will be specified for a parallelogram and a triangle. Three separate instances of the same member function can thus refer to three different classes.

Polymorphism can also be illustrated with an array of elements that refer to objects of different types (classes) as suggested in [MEY88, p. 225]. The array is shown in Figure 4-5 and includes pointers to different point types that are all derived from a superclass. In a programming language that does not support polymorphism, the corresponding structure would have to be implemented with a record whose components would refer to the different point types. The latter would be static references, whereas the polymorphic references could be dynamic.

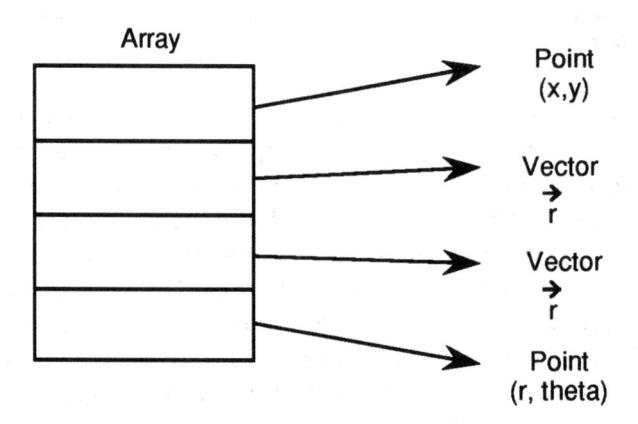

Figure 4-5. Polymorphic reference

4.8 BINDING

The concept of *binding* used in connection with a programming language pertains to the binding of a message (i.e., calling an operation associated with an object) and the code to be executed on behalf of the message. In a programming language with static binding, all references are determined at compilation time. Dynamic, or late, binding, however, means that the code to be executed in response to a message will not be determined until run-time. This is often used to implement screen windowing and pull-down menus where the "buttons" are associated with a set of messages that will activate a corresponding function.

Inheritance, polymorphism, and binding are closely related, and the execution of a call to an operation is associated with a polymorphic reference that depends on the type of the reference. During execution of the C++ program shown above, the appropriate reference to an Area member function will be made by the run-time system. The class association may be determined at compilation time or at execution time. The use of the *virtual* keyword tells the compiler that the association is deferred until execution time, as shown in our example for Area and pointInside. Whenever the virtual specifier is omitted, it is assumed that references are resolved at compilation time.

4.9 MODULARITY

The concept of modularity is related to how we "package" a system into manageable software entities to reduce the complexity of large systems. These entities can be ADTs, individual operations, entire libraries, and programs that are required for the creation of an executable image. The software entities we package are referred to as *modules*, and the creation of these modules have a profound effect on how we can reap the potential benefits of OT.

An important aim in the creation of modules is that the modules be compilation units. This can greatly reduce the amount of recompilation required for large systems when changes are made. It will also directly support an incremental development strategy of adding modules as additional system features are implemented.

The concept of a module implies some kind of identifiable boundary surrounding that module. As a general guideline, we try to create modules that implement encapsulation and information hiding. The general design principle for modular systems has not changed with the introduction of OT: high cohesion within each module, and loose coupling between modules.

A significant difference between the packaging of structured designs versus object-oriented designs is that the latter is based on ADTs. Modules based on structured design would, typically, include a set of operations and associated data structures. These data structures would not be hidden and could be modified throughout the program, resulting in a strong coupling to that data structure.

A typical C++ module will consist of a header file (.h file extension) that contains the specification of a C++ class as an ADT. This header file is imported (with the #include preprocessor statement) and represents the specification ("contract") to the client program using that ADT. A separately compiled ADT (.cpp file extension) source file contains the hidden implementation. The program file (.cpp file extension) includes the required *main* function and the remainder of the programming constructs to implement the required system features.

Here is a simple example of a C++ program module that outlines the use of the Stack class (constructors and a destructor have been omitted for the sake of simplicity):

```
// header file (stack.h)
class Stack { // specification
public:
    void stackInit();
```

```cpp
    long topOfStack();
    long pop();
    void push(long);
private:
    long stackItems[50];
    int stackPtr;
};

// source file (stack.cpp)
#include stack.h
// implementation
    void Stack::stackInit() { ... };
    long Stack::topOfStack() { ... };
    long Stack::pop() { ... };
    void Stack::push(long) { .. };
};

// program file (usestack.cpp)
#include stack.h

// global declarations here
void main () {
  newStack Stack;
  ...
  push( ... );
  ...
  pop();
  ...
};
```

The packaging issue of software modules is extremely important for attaining a high level of reusability. This will be revisited when we discuss the construction of C++ class libraries in later chapters.

4.10 GENERICITY

The concept of genericity refers to the creation of software entities with parameterized types that can be instantiated with different types at compile time.

This is usually referred to as a *parameterized* class, or *generic* class. The generic class is created as a template with formal parameters, and instances of the class are created by providing the corresponding actual parameters. This concept offers the ultimate in reusability, since the same class can be used with any number of types without resorting to inheritance relations of superclasses and subclasses.

Genericity is supported in C++ with the use of templates. Here is an example of a (simplified) generic stack to illustrate the concept:

```
template <class TYPE>
class Stack {
public:
  void reset();
  void push (TYPE);
  TYPE pop();
  TYPE topOf();
private:
  TYPE *stptr;
  int top;
  int length;
};
```

The parameterized type for the generic Stack class is TYPE, and we can now declare stacks of different types:

```
Stack<int> intStack;              // stack of integers
Stack<float> floatStack;          // stack of floats
Stack<complex> complexStack;      // stack of complex
                                  // numbers
Stack<char> charStack;            // stack of characters
```

The generic class represents a higher level of abstraction than the ADT described earlier. It supports reusability directly, since a multitude of instantiations can be made by simply varying the type or value of the actual parameters without rewriting the class for each type. The structure of a generic class is significantly simpler than the class hierarchies used with inheritance relations.

With a general understanding of the most important object-oriented concepts, we will now go on to describe the detailed features of classes and objects.

5

Classes and Objects

One of the most important concepts of object-oriented technology is the creation and description of classes and objects. These entities form the basis for how we partition a large system. They also determine how well we can realize reusable software components when the abstract entities created during the domain and requirements analysis phase are transitioned via the design phase to programming entities.

The primary concern of this chapter is to provide a "formal" (not formal in a mathematical sense) definition of classes and objects, and describe how we decompose large systems using the paradigms of inheritance, aggregation, and association.

5.1 DEFINITIONS

In this section, we will provide definitions for the two most important elements of object-orientation, i.e., classes and objects. Objects are defined first, to make it easier to define classes. We want to avoid a circular definition such as "a class is a collection of common objects, and an object is an instance of a class."

The definitions provided here will probably not satisfy the rigorous rules of a mathematician, but they will serve as a basis for our discussions of object-oriented paradigms.

5.1.1 Objects

A common definition for an object is that it is a tangible "thing," something that can be recognized visually or conceptually. Many objects have distinct physical boundaries, such as a chair or a desk. Other objects have more fuzzy boundaries, such as an organization or a staff.

An object can be defined using the following characteristics:

1. **An object is identified by a unique name.** An airplane, for example, can be identified by type and a unique tail number, such as Cessna N4GA or Mooney N9634N, or by a flight number, such as American Airlines 431. Of these three examples, the Cessna and the Mooney are objects that will persist for an indefinite time, whereas the American Airlines flight will only exist for the duration of the flight. This implies that we need additional attributes to fully describe an object within the framework of a particular system.

2. **An object has states.** These states will fully define the properties associated with an object, and the values of these properties for the lifetime of the object within the system boundaries. Examples of states for an airplane object within an air traffic control (ATC) system include: parked, taxiing, climbing, level flight, holding, descending, and landing.

3. **An object has a set of operations.** The behavior of objects within a system is described via a set of operations. These operations are used to obtain or change the state of an object, as well as to provide a means of communication between objects. Examples of operations for an airplane object within an ATC system include: calculate position, display target, estimate time of arrival, display weather information, and calculate ground speed. Operations are sometimes referred to as "methods." We will use "operations" to describe the general (language independent) behavior of objects. For C++, we will use the term *member functions*.

4. **An object has a set of attributes.** The attributes of an object contain state values throughout the lifetime of an object. They are usually implemented as hidden variables of the abstraction that the object represents. Examples of attributes for an airplane object include: cruising speed, range, amount of fuel onboard, and weight.

Even with this set of characteristics to describe an object, it is sometimes difficult to identify objects in the development process. An object takes on a number of different forms throughout the development cycle, and is referred to as an "object" at many different levels and in different development technologies. The real-world object shown in Figure 5-1 could be encountered during the domain analysis, and represents a high level abstraction.

Chapter 5 • Classes and Objects

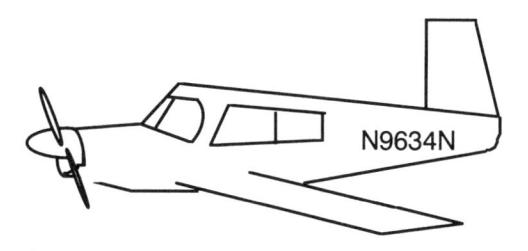

Figure 5-1. Real-world object

The Track Store data element shown in Figure 5-2 represents an abstract analysis object used in real-time structured analysis (i.e., not associated with object technology).

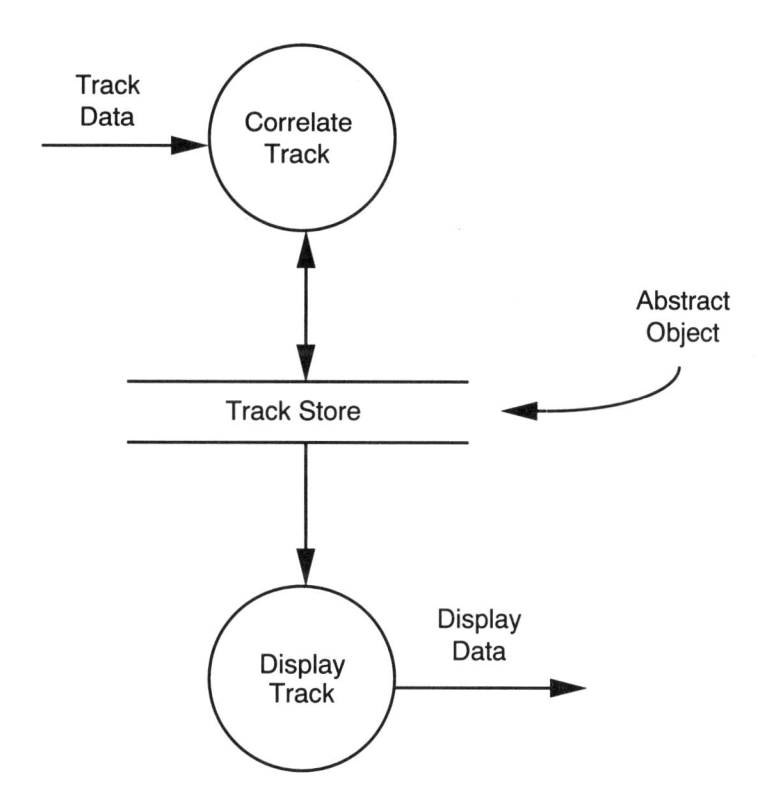

Figure 5-2. Abstract analysis object

The C++ class, String, shown in Figure 5-3 is an OOD/OOP entity also referred to as an "object." And, finally, the instance newString is a programming object created from the String class.

In most cases, we can tell from the context what kind of object is being referred to. Throughout this book, we will specify a domain analysis object, analysis object, design object, or programming object if the context is ambiguous.

```
class String {
public:
  String (char*);
  String (const String&);
  String ();
  ~String () { delete str; }

  String operator() (int, int);
  char& operator[] (int);
  String& operator= (const char*);
  // ...
  getLen () { return len; }
private:
  int len;
  char* str;
};

// ...
String newString;
```

Figure 5-3. OOP class object

An important concept in dealing with objects is the determination of how they relate to each other. The primary view is that an object interacts with another object via the operations associated with that object. An object sends a "message" to another object by calling an operation that is visible to the calling object. The direction of data passed can be uni- or bi-directional. This type of relationship is defined in [RUM91] as a *link* between two objects. An object can thus be looked upon as either a client using the operations of other objects, or a server providing operations to other objects.

5.1.2 Classes

Classes and objects are closely related, and having defined an object, we can now define classes in terms of objects.

An important difference between an object and a class is that an object is a concrete entity that has a finite time of existence within the system creating and using that object. A class, on the other hand, is only an abstraction and never exists in a concrete form. A general set of characteristics for the definition of a class include the following:

1. A class is a high level of abstraction. The abstraction is useful for describing a set of common characteristics of analysis and design entities. The class Aircraft, for example, can be used to describe attributes (characteristics) that are common to all specific instances of individual aircraft, such as landing gear, range, weight, cruising speed, and number of passengers. The class Radar can be used to describe different radars in terms of range and azimuth, revolutions per minute, and physical interfaces.

2. A class is a collection of objects. Each class represents a collection of objects with common attributes and a set of operations.

3. An object is a specific instance of a class. This represents the very close relationship between classes and objects. A unique object is a member of a particular class, and has a set of attributes and operations associated with that class. A particular Cessna 210 with the tail number N4GA is an instance of an Aircraft class. And a particular Doppler radar made by a specific manufacturer is an instance of the general class Radar.

4. A class has an implied hierarchy. Each class has a potential parent-child relationship where the hierarchy is represented as the concept of inheritance. A child class (subclass) can be derived from a parent (superclass) and inherit the attributes and operations of the parent class. An Aircraft class, for example, can be the parent of a number of subclasses, such as Fighter Aircraft, General Aviation, and Air Carriers. This characteristic of a class is an extremely important paradigm of object-oriented methods, and will be described in considerable length in various parts of this book.

With these definitions for classes and objects, we can now continue with the practical aspects of how classes and objects are used to support our development strategy.

5.1.3 Roles of Classes and Objects in OOA and OOD

Classes and objects are used to decompose a large system into real-world abstractions that can form the basis for analysis and design. During the domain analysis and requirements analysis phases, we determine high-level objects and their enclosing classes. These key abstractions are used as the basis for discussing the stated requirements with our customer and potential users. It is important that these initial artifacts have names that customers and users can relate to, and that implementation technology is left out of the requirements discussions.

During the design phase, the high-level classes and objects determined during the analysis phase are refined. Details are added by scrutinizing requirements for reusable attributes and operations, and suitable interfaces are constructed. Additional classes and objects are usually discovered or invented when we attempt to construct the design. The resulting architecture will enable the skeleton system to be realized with the chosen programming language during the implementation phase.

An important role played by classes in OOA/OOD is to provide the interfaces required for access to the attributes associated with instances of a particular class. The access is provided via the visible operations declared for each class. It is important to realize, however, that attributes and operations are associated with instances (objects) of a specific class, and not with the class itself. The operations declared in the class interface perform certain actions on each instance of the given class. The attributes declared in the class specification are referred to as *instance variables* and store the states of a particular instance. If we need attributes that are common to all instances of a class, we have to create *class variables*. This is supported directly in some programming languages. In C++, we will be using the *static* keyword to achieve the effect of a class variable. (See also the section on metaclasses below.)

5.2 CREATING CLASSES

The class/object concept is fundamental to object-oriented methods, and is used for OOA and OOD. With a programming language that supports OOP, we can directly implement the class/object structure from OOD.

The importance of the creation of classes and objects is that they support an object-oriented decomposition into real-world entities. The practical question is, "How do we create classes and objects for the various development phases?" The starting point for creating classes and objects is a set of guidelines for how system requirements can be classified into a number of class categories.

Since a class will function in a server role to the clients, we also need guidelines for the creation of a set of operations that can provide a suitable interface, i.e., the responsibilities of the class (and of the instantiated objects at the programming level).

5.2.1 Class Categories

The following set of class categories can be used as a guideline in the creation of classes from a set of system requirements:

1. **Device Interface Class.** Most of our systems will interface directly with hardware devices (e.g., radars, ATMs, and printers), and provide a readily identifiable class category (we are distinguishing these devices from user interface devices).

2. **External System Class.** This is an appropriate category for those systems that interface with similar external systems, e.g., an ATC center receiving a handover message from another center, or a banking system receiving information from a credit clearing institution.

3. **User Interface Class.** Most of our systems interface with users via a keyboard or graphical device. This may be subdivided into separate categories for each type of user interface device, e.g., keyboard, mouse, and lightpen.

4. **Computational Class.** This category is appropriate for systems that include significant computations to support the system requirements. Examples of this category include coordinate conversions for robot control and ATC systems, and the calculation of compound interest for a savings institution system.

5. **Role Class.** This category can be used where a person is an important part of the operational system. A Controller in an ATC or air defense system, for example, can take on the role of Supervisor, Trainer, Trainee, Approach Controller, or Tower Controller. In a banking system, a teller is one of the important roles.

6. **Data Abstraction Classes.** Classes in this category may not readily appear in the system requirements, but will become evident if we are employing data modeling as part of our development strategy. Entity relationship diagrams (ERDs), for example, may be used during the domain analysis. The major data entities in the ERDs are real-world

objects, and we can sometimes collect similar entities into data abstraction classes. Examples of data entities include radar and weather data for an ATC system, and user accounts for a banking system.

This set of class categories is the starting point for finding real-world classes and objects that can be used in the analysis and design of our systems. We will pursue the methods for finding classes and objects based on this classification in Chapter 8.

5.2.2 Operations Categories

The classes by themselves will be of little value as server entities unless they include proper interfaces that permit the clients to access the classes. An important activity during OOA and OOD is the identification of suitable operations for each class. These operations will, typically, be represented as procedural abstractions of a single functional entity, e.g., CalculateInterest, ReadATM, ValidatePIN, etc.

As an aid to the creation of a proper interface to a class, the operations necessary to manipulate instances of the class can be categorized as follows [LIP91, p. 223]:

1. **Manager Operations.** These operations will handle the creation, initialization and destruction of class instances (objects), assignment of one object to another, memory management, and type conversion (including the conversion of user-defined types). Many of the manager operations will be invoked automatically for classes and objects implemented with C++. These operations are usually part of the visible class interface.

2. **Implementor Operations.** The collection of these operations encompasses the functional requirements of the class abstraction. If we have a Windows class, for example, the implementor operations will include the registration, updating, moving, and repainting of Windows objects. These operations represent the primary class interface to the clients.

3. **Helping Operations.** These operations are used as auxiliary support functions to help out the operations in the two former categories, and are usually hidden to the clients.

4. **Access Operations.** Since the class attributes are encapsulated within the class structure, we have to provide a mechanism whereby the clients can get information about the hidden attributes. Access operations are also used to change the state values of class attributes, e.g., we

may have an operation to change the maximum number of lines in an edit screen.

We will return to these guidelines later when we start the decomposition of system requirements into sets of classes and objects.

5.3 INHERITANCE AND CLASS HIERARCHIES

An important consequence of the class inheritance relations discussed in Chapter 4, is the implied hierarchy of the derived classes (subclasses). A different view of the Window class shown in Chapter 4 is illustrated in Figure 5-4. This represents a hierarchical decomposition of a Window class. The first lower layer includes specialized versions of a Window. The second lower layer consists of specialized versions of a Control.

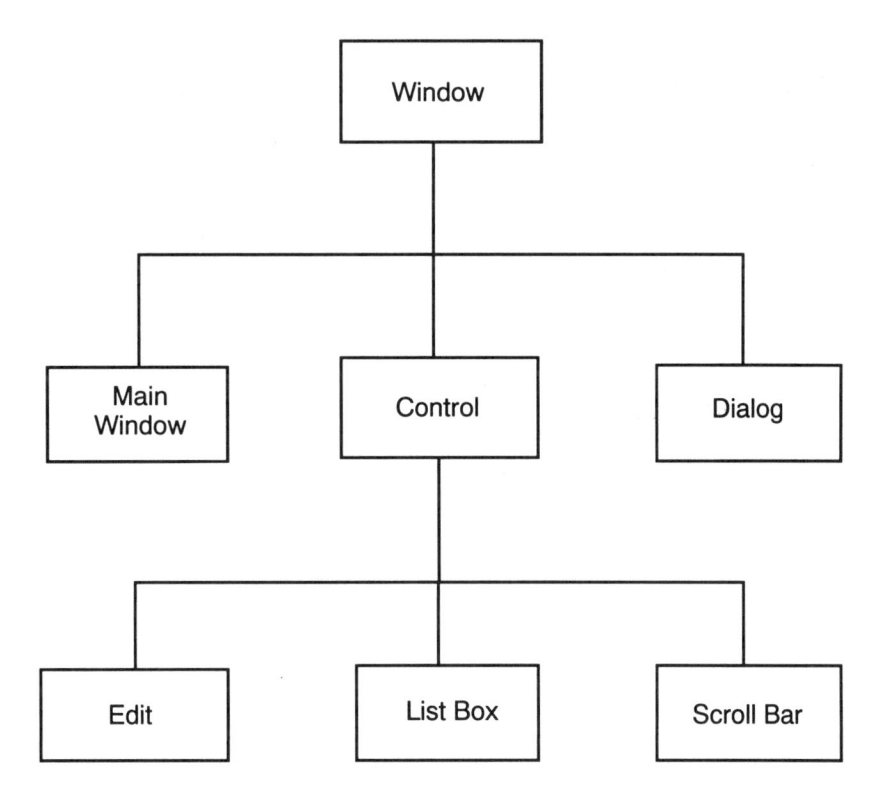

Figure 5-4. Class hierarchy

The nesting of classes to form lower level entities of higher specialization is one of the most important aspects of being able to decompose a large system into smaller, manageable parts. This form of generalization/specialization is the method we employ in everyday life to break down complex entities into something we can understand. The hierarchy resulting from the OOA and OOD phases can be implemented directly in OOP with a programming language that supports inheritance, such as C++.

The creation of a class hierarchy, and the associated inheritance paradigm, is only one way that classes are related for large, complex systems. The other two relations are aggregation and association, which are described in the next sections. It is very important to distinguish between these concepts, since inheritance is sometimes confused with aggregation, and may result in awkward implementations of an object decomposition.

5.4 AGGREGATION

Aggregation refers to a system being composed of a number of classes that are not related via a generalization/specialization hierarchy, but rather with a whole-parts relation. For example, an aircraft is composed of a fuselage, wings, engine, landing gear, and various electrical and hydraulic systems. The key term to aggregation is the "has-a" relation, as opposed to the "is-a" relation for a hierarchical structure as was shown in Figure 5-4.

The aggregation relation is illustrated in Figure 5-5 for some of the components of an airplane. An airplane is composed of (at least) a Wing, Engine, Fuselage, and Engine. The Airplane exhibits a has-a relationship to these components, i.e., the Airplane is the whole and the components the parts. It is clear from this illustration that a Wing is not an Airplane with an is-a relation. A Wing and an Electrical System have been further decomposed in their respective subcomponents. An aggregation is thus another form of hierarchy for which classes can be constructed, but not with an inheritance relationship.

The difference between inheritance and aggregation hierarchies can be further noted by comparing the Airplane has-a aggregation in Figure 5-5, and the Airplane is-a inheritance hierarchy in Figure 5-6. In the latter figure we have used the arrows to signify inheritance between parent-child entities. The OT literature is not consistent in this usage, however, and it is easy to confuse the two types of hierarchies.

Aggregation is sometimes referred to as composition, containment, and membership. These terms are used as synonyms throughout the OT literature.

Chapter 5 • Classes and Objects

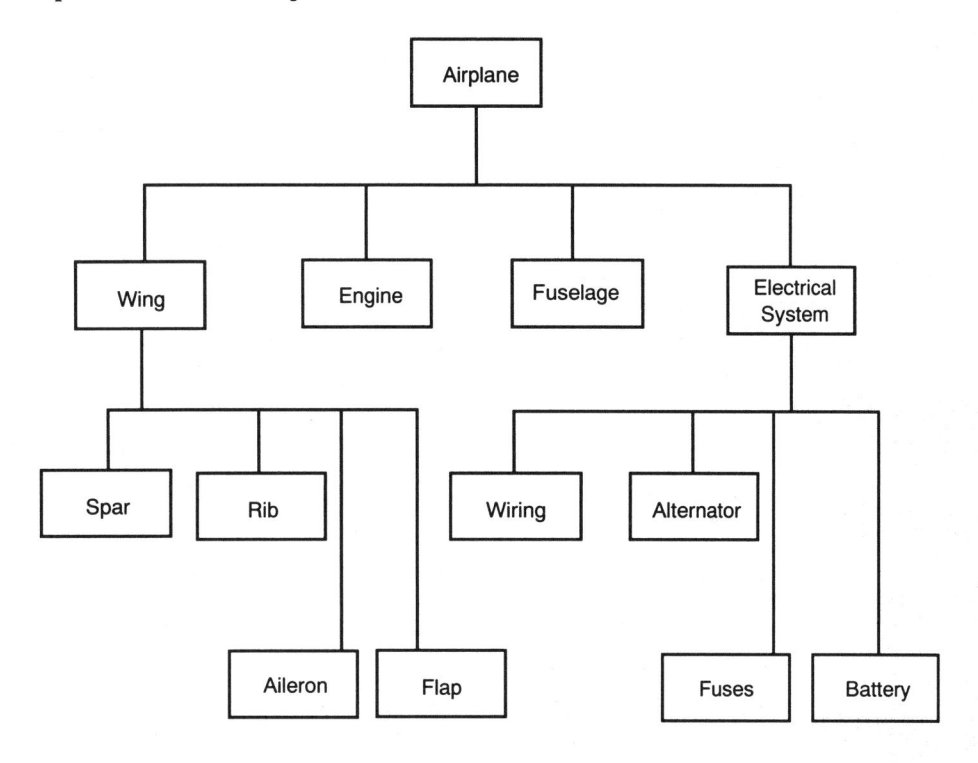

Figure 5-5. Aggregation relations

The differences between the relations in Figures 5-5 and 5-6 can be illustrated by C++ code skeletons. Here is an example of a base class Airplane and derived class Commercial corresponding to Figure 5-6, i.e., Commercial is-a Airplane:

```
class Airplane {
...
};

class Commercial : public Airplane {
            // class Commercial inherits
            // from class Airplane
...
};
```

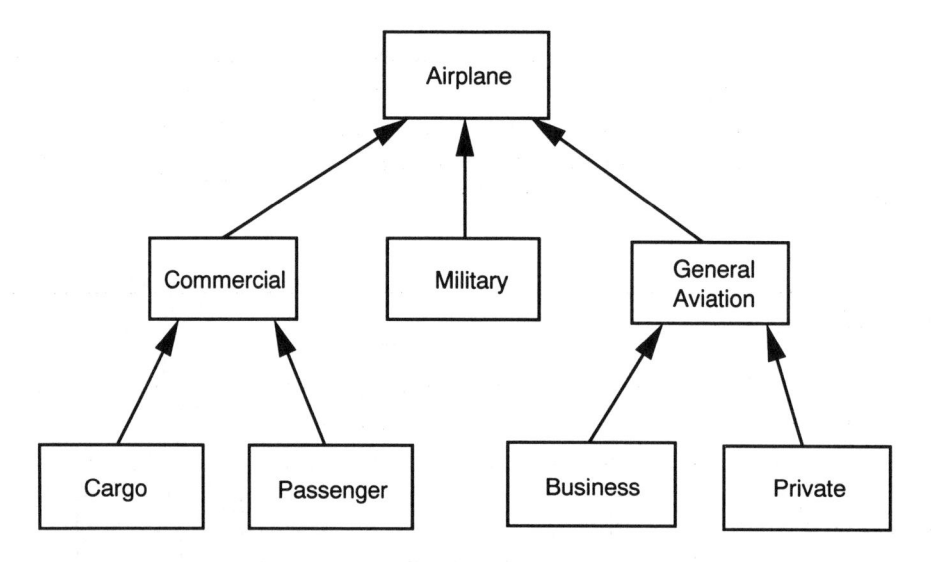

Figure 5-6. Inheritance relations

Here is an example of an Airplane class which has the classes Wing and Engine as member classes, i.e., the has-a relation in Figure 5-5:

```
class Wing {
...
};

class Engine {
...
};

class Airplane {
  Wing leftWing;
            // Wing class is member of Airplane class
  Wing rightWing;
  Engine rearEngine;
        // Engine class is member of Airplane class
  ...
};
```

The differences between aggregation and inheritance may have a profound effect on how well we construct our classes for reusability in the client/server sense. A common mistake is to use inheritance when we should be using aggregation. This topic will be covered in detail when we discuss OOP with C++ in Chapter 19.

5.5 ASSOCIATION

An association between classes refers to simple communication or a dependency between objects of different classes that do not fit the is-a or has-a relations. The establishment of an association defines the roles or dependencies between objects of two classes and their cardinalities (multiplicity), i.e., how many instances of each class can be involved in an association.

Each association forms a bidirectional dependency, unless it is specifically restricted to one direction. An Employee, for example, "works-for" a Company, and the Company "employs" the Employee. The "works-for" association is viewed from an Employee object to a Company object. The "employs" association is viewed in the opposite direction between the same two objects.

The same association may apply to multiple instances of the same class, and we, thus have the concept of cardinality or multiplicity. There are three basic categories of cardinality:

- one-to-one
- one-to-many (or many-to-one)
- many-to-many

A one-to-one association is illustrated in Figure 5-7 for objects of classes Person and Social Security Number (SSN). Each person has a unique SSN, and a given SSN refers to a single individual. We also notice the (implied) bidirectional relation between objects of these two classes. The role stated on the line (a Person "Has" an SSN) is read from left to right. The reverse relation (an SSN "identifies" a Person) is implied and is read from right to left.

```
┌─────────────────┐                    ┌─────────────────┐
│     Person      │                    │      SSN        │
├─────────────────┤       Has          ├─────────────────┤
│                 │────────────────────│                 │
│     Name        │                    │    Number       │
│    Address      │                    │                 │
│                 │                    │                 │
└─────────────────┘                    └─────────────────┘
```

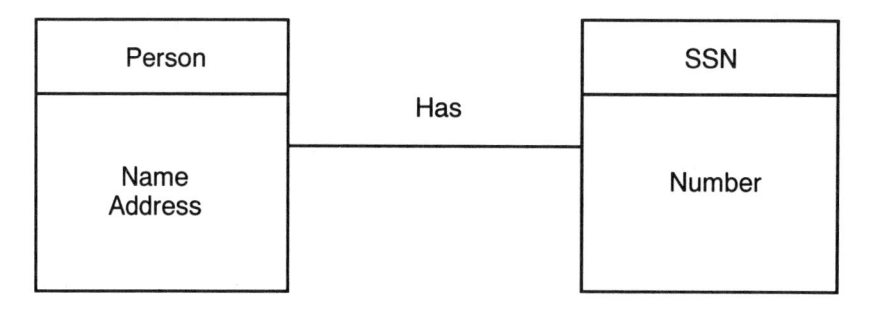

Figure 5-7. One-to-one association

A one-to-many association is illustrated in Figure 5-8 between a Person and the Company that person works for. We are assuming here that any one person only works for a single company.

If we assume that at least two intersecting lines form a point, and that a line can intersect multiple points, we have a many-to-many association between a Line and a Point class, as shown in Figure 5-9. The black circle represents many objects of a class, and the "2+" indicates at least two objects. This particular notation is taken from the Object Modeling Technique (OMT), described in [RUM91]. Notations for cardinality vary between OOA/OOD methods and must be observed for the particular method we choose. Variations in notation for OOA/OOD methods will be discussed further in Chapter 7.

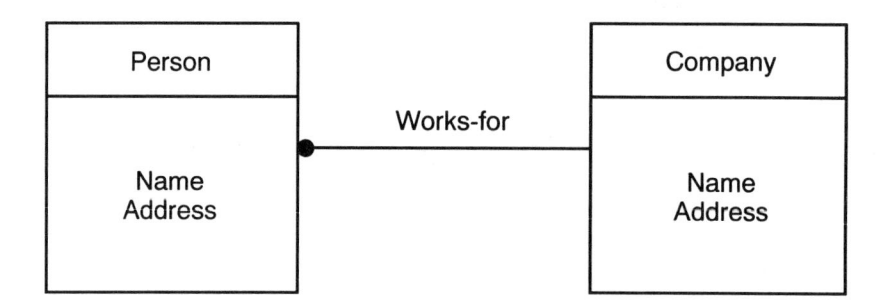

```
┌─────────────────┐                    ┌─────────────────┐
│     Person      │                    │     Company     │
├─────────────────┤     Works-for      ├─────────────────┤
│                 │●───────────────────│                 │
│     Name        │                    │     Name        │
│    Address      │                    │    Address      │
│                 │                    │                 │
└─────────────────┘                    └─────────────────┘
```

Figure 5-8. One-to-many association

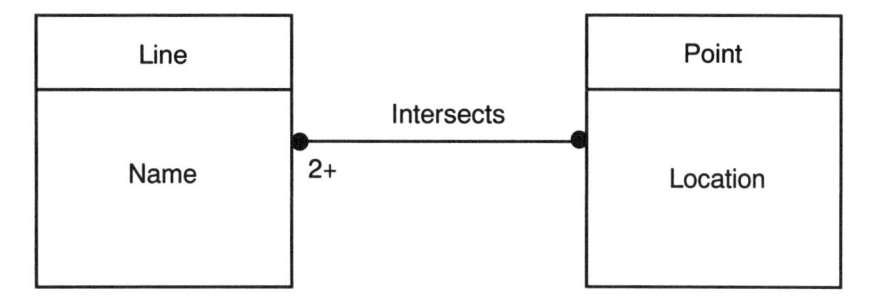

Figure 5-9. Many-to-many association

5.6 USING

A "using" relationship between classes and objects means that a reference is made to a class or object that is outside the current abstraction. An example of this relationship is the following ATM class, which is using an outside Account class:

```
extern class Account;
...
Account userAccount (...);

class ATM {
   ...
   float Balance (const char* accountNo);
   ...
};

...
float Balance (const char* accountNo) {
   ...
   return userAccount.GetBalance (accountNo);// using
}
```

One way to view this relationship is via the client/server role [BOO93, p. 130]. In our example, the ATM class is the client and the Account class the server. The using relationship is an important OT notation, and some of the methods discussed in Chapter 7 use a special notation to illustrate this.

5.7 MIXIN CLASSES

A "mixin" class [COP92, BOO93] is an independent class that does not have any superclass, i.e., a mixin class is not part of an inheritance hierarchy. A typical use for mixin classes is in the creation of a derived class that does not have a directly related parent class. This can simplify the class structure when multiple inheritance is required. One of the biggest problems in dealing with a deep hierarchy of derived classes is the identification of objects during the debugging phase. Use of mixins creates a single level in the hierarchy of the derived class, and may reduce debugging efforts.

5.8 CONTAINER CLASSES

Container classes [BOO93] are used to hold collections of objects, such as stacks, lists, sets, queues, etc. A homogeneous container class [MUR93] holds objects of the same type, whereas a heterogeneous container class includes objects of different types. Heterogeneous containers in C++ are usually derived from a common base class to provide ease of object access via the base class member functions. Homogeneous containers in C++ are, typically, implemented with the use of templates. Each type of object is specified in the template for the instantiation of the class.

5.9 METACLASSES

A metaclass is a highest-level class from which instances can be created as new classes, i.e., a class derived from a metaclass is an object. Metaclasses are useful for the treatment of high-level classes in a hierarchy, and for the creation of class variables. The derived high-level classes can be manipulated just like other objects [BOO93, p. 134].

C++ does not support the metaclass concept directly, but we can simulate class variables of a "metaclass" by using the *static* keyword. Static data members are shared by all instances of the "metaclass," and we thus have a way to create common variables that can be used or modified by all objects belonging to the same class. An example of the use of a class variable is to keep a count of how many instances are currently created of a given class. This is sometimes referred to as reference counting [COP92, p. 58].

5.10 REUSABILITY ISSUES

The type of reuse realized for any software development project comes in different forms, as shown in Figure 5-10. We have all used the common practice of cut-and-paste of individual lines of code from one program to another. This is a low-level form of reuse, and the primary selling point of OT is the potential for reusability in-the-large. This can be realized with the proper construction of individual classes. Mechanisms for extending the reuse of the classes include inheritance (creating subclasses from superclasses) and genericity (using templates for specifying the type of a particular object). Both of these mechanisms are supported by C++ and provide an excellent form for reusability.

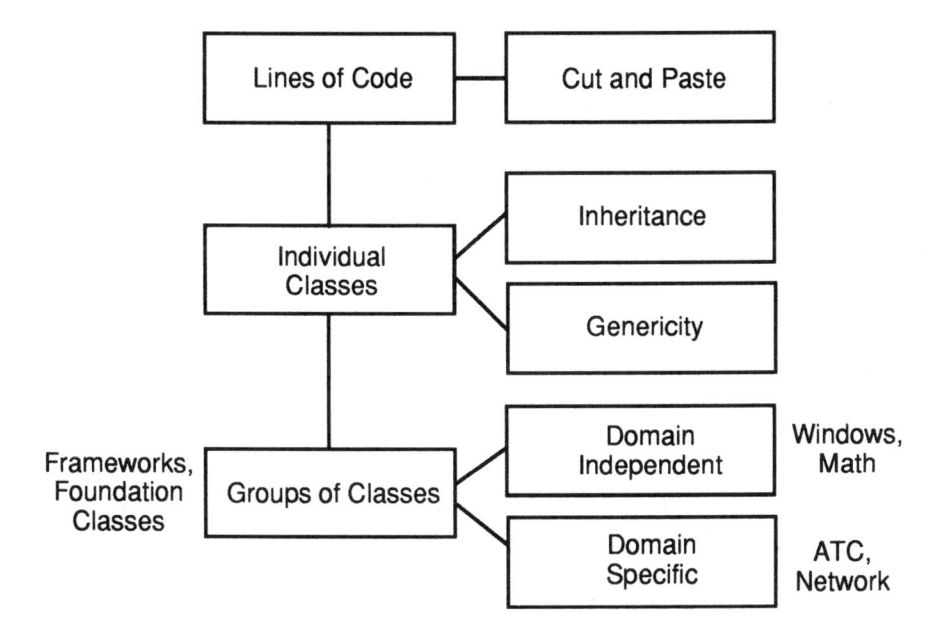

Figure 5-10. Levels of reuse

A higher form for reuse is the creation of frameworks or foundation classes. Each framework consists of a group of classes that can be domain independent or domain specific. Domain independent frameworks are available for Microsoft Windows applications and mathematics, e.g., the Microsoft Foundation Classes (MFC) and Borland's ObjectWindows Library (OWL 2.0). Domain specific frameworks can be developed for such applications as networking, air traffic control, and banking.

The realization of reusability in-the-large will not happen just because we use a programming language that supports the required OT mechanisms, such as C++. It is essential that reusability be planned and managed throughout the software development cycle. This includes management decisions to buy existing libraries versus development of new code. It also includes having a set of guidelines for design evaluations of existing and new code to be developed. These kind of guidelines will be discussed in various sections throughout the book.

6
Object-Oriented Analysis and Design Models

With an extension of an object orientation from the original object-oriented programming techniques to include the other major phases of the software development cycle (i.e., requirements analysis and design), a mixture of objects will be created. Some of these objects will be pure abstractions that will exist on paper only, whereas others will actually be implemented as statements in a programming language. It is highly desirable to have a consistent approach for the various phases in the development cycle. This should include a common nomenclature and a suitable set of tools to support the development process. Incorporated with the tools should be a set of graphical representations to illustrate the various design decisions made, and heuristics for transitioning from one development phase to the next.

It is unfortunate that a number of OOA and OOD techniques have emerged without a unifying notation or agreement for when a particular method should be used. Many of these techniques represent the same OT paradigms, but they use different graphical representations. A unifying description has been described [KOR90], but has not been adopted by the various vendors of OOA/OOD techniques and CASE tools.

The basic mechanism of all OT methods is a number of models used to describe certain analysis and design features of the system under consideration. These features capture static and dynamic views of the real-world entities that represent the system requirements and their corresponding architectural structures. The various models are discussed here, before we describe the methods themselves in the next chapter.

6.1 OBJECT-ORIENTED MODELS

All of the OOA/OOD methods in use today employ modeling tools to describe the relationships between the classes that represent the functional requirements of the problem domain and the architecture illustrating the design. Models are also used to describe the relations between objects created as instances of the various classes. OT models are used to represent abstractions of real-world entities and their relationships. These models depict various views of the system requirements and the architectures used in implementing the system.

There are potentially four sets of models that can be used for OT methods: OOA models, OOD models, class models, and object models. As we shall see later in this chapter, the same models can be used for both the OOA and the OOD phases. This is good news and bad news. The good news is that we use the same notation and graphical tools for the documentation items of both phases. The bad news is that using the exact same model for the two phases blurs the distinction between analysis and design and makes it more difficult to identify the transitioning between the two phases. In general, the primary difference between the OOA models and the OOD models is the higher level of abstraction for OOA objects and their relations.

The models used for relations between classes and objects, respectively, are identical and we will use the term "object model." If there is any ambiguity between these two models, we will refer to a "class model" for class relations only.

Having dispensed with the possible permutations of OOA/OOD and class/object models, we will now focus on the two sets of models that describe class/object relations for the analysis, design, and programming phases: static model and dynamic model. All of the OT methods described in the next chapter use combinations of these two sets of models, although the notation differs significantly between the various methods.

We will use the requirements of a simplified Automated Teller Machine (ATM) application to illustrate the various models, and to provide a comparative overview of the notations used by the different methods. A system diagram of an ATM application is shown in Figure 6-1. A number of ATMs are connected to a central computer which controls the ATMs. A consortium of banks has access to the central computer, and users furnished with an ATM card and an assigned personal identification number (PIN) can insert the card into any of the associated ATMs and withdraw cash or make a deposit. A user's bank account is associated with a single bank. Each bank computer commu-

Chapter 6 • Object-Oriented Analysis and Design Models   75

nicates with the central computer and updates a user's account after each ATM transaction is completed. We have simplified the system to include transactions only via ATMs, and have eliminated the personal bank tellers that are part of most banking systems. A complete description of the ATM requirements can be found in [RUM91, p. 151].

In the sections that follow we will be demonstrating the various general static and dynamic models used in OOA and OOD. The notation used for this demonstration will be the one associated with the Object Modeling Technique (OMT), which is discussed in the next chapter.

6.2 Static Models

The static model represents the relations between real-world objects in analysis and design, including their attributes and operations. The static representation does not take into account events and instruction sequencing that take place during execution of the implemented design model.

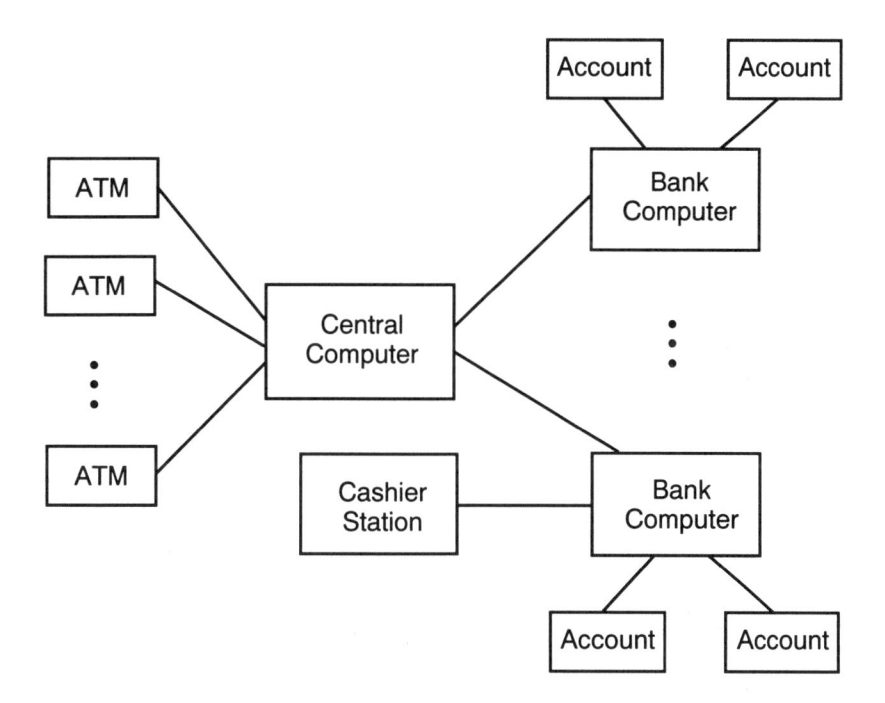

Figure 6-1. ATM system diagram

The static model is represented graphically showing object icons and their relations with other objects. An example of an object model diagram for the simplified ATM application is shown in Figure 6-2. The rectangular icons represent real-world objects such as Customer, ATM, Consortium, and Bank. The name of the object is given in the top of the rectangle, the attributes in the middle part, and the operations in the bottom part (operations are not included here). Relations between the objects are illustrated with annotated connecting lines. These relations are referred to as *associations* in some of the methods. Some object diagrams omit the attributes and operations, and thus contain less detailed information. This may be used for OOA models during the domain and requirements analysis, where the emphasis is placed on finding the key real-world abstractions.

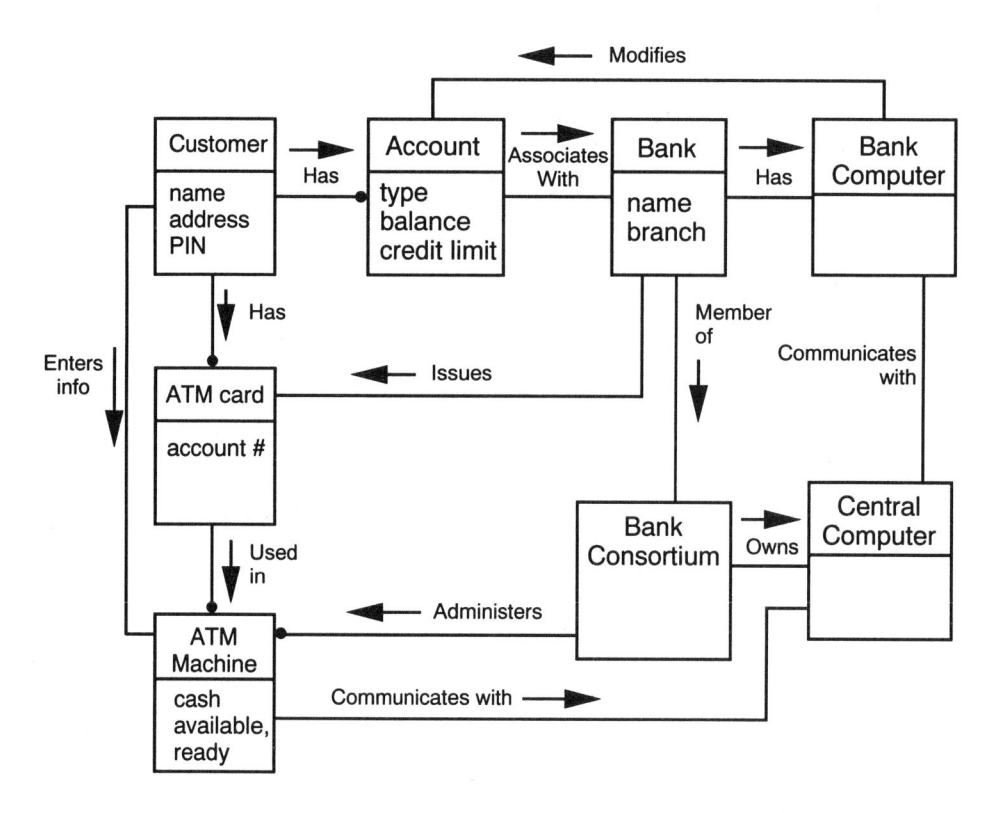

Figure 6-2. Object model of ATM application

Chapter 6 • Object-Oriented Analysis and Design Models

A static model used to illustrate object decomposition is shown in Figure 6-3, and represents a more detailed look at the ATM Machine object. Aggregation is depicted for a whole-part relationship between the ATM machine and the components Customer Display, Transaction, and Printer. Inheritance is shown with Cash Withdrawal and Check Deposit as derived objects from the parent Transaction.

Another form of a static model is the module architecture diagram shown in Figure 6-4. This is used for the OOD phase and illustrates static architectural entities and their interfaces. Each design icon depicts the interface used for receiving and sending messages to and from the object encapsulated within the icon boundary. The message flow can be indicated by the direction of arrows on the lines connecting the objects.

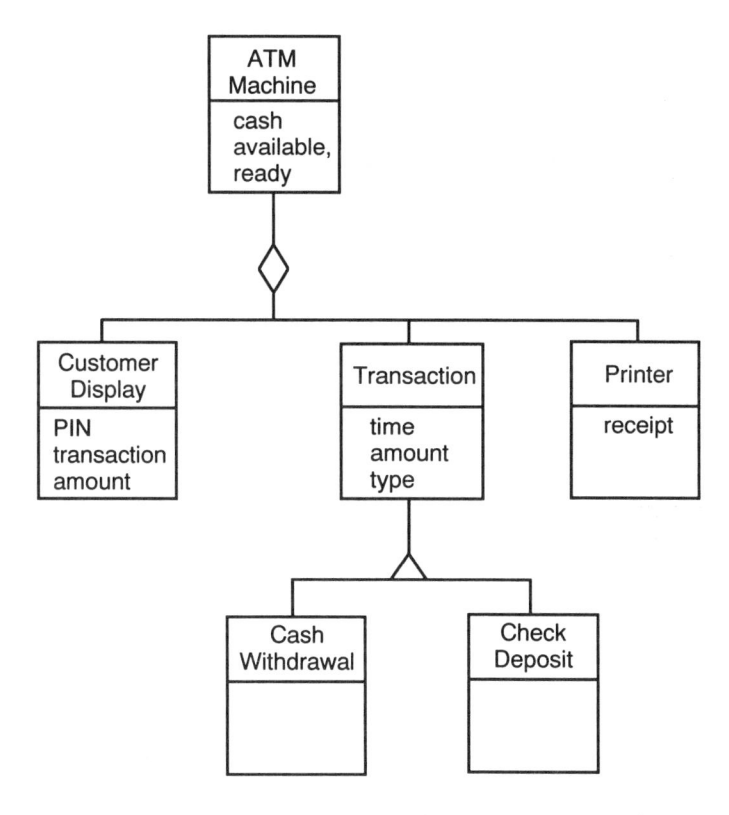

Figure 6-3. Inheritance and aggregation model

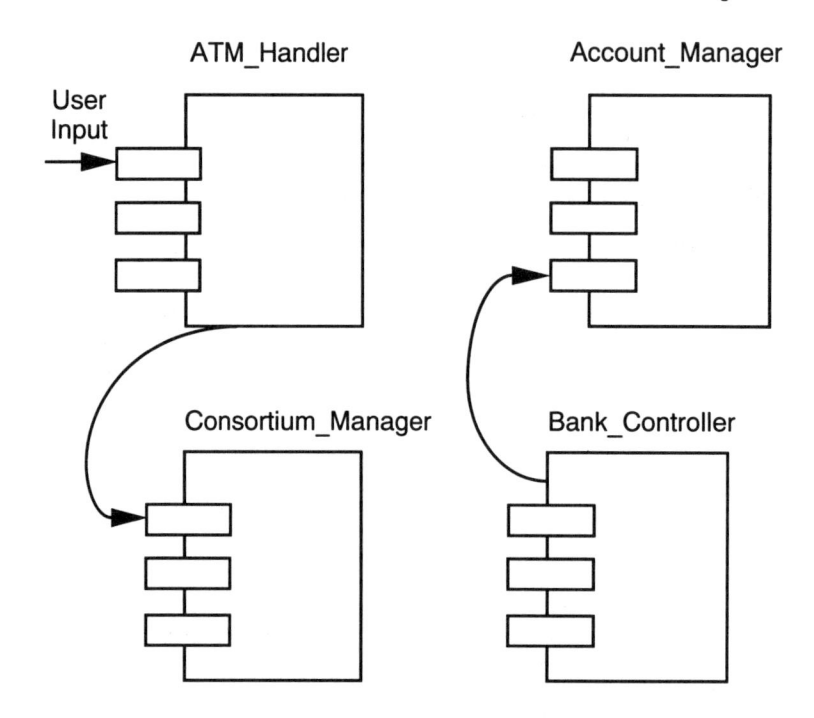

Figure 6-4. Module architecture diagram for ATM application

6.3 DYNAMIC MODELS

Dynamic models are used to describe objects and their relations with regard to the system changing with time. The dynamic behavior includes system state changes, sequencing of events, and external input and output (e.g., incoming interrupts and outgoing signals sent to hardware devices).

An example of a dynamic object model for the ATM application is shown in Figure 6-5. This is an object flow model depicting the messages that flow between the objects. Some OT methods consider all of these objects as high-level concurrent entities, and use this model to determine the elements of subsystems.

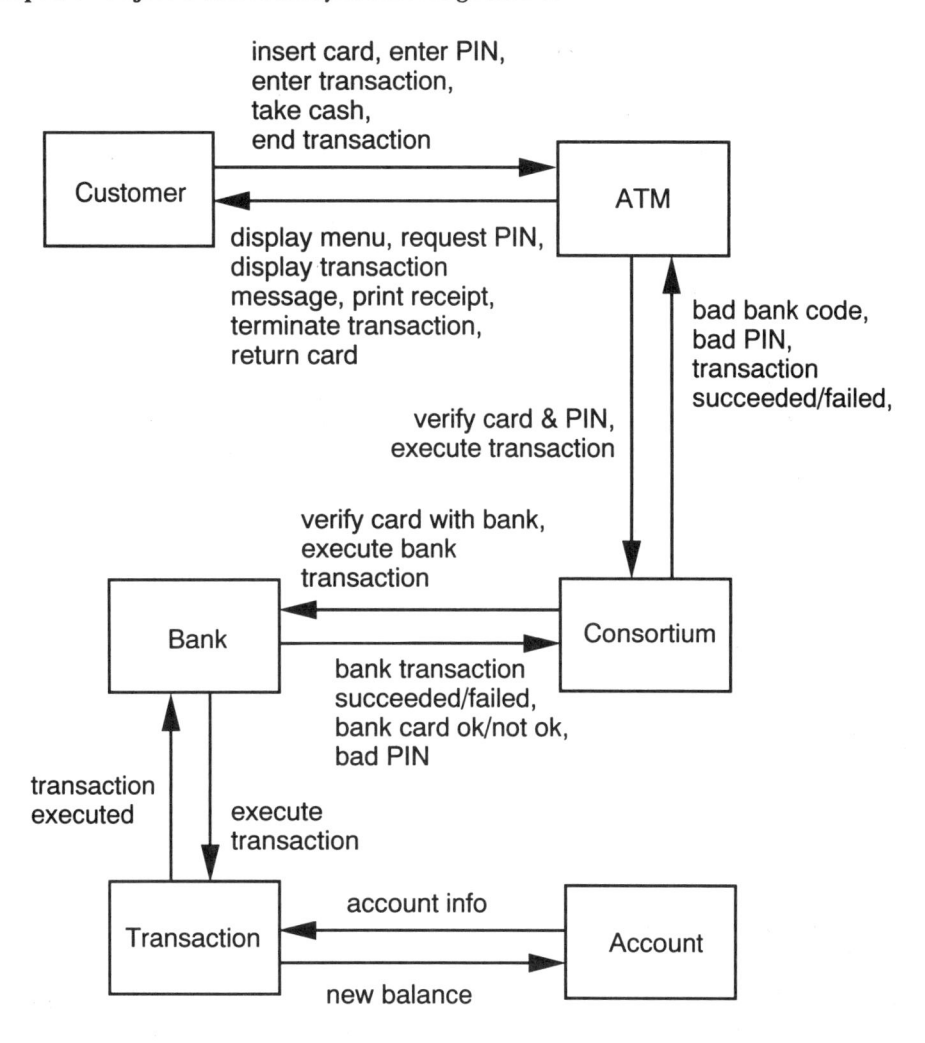

Chapter 6 • Object-Oriented Analysis and Design Models

Figure 6-5. Object flow model of ATM application

A second form of a dynamic object model is the event trace diagram for the ATM application shown in Figure 6-6. This illustrates the time-ordered events that take place between the real-world objects depicted in the object model (see Figure 6-2) or the object flow model (see Figure 6-5). The heavy vertical lines in Figure 6-6 represent the major ATM objects, and the annotated connecting lines represent the events that flow between the objects. Time is measured from top to bottom, but is not to scale.

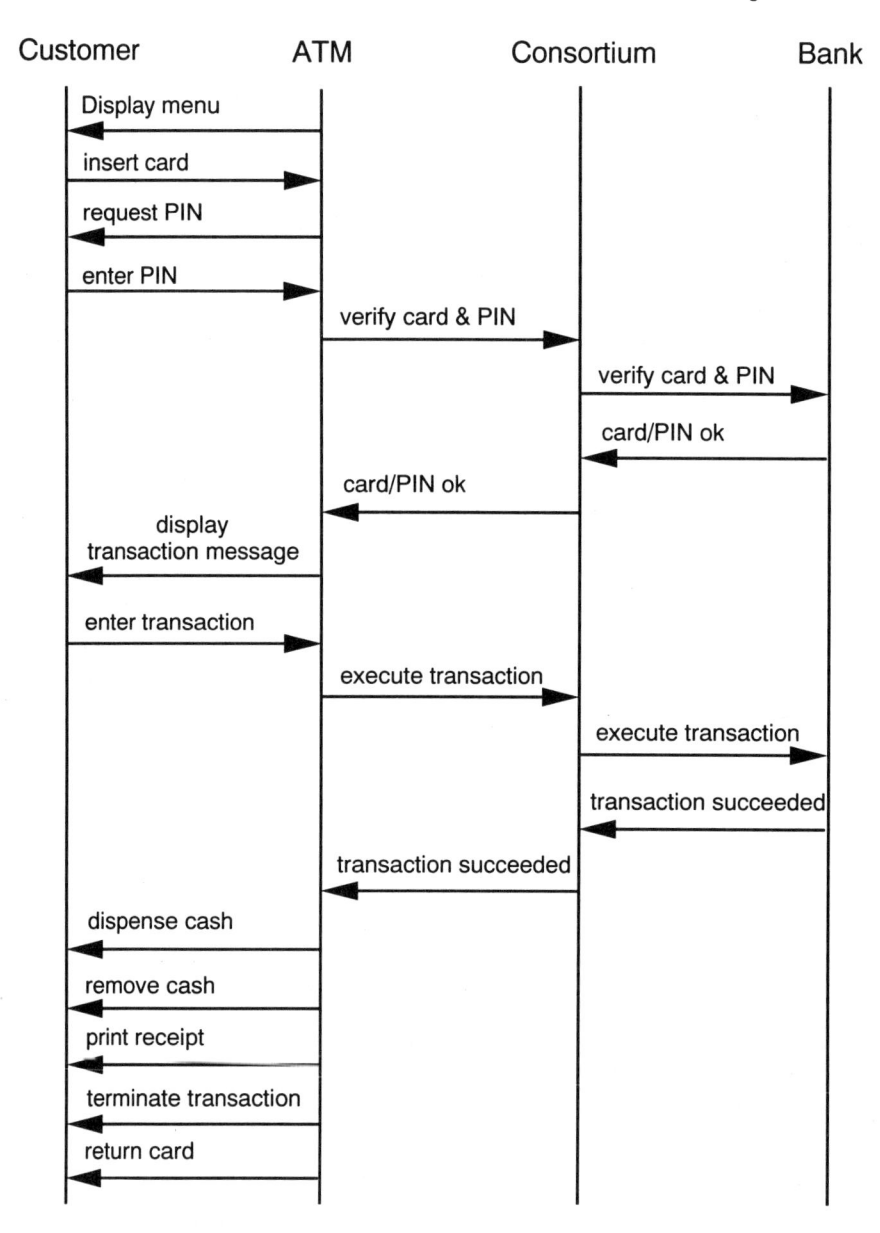

Figure 6-6. Event trace diagram for ATM application

A third form for a dynamic model is the state transition diagram (STD) for the ATM application shown in Figure 6-7. Each rectangle represents a given

Chapter 6 • Object-Oriented Analysis and Design Models

system state, and the annotated connections are the events that trigger the actions that cause the state changes. The STDs do not scale up well for large systems, due to the number of complex details required for a system STD. The only way to manage state changes for large systems is to use STDs at the object level, rather than at the system level.

The dynamic model includes several graphical representations that depict dynamic behavior. Each representation illustrates a different view of the interacting objects, and is used to describe certain aspects of the analysis or design effort with varying levels of abstraction.

It should be noted that complicated charts such as STDs and event trace diagrams include a great amount of detail and may not be suitable for discussing system requirements with a customer. There may thus be a natural distinction between the models used for the analysis phase versus the design phase. Higher levels of abstraction are more suitable during the analysis phase. More detail is required for the design phase. We can make a rule that only the dynamic object model should be included for the analysis phase. STDs and event traces are added for the design phase.

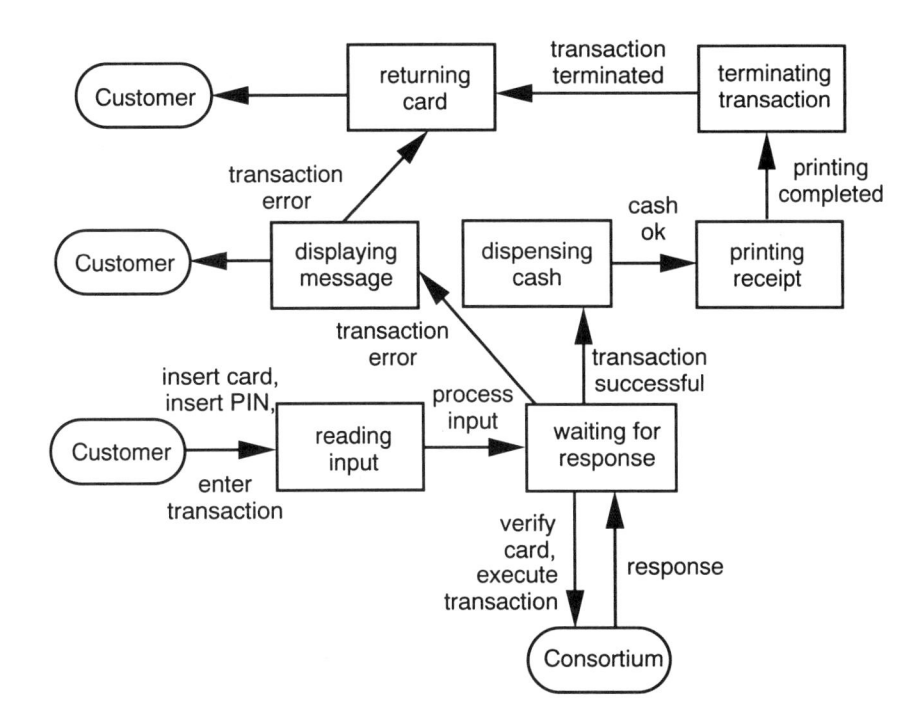

Figure 6-7. STD for ATM application

6.4 SYSTEM DESIGN MODELS

The system design model is used to illustrate the architecture of the hardware elements and their interfaces in a distributed system. An example of a system design model for the ATM system is shown in Figure 6-8. The rounded rectangles represent subsystems that will correspond to hardware nodes in the distributed architecture. This particular model does not depict the allocation of system requirements to hardware and software; DFDs at the system level can be used for that purpose.

A different form of a system design model is shown in Figure 6-9 for a robot controller in a distributed architecture. The rectangles represent hardware nodes that include at least one CPU, and their associated local memory. This view is more hardware oriented than the model shown in Figure 6-8, and illustrates hardware elements and their interfaces at the bus and LAN levels. Each named processor represents a physical node with which a set of software modules will be associated.

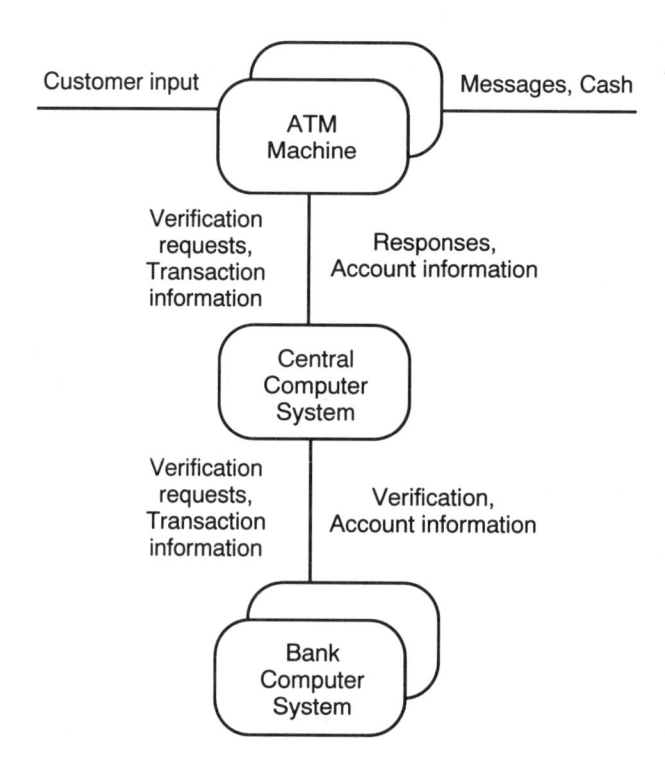

Figure 6-8. ATM system architecture diagram

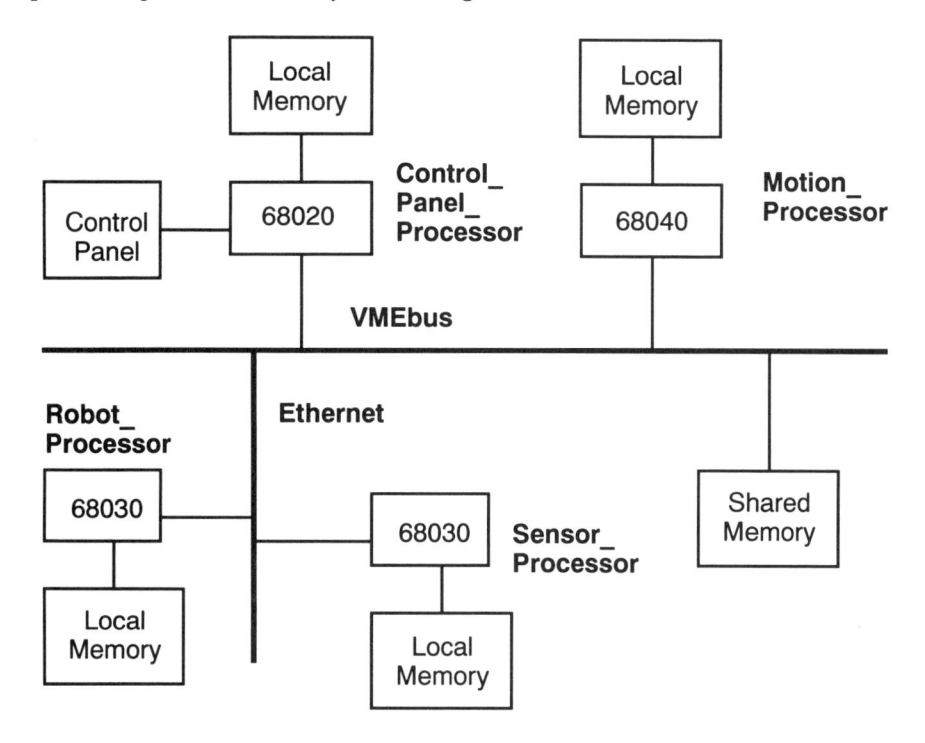

Chapter 6 • Object-Oriented Analysis and Design Models

Figure 6-9. Robot controller system architecture diagram

6.5 CONCURRENCY MODELS

A weakness of most of the OT methods in current use is that they do not adequately consider real-time systems and concurrency issues. One of the paradigms borrowed from real-time structured design (RTSD) is process abstraction [GOM84, NIE92]. The process structure chart shown in Figure 6-10 is used to depict processes as independent schedulable entities (task or process) that compete for the services of the same CPU. Each parallelogram represents a task or process. The annotated connecting lines represent messages passed between the processes. The various forms for passing data are shown in the legend.

Exactly how the processes will be implemented cannot be determined from the process structure chart, and depends on the programming language and run-time support. In C++, for example, they can be implemented as processes or coroutines using real-time libraries, or by accessing low-level scheduling mechanisms directly.

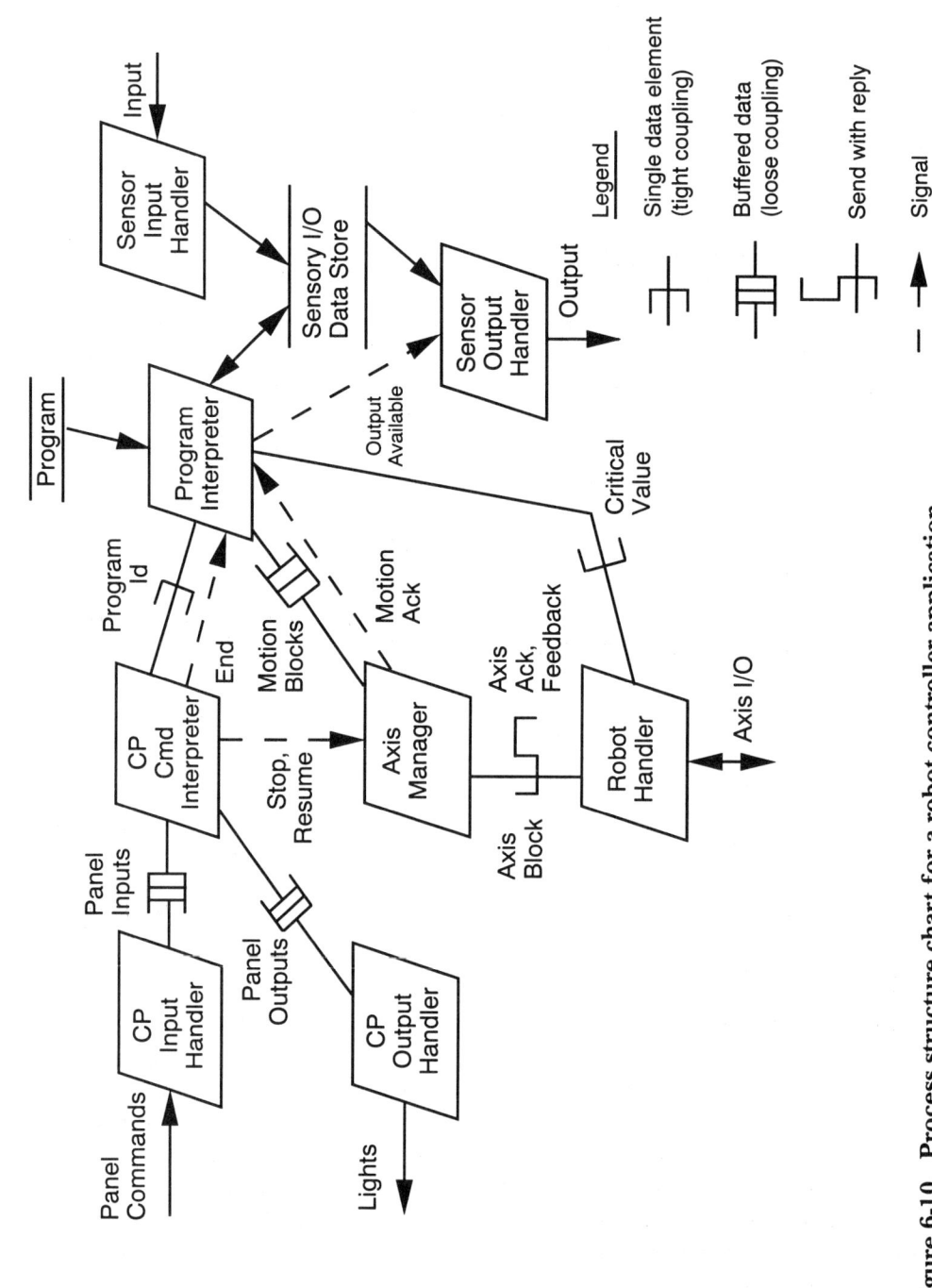

Figure 6-10. Process structure chart for a robot controller application

Note the difference between the process structure chart and the object flow diagram. The former deals explicitly with communication and synchronization between the processes. The latter only considers the message flows between the concurrent objects, and these objects may end up as entire subsystems rather than individual tasks.

6.6 FUNCTIONAL MODELS

Functional models used with structured methods can be used to complement the OT models. We have already seen how STDs can be used at the object level to depict dynamic state changes within an individual object.

The event trace diagram provides a view of the synchronization of events between major objects.

DFDs can be used to determine the allocation of system requirements to hardware and software where an object is split between two or more subsystems. The ATM system diagram shown in Figure 6-1 can be considered a top-level DFD.

The process structure chart can be used to analyze message passing between tasks, and to determine the proper control and synchronization of the tasks.

6.7 SUMMARY

OT methods use several different static and dynamic models. These models are used to describe analysis and design features of a system at various levels of detail.

The most important static model for analyzing objects and their interfaces is the object model. This is also used to decompose large objects via inheritance and aggregation. Other static models include the module architecture for the software structure, and system architecture for determining the subsystems.

Dynamic models include the object flow model, event trace diagram, and STD. These all represent different levels of abstraction and views for understanding the dynamic behavior of the system.

The process abstraction model is a low-level view of tasks and their interfaces. The process structure chart includes graphical symbols for the various modes of data passed between tasks in terms of synchronous versus asynchronous message passing.

7

Object-Oriented Methods

The basic mechanism of all OT methods is the use of the analysis and design models described in the previous chapter. The objective of this chapter is to discuss some of the most popular OT methods in use today. The discussion will be based on the various models supported, notations used in those models, and the level of heuristics and guidelines included with each method. The material is organized in terms of the models used during OOA, system design, and OOD. Support for real-time features and concurrency, and the availability of CASE tools are also discussed.

7.1 OBJECT MODELING TECHNIQUE (OMT)

We used some of the OMT notation above to illustrate the general static and dynamic models used in the various OT methods. OMT supports both the analysis and design phases [RUM91]. The notation is rich and supports all of the modeling views listed in Chapter 6 as well as all of the class/object relationships described in Chapter 5.

OMT is based on the following three models:

- *Object Model.* Used to describe classes and objects and their static relationships. Views supported include generalization/specialization, association, and aggregation. Class/object diagram adornments include cardinality, links, attributes, and operations. The result of the object modeling activity is a view of the key real-world abstractions and their static relationships.

- *Dynamic Model.* Uses STDs at the object level to describe state changes and event traces to describe time-ordered events. Event flow diagrams are used to depict events flowing between objects without regard for any time sequencing. These diagrams represent the dynamic equivalent of the corresponding static object diagrams. The result of the dynamic modeling activity is a view of the time-ordered events, event flows between the key abstractions, and the state changes that may take place within each object.
- *Functional Model.* Describes functional decomposition and relationships between functional entities. The notation in this model is a hierarchy of DFDs. The result of the functional model is a set of DFDs that show the flow of data between the major functional components of the system. The bubbles ("processes") on a DFD correspond to activities and actions in STDs. The data flows shown in a DFD correspond to objects and attributes in the object diagram. Even though this model is described as being part of the overall OMT approach, its use is discouraged in favor of the other two models [ACC93a].

An example of the OMT object model was shown in Figure 6-2 for the ATM application. This is the static model of the real-world abstractions obtained from the system requirements. The cardinality associations (multiplicities) are indicated with open and closed dots at the class/object boundary, with additional notation for specific numerical restrictions. Open and closed dots are used to describe has-a and using relationships, respectively, in the Booch'93 notation, and this represents one of the major problems we are faced with in the absence of an agreed-upon unified notation. The details of how the various versions of multiplicity are depicted with the object model in OMT is shown in Figure 7-1.

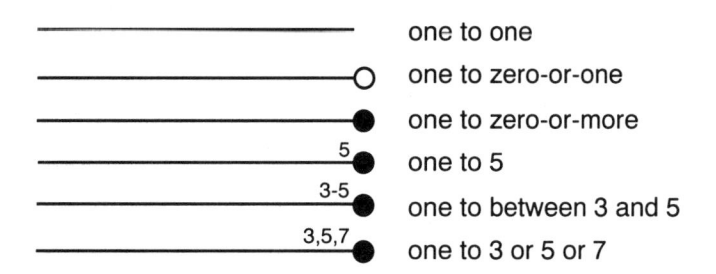

```
─────────────────      one to one
──────────────○      one to zero-or-one
──────────────●      one to zero-or-more
            5●      one to 5
          3-5●      one to between 3 and 5
         3,5,7●      one to 3 or 5 or 7
```

Figure 7-1. Multiplicity in OMT

Chapter 7 • Object-Oriented Methods 89

A module architecture diagram for the ATM application was shown in Figure 6-4. OMT does not have a comparable model to depict the static view of software modules. The system architecture diagram shown in Figure 6-8 is used by OMT to describe subsystem elements.

The dynamic models used by OMT include the object flow model shown in Figure 6-5 (called an event flow diagram in OMT), the event trace diagram shown in Figure 6-6, and STDs at the object level (using Harel notation).

We now describe OMT as it is applied to the three major phases specified for this method: OOA, system design, and OOD.

7.1.1 OOA

The OMT method consists of the following steps during the OOA phase:
1. **Create the Object Model.**
   - determine an initial set of objects and classes from the requirements specification
   - eliminate redundant, trivial, and irrelevant classes and objects
   - prepare a data dictionary
   - determine candidate class/object associations
   - eliminate unwanted associations
   - identify attributes and operations
   - determine inheritance hierarchies using generalization/specialization criteria
   - group classes into modules (logical subsets)
2. **Create the Dynamic Model**
   - prepare scenarios
   - identify events associated with a given scenario
   - prepare event trace diagram for each scenario
   - prepare event flow diagrams
   - create STDs for each object
3. **Create the Functional Model.**
   - identify input and output values and prepare a system diagram
   - prepare DFDs showing functional dependencies

- describe functional entities
- identify constraints between objects
- specify optimizing criteria in terms of time and space parameters

An extensive set of heuristics is available for the creation of classes and objects. As an initial guide to establishing a model of concurrent entities, all objects appearing in the object model are considered concurrent. This view is modified during system design with the creation of subsystems and the allocation of subsystems to processors and tasks.

7.1.2 System Design

It is recommended that the analysis phase be followed by a system design with a partitioning of system requirements into hardware and software components. The resulting structure will represent the system architecture. This activity is to be completed before the OOD phase is started. The steps involved in this phase include the following:

- organize the system into subsystems
- identify inherent concurrency
- allocate subsystems to processors and tasks
- choose an approach for management of data stores
- prescribe a mechanism for access to global resources
- choose a mechanism for software control of external and internal events
- determine a mechanism for system initialization, termination, and exception handling
- set development and hardware resource trade-off priorities

Specific guidelines are included in [RUM91] for many of these steps. More extensive heuristics are included in [ACC93b]. Subsystems are created by combining related classes and objects that collectively will form a well-defined client/server interface to the outside world. The lowest level of a subsystem is a module, which is a logical grouping of classes, associations, and generalizations. Subsystem boundaries typically align with module boundaries. A recommendation is made to keep the number of subsystems small: 20 is too many.

Concurrency is treated by determining whether objects can be active together, and by folding mutually exclusive objects into a task. STDs are used to determine if objects can be combined, but the notation is very complex (Harel notation).

Each subsystem is considered a concurrent entity that must be allocated to a hardware component. The steps included in this activity are:

- estimate hardware resource requirements
- draw a hardware architecture diagram
- allocate hardware and software requirements for each subsystem
- assign software requirements to processors
- determine physical connectivity of the subsystems

An example of a hardware architecture diagram is shown in Figure 7-2. The same icons that are used in the object model diagram and event flow diagram are sometimes used to depict subsystems. This type of icon overloading can be avoided by using, for example, the rectangles with rounded corners, as illustrated in Figure 7-2 (we'll get back to this notation in Chapter 11).

Upon completion of the system design phase, all of the system requirements have been allocated to subsystems, and hardware and software requirements have been allocated within each subsystem. The following considerations are recommended for determining the allocation of concurrent subsystems to hardware units [RUM91, p. 203]:

- estimate performance requirements and the resources needed to satisfy them
- determine whether a subsystem should be implemented in software or hardware
- allocate software subsystems to processors that will satisfy the performance requirements and minimize interprocessor communication
- determine the connectivity of the physical units that make up the subsystems

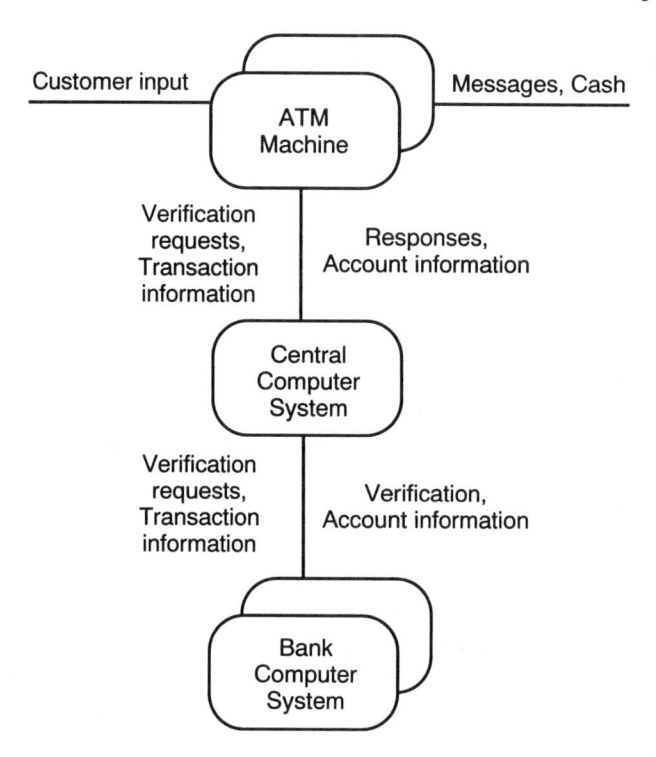

Figure 7-2. Hardware architecture diagram

7.1.3 OOD

The transitioning between OOA and OOD is fuzzy: " . . . there is no need to transform from one model to another, as the object-oriented paradigm spans analysis, design, and implementation" [RUM91, p. 227]. The OOD phase is viewed as an activity to flesh out the analysis model to provide a basis for implementation. Specific steps recommended for the OOD phase include the following:

- combine the object, dynamic, and functional models to obtain operations on classes
- design algorithms to implement the operations
- optimize access paths to data
- implement control for external interactions

- adjust class structure to increase inheritance
- design the associations
- determine object representations
- package classes and associations into modules

7.1.4 Real-Time Aspects and Concurrency

OMT is vague regarding guidelines for the creation of concurrent elements from objects or modules. Suggestions are made for examining the STDs, and folding objects together into a thread (task). But specific transitioning guidelines from STDs to tasks are not included. It is recommended that events be implemented as inter-task calls by using available features of the programming language or operating system.

7.1.5 CASE Tools

Reasonably priced CASE tools available for the OMT method that run on PCs include OMTool and C++ Designer. More expensive tools running on workstations under Unix include IDE's Software through Pictures (StP) and Cadre's TeamWork.

7.2 OBJECT-ORIENTED SOFTWARE ENGINEERING (OOSE)

OOSE [JAC92] is more than a single OT "method" and can support the entire software development process described in Chapter 2. OOSE is derived from the much larger Objectory (Object FactOry), a proprietary product belonging to the Swedish company Objectory AB.

One of the most promising aspects of OOSE is the "use case" driven approach. The more familiar term "scenario" driven will be used here, and describes user interactions with the system. A number of scenarios can be determined for all the user interactions, and the analysis, design and implementation is focused around each scenario. System requirements can thus be traced directly from the definition of user interfaces to the implementation and testing.

Another direct benefit of the scenario approach is that it supports an incremental development strategy. Whereas the various class/object modeling views in OMT are at the system level, OOSE presents the corresponding views at the scenario level. OMT also uses scenarios, but they are not defined until after the object model is completed, and they are used primarily to determine the dynamic model.

An example of the scenario model is shown in Figure 7-3 for a simplified recycling machine [JAC92, p. 155]. Scenarios are created from the system requirements prior to the analysis phase, and the set of scenarios is referred to as the requirements model. Guidelines are provided in [JAC92] for the creation of scenarios.

OOSE includes the following analysis and design models:

- *Scenario (Use Case) Model.* Models the roles of users and external systems interfacing with the system to be built.
- *Domain Object Model.* Forms the basis for understanding the concepts of the problem domain.
- *Analysis Model.* Identifies classes, objects, attributes, operations, and their associations. Classifies objects into interface, entity, and control objects.
- *Subsystem Model.* Groups objects and other subsystems into managing units.
- *Design Model.* Transitions analysis objects into implementations as "blocks." Object modules are developed as classes.

7.2.1 OOA

Note that the analysis phase described above for the OMT method is preceded in OOSE by a requirements modeling activity to create scenarios, and a domain analysis to understand the problem concepts. This sequence of activities follows very closely our recommended modeling approach (see Chapter 8).

Chapter 7 • Object-Oriented Methods

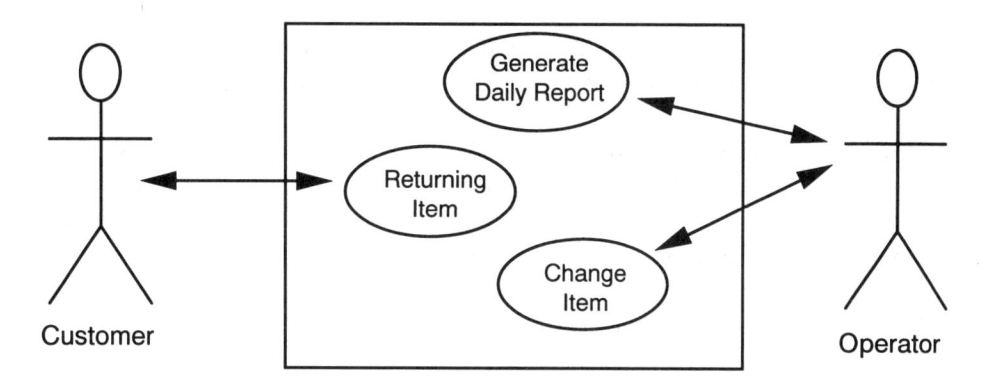

Figure 7-3. Scenario diagram for recycling machine

OOSE uses all of the static and dynamic models described in Chapter 6. A unique aspect of OOSE is the method used to classify objects in the behavior, presentation, and information space. Three types of objects are placed in these three dimensions, as illustrated in Figure 7-4. Entity objects represent the requirements of the key abstractions expressed in the real-world objects, and are associated with the information axis in the three dimensional presentation space shown in Figure 7-4. Interface objects model information representing the external system interfaces and are aligned with the presentation axis. Control objects represent the handling of short-lived state changes within the system and align themselves with the behavior axis. An example of the scenario view for interface objects belonging to the recycling machine domain is shown in Figure 7-5.

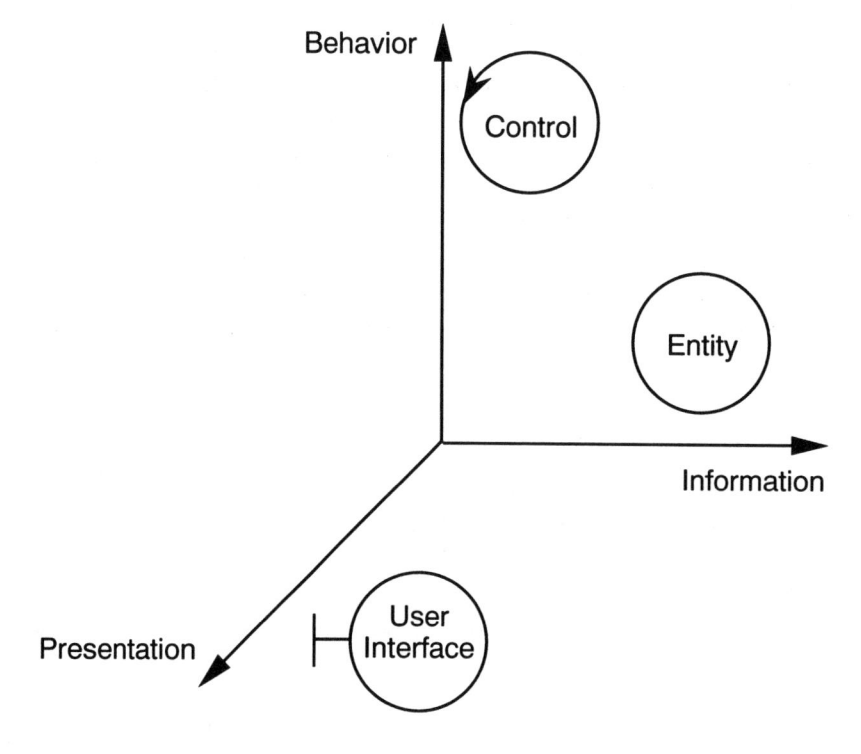

Figure 7-4. Objects in the information space

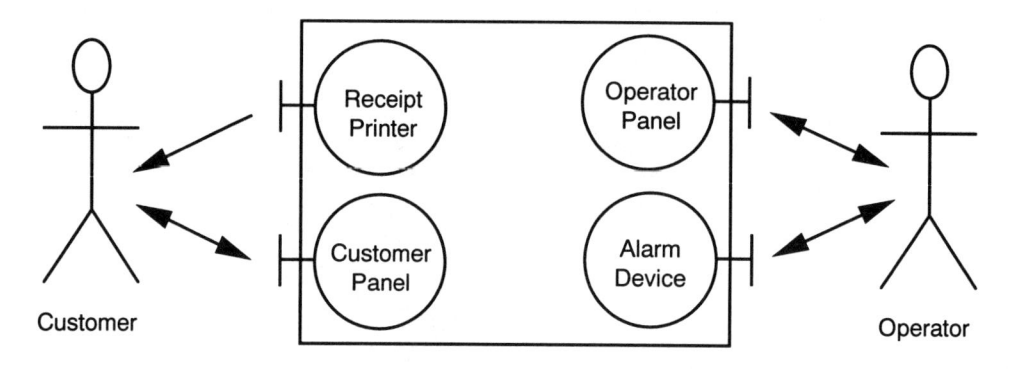

Figure 7-5. Interface objects for the Return Item scenario

Chapter 7 • Object-Oriented Methods

OOSE uses the class/object models described in Chapter 6 to support the views of each scenario. An example of the interface objects associated with the Customer Panel abstraction is shown in Figure 7-6. For this view, we have used the OMT notation with an adornment (I) in the lower right hand corner to denote that the objects are of the interface type. Similar views are created for the object models of the entity and control objects for the same scenario (the roles of these three types are discussed in detail in Chapter 10).

A combined view for all the three types of objects is presented in the event flow diagram in Figure 7-7. This is a dynamic view that illustrates the message flows between the objects during the execution of the system.

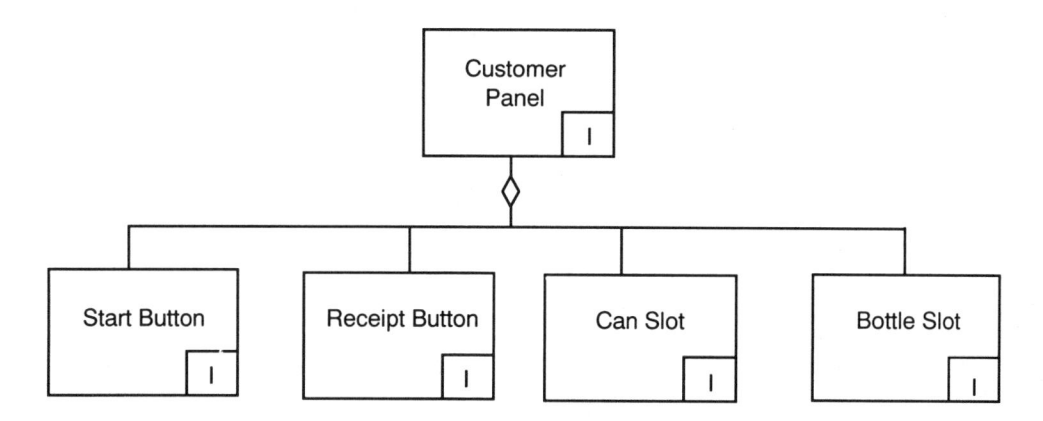

Figure 7-6. Aggregate of the Customer Panel interface objects

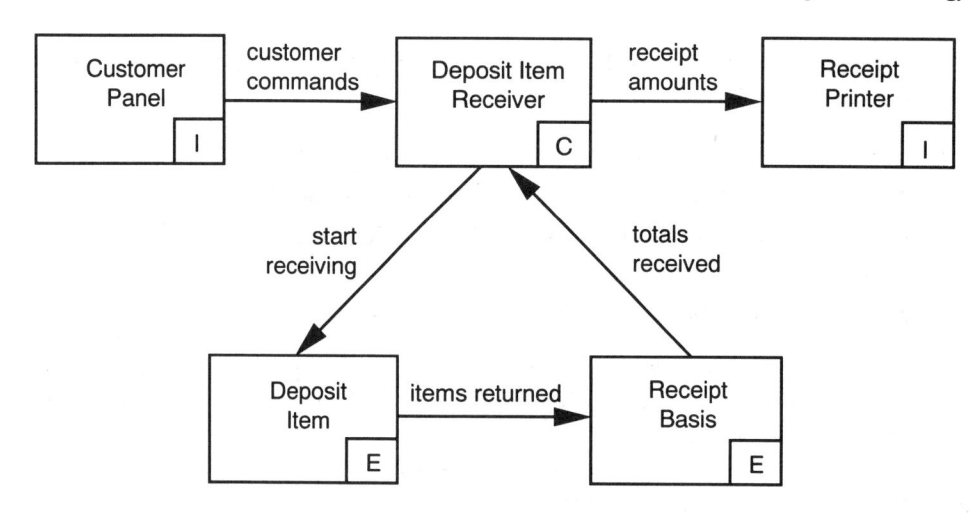

Figure 7-7. Event flow diagram for the Returning Item scenario

Figures 7-6 and 7-7 demonstrate the flexibility of OOSE: We have used the OMT notation here, but could have used Booch'93, Shlaer-Mellor, or Coad-Yourdon just as well. This further enforces our perception that a method is just a tool to support the overall development process.

The dynamic models used in OOSE include STDs (Mealy notation [HAT87]), interaction diagrams (event trace diagram), and event flow diagrams.

7.2.2 System Design

The objects created during the analysis phase are collected into subsystems to reduce complexity and to provide clean interfaces for the integration of modules. The lowest level subsystems are considered "change units," i.e., entities that can be replaced as components without affecting the overall system design, and are referred to as "service packages."

Heuristics are included for grouping objects into subsystems based on loose coupling between subsystems, and strong functional cohesion between objects clustered in a subsystem. Heuristics for determining strong functional cohesion between two objects are based on answering the following design decisions [JAC92, p. 191]:

- Will changes in one object create changes in the other object?
- Do the two objects communicate with the same actor?
- Are both objects dependent on a third object, such as an interface or entity object?
- Does one object perform several operations on the other?

An example of a subsystem diagram for the recycling machine is shown in Figure 7-8. This is the same view as the hardware architecture diagram used in OMT (see Figure 7-2). The subsystem model retains the icons to distinguish between entity, control, and interface objects. It also includes the inheritance relations between objects.

OOSE does not include specific guidelines for the allocation of hardware and software requirements to subsystems.

7.2.3 OOD

Extensive guidelines are provided for creating classes and objects, and for transitioning between the analysis and design phases. A deliberate effort is made to distinguish between the products of the OOA phase and the OOD phase by using different icons for the object model in the two phases, and by calling the OOD objects "blocks."

The initial part of the transitioning phase from OOA is to first transform the analysis objects to design objects, referred to as "blocks." Analysis objects emphasize modeling requirements, whereas blocks are refined to include the semantics of the implementation environment. During the refinement of the initial blocks, there are usually a number of new design objects that must be added for a proper architecture that can be implemented. Other activities during OOD include the establishment of considerations for system performance, real-time aspects, and fault tolerance. An example of an object model for OOSE blocks is shown in Figure 7-9 for the recycling machine. Note the use of rectangular icons to describe the blocks, as opposed to circles for the analysis object model.

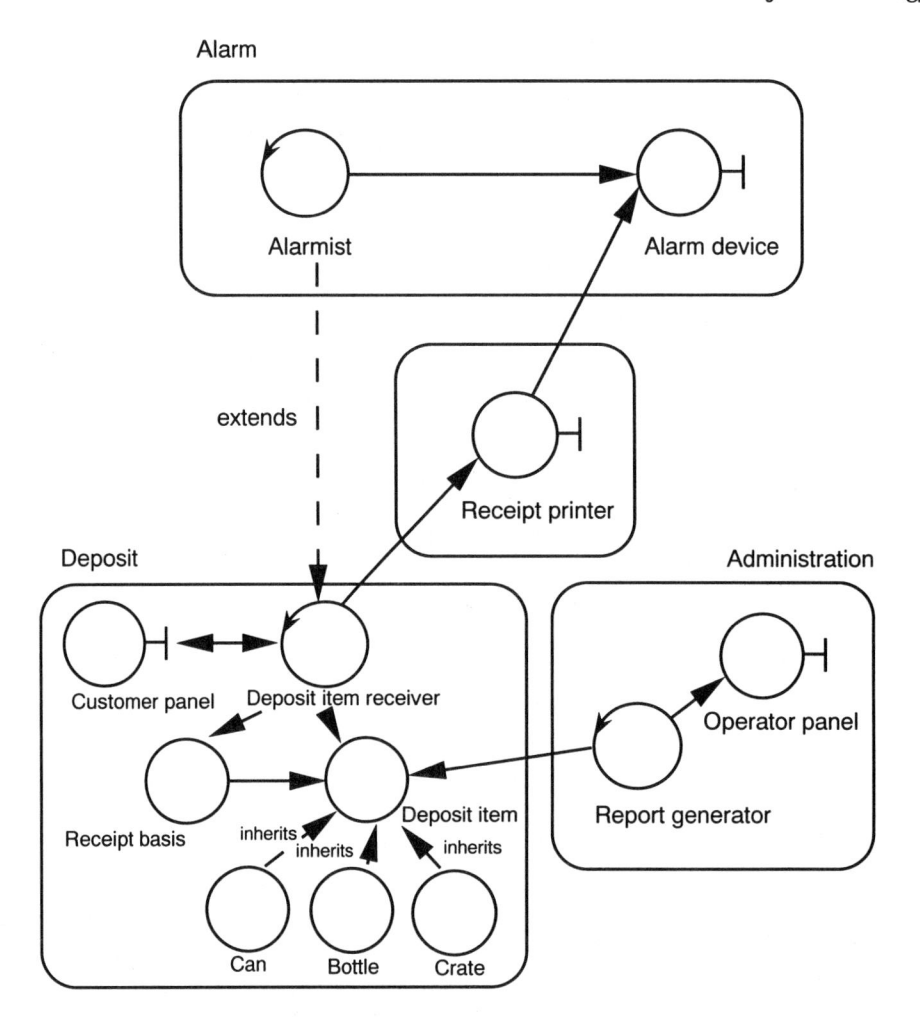

Figure 7-8. Subsystem diagram for recycling machine

An important element of the distinct transitioning activity from OOA to OOD in OOSE is the resulting requirements traceability from user requirements via analysis objects to the blocks. This kind of traceability is made very difficult in other OT methods when changes occur in the requirements or the design. With only a vague separation between OOA and OOD products, the OOD structure tends to predominate the development, and the OOA products get lost. There is no longer a clear trace between requirements, analysis, and design in either direction.

Chapter 7 • Object-Oriented Methods

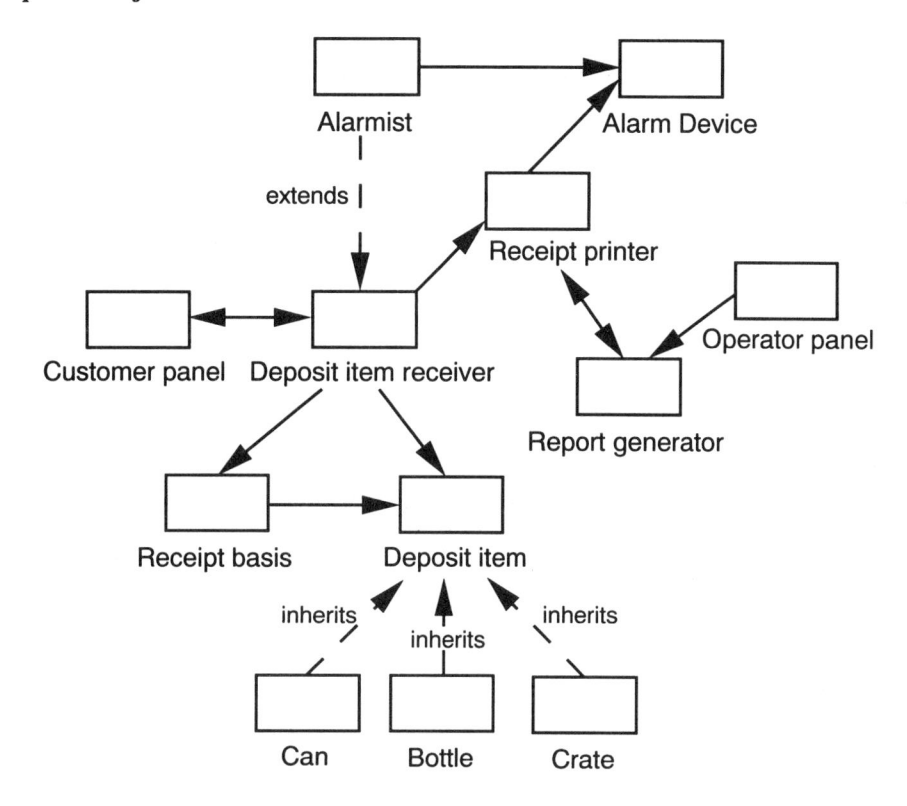

Figure 7-9. Design objects for recycling machine

Interaction diagrams (event trace diagrams) are used for each scenario to show how the objects are interacting with each other. An example of an interaction diagram for the scenario Returning Item is shown in Figure 7-10. A distinction is made between messages (closed arrowhead) and signals (open arrowhead) used for communication between concurrent elements or between the system and the external interfaces. Messages are transformed during the latter part of the design phase (detailed design) to C++ calls, and signals to synchronous or asynchronous mechanisms to control interrupts, concurrent activities, etc. STDs (using Mealy notation) are used to further elucidate the dynamic behavior of individual objects.

The final activity of the OOD phase is the preparation of the block interfaces for an anticipated implementation as programming language modules such as C++ classes or Ada packages. Included in this activity is the determination of the level of information hiding regarding attributes and operations.

7.2.4 Real-Time Aspects and Concurrency

OOSE includes considerations for real-time systems and the creation of concurrent elements (processes). Guidelines are included for the creation of a process structure as part of the analysis phase. One suggestion is to look for concurrent elements among the interface objects. The semantics for communication and synchronization is not part of the method, and must be implemented with whatever services are available via the operating system or programming language. An example of a process structure chart is shown in Figure 7-11 for a telecommunications application [JAC92, p. 416]. The parallelograms encapsulate related tasks (open rectangles), and some of the tasks are controlled by semaphores (shaded rectangles). This process view is based on a specific scenario.

Real-time requirements are determined by associating time attributes to the operational sequences in the scenarios. Concurrency is associated with scenarios in two different ways: multiple, simultaneous activities may be performed within a scenario, and scenarios may be performed in parallel.

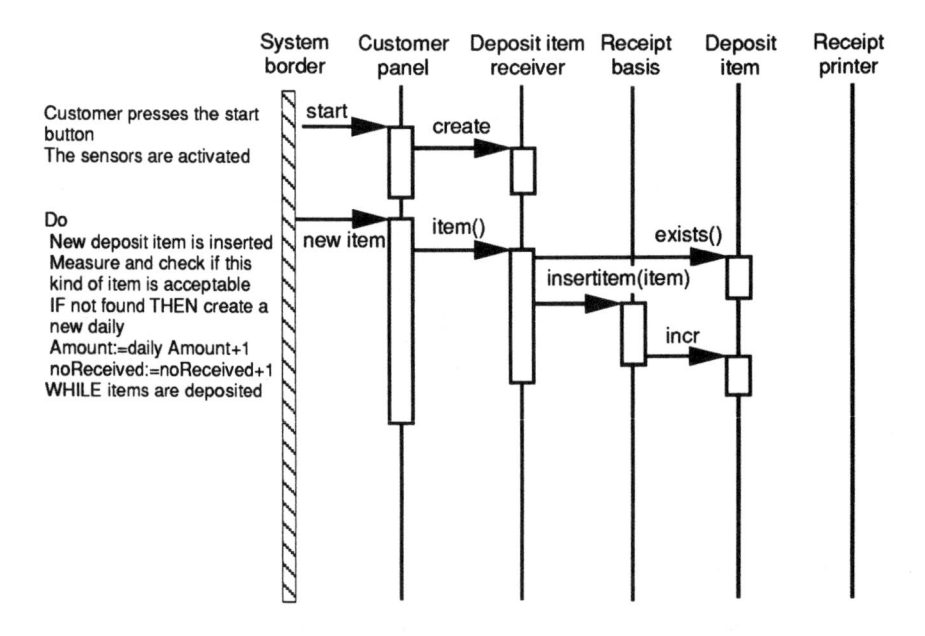

Figure 7-10. Interaction diagram for Returning Item

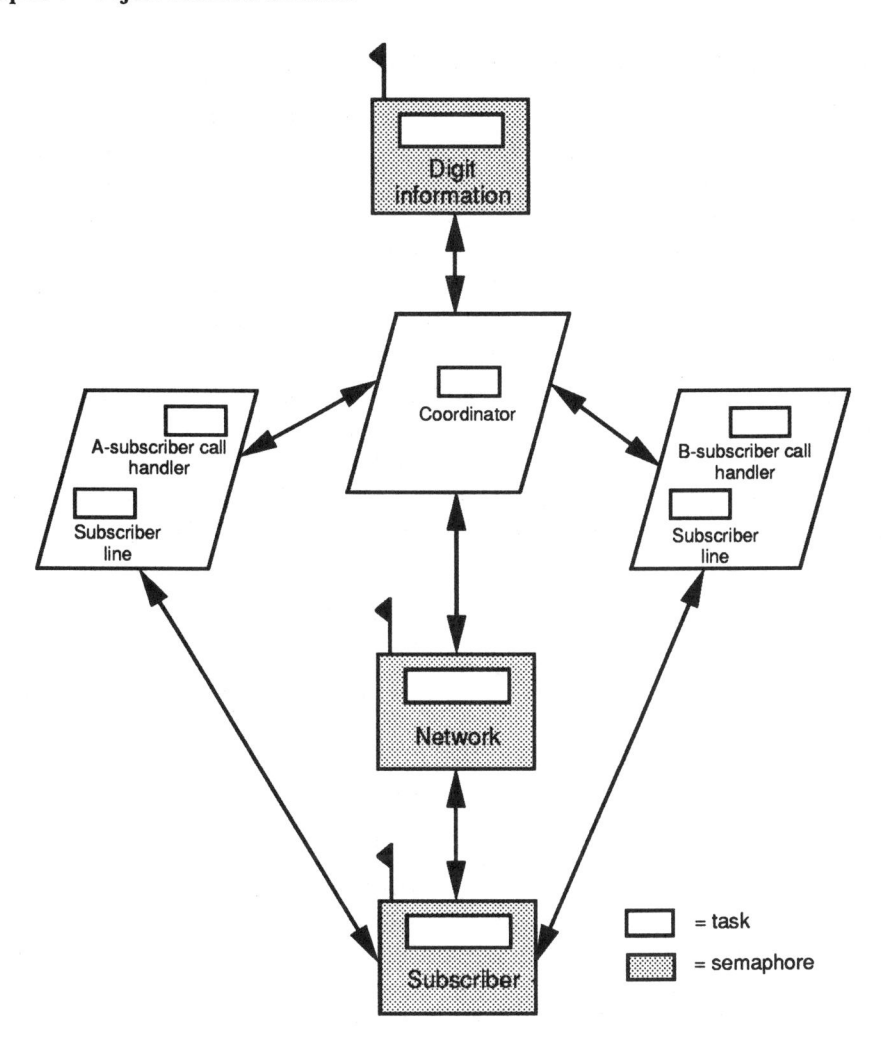

Figure 7-11. Process structure chart

7.2.5 CASE Tools

A CASE tool is available for the entire Objectory process [JAC92], but not for the simplified OOSE. The CASE tools available for individual methods, such as OMT (OMTool and C++ Designer) and Booch'93 (Rose), can be adapted for use with OOSE, but will then suffer the inherent restrictions of the respective tool.

OOSE forms the basis for our recommended modeling approach and is discussed further in Chapter 8, and again in Part III as we apply OT to the software development process.

7.3 BOOCH'93

The original Booch method [BOO91] focused on modeling objects in terms of their behaviors, responsibilities, and collaborations and was mostly intended for object-oriented design. The method has recently [BOO93] been augmented with notations for describing attributes and associations, and is now quite suitable for both the OOA and OOD phases. All of the static and dynamic models are included in the method, and extensive analysis and design guidelines are provided in the primary reference [BOO93].

7.3.1 OOA/OOD

Booch's method can be summarized briefly with the following development steps:

- identify classes and objects at the appropriate abstraction level
- determine the semantics of the classes and objects
- determine the relationships between the classes and objects
- specify the interfaces of the classes and objects
- implement the classes and objects using the chosen programming language

The notation is quite different from the other OT methods, and a CASE tool is required for creating and maintaining analysis and design representations. One of the major differences between, for example, OMT and Booch'93 is the depiction of cardinality and the various relationships between classes and objects. Another difference is the shape of the class and object icons. As we saw above, the OMT classes and objects are depicted as rectangles. In Booch'93, classes and objects are represented as clouds, with a dashed-line boundary for classes and continuous lines for objects. The rationale for the cloud shape [BOO93, p. 177] is that the icon suggests an abstraction that does not necessarily have plain or sharp edges, and that the rectangular icon used in OMT (and other methods) is heavily overloaded on several different models with different views.

Chapter 7 • Object-Oriented Methods

An example of a class diagram for an ATM application is shown in Figure 7-12 and illustrates the notation. Note that what OMT uses for cardinality, Booch'93 uses for inheritance, aggregation, and using relationships. The cardinality in Booch'93 is written explicitly near the corresponding class or object. The class diagram is used during OOA to document the classes and their relationships. During OOD, it is used to determine the class structure that will form the architecture of the system.

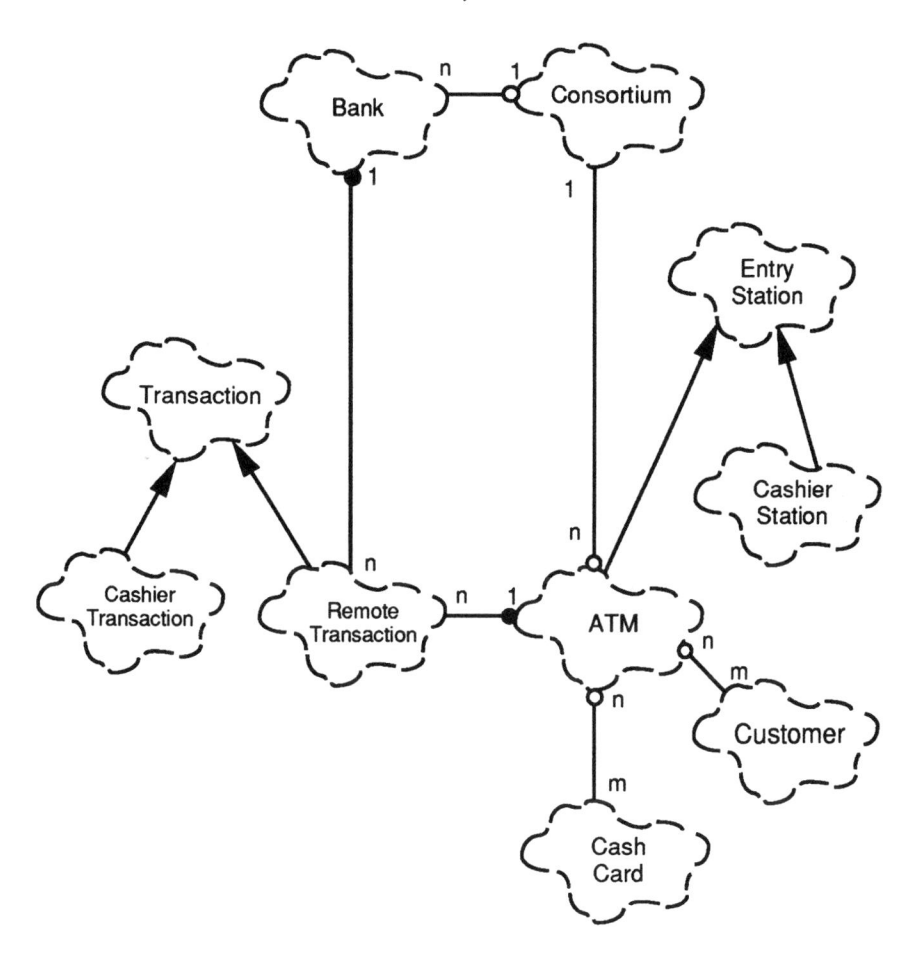

Figure 7-12. Class diagram for the ATM application

A partial object diagram for the ATM application is shown in Figure 7-13. This is similar to the OMT object flow diagram shown in Figure 6-5. The object diagram is used during OOA to represent a view of the object structure of the system for a set of class instances. During OOD, this diagram is used to illustrate the dynamic behavior between objects. In general, the class diagram is used to determine the decomposition and class hierarchies of the system. The object diagram is used to identify the interactions between a typical set of objects derived from the class structure.

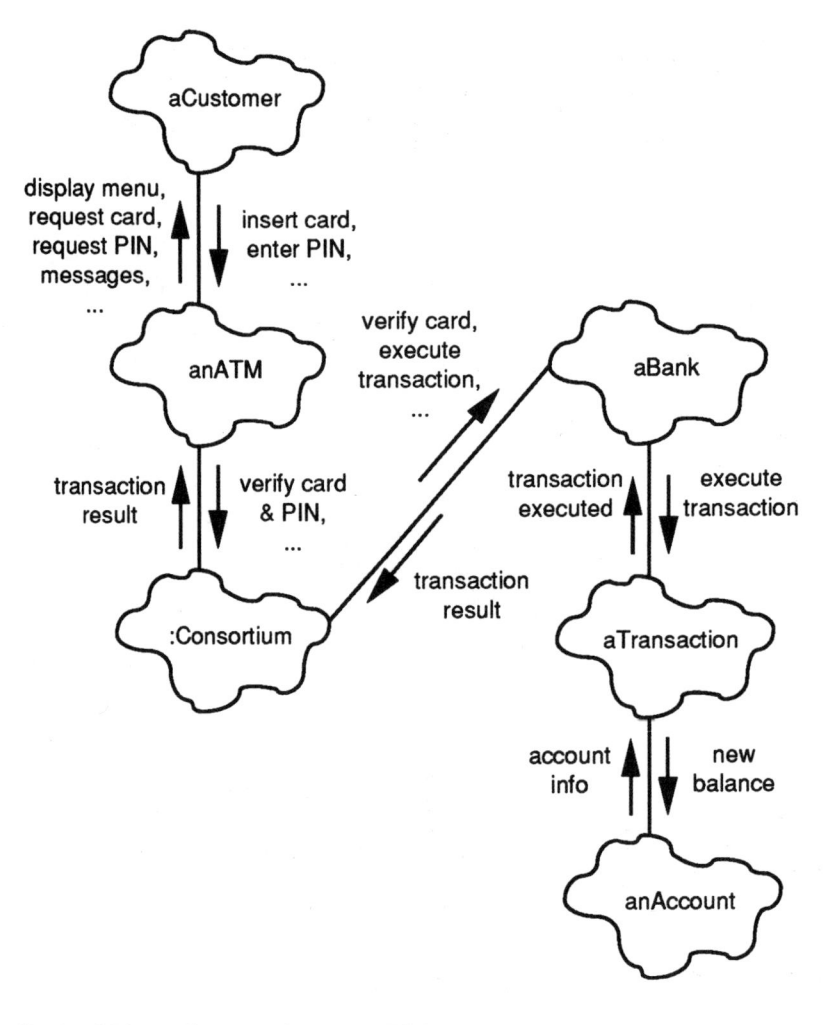

Figure 7-13. Object diagram for the ATM application

Another dynamic model is the STD as shown in Figure 7-14 for the ATM system. The notation has been adopted from Harel [HAR87] and is quite similar to the notation used in OMT. Booch '93 also uses system interaction diagrams which are almost identical to the event trace diagrams used in OMT. Script diagrams similar to the OOSE interaction diagrams are used to describe complex scenarios.

The Booch'93 method applies to both analysis and design, and there is not a sharp distinction between these two phases.

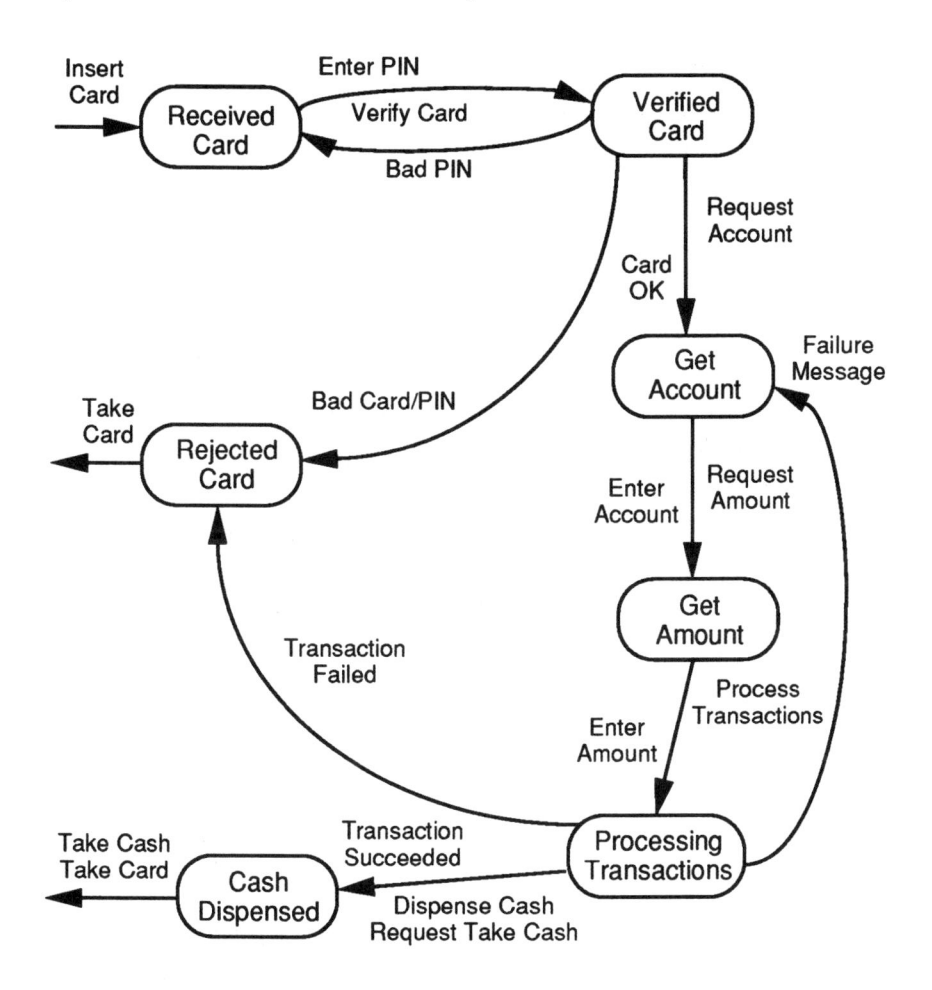

Figure 7-14. STD for the ATM application

Guidelines are included for the identification of classes and objects, using, potentially, a three step process:

1. Identify classes and objects first, based on the properties of the problem domain, i.e., tangible things, roles, events, places, etc.
2. If the first step does not provide a satisfactory set of real-world abstractions, focus on the dynamic behavior of the primary sources for classes and objects. Consider forming classes from groups of objects that exhibit similar behavior.
3. If both of the prior steps fail, consider classification by association, i.e., clusters of objects are identified in terms of some close resemblance to a prototypical object. An example in this category is a game, since there is not a common group of properties shared by all games.

The use of CRC cards is recommended as an effective way of brainstorming during the initial class/object identification phase.

7.3.2 System Design

A systems analysis phase is recommended for hardware-intensive systems, and starts by considering the hardware that will host the software. A process diagram is used to model the hardware layout using three dimensional cubes to depict hardware entities. The process diagram includes the three main parts of a hardware architecture: processors, devices, and connections. A processor is defined to be a piece of hardware capable of executing application programs. A device is a piece of hardware incapable of executing application programs (it can execute firmware or hardwired programs such as A/D or D/A). Connections are the undirected lines between processors and devices. Connections are assumed to be bidirectional, unless otherwise indicated with an annotated arrow.

An example of a system process diagram is shown in Figure 7-15. The cubes with a shaded side indicate processors; the unshaded cubes are devices. The process diagram is equivalent to a high-level hardware architecture diagram, except with fewer details than what we saw earlier.

The process diagram is also used to show the allocation of processes to processors, where the processes are listed below their corresponding host processor.

Specific guidelines for allocating hardware and software requirements are not included. Booch maintains [BOO93, p. 295] that "...changing the hardware/software boundary is largely immaterial to our object-oriented architecture. Changing the details of the system's hardware only impacts our abstraction of the lower layers of the system."

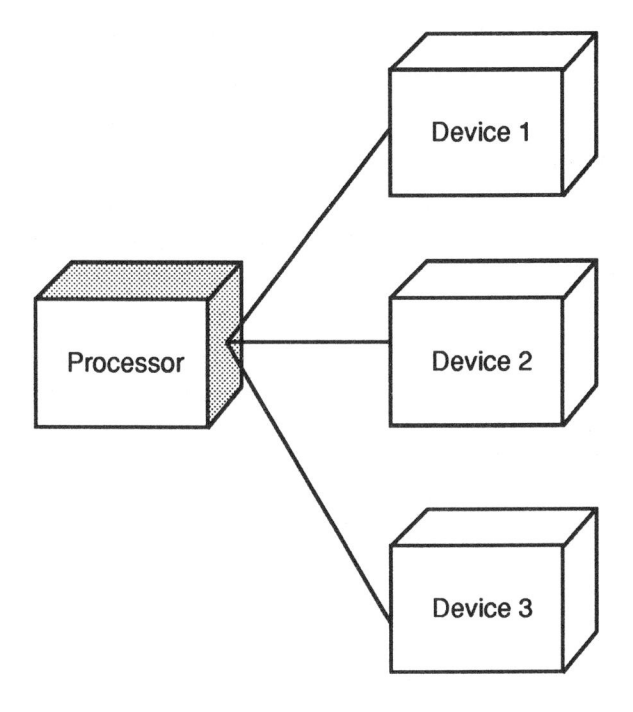

Figure 7-15. System process diagram

The products of the analysis phase will include sets of object diagrams, class diagrams, and STDs. The products of the design phase (including system design) will include sets of class diagrams, object diagrams, interaction diagrams, script diagrams, module diagrams, and process diagrams.

7.3.3 Real-Time Aspects and Concurrency

As an aid to the specification of how the various processors are scheduled, Booch suggests the following adornments for the processors (assuming a fair scheduling algorithm):

1. **Preemptive.** A higher priority process that is ready to run may preempt a lower priority process that is currently running.
2. **Nonpreemptive.** The process that is currently running will complete its execution, and then relinquish control back to the scheduling entity of the operating system.
3. **Cyclic.** Each process is allocated a fixed time slice or frame, and execution proceeds cyclically between processes.

4. **Executive.** A specified algorithm controls the process scheduling.

5. **Manual.** An operator specifies the process scheduling before the execution of the program is started.

Some guidelines for the selection of processes as independent schedulable entities are included in Booch'93.

7.3.4 CASE Tools

Rational provides a development tool called Rose that runs on PCs and Unix machines. Rose supports class and object diagrams, STDs, architecture diagrams, and process diagrams. The tool distinguishes between class and object diagrams, and can be used for the OOA and OOD phases.

7.4 SHLAER-MELLOR

The Shlaer-Mellor method has evolved from their initial data modeling technique [SHL88], through the inclusion of dynamic behavior [SHL92], to the approach of recursive design [SHL90, SHL93]. The combined development approach is referred to as OOA/RD. This is probably one of the more difficult OT approaches to learn for the novice, and significant hand-holding is recommended for the initial project attempting to use this method. A successful use of OOA/RD (including the required hand-holding) for a communications system is reported in [HIN94].

The general approach of applying OOA/RD can be described as follows [SHL93]:

- partition the system into domains
- analyze each domain (OOA)
- verify the analysis through simulation
- specify the translation of OOA models (specification of RD)
- build the translation components (construction of RD elements)
- translate the OOA models of each domain (application of RD)

This list of steps is not intended to imply a strictly sequential application of the steps. Significant overlap and iteration is expected of and between the steps. An overview of the development steps will be described below using the models given in [SHL93].

7.4.1 OOA

The system partitioning results in the creation of a number of independent, distinct partitions:

- *An Application Domain.* This describes the part of the system that concerns the end users of the delivered system. There may be more than one application domain for very large systems.
- *Several General (Service) Domains.* These domains include GUIs, sensor and actuator domains for real-time systems, etc.
- *An Architectural Domain.* This is a description of the system design.
- *Implementation Domains.* These domains include technology dependent elements, such as operating systems, networks, and the expected programming language(s) to be used for implementing the design.

The result of the initial partitioning is depicted in the domain chart shown in Figure 7-16. The ovals represent domains, and the thick arrows represent client/server relationships, with the arrowhead pointing to the server. Each relationship is referred to as a *bridge*. Textual descriptions are used to supply additional information about the domains and bridges.

The application domains are analyzed using an object-oriented version of well known structured techniques. The result of the analysis includes an information model (very close to traditional ERDs where the traditional entities are replaced by real-world objects), STDs for each object, and action DFDs (ADFDs) for each state in the STD. The primary differences between traditional DFDs and ADFDs are that ADFDs depict transforms for each state on an STD, and that the actions for the corresponding state are the data flows. There is thus one ADFD for each state on the STD, and it provides a finer level of detail than shown on the STD. A traditional DFD does not deal with dynamic state changes, and merely provides a view of the transformations and the data flows between them.

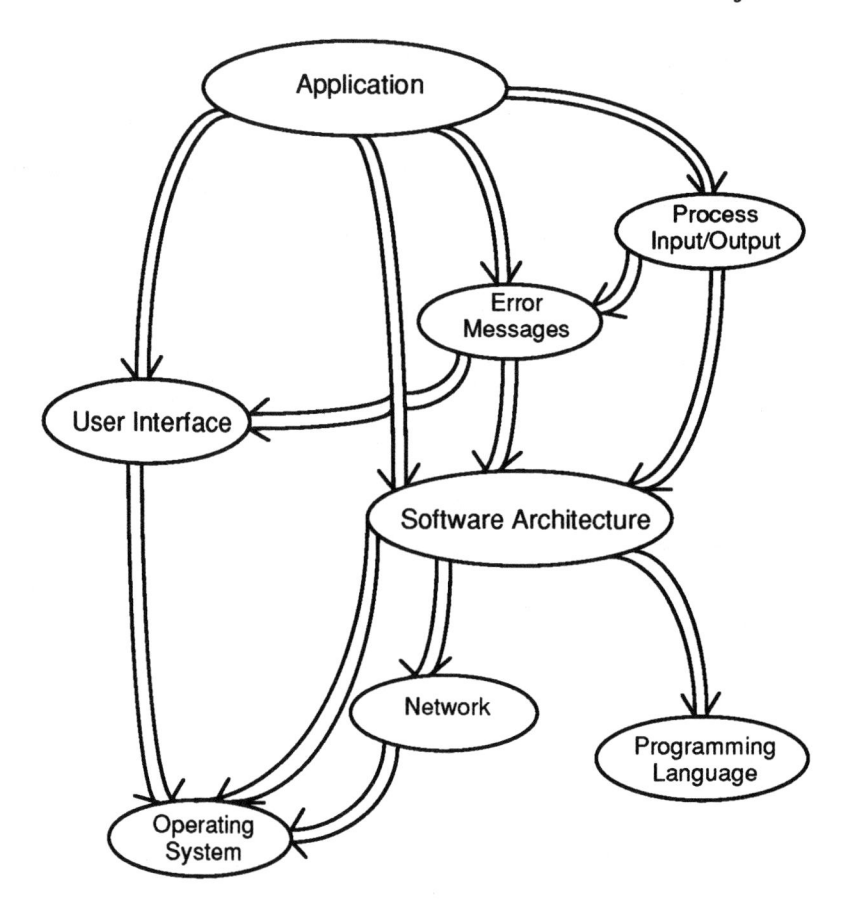

Figure 7-16. Domain chart

The next step is to verify the analysis of each domain with a simulated execution of the analysis models. The following steps are suggested for the simulation:

1. Create the desired initial state of the system using data values in the information model.
2. Initiate the desired dynamic behavior with a known event sent to a state model.
3. Execute the processing using the transforms and actions in the ADFDs and the sequences from the corresponding STD.
4. Evaluate the outcome against the expected results.

As the analysis of the application domain evolves, service domains are identified. These may include mechanisms for providing persistent data, data communications, and operator communications. The same analysis is applied to the service domains after the application domain analysis is completed.

As a way of formalizing the OOA phase, 72 rules (conditions) have been created [LAN93] to determine the validity and completion of the OOA phase.

7.4.2 System Design

System design is the subject matter of the architectural domain. The primary activity of this phase is the translation of the OOA models into structural design entities. This includes the specification of mechanisms and structures for managing data, the control of the system as a whole, and performance requirements.

The creation of subsystems is managed by slicing large domains into smaller, manageable portions that can be worked on by two to four persons. Another approach to the creation of subsystems is the clustering of related objects into cohesive entities that can form a well defined interface to other subsystems.

Specific guidelines for allocating hardware and software requirements are not included.

7.4.3 OOD

Objects from the information model are converted into classes and the associated data attributes. State models are used to specify the operations available for each class (i.e., the class interfaces). The process model (using ADFDs) is used to specify how the operations are performed (i.e., the implementations of the class operations).

The OOD activity uses a special notation referred to as Object-Oriented Design LanguagE (OODLE) [SHL92] and is based on the following graphical charts:

1. **Inheritance Diagram.** This shows the class inheritance with the usual layered hierarchy employed by the other methods.
2. **Dependency Diagram.** This illustrates the client/server relations between classes. It also includes "friend" relations. In C++, a friend class has access to the private members of the server class. An example of a dependency diagram is shown in Figure 7-17. Client objects making calls to server objects are indicated with a single arrow. Friend relations are indicated with a double arrow.

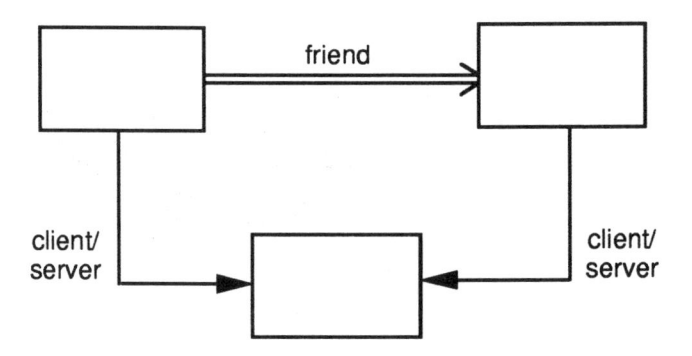

Figure 7-17. Dependency diagram

3. **Class Diagram.** This shows the external view of a class, and is similar to the notation Booch used for depicting Ada packages [BOO87]. An example of a class diagram for the class Date is shown in Figure 7-18. Visible operations are shown as rectangles inside the class boundary. Hidden data elements are represented as polygons inside the class. Input and output are shown above and below a horizontal reference line, respectively. The descriptions inside the polygons include the name of a the data object and the corresponding type underneath.

4. **Class Structure Chart.** This shows the internal structure of the implementations of the operations associated with a single class. An example of a class structure chart is shown in Figure 7-19. The rectangles correspond to the operations listed inside the class diagram in Figure 7-18. The polygons represent the data elements passed between the operations.

5. **Object Communication Diagram.** This diagram is used to show the event flows between the major objects. An example of a partial object communication diagram is shown in Figure 7-20 for the ATM application. The label preceding each event will typically be listed in an event table for each object. Each event table contains a list of the events that enter that object. Terminating objects are depicted as straight rectangles rather than the rounded rectangles used for the internal objects. Each object is considered a concurrent element that may be used as the basis for determining subsystems, or tasks that will compete for the services of the same CPU.

Chapter 7 • Object-Oriented Methods

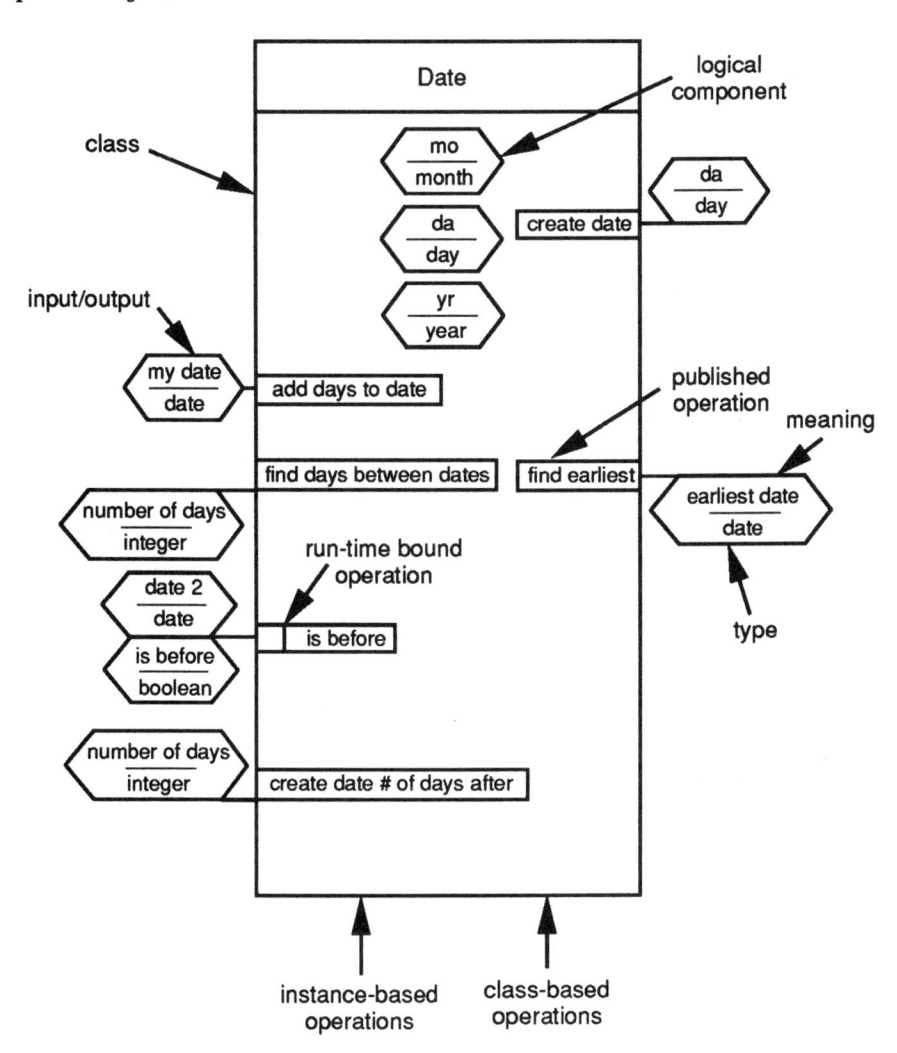

Figure 7-18. Class diagram

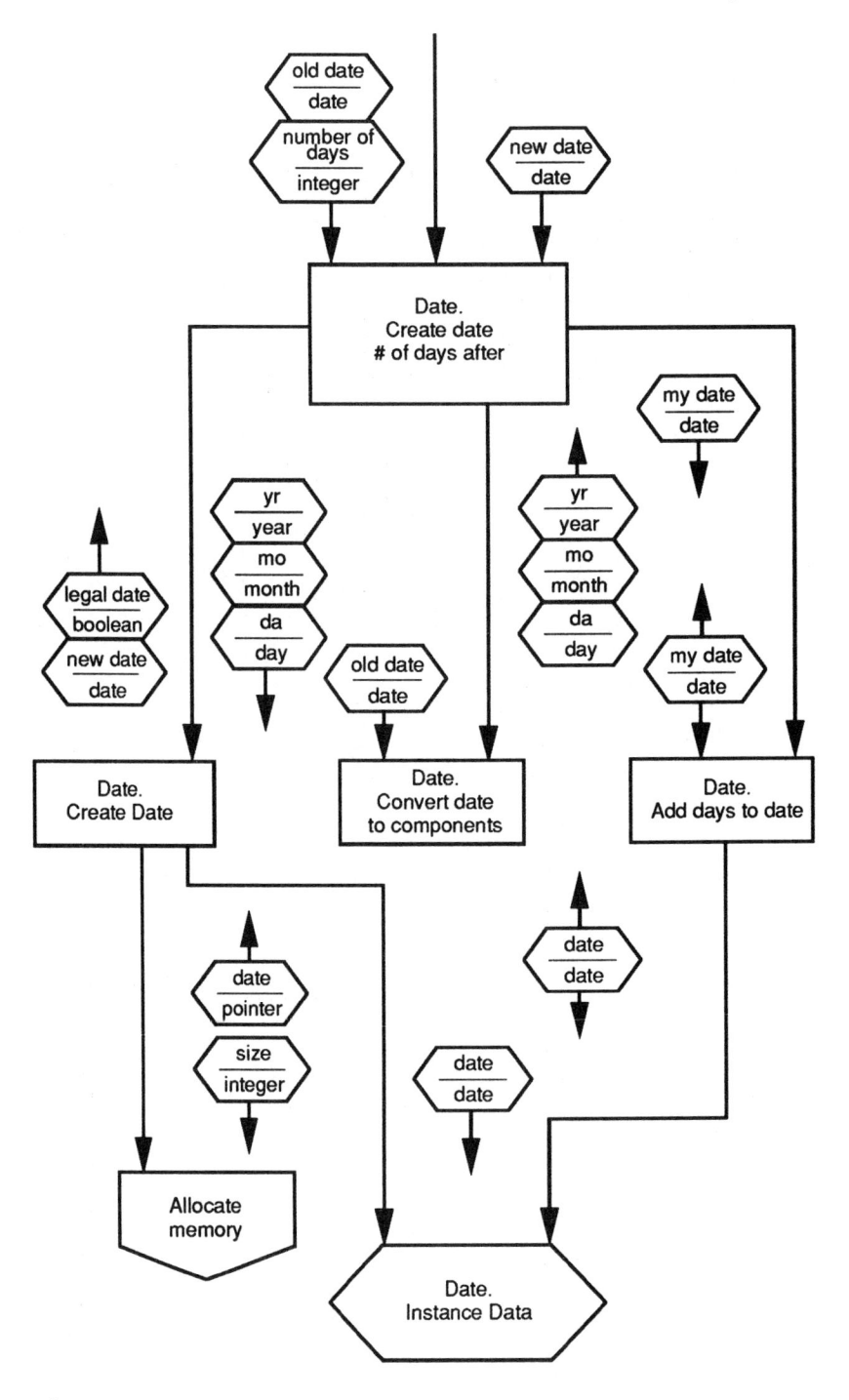

Figure 7-19. Class structure chart

Chapter 7 • Object-Oriented Methods

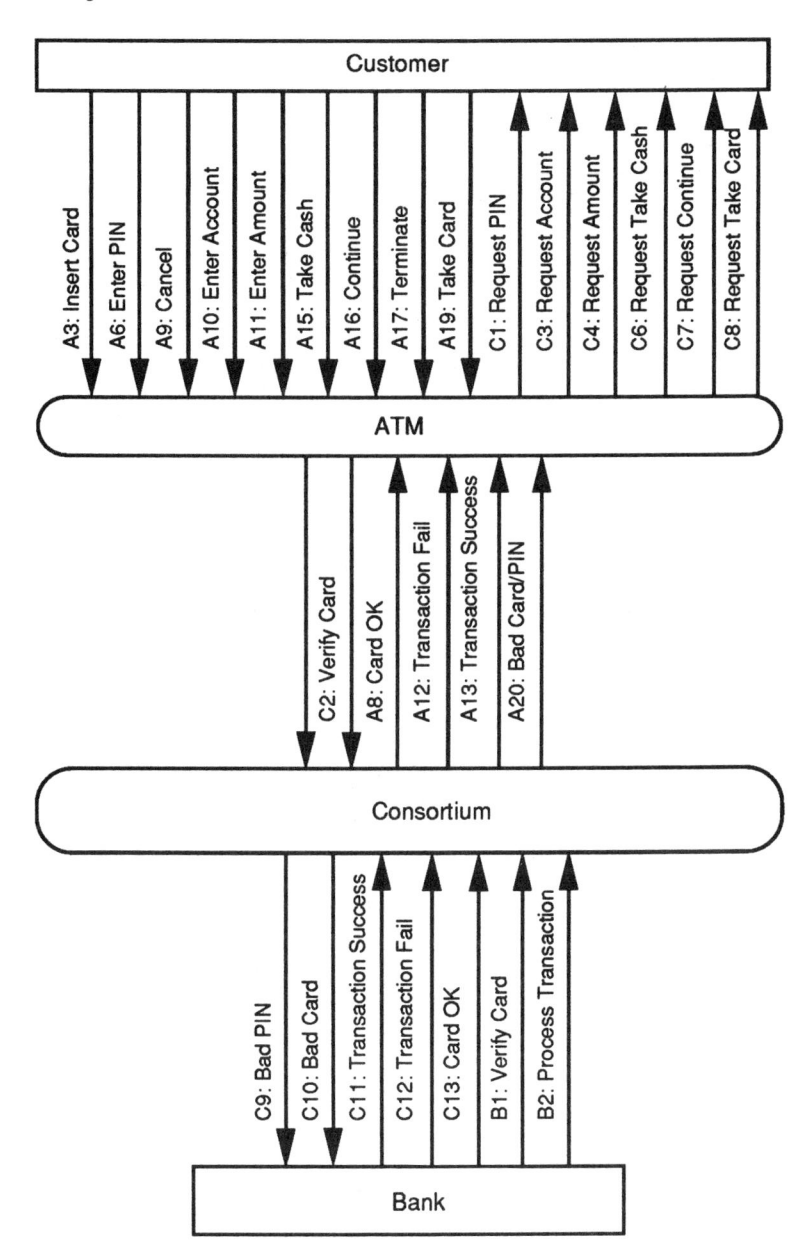

Figure 7-20. Object communication diagram

7.4.4 Recursive Design

The concept of RD needs some further explanation. Most programmers will associate the term "recursive" with a procedure that calls itself until one or more pre-specified stopping criteria are satisfied. The notion of RD is to apply a set of rules repeatedly ("recursively") for each domain until all the rules have been applied ("stopping criteria"). The rules are used to translate OOA objects to OOD objects, and the primary domains for this translation are the application and service domains. Applying the same set of rules to all these domains, will assure a uniform translation from analysis to design, and may allow for some automation of the transformation. At least, it provides a set of design evaluations for the resulting OOD objects.

One view of OOA/RD [MEL93] is shown in Figure 7-21. The design rules defined in the software architecture domain are applied to the OOA models in each domain. Templates can be used to create code skeletons from the OOD entities. The skeletons can then be filled in with actual code during the implementation phase.

The primary advantage of using OOA/RD is that when a change is required for the mapping of OOA to OOD entities, the appropriate rule is changed and then reapplied uniformly to all of the various domains.

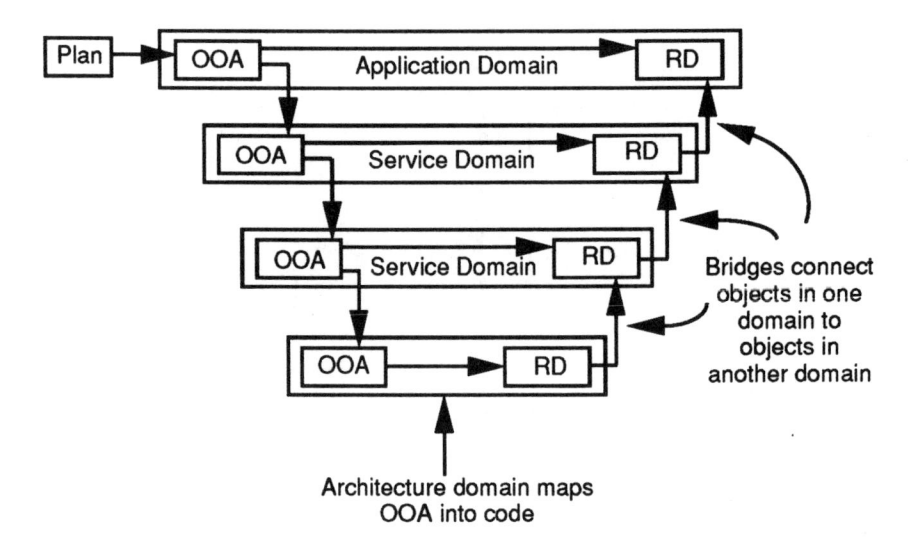

Figure 7-21. Applying RD to analysis domains

7.4.5 Real-Time Aspects and Concurrency

The object communication model (OCM) is used to show objects and the messages (events) passing between objects (see Figure 7-20). Each object is assumed to be an independent entity that can operate simultaneous with the other objects. Elements of the OCM include synchronization and control between the objects.

The selection of processes is suggested via a layering mechanism: Objects that interface with hardware devices are placed in the lowest layer and hide the interfacing mechanisms. Objects that handle real-world system events, and guide objects at the lowest layer, are placed in the highest layer and are considered actors in an object-oriented sense, i.e., they are acted upon by users and external systems interfacing with the system to be built. Middle layer objects are considered agents, and act on behalf of other objects. They may, typically, receive events from objects in the upper layer and forward these events to objects on the lowest layer.

7.4.6 CASE Tools

Elements of the OOA/RD methods are available in Cadre's TeamWork, Objective Solutions' ObjectiveAnalyst, StructSoft's TurboCASE, and SES's ObjectBench.

7.5 RDD AND CRCS

The responsibility-driven design (RDD) method has been applied to both object-oriented analysis and design. The method is described by Wirfs-Brock et al. [WIR90] and is based on the use of class, responsibility, and collaboration (CRC) cards. A CRC card includes the name of a class, its associated responsibilities (operations), and its collaborations with other classes (i.e., how the class interacts with other classes).

7.5.1 OOA

This method assumes the existence of a system requirements specification, or the participation of domain experts who can transform requirements into real-world objects and classes. A CRC card is prepared for each real-world entity. The entity is given a class name, and the associated operations (responsibilities) are listed on a 3x5 inch card (or electronic media). Class collaborators are also listed on the card, and specify the type of interfaces the given class makes with other classes. The collaborations are viewed in a client/server relationship, where the class named on the card is the server and the classes listed as collaborators are clients. An example of a CRC card for the ATM application is shown in Figure 7-22. The only collaborator for the Customer class is the ATM class, with the ATM class as the client.

The last activity of the responsibility-driven approach is the grouping of responsibilities into contracts. A *contract* represents the server interface, i.e., the set of messages (calls) that a client can send to a server. The primary significance of a contract is that during the transitioning from analysis to design, the contract becomes the visible interface. Considerations affecting a class contract can be implemented in C++ with constructs such as *friend* and *protected*.

An iterative approach will usually result as the CRC cards are produced, since we cannot define a collaborating class before that class is defined.

The CRC notation is not particularly powerful, but the method provides a simple and straightforward approach to the initial determination of classes. The method is also useful for initial brainstorming about system entities that can be viewed as real-world objects and their relationships.

Class: Customer	
Responsibilities:	Collaborations:
provides ATM card	ATM
retrieves ATM card	ATM
provides withdrawal amount	ATM
accepts cash	ATM
provides account number	ATM
accepts receipt	ATM
accepts continue query	ATM

Figure 7-22. CRC card for the Customer class

Chapter 7 • Object-Oriented Methods

An interesting aspect of the responsibility-driven approach is that it focuses on operations and class interfaces. Attributes (i.e., data entities) are not important for the analysis or design decisions to be made. Attributes can be annotated to the CRC cards, but are probably better kept in a separate data dictionary.

7.5.2 OOD

There is no separation between analysis and design models for this method. CRC class cards can be used to supplement any of the other OT methods for the identification of objects and classes during both the OOA and OOD phases.

7.5.3 System Design

The method does account for a clustering of classes into subsystems, but does not deal with the allocation of hardware and software requirements. The collaboration graph shown in Figure 7-23 can be used for subsystems as well

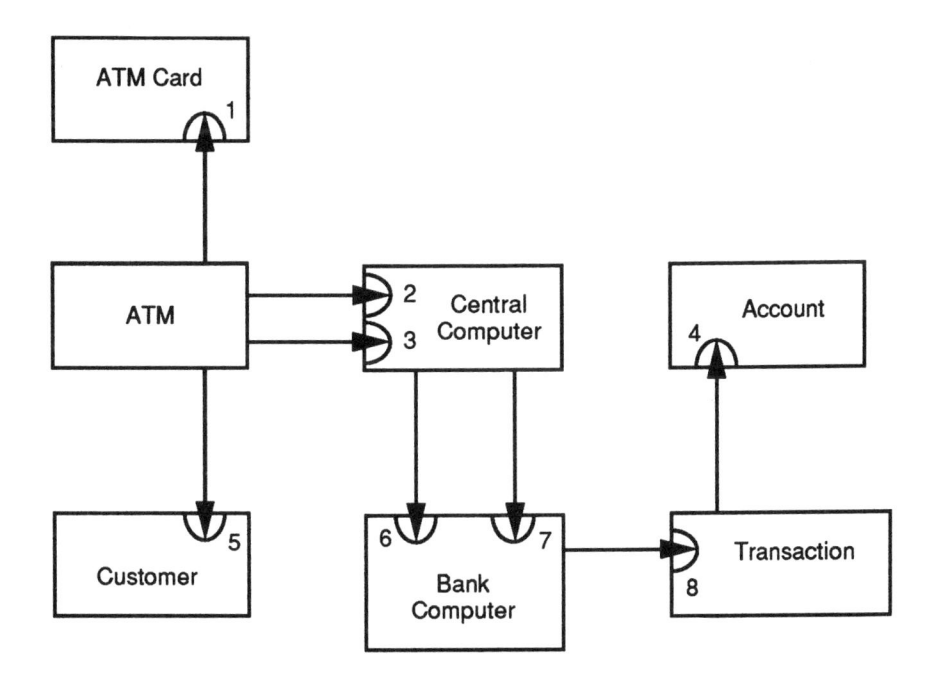

Figure 7-23. ATM collaboration graph

as for individual class interfaces. Each rectangle represents a class, and the directed graphs show the client/server relations, i.e., the arrowhead points toward the server. The number next to the small circles indicates the contract number and represents the collection of responsibilities for that class. Contract #5, for example, corresponds to the responsibilities listed for the Customer class in Figure 7-22.

7.6 COAD-YOURDON

The elements of the Coad-Yourdon method that pertain to OOA are described in [COA90, and COA91], and the OOD features are described in [COA91a]. This method is the antithesis to the Shlaer-Mellor method. Almost no rules are applied, and the diagrams are few and simplistic.

7.6.1 OOA

The OOA model is described in terms of attempting to establish five separate layers:

1. **Class and Object Layer.** Classes and objects are identified as real-world abstractions by searching for structures, other systems, devices, things or events remembered, roles played, operational procedures, sites, or organizational units. Classes and objects (instances) are depicted with an inner rectangle as the class and an outer rectangle as an instance. Figure 7-24 illustrates the notation for a Building class, with attributes added inside the class/object icon, and an Aircraft class, with a set of services (operations) added. Both attributes and operations can be annotated to the class/object icon, as indicated by the two empty areas.

Chapter 7 • Object-Oriented Methods

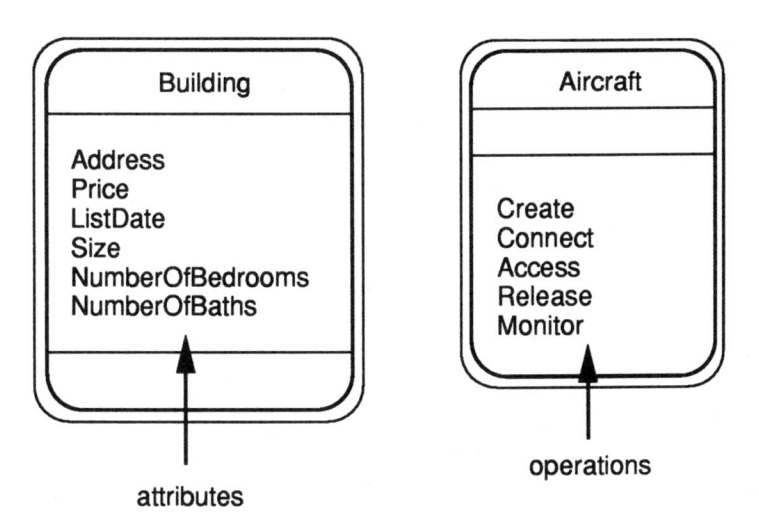

```
┌─────────────────────┐         ┌─────────────────────┐
│      Building       │         │      Aircraft       │
├─────────────────────┤         ├─────────────────────┤
│  Address            │         │                     │
│  Price              │         │  Create             │
│  ListDate           │         │  Connect            │
│  Size               │         │  Access             │
│  NumberOfBedrooms   │         │  Release            │
│  NumberOfBaths      │         │  Monitor            │
└─────────────────────┘         └─────────────────────┘
            ↑                               ↑
        attributes                      operations
```

Figure 7-24. Class/object icon

2. **Structure Layer.** The Generalization-Specialization (Gen-Spec) structure is used to describe inheritance (is-a) relationships between classes. The Whole-Part structure is used to describe aggregation (has-a) relationships. An example of the notation used for these structures is shown in Figure 7-25 for the ATM application.

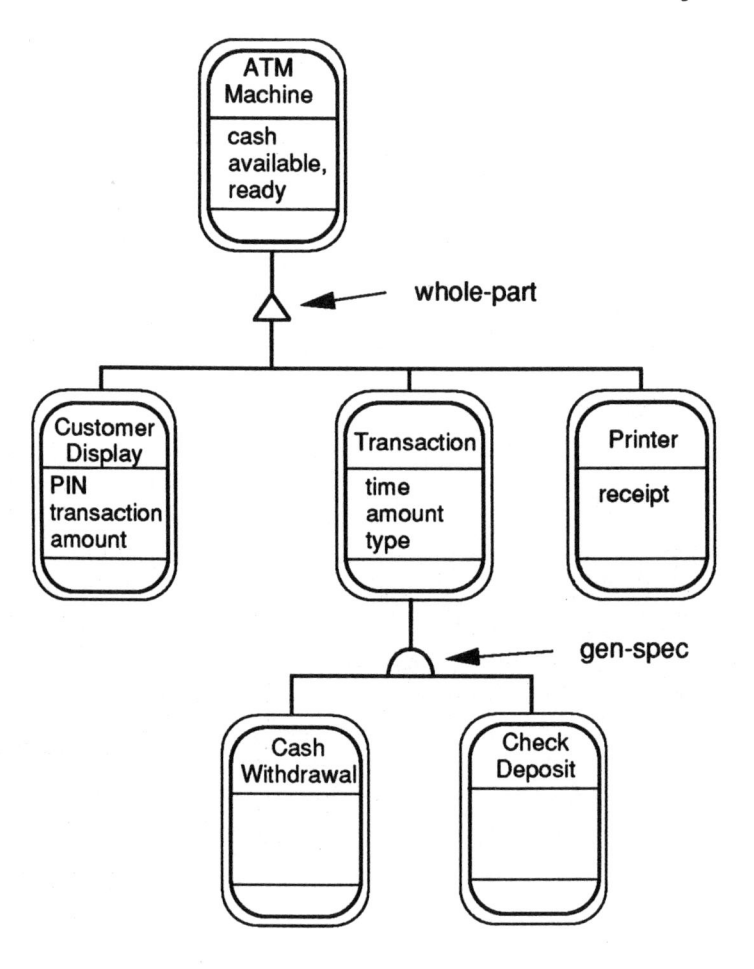

Figure 7-25. Class structures

3. **Instance Connections.** This is equivalent to the static object model used by other OT methods, and include cardinality notations as shown in Figure 7-26 for the ATM application.

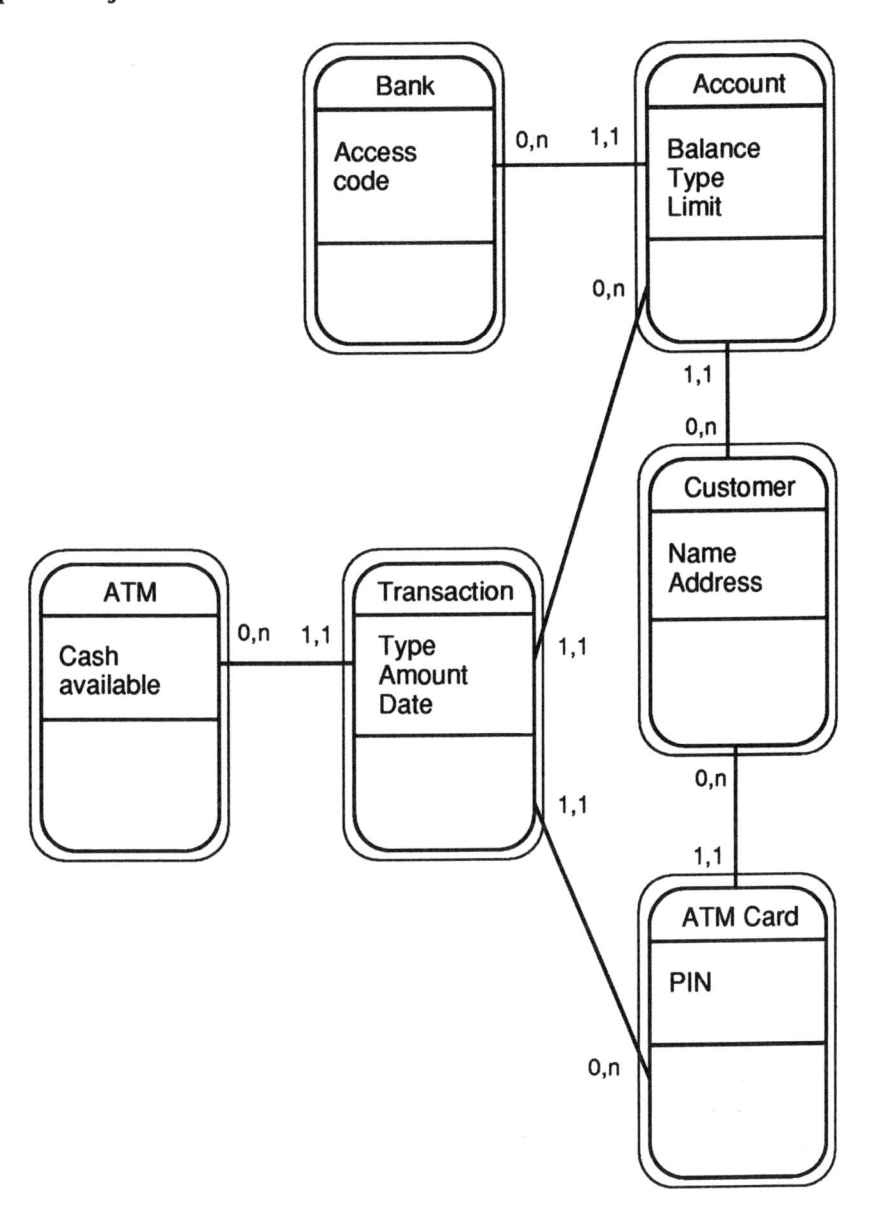

Figure 7-26. Instance connections for the ATM application

4. **Subject Layer.** This typically represents a clustering of about five to nine objects to reduce the number of objects to something manageable, and to reduce multiple levels of diagrams. A guide to the selection of a subject is to promote the uppermost class in each structure to a subject. Then, to promote each class/object not in a structure upwards to a subject.

5. **Attribute Layer.** Class attributes are identified as state variables associated with each object. They are shown as an adornment in the middle section of the class/object icons as shown in Figure 7-24 for the ATM application. Suggestions for specifications of attributes are made in terms of such things as units, range of values, precision, and default value.

6. **Service Layer.** Services (operations) are defined to affect the behavior of the object they are associated with. Services are created by applying the following steps:

    - identify object states
    - identify the required services
    - identify message connections
    - specify the services
    - put the OOA documentation set together

A service chart is used to show the procedural abstraction of a service. An example of a service chart is shown in Figure 7-27 for an ATM operation.

7.6.2 System Design

The method does not describe a systems design activity, but it refers to "subjects" as the equivalent of subsystems in OOSE, OMT, and Shlaer-Mellor, and class categories in Booch'93. Guidelines for allocating software and hardware requirements are not included.

7.6.3 OOD

The underpinning of the Coad-Yourdon method is to have a uniform notation for models used in OOA and OOD. The purported major benefit of this representation is that no transitioning is required from the OOA to the OOD phase. Classes and objects and their relationships are simply refined during the OOD phase, and additional classes and objects discovered during this phase are added to the design entities.

Chapter 7 • Object-Oriented Methods

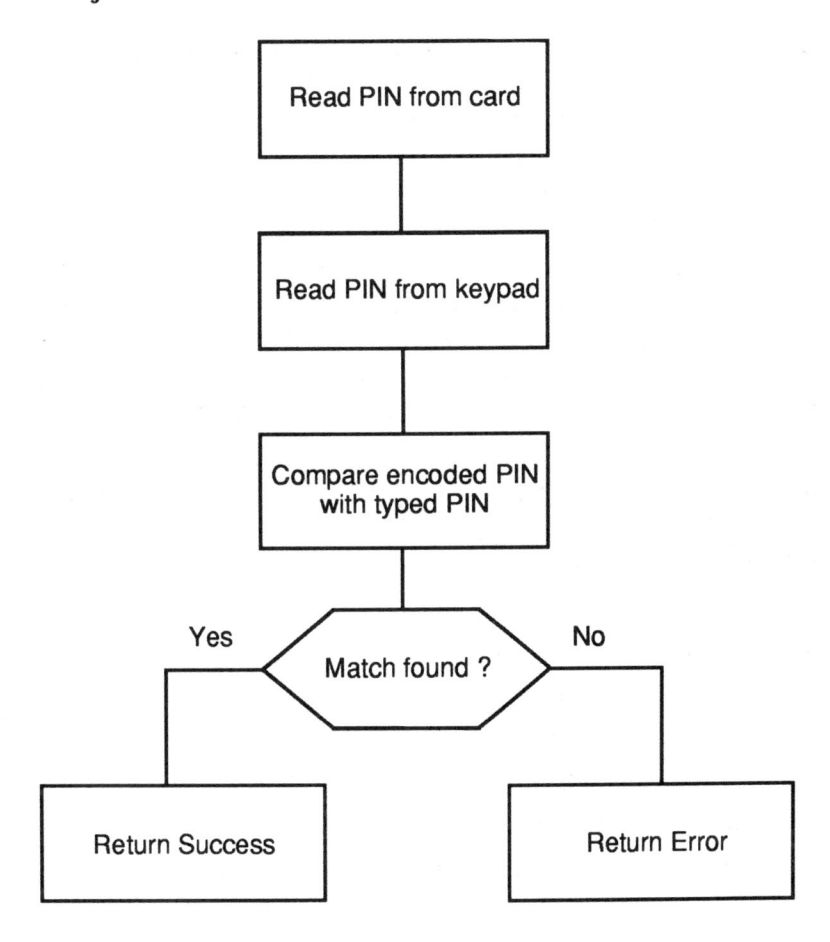

```
         ┌─────────────────────┐
         │  Read PIN from card │
         └─────────────────────┘
                    │
         ┌─────────────────────┐
         │ Read PIN from keypad│
         └─────────────────────┘
                    │
         ┌─────────────────────┐
         │ Compare encoded PIN │
         │   with typed PIN    │
         └─────────────────────┘
                    │
      Yes      ╱ Match ╲      No
        ┌─────< found ? >─────┐
        │      ╲       ╱      │
┌───────────────┐      ┌───────────────┐
│ Return Success│      │ Return Error  │
└───────────────┘      └───────────────┘
```

Figure 7-27. Service chart for the VerifyPIN operation

The OOD phase applies the whole-part paradigm to describe the following four major design models:

1. **Problem Domain Component.** OOA results are placed directly into this component.
2. **Human Interaction Component.** This includes actual displays and inputs needed for effective human-computer interaction.
3. **Task Management Component.** This component includes task definitions, communication mechanisms, and concurrency control. It also incorporates hardware allocation considerations, and external system and device protocols.

4. **Data Management Component.** This component includes access and management of persistent data.

The major activities of OOD are the creations of the four component models listed above in terms of the same five layers that were used for OOA: class and object, structure, subject, attribute, and service layers. The major reference for the OOD phase ([COA91a]) provides some guidance to the activities, but it is difficult to determine the results of the OOD phase (i.e., there are no stopping criteria). The major products are the refined classes and objects from the problem domain, plus additional classes and objects in the other three components.

Evaluation guidelines are provided for the degree of coupling and cohesion between OOD entities. A desired low coupling is suggested by keeping the number of parameters in a message (procedure or function call) to three or less. A desired high coupling for the gen-spec paradigm of inheritance is measured by the number of attributes and services the specialized class inherits. Strong cohesion for a service is obtained when the service only performs a single operation. Strong cohesion for a class is reflected in services that perform operations related to the same abstraction. Strong cohesion for the gen-spec relationship is measured by how well the specialized class relates to the general class.

7.6.4 Real-Time Aspects and Concurrency

The Coad-Yourdon method does address real-time aspects and concurrency requirements. The following task selection rules are suggested to populate the task management component:

1. **Identify Event-Driven Tasks.** These tasks are typically triggered by an event from an external device or external system in the form of an interrupt.
2. **Identify Clock-Driven Tasks.** These tasks execute for certain pre-determined time periods, and may be periodic or aperiodic.
3. **Identify Priority Tasks and Critical Tasks.** Tasks used in hard real-time systems require high priorities to prevent the loss of critical data. Background tasks can time slice their executions and are given low priorities.
4. **Identify a Coordinator.** A coordinator task can be added to a concurrent system with three or more tasks. The new task will encapsulate the coordination activity, but adds run-time overhead.

5. **Challenge Each Task.** The total number of tasks in the system (that compete for the services of the same CPU) should be kept to a minimum, since the addition of each task adds run-time overhead.
6. **Define Each Task.** Each task is defined in terms of task coordination, periodicities, priorities, communication, and services provided.

7.6.5 CASE Tools

The OODTool includes drawing and interface checking support for the OOD phase. This tool runs on PCs, Macintoshes, and Unix machines.

7.7 OTHER METHODS

The OOA/OOD methods described above represent most of the popular OT methods that are currently being used as language independent tools. Numerous other methods have been described in the literature, some of them have a definite programming language bent, e.g., Firesmith's Ada-leaning OORA/OODL [FIR93]. Texts describing other methods and OT paradigms include [GRA94], [CHA93], [BER93], and [ODE92].

7.8 SUMMARY

A large number of methods are available to implement an OT approach. Many of these methods use the same models, but, unfortunately, employ widely different notations to illustrate the same concepts. Some of these notations are extremely complex and require the use of CASE tools to manage the diagrams used to illustrate the various models.

The methods described above differ significantly in their approach to distinguishing between the various development phases. Coad-Yourdon, OMT, and Booch '93 have a blurred distinction between the OOA and OOD phases. Shlaer-Mellors's OOA/RD and Jacobson's OOSE make sharp distinctions between these two phases.

The methods differ significantly in their approach to provide guidelines and rules for transitioning between the various phases. OOA/RD and OOSE include valuable transitioning criteria between the OOA, OOD, and OOP phases. OOA/RD is rule-based and includes 72 rules (conditions) to determine the validity and completion of the OOA phase.

Some of the methods, e.g., Coad-Yourdon, include guidelines for task selections and measures of coupling and cohesion.

CRC cards are simple and effective for determining the client/server class contract relationships. They can be used to supplement the other methods during the OOA and OOD phases. The focus of the CRC approach is on responsibilities (operations) and does not consider attributes.

8

Using Object-Oriented Methods

The most important aspect of adopting a new software development approach is the level of risk associated with switching to new techniques. A significant investment is required for a successful organization-wide implementation of a new development approach. This investment includes the training of the development staff, acquisition of CASE and compilation tools, and a potential reorganization of the development staff. The risk is directly related to the kind of returns that can be expected after the new software development approach is in place. That return is primarily measured by the amount of reusable software that can be realized for current and future projects, any increase in productivity, and the quality of the software produced.

There has been a significant amount of controversy over the "orthogonality" of OOA/OOD and traditional structured analysis and structured design (SA/SD). The OT proponents have steadfastly maintained that OOA/OOD cannot be used in conjunction with SA/SD, whereas the traditional SA/SD methods camp argue that the two approaches complement each other. The current attitude seems to prevail that OT methods are "good," and structured methods are old-fashioned, and will produce less reliable software products.

The objectives of this chapter are to:

- discuss the use of OT methods and traditional structured methods
- provide guidelines for picking the "right" method for a particular project
- provide guidelines for creating real-world entities
- suggest a transitioning strategy from structured to OT methods

8.1 BENEFITS OF OBJECT-ORIENTED METHODS

Some of the major benefits of using object-oriented methods to support the software development process include the following:

1. The analysis model is developed in terms of key abstractions that are described with real-world entities. These entities have names and attributes our customers and users can understand, and make the system requirements definitions easier.
2. System requirement changes are relatively easy to identify and transform to analysis and design entities. A high level of traceability from requirements to implementation is attained via the localization of requirements to clearly identified objects.
3. Reusability in-the-large can be realized by the transformation of real-world entities into software modules and, possibly, entire subsystems. The OT paradigms, including encapsulation, data hiding, classes, objects, inheritance, and aggregation can be transitioned from OOA to OOD to OOP.
4. The creation of classes and class libraries supports reusability and can provide improved productivity and quality, since less code needs to be tested and debugged and code already debugged is reused.
5. The transformation from analysis to design is made a distinct part of the development process, and provides direct correlations between analysis and design products.
6. Maintenance is simplified by replacing entire objects when system requirements change or enhancements are necessary.
7. The development of objects can support an early demonstration of operational concepts, GUIs, etc., to provide user feedback on system requirements.

The use of OT methods does not guarantee an automatic realization of the suggested benefits. A significant effort, starting with a strong commitment of support by management, will be required for the success of using OT methods.

8.2 POTENTIAL PROBLEMS WITH OBJECT-ORIENTED METHODS

OT methods are now used by many software development organizations, and the use of these methods is associated with "good" software engineering practices. A large number of established software organizations have successfully used some form of SA/SD over the last two decades, and it has not yet been shown that the tremendous productivity gains and reuse suggested by the OT community can readily be realized. The latter organizations are reluctant to switch to the use of OT methods because of a number of potential problems and risks associated with their use.

8.2.1 Problem Areas

Some of the problems associated with the use of OT methods include the following:

1. **Little Delineation between OOA and OOD.** Many OT methods do not distinguish between the OOA and OOD phases, resulting in problems with requirements traceability when changes occur. Some organizations developing large projects receive partial payments from their customers based on the successful completion of distinct analysis and design phases.

2. **Immature CASE Tools.** Most of the existing CASE tools are immature and do not support a full complement of OOA/OOD paradigms.

3. **Complex Class Hierarchies.** Undisciplined use of class hierarchies may render designs incomprehensible and make software certification more difficult by the inheritance relations. Any change or problem occurring in a parent class will have to be evaluated and tested in all child classes.

4. **Emphasis on Data Abstraction.** A shortcoming of current object-oriented design approaches is that they are based entirely on data abstraction and do not address the problem of determining the concurrent elements of a real-time system, i.e., process abstraction.

5. **Training Required.** A significant training effort is required to install a software development process using OT methods. An adequate understanding of a particular OT method used for OOA/OOD and an OOP language may take six to twelve months.

6. **Lack of Development Tools.** Sophisticated browsers are required to rapidly locate the hierarchy or path of an entity contained in a low-level subclass.

7. **Lack of Support for Concurrency.** Many of the current OT methods

do not adequately address concurrency issues. This is of particular importance for real-time systems.

8. **Multiple Methods in Use.** Different software development organizations within the same company may already be using their own favorite methods, which differ from organization to organization. This will complicate an effort to establish unified training material and development approaches.

The potential problem areas listed above may provide a significant risk against a successful development with OT methods. This is particularly important for the first few projects that are switching from traditional structured techniques to OT approaches.

8.2.2 Risk Areas

A number of risk areas are associated with the use of OT methods:

1. **Longer Development Time.** The first few development projects using OT methods may take longer and cost more when compared to the use of traditional methods. This can be caused by the amount of training required, and the higher complexity of multi-layered designs.

2. **Added Maintenance.** The use of inheritance and polymorphism in C++ may add greatly to the complexity of the software produced and thus make maintenance more difficult and costly, compared to C or Ada.

3. **Poor Performance.** Compilation times may be significantly longer, and the use of dynamic binding may take extra execution time compared to the use of more traditional programming languages.

4. **Unrealized Return on Investment.** The added investment in training and tools may not provide the expected return on investments. Reuse efforts may fail to materialize if only half-hearted support is provided.

5. **Dissension between Development Organizations.** The method we pick to support the company-wide development process may be different from one or more methods that are already in use by some development organizations within a large company.

Despite the many potential problems and their associated risks, the use of OT can greatly enhance the development process. In the next few sections, we will discuss the beneficial use of OT and a recommended approach.

8.3 WHEN TO USE OBJECT-ORIENTED METHODS

For development organizations already using OT methods exclusively, this will be a non-issue. For organizations using structured methods, however, the issue of why and when to switch to object-oriented techniques can be extremely important. Here are some suggestions for the latter organizations:

1. **The Customer Demands It.** A customer may require a potential contractor to use OT methods. It behooves the contractor to get a very clear understanding of what the customer means by "object-oriented," does it mean a particular OT method, for example?

2. **Switching to an Object-Oriented Programming Language.** Using an OOA/OOD approach will provide a smoother transition from the design phase to programming if paradigms including classes, objects, and inheritance are incorporated into the development approach.

3. **Overall Reuse Strategy.** If the development staff is already trained in the use of OT methods, it makes sense to switch to an object-oriented approach for the implementation of a reuse strategy involving the creation of domain dependent class libraries.

4. **Currently Hacking.** If no development process exists within a software organization, the use of an object-oriented approach will impose a uniform development strategy for the various development teams. (This is, of course, also true for adopting a structured approach.)

5. **Support of Prototyping.** The use of scenarios and real-world entities lend themselves to the development of prototypes for identifying and refining user requirements. The use of structured methods has created problems in the past in discussing requirements with the customer. The use of DFDs (the structured method used for requirements analysis) tends to be design oriented and may complicate communication with customers.

6. **OT Development Tools.** The successful implementation of any development process is highly dependent on the availability of development tools that support the process. The availability of OT tools simplifies the transitioning from structured to OT methods.

7. **Ease of Identifying Subsystems.** Subsystems are sometimes readily identified as abstract real-world entities, e.g., an ATM machine and a central computer system.

Software development organizations using a structured approach do not need to toss out their entire process as they switch to using OT methods. A coexistence of structured and OT methods is quite realistic. The important aspect is to have an overall development approach and to incorporate OT methods to support some, or all, of the development phases.

8.4 MIXING OBJECT-ORIENTED AND STRUCTURED METHODS

Many large, established software development organizations have successfully used some form of SA/SD over the last two decades. The tremendous productivity gains and large-scale reuse suggested with the use of OT methods are not automatically realized. It may be, for example, that the creation of a design with deep inheritance layers will add to the complexity of the software produced, and thus make maintenance more difficult and costly, compared to software created from a structured design.

Some software organizations with established structured methods may use these methods for the analysis phase and still employ OOD for the design phase with a straightforward transitioning from design entities to the C++ coding phase. In general, structured analysis methods and object-oriented design methods are complementary, not "orthogonal," where orthogonal is used in a connotation of "does not mix well."

If the requirements for a given application implemented in C, for example, have not changed dramatically, and we want to take advantage of the greater reuse potential with C++, a redesign using OT methods is quite reasonable. One potential problem with using structured analysis as a front end to OOD is that the level of DFDs may be too detailed and already reflect design decisions.

Some structured methods are better suited to handle concurrency than OT methods, and can be used for the selection of processes in real-time systems. The use of structured methods may also make sense where objects tend to be split between subsystems, and there is a need to determine the requirements allocation of hardware and software to subsystems.

One instance where mixing structured and OT methods may make sense is during the transitioning period from structured to OT methods. Rather than risk a higher development cost and longer development schedule for the entire project, structured methods can be used for the requirements analysis phase and OT methods for the design phase. A fall-back position for a late project can then be to complete the project using familiar structured design techniques.

The primary problem with mixing structured and OT methods is the existence of two different sets of notations and development tools. Another problem is that forward and backward requirements traceability becomes more difficult when requirements or designs are changing.

The use of structured techniques is further discussed where appropriate in Part III when we describe the various development phases.

8.5 SELECTING THE "RIGHT" METHOD

In light of the constant debate over the selection of the "right" OT method, [TOP94], [MON93], and [FIC92], it would be presumptuous to claim a magic formula for this choice. Picking a suitable OT method is fraught with difficult trade-off decisions. The various OOA/OOD methods discussed in Chapter 7 have their strengths and weaknesses, and neither one represents a perfect choice to support our development process. We can, however, provide a number of guidelines to make the selection process simpler.

Our development strategy must result in software that contains a high degree of reusability to support an ever-toughening competitive marketplace. Software organizations cannot rely on cushioned cost-plus contracts, but must compete in a shrinking market for fixed-cost contracts. The development of new applications is highly cost-competitive, and it becomes important that small, medium, and large software systems can be constructed from a core of common modules available for a given problem domain.

Current practices for employing a system development process can be classified roughly into three approaches that apply to both structured and object-oriented techniques:

1. Pick one or more methods that can support the various development phases, and try to find Computer Aided Software Engineering (CASE) tools that implement these methods.

2. Pick a CASE tool and let this tool dictate which methods are used to support the process.

3. Leave the choice to an in-house guru who has some experience with software development methods.

Neither of these approaches is ideal, since there is no CASE tool in existence that can support a wide variety of methods. The first approach usually leads to the acquisition and use of a number of tools that employ different notations for similar analysis and design concepts. The second approach limits the use of methods to those embedded within the CASE tool. The third approach is likely to be based on the guru's personal preferences without a proper trade-off study.

The selection process should first include the establishment of a set of evaluation criteria, followed by an evaluation and comparison of potential OT methods that support these criteria. The selection should not be based on a personal bias by an individual who happens to be familiar with a particular method.

8.5.1 Evaluation Criteria

Picking the "right" method is no simple task, especially since more than one method may support the development process. A selection process should be undertaken to compare the features of the methods deemed suitable for adaptation. Here are some guidelines for evaluating OT methods:

1. **Support the Development Process.** Any object-oriented method considered must support the overall development process, i.e., the models and views employed must cover all of the various development phases, and scale up to the kind of systems to be developed. It is important that the method does not become the development process.

2. **Method is Teachable.** Training is the key to a successful transitioning from a structured to an object-oriented approach. The method we pick must be straightforward to teach. Course material and instructors must be available so that a "train-the-trainers" program for further in-house training can be accomplished.

3. **Guidelines.** Guidelines must be incorporated into the method, e.g., for identifying classes and objects, and for transitioning between development phases.

4. **Development Tools.** Development tools that support the notation of the various models should exist. This is especially important for a method with notations that are significantly different from structured notation, and for methods that use many different icons and adornments on the model diagrams. Development tools can include:

   - CASE tools
   - compilation and run-time systems
   - browsers
   - configuration management and versioning

- management and tracking
- class libraries
- test tools

5. **Real-Time Support.** The chosen method must support the type of applications we are developing. If we are developing real-time systems, for example, the chosen approach must support the design of such systems and include considerations for concurrency and distributed architectures.

6. **Complements Current Approach.** OT methods should be incorporated gradually into the current development approach. The transitioning from structured to OT methods can be made more smoothly if the new methods fit well with the current structured approach. If ERDs are used in the current structured approach, for example, it is relatively simple to incorporate the object model with the real-world entities matching the entities on the ERDs.

7. **Language Dependence.** The preferred OT method is not language dependent in the support of the domain analysis, OOA, and OOD phases (except for detailed design).

8. **Cost.** A cost estimate should be made for the implementation of a particular method. This should include training, acquisition of tools, and management support.

8.5.2 Picking OT Methods

By using the above guidelines for evaluating OT methods, we can now pick the OT method that will support our development approach.

Development guidelines can be established by picking the best suggestions from the various methods. This can, for example, be applied to:

- identification of classes and objects
- process selection
- creation of subsystems
- evaluation of objects

Once the methods, rules, and guidelines have been established, it is imperative that they be implemented uniformly within all the various development organizations of the company. This will require a strong management edict and the availability of senior developers who can teach and enforce the new approach.

It should be recognized that any development approach will evolve over a period of time, and that improvements are likely to be incorporated from one project to the next. Significant changes in notation, rules, and guidelines are not recommended once a project is well advanced in the development process.

8.5.3 Rule-Based Development

Rule-based development can be established by incorporating the best of the rules from several different methods. This is especially important for the first few projects, as the development teams need guidance in moving from one phase to the next. Specific rules and guidelines should be developed for the following:

- creation of scenarios
- creation of classes and objects
- creation of subsystems and object clustering
- transitioning from OOA to OOD
- adding attributes and operations to OOD classes
- transitioning from OOD to OOP
- process (task) selection rules

One of the important contributions of Shlaer-Mellor's OOA/RD method is the development of rules and conditions. Rule-based transformations can be used to create OOD entities from the OOA entities. Rules and conditions can also be used to determine stopping criteria for an individual development phase. Here are some of the rules used in OOA/RD for transitioning from the OOA to the OOD phase [LEE93]:

- objects => classes
- attributes => instance data
- relationships => inheritance
- events => architecture class
- state transitions => architecture class
- state actions => operations (state dependent)
- accessors => operations (state independent)
- process models => program structure

These kind of rules should be included in the overall process as part of the transitioning guidelines and can also be used for analysis and design evaluations.

Additional sets of rules will be established in Part III as we apply OT paradigms to the various development phases.

8.6 RECOMMENDED MODELING APPROACH

The chosen modeling approach should support all of the different views and models required to develop design entities that can be implemented with C++ constructs. The approach must scale up and be usable for the development of small, medium, and large systems.

The modeling approach suggested in the following subsections is based on the development phases described in Chapter 2, the OOA and OOD models in Chapter 6, and the OT methods discussed in Chapter 7.

8.6.1 System Model

The system view is the highest level abstraction of the system requirements and illustrates the relations between system elements and external entities without regard for architectural structure. One example of a system model is shown in Figure 8-1 for the elements of an ATM system. The emphasis of this model is on the relations between the various elements that comprise an ATM system.

Another system view for a software-intensive air traffic control system (ATCS) is shown in Figure 8-2. This model is the context diagram familiar to developers using structured methods, and is considered the top-level DFD. The focus of this model is on the data passed between the system to be developed and the external interfaces.

8.6.2 Scenario-Driven Approach

The use of a scenario-driven approach from Jacobson's OOSE is highly recommended for systems that involve user interfaces and interfaces to external systems. A number of scenarios can be determined for all the user interactions, and the analysis, design and implementation is focused around each scenario. System requirements can thus be traced directly from the definition of user or external system interfaces to the implementation and testing.

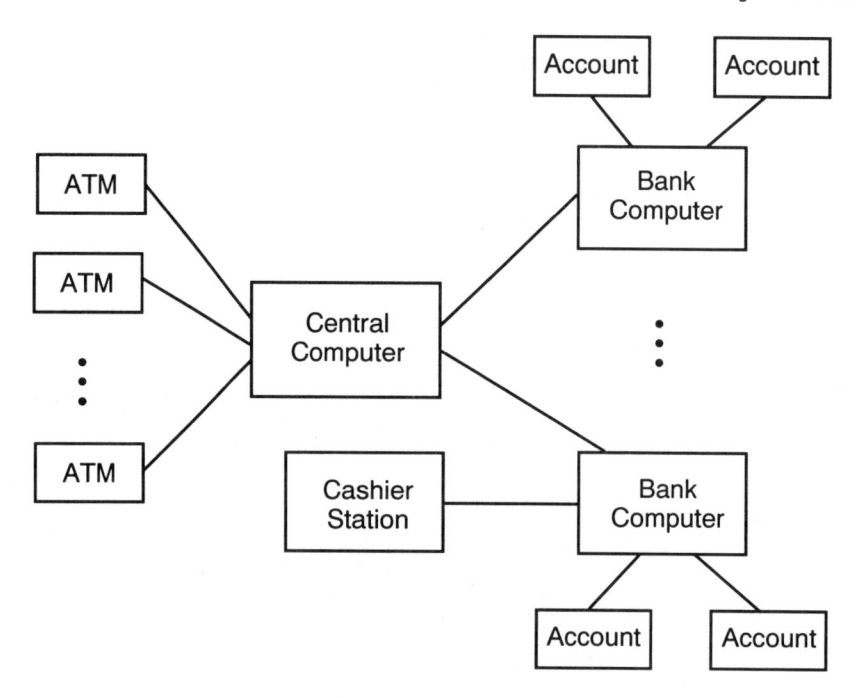

Figure 8-1. ATM system diagram

Another direct benefit of the scenario approach is that it supports an incremental development strategy. This approach presents the various class/object modeling views at the highly abstract scenario level, rather than at the lower abstraction of the system level.

The creation of scenarios should start with the domain analysis, as the incremental "build" structures and prototyping efforts are defined. An example of a single scenario for a simplified recycling machine [JAC92, p. 155] is shown in Figure 8-3.

Chapter 8 • Using Object-Oriented Methods

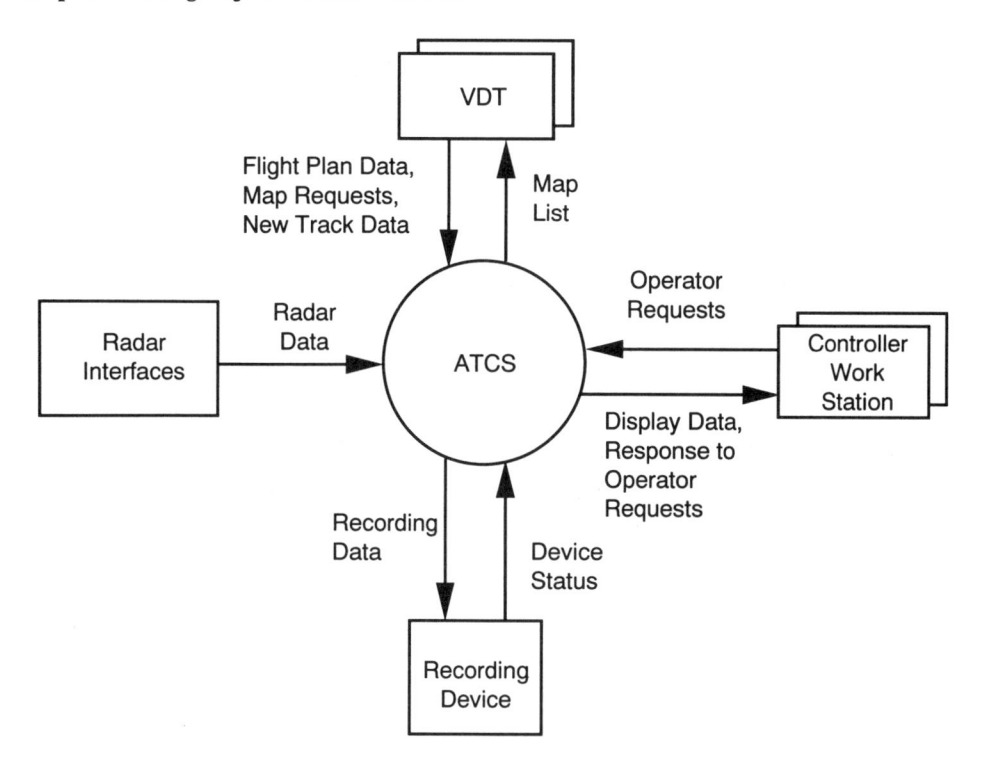

Figure 8-2. ATC context diagram

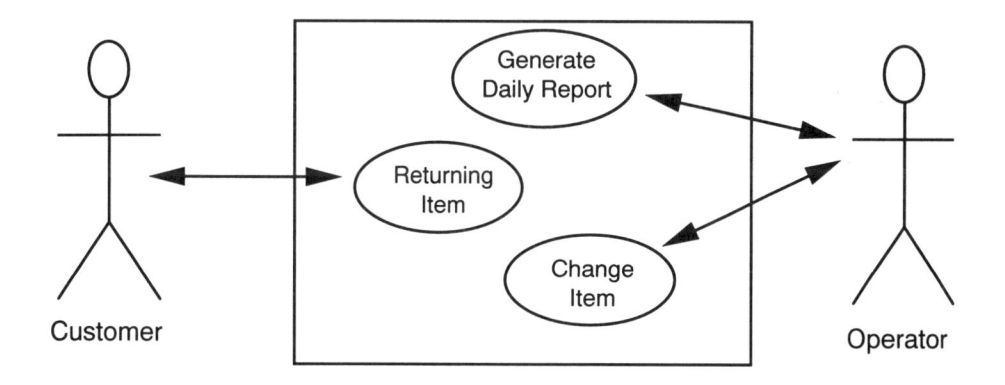

Figure 8-3. Scenario diagram for recycling machine

8.6.3 Static Models

Static models are used in both the OOA and OOD activities. An example of an object model is shown in Figure 8-4 for an ATM system, and illustrate the major objects and their relations or associations. This is one of the primary models used for OOA in finding the key real-world abstractions of the system.

Another static view, which is used to illustrate object decomposition, is shown in Figure 8-5, and provides a more detailed look at the ATM Machine object. Aggregation is depicted for a whole-part relationship between the ATM Machine and the components Customer Display, Transaction, and Printer. Inheritance is shown with Cash Withdrawal and Check Deposit as derived objects from the parent Transaction.

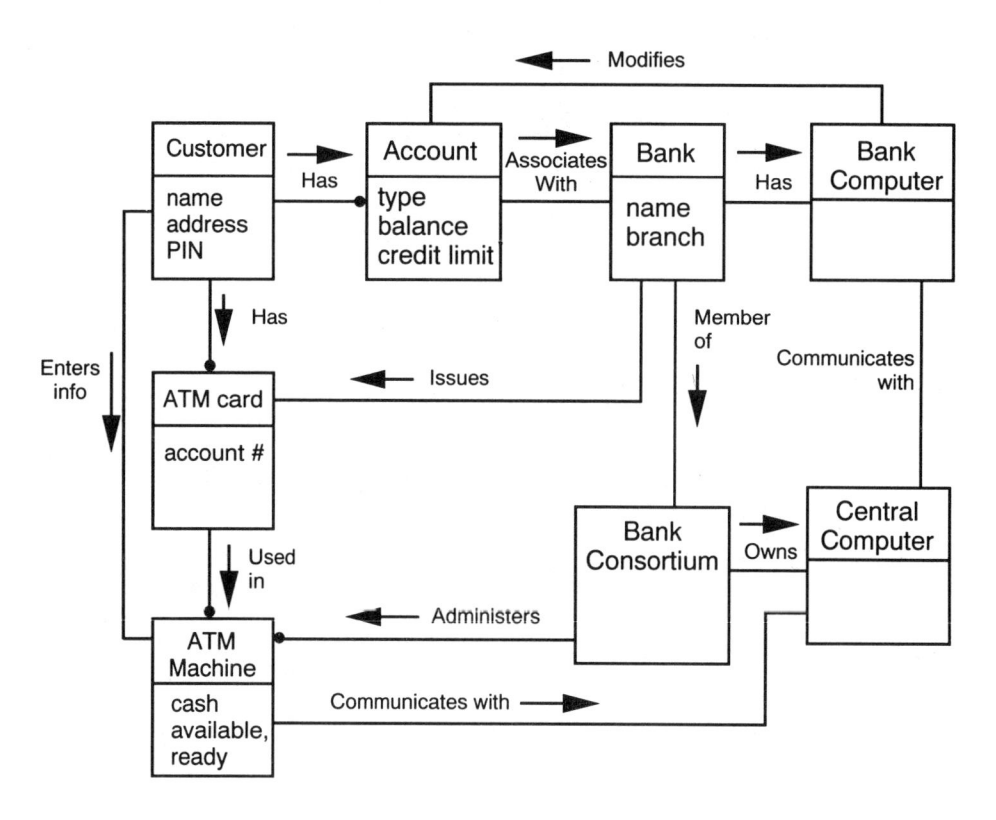

Figure 8-4. Object model of ATM application

Chapter 8 • Using Object-Oriented Methods

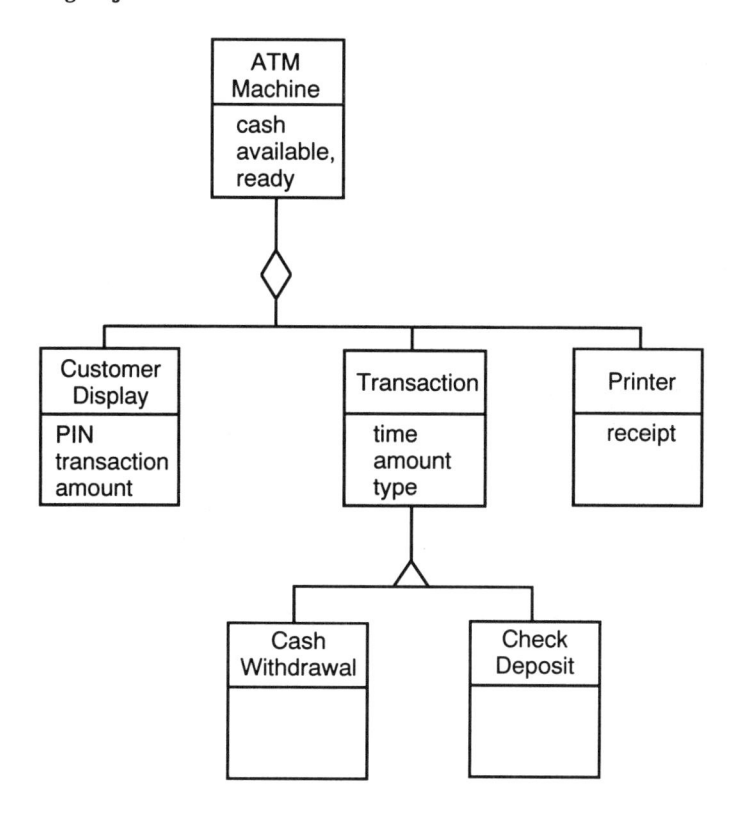

Figure 8-5. Inheritance and aggregation model

Another form of a static model is the module architecture diagram shown in Figure 8-6. This is used for the OOD phase and illustrates static architectural entities and their interfaces. Each design icon depicts the interface used for receiving and sending messages to and from the object encapsulated within the icon boundary. The message flow can be indicated by the direction of arrows on the lines connecting the objects.

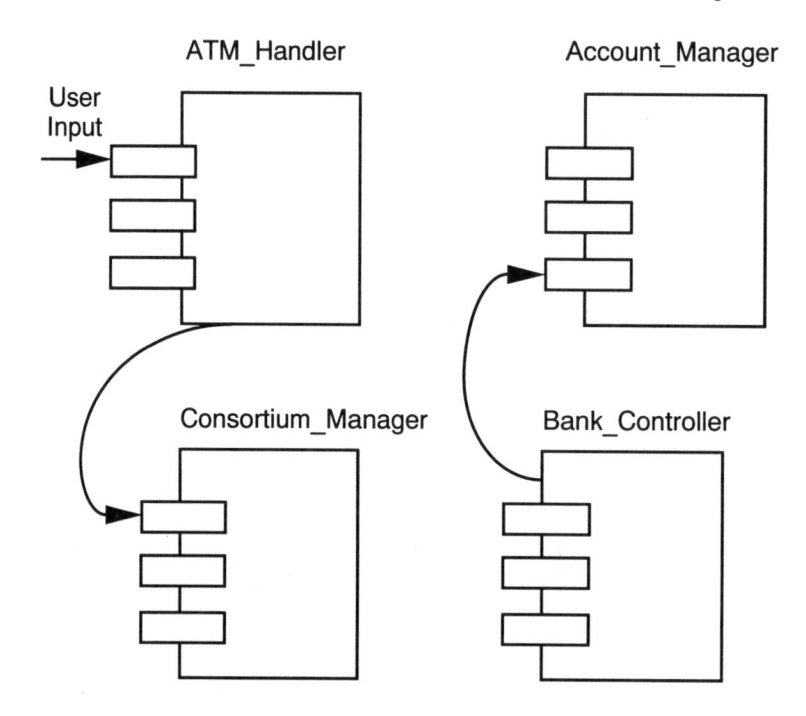

Figure 8-6. Module architecture diagram for ATM application

8.6.4 Dynamic Models

Dynamic models are used to describe objects and their relations with regard to the system changing with time. The dynamic behavior includes system state changes, sequencing of events, and external input and output (e.g., incoming interrupts and outgoing signals sent to hardware devices).

An example of a dynamic object model is shown in Figure 8-7 for the ATM application. This is an object flow model depicting the messages that flow between the objects. Some OT methods consider all of these objects as high-level concurrent entities, and use this model to determine the elements of subsystems.

Chapter 8 • Using Object-Oriented Methods

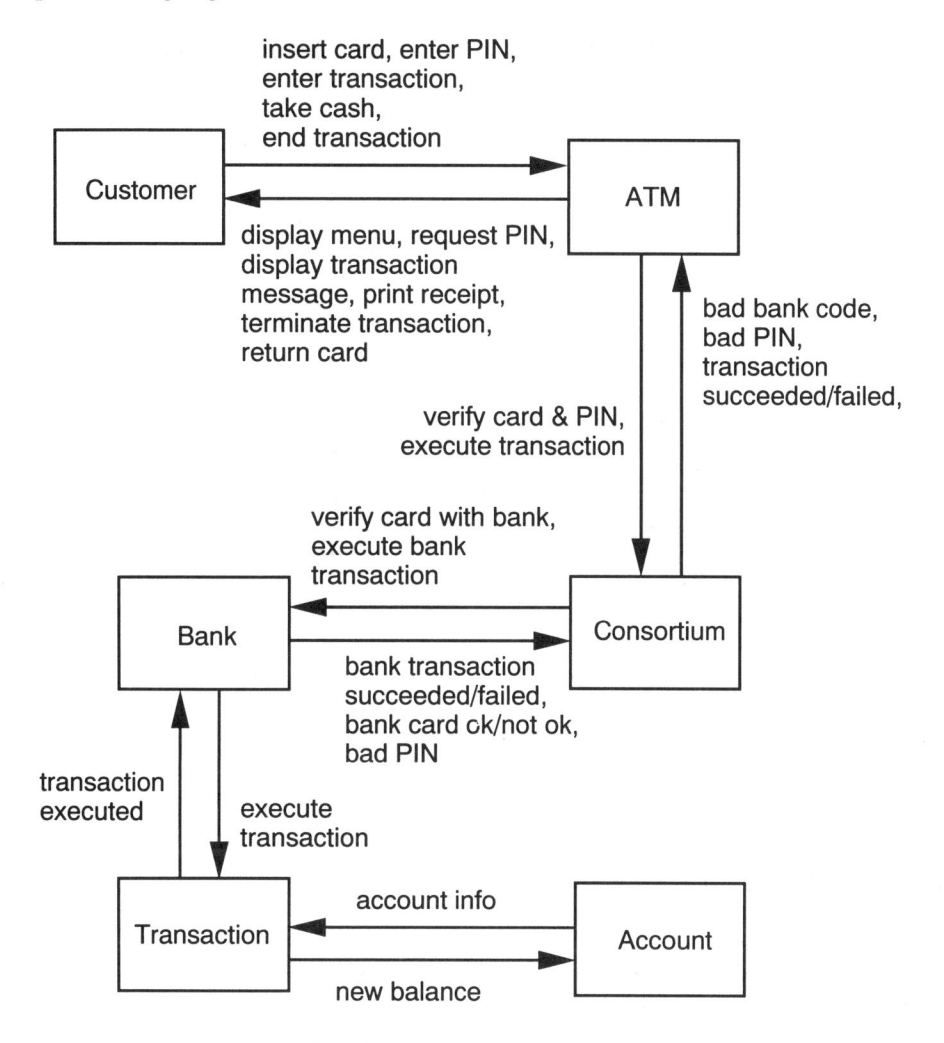

Figure 8-7. Object flow model of ATM application

A second form of a dynamic object model is the event trace diagram for the ATM application shown in Figure 8-8. This illustrates the time-ordered events that take place between the real-world objects depicted in the object model (see Figure 8-4) or the object flow model (see Figure 8-7). The heavy vertical lines in Figure 8-8 represent the major ATM objects, and the annotated connecting lines represent the events that flow between the objects. Time is measured from top to bottom, but is not to scale.

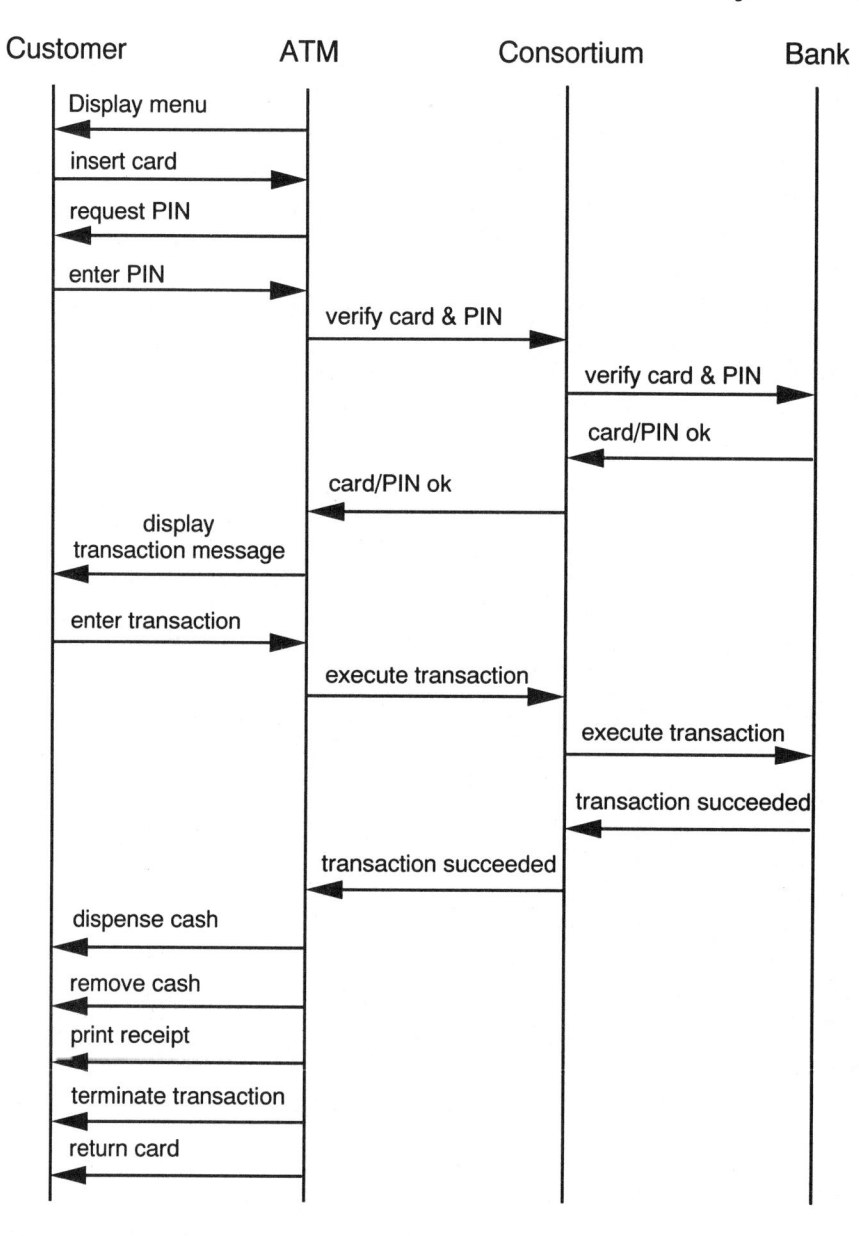

Figure 8-8. Event trace diagram for ATM application

Chapter 8 • Using Object-Oriented Methods   149

A third form for a dynamic model is the state transition diagram (STD) for the ATM application shown in Figure 8-9. Each rectangle represents a given system state, and the annotated connections are the events that trigger the actions that cause the state changes. The STDs do not scale up well for large systems, due to the number of complex details required for a system STD. The only way to manage state changes for large systems is to use STDs at the object level, rather than at the system level.

The dynamic model includes several graphical representations that depict dynamic behavior. Each representation illustrates a different view of the interacting objects, and is used to describe certain aspects of the analysis or design effort with varying levels of abstraction.

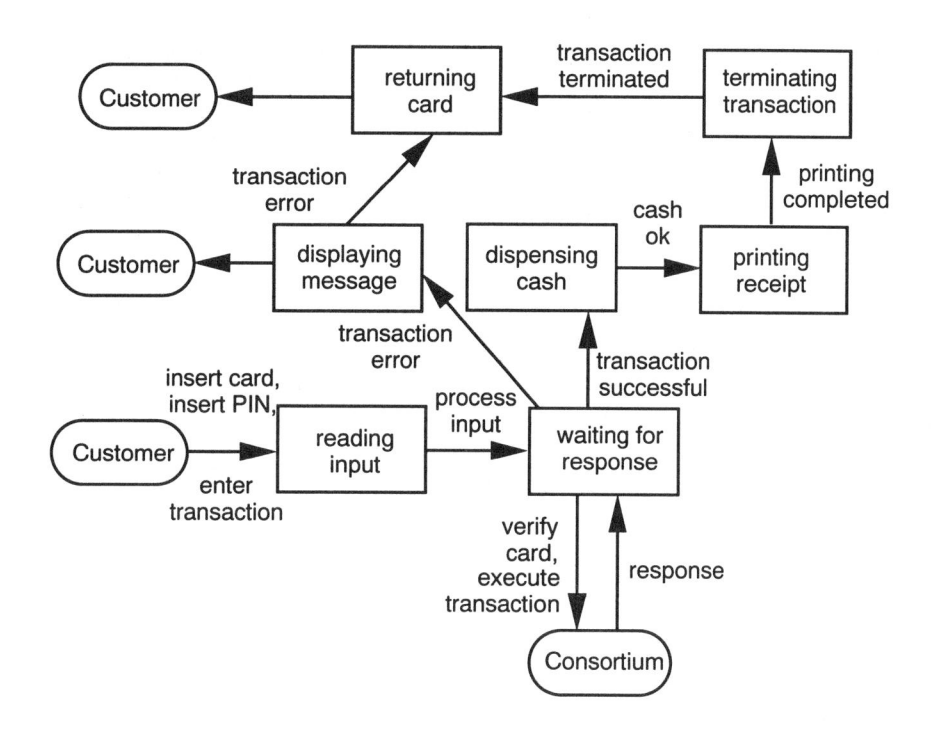

Figure 8-9. STD for ATM application

8.6.5 Subsystem Model

Models depicting subsystems are created during the system design phase, and are used to illustrate the architecture of the hardware elements and their interfaces in a distributed system. An example of a system design model is shown in Figure 8-10 for the ATM system. The rounded rectangles represent subsystems that will correspond to hardware nodes in the distributed architecture. This particular model does not depict the allocation of system requirements to hardware and software; DFDs at the system level can be used for that purpose.

A different form of a system design model is shown in Figure 8-11 for a robot controller in a distributed architecture. The rectangles represent hardware nodes that include at least one CPU, and their associated local memory. This view is more hardware oriented than the model shown in Figure 8-10, and illustrates hardware elements and their interfaces at the bus and LAN levels.

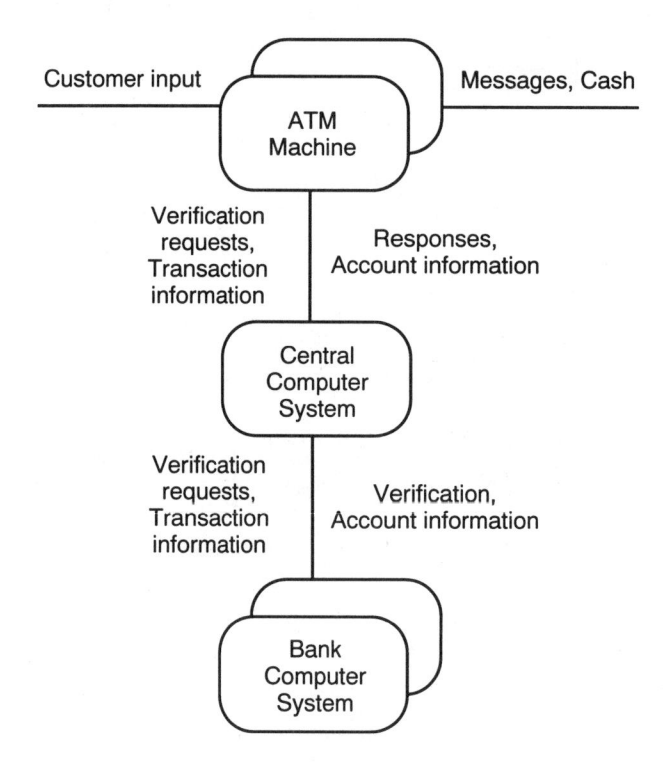

Figure 8-10. ATM system architecture diagram

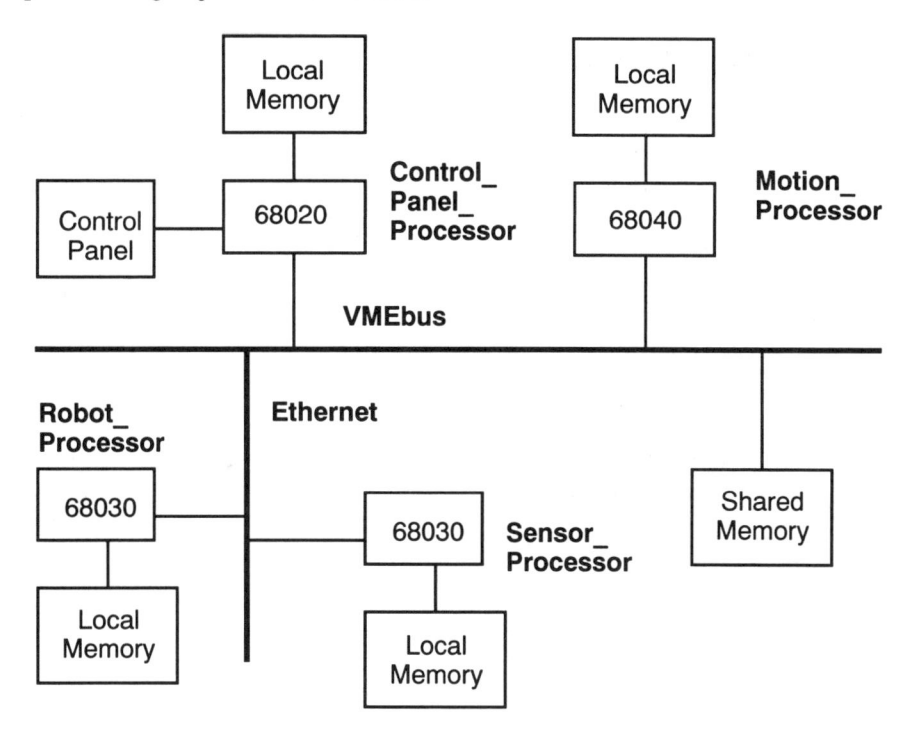

Figure 8-11. Robot controller system architecture diagram

8.6.6 Concurrency Model

One of the paradigms borrowed from real-time structured design (RTSD) is process abstraction [GOM84, NIE90, NIE92]. The process structure chart shown in Figure 8-12 is used to depict processes as independent schedulable entities (task or process) that compete for the services of the same CPU. The annotated connecting lines represent messages passed between the processes.

Exactly how the processes will be implemented cannot be determined from the process structure chart, and depends on the programming language and run-time support. In C++, for example, they can be implemented as processes or coroutines using real-time libraries or by accessing low-level scheduling mechanisms directly.

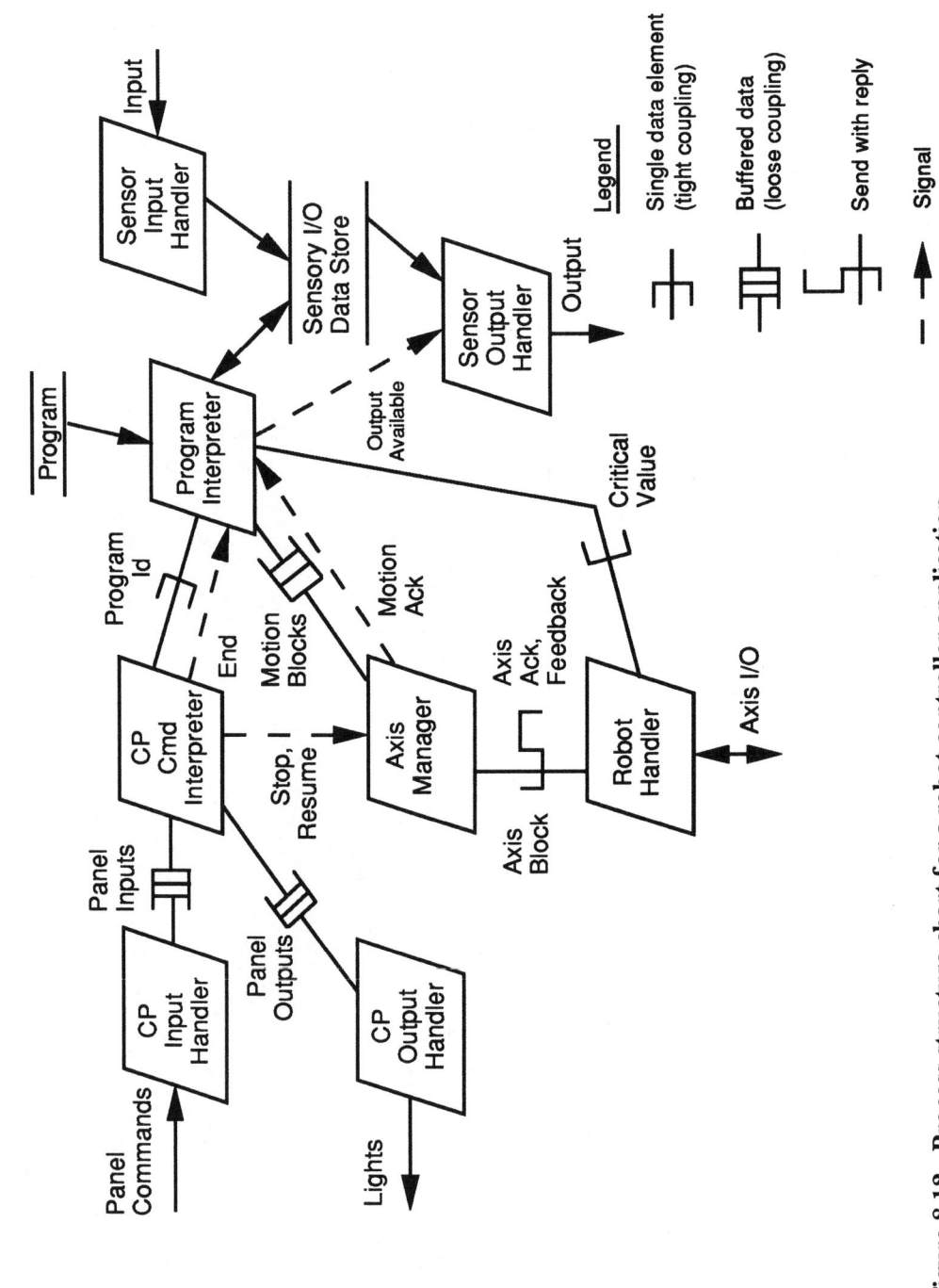

Figure 8-12. Process structure chart for a robot controller application

Note the difference between the process structure chart and the object flow diagram. The former deals explicitly with communication and synchronization between the processes. The latter only considers the message flows between the concurrent objects, and these objects may end up as entire subsystems rather than individual tasks.

The legend shown in Figure 8-12 illustrates different communication and synchronization mechanisms between the processes. A single data element can be passed from one process to another with a tight coupling between the two processes during the data transfer. This represents a synchronous data transfer, as the producer waits until the consumer has received the data. Buffered data is used to create a loose coupling between two processes. This represents an asynchronous communication mode, as the producer puts data elements into a buffer, and the consumer retrieves the data when it is ready. The producer does not wait for the consumer in this mode. A different synchronous mode is where the producer sends a data element and waits for a reply. The last symbol in the legend, illustrates the passing of a signal from a producer to a consumer. No actual data elements are passed in this mode.

The various communication and synchronization mechanisms described above are implemented using a variety of primitives, such as mailboxes, semaphores, agent tasks, and rendezvous. The exact implementation will depend on the primitives available with the programming language and associated runtime system.

8.6.7 Functional Models

Functional models used with structured methods can be used to complement the OT models. We have already seen how STDs can be used at the object level to depict dynamic state changes within an individual object.

The event trace diagram provides a view of the synchronization of events between major objects.

DFDs can be used to determine the allocation of system requirements to hardware and software where an object is split between two or more subsystems. The ATCS context diagram shown in Figure 8-2 can be considered a top-level DFD.

The process structure chart can be used to analyze message passing between tasks and to determine the proper control and synchronization of the tasks.

The use of functional models for depicting architectural elements at the subsystem level will be described in Chapter 11.

8.6.8 Notation

The notation for the various modeling diagrams should be from a single method. We do not recommend mixing the notation of Booch'93, Shlaer-Mellor, and OMT, for example. Using notations from different methods will confuse the customers and the various development teams that are working on different phases of the development process.

Most of the examples shown above for the static and dynamic models use the notation specified for OMT. The STD notation specified in OMT is unnecessarily complex (based on Harel's notation [HAR87]), and we recommend instead the Moore notation [HAT87].

It should be noted that complicated charts such as STDs and event trace diagrams include a great amount of detail and may not be suitable for discussing system requirements with a customer. There may thus be a natural distinction between the models used for the analysis phase versus the design phase. Higher levels of abstraction are more suitable during the analysis phase. More detail is required for the design phase. We can make a rule that only the dynamic object model should be included for the analysis phase. STDs and event traces are added for the design phase.

The notation used to describe inheritance (is-a) can take two different forms, as shown in Figure 8-13. The relation on the left in this figure includes an arrow from the derived object or class to the parent. The OMT notation on the right uses a special symbol to designate the inheritance relation. Any CASE tool for the OMT method (e.g., C++ Designer and OMTool) uses the special symbol shown on the right. The symbolism shown on the left is probably easier to understand intuitively.

The notations used to designate aggregation (has-a, composition, or whole-part) relation are shown in Figure 8-14. The notation on the left includes arrowheads that point to the components. The notation on the right uses the special OMT aggregation symbol. Again, OMT CASE tools use the symbol depicted on the right, whereas the arrow notation is probably more intuitive.

The usual notation for showing an association between two objects is to draw an arc between them. The direction of an association is sometimes difficult to determine. To alleviate this problem, we can add an annotated arrow, as shown in Figure 8-15. This was the notation used in Figure 8-4 for the object model of the ATM application. One problem with this approach is that it is not strictly part of OMT and is not supported by the OMT CASE tools.

Chapter 8 • Using Object-Oriented Methods

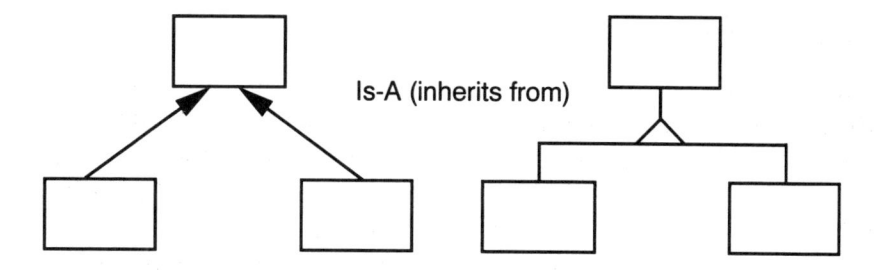

Figure 8-13. Inheritance and is-a

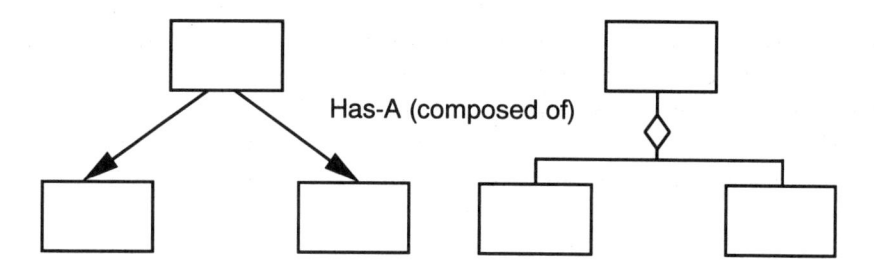

Figure 8-14. Aggregation and has-a

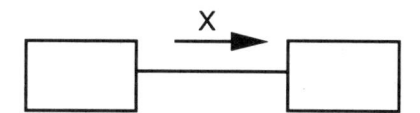

Figure 8-15. Association

The particular notation for each development phase will be illustrated further in Part III, as we describe the use of OT paradigms for the various development phases.

8.7 IDENTIFYING REAL-WORLD CLASSES AND OBJECTS

The identification of classes and objects is the cornerstone of using OT methods. Categories of classes are used to group objects at various levels of abstractions as we move through the development process. At the highest level, we have the key abstractions that represent real-world entities and reflect the system requirements. At the lowest level, we have design entities that are implemented with C++ constructs.

For the initial effort of identifying classes and objects, we will use a functional classification scheme. This takes place during the domain analysis phase.

After scenarios have been developed, we create additional classes and objects in terms of interface, entity, and control objects. This takes place during the system requirements analysis phase, or the software requirements analysis phase if the former phase is not performed.

8.7.1 Classes and Objects Based on Functionality

The following class categories can be used to identify the initial, high-level real-world abstractions :from a set of system requirements:

1. **Device Interface Class.** Most of our systems will interface directly with hardware devices (e.g., radars and printers), and provides a readily identifiable class category (we are distinguishing these devices from user interface devices).
2. **External System Class.** This is an appropriate category for those systems that interface with similar external systems, e.g., an ATC center receiving a handover message from another center, or a banking system receiving information from a credit clearing institution.
3. **User Interface Class.** Most of our systems interface with users via a keyboard or graphical device. This may be subdivided into separate categories for each type of user interface device, e.g., keyboard, mouse, and lightpen.
4. **Computational Class.** This category is appropriate for systems that include significant computations to support the system requirements. Examples for this category include coordinate conversions for robot control and ATC systems, and the calculation of compound interest for a savings institution system.
5. **Role Class.** This category can be used where a person is an important

part of the operational system. A Controller in an ATC or air defense system, for example, can take on the role of Supervisor, Trainer, Trainee, Approach Controller, or Tower Controller. In a banking system, a teller is one of the important roles.

6. **Data Abstraction Class.** Classes in this category may not readily appear in the system requirements, but will become evident if we are employing data modeling as part of our development strategy. Entity relationship diagrams (ERDs), for example, may be used during the domain analysis. The major data entities in the ERDs are real-world objects, and we can sometimes collect similar entities into data abstraction classes. Examples of data entities include radar and weather data for an ATC system, and user accounts for a banking system.

This set of class categories is the starting point for finding real-world classes and objects that can be used in the analysis and design of our systems. We will pursue the methods for finding classes and objects based on this classification in Chapters 9, 10, and 12.

Most of the requirements specified for a system will reflect objects that can be placed in one of these class categories. These objects will represent the key abstractions of the system, and will form the basis for all further development efforts. It is extremely important that the initial classes and objects be carefully evaluated.

8.7.2 Classes and Objects Based on Scenarios

After the initial scenarios and key abstractions have been identified during the domain analysis phase, additional objects can be defined.

The initial high level abstractions are first transitioned to entity objects. Additional objects are then defined as interface objects and control objects for each scenario:

1. **Entity Objects.** Represent the requirements of the key abstractions expressed in the real-world objects.
2. **Interface Objects.** Model information representing the external system interfaces.
3. **Control Objects.** Represent the handling of short-lived state changes within the system.

The use of this classification scheme is one of the major paradigms of OOSE, and will be described in detail in Chapter 10, as we apply OT paradigms to the system requirements analysis phase.

For some systems, such as the development of a class library (see Chapters 17 and 22), the use of scenarios does not make sense, since there are no external users involved. The primary emphasis for these types of systems is the creation of classes and their interfaces. The identification of classes and objects should then be based on the functional classification, rather than on objects to support a given scenario.

8.8 TRANSITIONING FROM STRUCTURED TO OT METHODS

Software development organizations wanting to use OT methods can switch from their current approach in a number of ways:

- cold turkey
- gradually, by introducing OT methods into selected development phases
- prototyping, by picking a trial project

Selecting a brand new development approach for a large project is associated with a tremendous risk, and should be avoided. The only rationale for adopting OT methods cold turkey would be if a customer demanded it, or there is no current development process in place.

The recommended strategy for transitioning from structured to OT methods is a gradual, evolutionary approach. Careful planning is required to successfully move a large software development organization into the realm of OT.

A gradual transitioning by employing OT methods on selected development phases can be done. One problem with this approach is that two different sets of notations will have to be maintained. There may also be problems in transitioning between the various development phases.

The preferred transitioning strategy is to pick a well-defined project that can be used as a prototype for the new OT methods. The size of the project must be large enough to ensure that the methods will scale up to the real applications that are normally developed. The OT methods should be employed in all the development phases.

The most important part of transitioning from structured to OT techniques (aside from management support!) is training. The training activity should emphasize hands-on exercises, and should be geared to training in-house trainers. Course material and guidelines for analysts and designers are the most important products. The OT methods picked for the training should include rule-based guidelines and heuristics for the creation of classes and objects, transitioning from OOA to OOD and from OOD to OOP, etc. These guidelines and heuristics will form the basis for how future OT-based projects will be run.

Since the primary impetus for switching to OT methods is the potential for reusability in-the-large, a reuse strategy should be planned. The initial effort can focus on available C++ classes and libraries that can be of immediate use for upcoming applications. A longer-term plan should include the establishment of a reuse repository for documentation, design products, and C++ code. The key to such a repository is how easily the elements can be found and retrieved. A reuse repository should include a GUI with suitable browsers for locating and retrieving the information.

8.9 EFFECT ON STEPS IN THE DEVELOPMENT PROCESS

We should not expect that the use of OT methods will impact the overall development process shown in Figure 8-16. We have made the point earlier that the use of an OT method simply supports the overall process, and does not dictate which steps should be performed.

The only considerations that may affect the development steps is the size of the system to be developed and the amount of reusable entities that are available.

8.9.1 Large Systems

The development of large systems should employ all of the development phases. The domain analysis is particularly important for the management of the system, and the determination of reusable elements. None of the steps shown in Figure 8-16 should be skipped.

8.9.2 Medium-Size Systems

A medium-size system that is software intensive can skip the system requirements analysis and the system design phases, and go directly to the software requirements analysis step. Whether or not these steps should be skipped is determined during the domain analysis.

```
        Domain Analysis
              │
              ▼
    System Requirements
         Analysis
              │
              ▼
       System Design
         ╱         ╲
        ▼           ▼
Hardware Requirements   Software Requirements
     Analysis               Analysis
        │                       │
        ▼                       ▼
  Hardware Design         Software Design
        │                       │
        ▼                       ▼
Hardware Construction        Coding
   and Assembly
        │                       │
        ▼                       ▼
     Testing  ◄──────────►   Testing
```

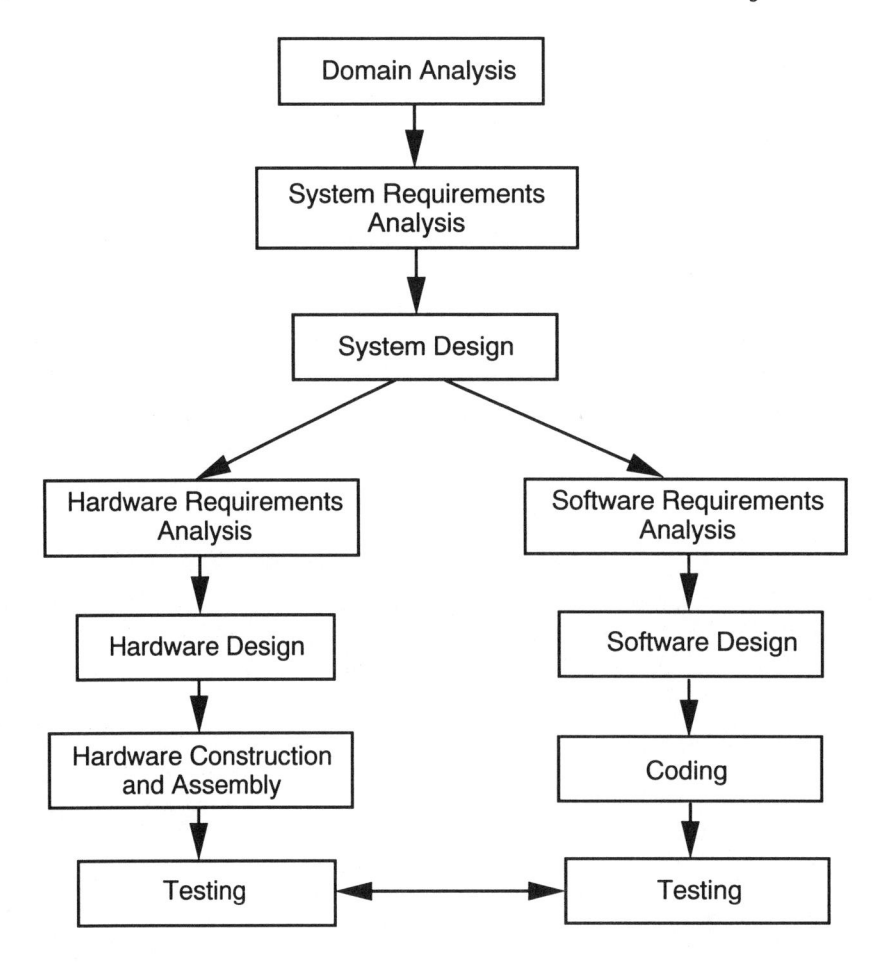

Figure 8-16. The development process

A medium-size system that is being developed as part of a product line, will eventually have to be subjected to a system design when the software is configured for a particular customer. Reusable components will then be combined into software modules and allocated to hardware nodes.

8.9.3 Small Systems

Small systems that will reside on a single hardware node can skip the system requirements analysis and the system design phases and go directly to the software requirements analysis step. This will be the case, for example, if we are developing a C++ class library. The only hardware considerations to be made are how much storage is necessary to host the library code, and the required speed of the CPU for the applications that will be importing the services of the library.

The domain analysis is required even for small systems, since one of the major activities of this phase is the determination of reusable elements and their storage and retrieval mechanism.

Small systems that will execute in a single-thread fashion can skip the process abstraction step of the software design phase. There is no need for the creation of multiple processes and considerations for associated tasking primitives.

8.10 SUMMARY

Even though there are risks associated with switching from a structured development approach to the use of OT methods, the potential benefits are substantial:

- localization of system requirements to better manage requirements changes
- development of real-world, key abstractions that can readily be transitioned to design entities that can be implemented with C++ constructs
- objects promote the facilitation of prototyping models for early user feedback and concept demonstration
- reusability in-the-large with classes and class libraries
- simplified maintenance by replacing entire objects when system requirements change or enhancements are necessary

OT methods can coexist with structured methods to support the overall development strategy. A gradual introduction of OT methods can be incorporated into the development process as the staff is being trained.

Rule-based development should be employed to provide guidance for the first few projects using new OT methods. This is particularly important for the transitioning between the various development phases.

The recommended modeling approach includes the following:

- development of scenarios to support an incremental "build" structure, and the creation of prototypes

- the use of static and dynamic models for class/object hierarchies, associations, and message flows
- subsystem views for architectural structures
- concurrency model for process abstraction

The identification of classes and objects is based on a functional classification scheme in the domain analysis phase, and on a scenario view in the system requirements analysis.

The key to a successful transitioning from structured to OT methods is training. The training effort should be geared toward training in-house trainers as future instructors. Training materials should include guidelines and heuristics that will form the basis for a rule-based strategy for future projects using OT.

PART III

Using OT in the Software Development Process

After having described the overall software development process and object-oriented methods, we will now discuss how to apply OT to the various software development phases.

Using OT paradigms doesn't preclude the use of structured techniques. The two strategies can coexist and can complement each other in areas where one strategy is better suited than the other.

The use of OT doesn't alter the overall development process. The same steps are employed even if different models are used to document the various views used in the decomposition process.

Only minimal use of OT is employed in the domain analysis phase. The primary OT paradigm for this step is the determination of high-level, real-world abstractions that we use to determine the potential for reuse. Major objects determined in this phase may form the basis for subsystems used during the system design activity.

A full complement of OOA models is applied to the system requirements analysis phase. The classes and objects defined during OOA are transitioned to OOD entities at the start of the design activity. Classes and objects are refined in the OOD phase and implemented with C++ class constructs during the implementation phase using OOP paradigms. The OOP activity includes the creation of C++ constructors, destructors, and class access-level mechanisms.

9

Domain Analysis

The logical starting point for any major system development project is to carefully analyze the requirements of the project and try to match those requirements with available products that can be successfully reused. Such a starting point is a *domain analysis* (shown as the first step depicted in the overall software development process in Figure 9-1) that will

- result in a clear understanding of the system to be built
- have a mapping of requirements to reusable software hardware, documentation, and in-house expertise
- present a risk reduction plan

Large systems are developed by teams of analysts, software engineers, programmers, and managers. The domain analysis sets the stage for how the development process will be carried out. A major role of this phase is to determine a preliminary "build" structure for incremental development. This will include the determination of prototyping efforts to mitigate high risk areas, and help to define obscure or poorly defined system requirements.

One of the important activities of domain analysis is the identification of abstract real-world classes and objects that are common to related applications within a specific problem domain. Examples of such problem domains include air traffic control, avionics, banking applications, and satellite tracking systems. The result of this activity will aid us in determining the degree of reusable entities that are available in the form of in-house or commercial products.

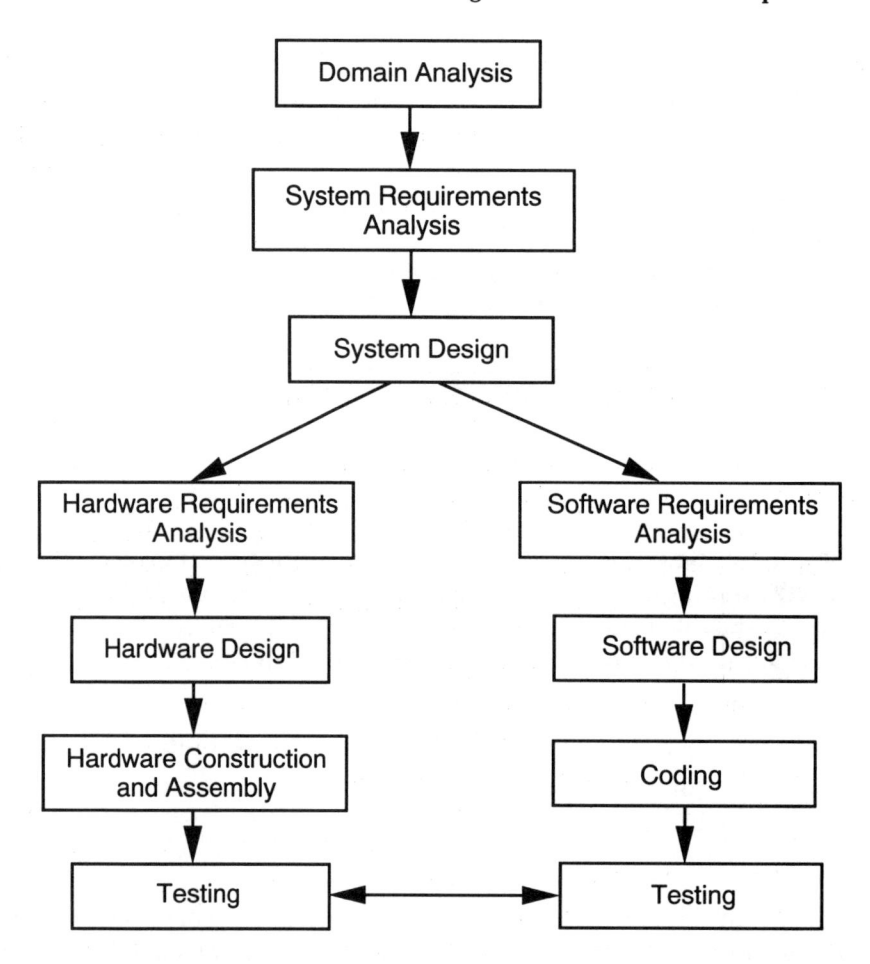

Figure 9-1. Steps in the software development process

We could perform the domain analysis using a strictly functional strategy. This can help us identify reusable products, but if no products are available for reuse, the functional view will not aid us in the further development process. An early object orientation can be transformed into an object-oriented analysis (OOA) approach and to object-oriented design (OOD). High-level abstractions identified during the domain analysis may form the basis for creating subsystems in a distributed solution.

The use of a domain analysis is particularly important for a company that is looking for the highest possible reuse with a product line. The key to understanding the marketplace in which the company wants to participate is to analyze carefully the problem domain and to develop a set of core capabilities that can be tailored for a wide variety of system requirements.

One of the major benefits of performing a domain analysis is to gain a sharp focus of the development *process* at the start of the project. This includes an early identification of risk areas and a chance to modify the process, methods, and tools. The larger the project to be developed, the more important the domain analysis phase becomes.

9.1 UNDERSTANDING THE PROBLEM DOMAIN

The domain analysis precedes the usual system requirements analysis (see Figure 9-1) and takes into account known requirements from previous, current, and expected contract awards or projects. A common subset of requirements can usually be identified for problem domains, such as air traffic control systems, robotics, avionics, air defense, communications and networking, and banking systems.

The primary inputs to this analysis are available system specifications and the expectations of future customer requirements. A System Specification document is the initial source for the identification of real-world classes and objects. For an air traffic control domain, for example, system requirements will be specified for radar data processing, flight data processing, data display, human-machine interface, data recording and playback, and meteorological data processing [FIE85, NOL90]. Real-world abstractions can then be specified for each system requirement.

The classes and objects identified in this phase are used to determine the potential for reusability in terms of existing software and associated documentation and in-house expertise, i.e., we are striving for reusability in-the-large. Substantial objects can be used to define subsystems within the overall, distributed solution.

The identification of the common requirements will normally create a set of functional capabilities that can form the basis for creating classes and objects.

Specific elements of the analysis include the following:

1. **System Features.** Basic system features to be determined include real-time, distributed, database oriented, message driven, time critical, etc.
2. **System Requirements.** The major functional areas within the problem domain should be determined. For an air traffic control system, for

example, these areas will include radar data processing, flight data processing, monitor and control, human-computer interface, data recording, playback, and simulation.

3. **System Architecture.** This will include a determination of the range of systems to be developed, e.g., small, medium, and large with regard to the required functionality. The expected hardware architectures and associated operating systems should be specified. Examples include Sun/Unix workstations, Ethernet or TCP/IP communication, PowerPC-based Macintoshes, and Pentium-based PCs running Windows.

4. **Real-World Classes and Objects.** This represents an abstraction of the major functional areas and is used as an aid to understanding the complexity of large systems. The classes and objects should be associated with a level of stability (i.e., resistant to change) for a range of systems. The attributes should be evaluated for their potential volatility, i.e., how they will change from system to system within the problem domain.

The general domain analysis process is illustrated in Figure 9-2. The combination of existing requirements, anticipated future requirements, and in-house expertise serves as the basis for the identification of a common set of functions. These functions are described in documents that can be used as marketing material and a system functional specification. The common functions are subsequently expanded into the key abstractions from which classes and objects can be derived.

The domain analysis will lay the foundation for the planning and effort required in establishing the amount of software to be developed, and the functionality of potential software available for reuse.

9.2 CAPTURING EXISTING EXPERTISE AND SOFTWARE

Unless an organization is developing a brand new product and intends to start the software development from scratch, there is most likely a significant amount of in-house expertise available from previous projects. Before any software development gets started, an attempt should be made to match this expertise to the common requirements determined during the domain analysis.

It is quite likely that a significant amount of software (maybe even complete subsystems) exists that can be reused in one form or another for an upcoming project. And, if a product orientation is the goal, from this point forward, the primary emphasis within the organization should be to develop a set of reusable components that can be tailored for small, medium, and large systems within the specific problem domain.

The actual development of the core functions may involve a combination of transitioning existing software to C++ and developing all new software required in C++ only. A company may, for example, have a collection of Fortran and C modules which have been used in previous projects.. These modules can be transitioned to C++ via a partial redesign and/or translation, or the modules may be imported directly into a C++ program with the *extern* "C" construct.

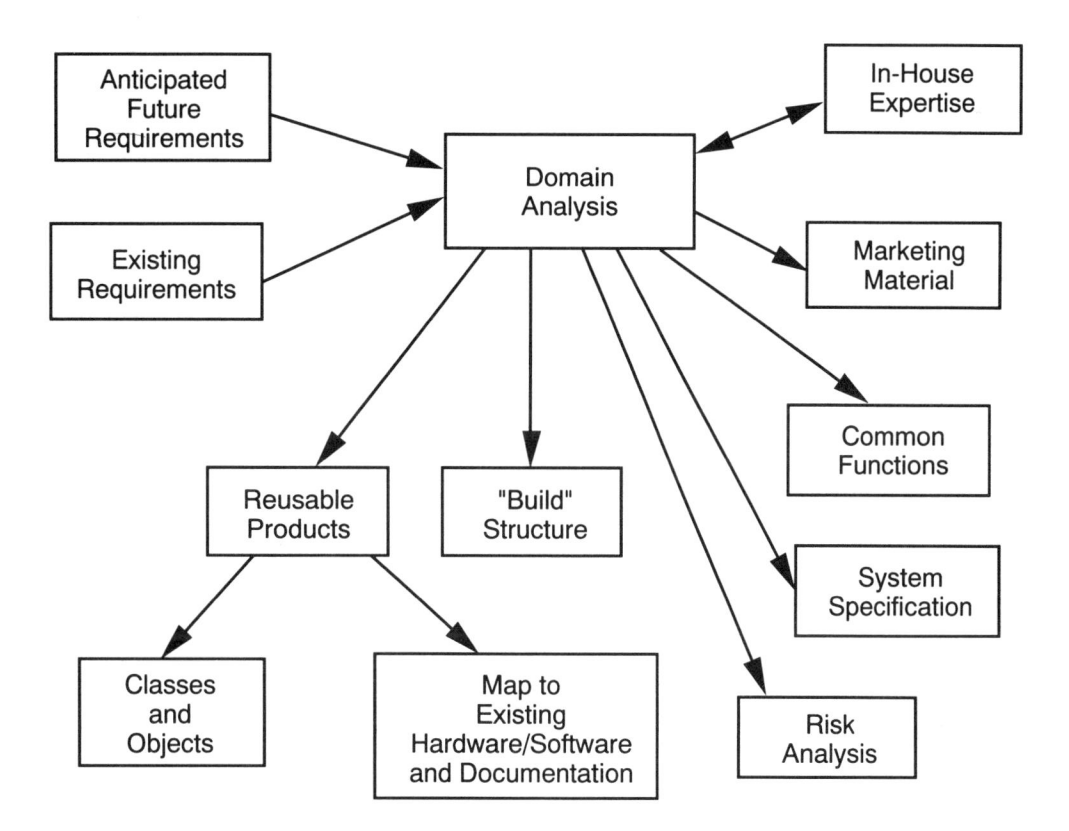

Figure 9-2. Domain analysis relations

Another aspect of identifying existing software and systems is the determination of available commercial products. This can encompass entire subsystems, software libraries, and graphical user interfaces. The cost of buying and adapting commercial products is traded off against in-house development. The cost of buying should include training, licensing, maintenance, and, possibly, required modifications.

9.3 CREATING REAL-WORLD CLASSES AND OBJECTS

Key abstractions of the problem domain are identified in terms of real-world objects. For an air traffic control system, for example, some of the key abstractions include controller workstations, situation displays, weather displays, aircraft tracks, communications system, and flight plans. Some of the operations associated with these abstractions include the creation of situation and tabular displays; algorithmic tracking and display of aircraft trajectories; and activation, distribution, and closing of flight plans. These abstractions and operations are common to all ATC systems regardless of the complexity of the operations within a given airspace. They apply to small airport operations that only service general aviation aircraft, as well as to the major metropolitan airports, such as LAX in Los Angeles, O'Hare in Chicago, and Heathrow in London.

In this phase, we are looking for primary, large real-world objects and classes. Objects with common characteristics can be collected into classes that can be reused for a given system implementation. A class can, for example, be identified as Displays with subclasses of Situation Displays for depicting aircraft positions and Tabular Displays for arrival and departure lists. Objects can then be created as instances of a given subclass to satisfy a specific requirement for a system implementation.

The gross objects identified during the domain analysis phase are refined during the subsequent system requirements analysis. At that time, we expand the analysis to include the relations between the objects.

9.3.1 Classification

An object is sometimes categorized as a person, place, or thing, but this does not always suffice for the kinds of systems we are dealing with. We would like to have a general classification scheme that can be used for the determination of classes and objects for a wide variety of systems. An object can take on an infinite number of representations, and it is easier to look for objects that fit in certain classes.

The following list of classes can be used as a guide in the original determination of objects and classes based on the functional requirements:

1. **Device Interface Class.** Most of our systems will interface directly with hardware devices, and provide a readily identifiable class category (we are distinguishing these devices from user interface devices).

2. **External System Class.** This is an appropriate category for those systems that interface with similar external systems, e.g., an ATC center receiving a handover message from another center.

3. **User Interface Class.** Most of our systems interface with users via a keyboard or graphical device. This may be subdivided into separate categories for each type of user interface device.

4. **Computational Class.** This category is appropriate for systems that include significant computations to support the system requirements. Examples of this category include coordinate conversions for robot control and ATC systems, and pairing of tracks for ATC and air defense systems.

5. **Role Class.** This category can be used where a person is an important part of the operational system. A controller in an ATC or air defense system, for example, can take on the role of Supervisor, Trainer, Trainee, Approach Controller, or Tower Controller.

6. **Data Abstraction Classes.** Classes in this category will become evident if we are employing a data modeling technique with entity relationship diagrams (ERDs) during the domain analysis. The entities in the ERDs are real-world objects, and we can sometimes collect similar entities into classes.

This classification is primarily used to define coarse-grained objects for high-level abstractions. The other type of classification of entity, interface, and control objects which was introduced in Chapter 7 and associated with Jacobson's OOSE method, is used in the software requirements analysis, after the major key abstractions have been identified.

9.3.2 Finding Classes and Objects

The identification of classes and objects should be performed by domain experts who are able to uncover additional or derived requirements that are not fully documented. We are assuming here that the system requirements are documented in the traditional fashion with functional descriptions.

Classes and objects that fit in categories 1 through 5 can all be derived directly from reading the system requirements. Classes that belong in the data abstraction category are often discovered as a derived requirement, e.g., a Track Store to support general tracking functions. Even though the domain analysis is only intended to determine high-level classes and objects, object models or ERDs can be used to uncover the derived requirements.

Additional classes and objects will usually be discovered during the prototyping activities, or in discussions with the customer regarding the details of the system requirements.

The class categories are useful even if we only discover a single object within a given category. We will then have an object rather than a class to describe a particular real-world entity. Examples of real-world classes and objects for an ATC system and their corresponding class categories include those listed in the following chart:

Class/Object Name	Class Category
Radar Interfaces	Device Interface
External Comm. Interfaces	External System
Recording Devices Interfaces	Device Interface
Controller Work Station Interface	User Interface
Track Store	Data Abstraction
Pairing	Computational

9.3.3 Class/Object Descriptions

An example of a class description for a Track Store, including attributes and operations, is the following:

Object Name: Track Store

Abstraction: Data abstraction class that defines track data attributes and operations.

Hidden Information: Hides the internal representation of a track (or target).

Anticipated Changes: Additional attributes and operations may be required. Data now envisioned to be in the Track File object may be included here.

Attributes:	Track Id	Track Status	Squawk
	Speed	Heading	Altitude
Operations:	Initiate a track	Drop a track	Add a track
	Read a track	Read all tracks	Update a track
	Correlate tracks	Extrapolate tracks	Correct Mode C

Usage Constraints: None

Undesired Events: Track Store empty, Track Store full. Unable to access group of tracks within requested region

Effects: Track positions are extrapolated if no new position data received in adaptable seconds

Traceability: Radar Data Processing

Objects: Track Store Monitor, Track File Monitor

The specification of operations and attributes is not strictly required for the domain analysis and can be delayed until the requirements analysis phase.

9.4 EVALUATION OF OBJECTS

The high-level objects created during the domain analysis should be carefully evaluated for their suitability as abstract entities. Evaluation criteria should include, at least, the following:

1. **Real-World Entities.** The objects identified should readily be associated with the requirements of the problem domain. They should have real-world names that a customer or end-user can easily identify with; avoid the use of all uppercase letters and underscores in object identifiers. This will simplify requirements reviews and discussions with customers and end-users.

2. **Completeness.** The set of identified objects should represent all the requirements for the problem domain. If there are additional objects that do not seem to fit, they may represent derived requirements and should be included in the analysis.

3. **Size.** The granularity of abstract objects should be at a high level. Small objects with too much detail tend to be treated as design entities, which they should not be at this stage of the development. Objects that are too small can be combined into larger entities that will form a better abstraction. Objects that appear too large may be treated as subsystems if a "black box" can be identified as a reusable product. Otherwise, the object should be decomposed into smaller abstractions.

4. **Development Category.** Each object should be identified with regard to its development category: reusable in-house product, commercial product, Government Furnished Equipment (GFE), or new development.

5. **Object Classification.** Each object is associated with a class category, as was suggested in Section 9.3.1. The object classification should be checked for its appropriateness. If any of the classes do not contain any objects, perhaps the analysis is incomplete.

6. **Attributes.** The listed attributes should be closely associated with the class. If the description of an attribute is too general, e.g., "display data," it should be made into a separate object, and will most likely represent a derived requirement.

7. **Operations.** The operations associated with the class do not have to represent a complete set at this stage of the development. Each operation must include a unique description that identifies a single action to be associated with an object, e.g., Update a Track.

9.5 WORK PRODUCTS

A number of products will be produced during the course of the domain analysis. The major products will include at least the following:

1. **System Functional Specification.** This document will specify the system requirements of the problem domain. It can use a formal format specified in a standard documentation series (e.g., U.S. DoD Mil-Standard 2167A, [DOD88]) or an informal description. This document will serve as a precursor to a formal System Requirements Specification document to be prepared during the requirements analysis phase. The functional specification can also serve as a marketing tool used by the sales force. Other information associated with this document includes

size and costing data of the software components. Initial size estimates can be made based on existing modules. More exact information can be filled in as the components are created.

2. **Classes and Objects.** This includes conceptual, high-level abstractions of the major elements of the system. For an ATC system, for example, a class may be Radar Interfaces. An object within the class may be a particular Swedish, Russian, or American radar. The attributes associated with the object could include electrical interfaces, message types and content, and the radar scan rate. Operations could include the reception of radar data, sending track or plot messages, and sending radar configuration messages.

3. **Checklists for Classes and Objects.** Checklists are used as an aid in evaluating the efficacy of the abstract objects and classes. It is particularly important that unnecessary detail be avoided during this phase, so that a "design" is not created prematurely.

4. **Existing Software.** A list of existing software for the corresponding functionality should be made for each set of class and object combination. The software should be evaluated for potential reuse with regard to programming language and available documentation. The evaluation should include a quantitative analysis of the estimated effort required for reuse, "lift" (reusing a software module without any associated documentation), redesign, or direct translation.

5. **In-House Expertise.** It is highly likely that there are several individuals who are experts in different areas of the problem domain. This will include both analysts and software engineers. These individuals should be identified with their particular area of expertise and potential availability for supporting the project. The availability of such a talent pool is extremely important for the success of the project, and a total lack of such individuals should spur efforts to start an active recruiting campaign.

6. **Risk Reduction Plan.** A number of high risk areas can be identified for potential prototyping. In a distributed system, this could include the interprocess communication (IPC) mechanism, fault tolerance, or database design. Another important area is to determine display requirements with a flexible design to satisfy different personal preferences. The prototyping effort may or may not be associated with throw-away code. If possible (i.e., if the schedule permits), the prototyping functions should be carefully selected and implemented with well defined

interfaces so they can readily be integrated with the rest of the system that will be developed later. Prototyping efforts are also used to evaluate the steps of the development process to make sure they "scale up" to large systems.

7. **Preliminary "Build" Plan.** Large systems are developed with incremental functionality, and a build corresponds to a given set of customer requirements. Each subsequent build includes an identified additional functionality that will be demonstrated to the customer. This plan forms the basis for the thread analysis and the determination of scenarios ("use cases") [JAC92] in the system requirements analysis phase. The prototyping activities are closely aligned with the development of each build and support the functionality to be demonstrated.

8. **Checklist for Domain Analysis Objects.** The object evaluation discussion presented in Section 9.4 can be used as a guide for the preparation of the checklist shown in Figure 9-3.

The conclusion of the domain analysis serves as the starting point for the system requirements analysis. At this time, the functionality is well known, and reasonable estimates should have been obtained for the magnitude of the software development effort. The effort can then be divided among the prototyping tasks and the system development tasks. One team of developers can start the transformation process of existing subsystems and software, another team can start the system requirements analysis for the development of the new subsystems and software required, a third team can start the prototyping effort, and a fourth team can start to analyze the storage and retrieval system for the reusable elements.

9.6 RISK AREAS

There is almost no risk associated with the use of OT for this phase. The OT notation used is minimal, no graphical representations are required if we don't use the object model for data modeling, and very little training is required to use the OT concepts. The only use of OOA concepts is the creation of objects based on a set of class categories.

Chapter 9 • Domain Analysis

Object Id: _____   File/Location: _____

Review Item		Comments
1. Real-World Entity		
2. Completeness		
3. Size		
4. Development Category		
5. Object Classification		
6. Attributes		
7. Operations		

Reviewer: _____   Date: _____

Corrective action required (Yes/No): _____

Further review required (Yes/No): _____

Corrective action completed, date: _____   Reviewer: _____

Page ____ of ____

Figure 9-3. Checklist for domain analysis objects

10

System Requirements Analysis

The purpose of the system requirements analysis is to structure the system independent of any implementation environment. This phase will determine system behavior and limitations, and the system will be described in terms that can easily be discussed with customers and end users.

The structure we create should be sufficiently robust to withstand the requirements changes that are inevitable for large systems. The robustness is achieved by creating an ideal, logical, and stable structure in the form of independent objects with well-defined interfaces.

The approach presented here is to combine the creation of scenarios with an object-oriented technique. The scenarios are determined first, and then a set of objects is identified to support each scenario.

The use of scenarios supports a "build" structure for incremental development of large systems. It also provides a basis for the construction of prototypes. This approach enhances the management of large system development by aligning the products of each development phase with the organizational units.

The system requirements analysis activity represents the second major development phase of the overall process, as was illustrated in Figure 9-1. The approach presented here makes a deliberate effort to separate analysis and design. We are assuming that the requirements allocation to hardware and software is accomplished during the system design phase. The analysis approach presented here can be used even if a domain analysis has not been performed prior to this activity.

10.1 USING SCENARIOS

A common approach to object-oriented methods is to focus exclusively on objects and their relations. This may work well for small programs where relatively few developers are involved and the development is managed in a single physical location. When requirements changes are necessary, or demanded by the customer, the changes can be communicated to all the developers with relative ease. How much perturbation a particular change will cause, depends on how far along the analysis phase has progressed and how much of the documentation must be changed.

Large programs are developed in parallel by several teams of engineers who may be working in separate physical locations. The implementation of requirements changes can be quite costly and time consuming, unless the development can progress with the changes being isolated to a particular development effort.

The overall strategy of using scenarios to drive the development is to have a well-defined effort for each development team where requirements changes won't affect all the teams working in parallel. The objects to be developed will merely support the identified scenarios, rather than driving the entire development. When requirement changes occur, they can be localized to particular objects rather than permeating throughout the entire development.

Scenarios are used to identify "builds" for incremental development and prototypes for proof of concept and verification of methods and tools. Scenarios represent the basis for all of the development phases including analysis, design, implementation, and testing. Objects are developed to support the scenarios. Some objects may be used in more than one scenario and may be given higher priorities in the development order.

10.1.1 What Is a Scenario?

A scenario is a sequence of actions that takes place within the system. The starting point is a stimulus from an external source, e.g., a user hitting a command from the keyboard, and the end point is the logical termination of a particular sequence, e.g., a message being printed on a console or the system waiting for another stimulus from the user.

The scenario approach suggested here is based on the *use case* model described in [JAC92]. The external stimuli are coming from *actors* (a class) and *users* (specific instances of an actor). An actor does not have to be a person, e.g., an air traffic controller, but also includes other interacting systems, e.g., a handoff message coming from another air traffic control center. The user is the actual person or message that stimulates the system, whereas an actor represents the role a user can play.

Each time a user activates the system, a sequence of actions takes place within the system. This sequence represents a scenario. (A scenario is called a *use case* in [JAC92].)

A significant difference between a user and objects within the system, is that user actions are non-deterministic. We don't know, for example, in which particular order a user may pick items from a pull-down menu. The objects we develop to support the scenarios are deterministic, and we know their states and behavior. By the same token, a particular scenario can be considered an instance of a scenario class. Each scenario will undergo a number of state changes with known behavior.

10.1.2 Properties of Scenarios

The concept of a scenario is not new. A number of researchers have used this notion in various lifecycle contexts (see, for example, Harel [HAR87], and Deutsch and Nielsen [DEU88, DEU91]). The scenario represents a descriptor of system behavior in application terms across multiple lifecycle phases that involve multiple job disciplines. Scenarios can also play a role in exposing uncertainties, errors, and omissions in system behavior.

The dominating property of the scenario is its ability to provide a level of communication between non-computer trained applications experts, such as users and customers, and the software engineers who are developing the system. A scenario can be described as an entity that:

- connects an external stimulus with an external response to depict a user perceivable behavior path
- contains data events, control events, and conditions
- is both a specification and an implementation
- can be implemented in either hardware, software, by manual actions, or a combination of these

A thread can be followed from the external stimulus via the internal processing of a number of system requirements to a graphical or textual representation a user can recognize.

Both a stimulus and a response can contain data events, control events, and conditions or a subset, as in Figure 10-1, where a network of interconnected scenarios is shown. Data events are simply traditional inputs and outputs. A control event can be either a signal or the initiator/terminator of a process.

A condition represents a "snapshot" of the transient status of each external entity and, perhaps, internal entities that play a role in the scenario. Thus, the parallel conditions of multiple relevant objects are represented. The composite of the conditions represents the state of the system at the moment of the stimulus and the changed state at the moment of the response. The relationship of the response in a predecessor scenario with the stimulus in successive scenarios influences the concurrency structure of event-driven systems.

We would prefer a one-to-one correspondence between the specification (a scenario) and a structural element, such as one or more abstract objects that can later be transitioned to design objects and implemented as, for example, Ada packages or C++ classes. The guiding system engineering principle is to attain a direct correspondence between system architecture and operational usage scenarios.

A scenario may be wholly or partially implemented by manual actions. An allocation of functional behavior to the manual domain may yield derived requirements for software or hardware support. The interaction of all three domains must be factored into system validation. The scenario object provides significant support for these system engineering considerations.

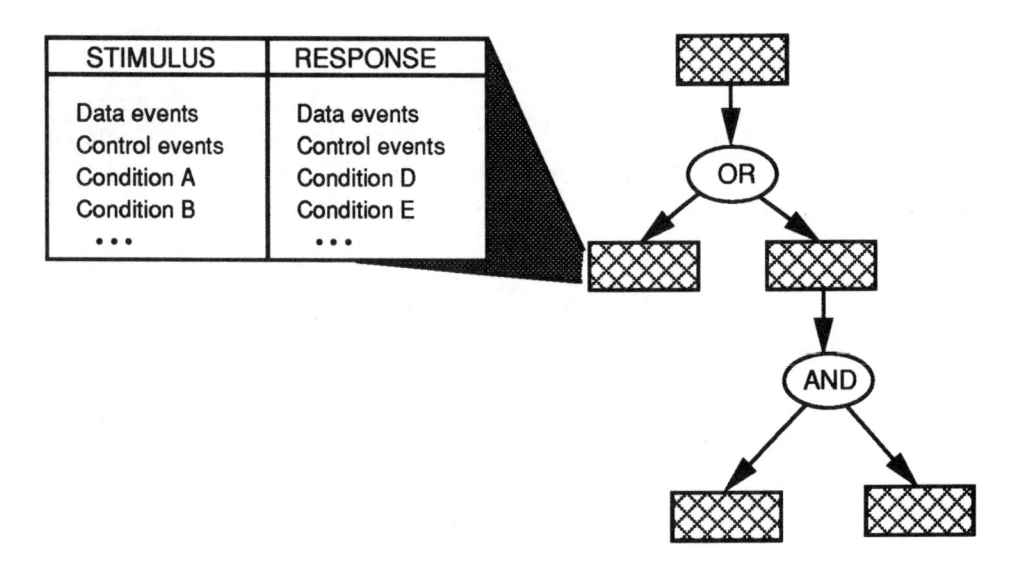

Figure 10-1. Contents of a scenario

10.1.3 Finding Scenarios

Scenarios are determined by first establishing the user interfaces (or external system interfaces) with the system. For each such starting point, we trace the activities triggered by the stimulus to a logical end point and record the sequence of events. This is sometimes referred to as *thread analysis*. The sequence of internal activities, initiated by a certain stimulus, represents a particular scenario.

The scenario analysis can be approached by mentally rehearsing the working profile of the system under analysis, and by keying on the stimuli originating in the external environment and asserting the necessary responses back into that external environment. Data events, control events, and conditions of the system and environment objects should be considered in each stimulus and response.

Scenarios can be identified via the actors of the system. Each complete sequence of events initiated by an actor represents a scenario. As an aid to finding the scenarios, we can ask a series of questions related to the potential actors of the system [JAC92, p. 155]:

- What are the main tasks of each actor?
- Will the actor have to read/write/change any of the system information?
- Will the actor have to inform the system about outside changes?
- Does the actor wish to be informed about unexpected changes?

To illustrate the process, we can use a simplified air traffic control (ATC) system with the context diagram shown in Figure 10-2. The system context diagram is one of the primary tools that can be used for identifying the actors of the system. One way to get started with the identification of scenarios is to proceed chronologically, focusing first on a single physical object in the external environment. Flight plan (FP) data, for example is entered by an operator (actor) via a Visual Display Terminal (VDT), with the stimulus-response characteristics shown in Table 10-1. Additional scenarios are created by considering other stimuli that originate with each actor in the external environment.

Scenarios are identified with a name and/or a unique identifier. For the example shown in Table 10-1, the name is Normal FP Entry, and the identifier is "1." Collections of scenarios will be associated with a "build" for incremental development, and the name or identifier may reflect the build number.

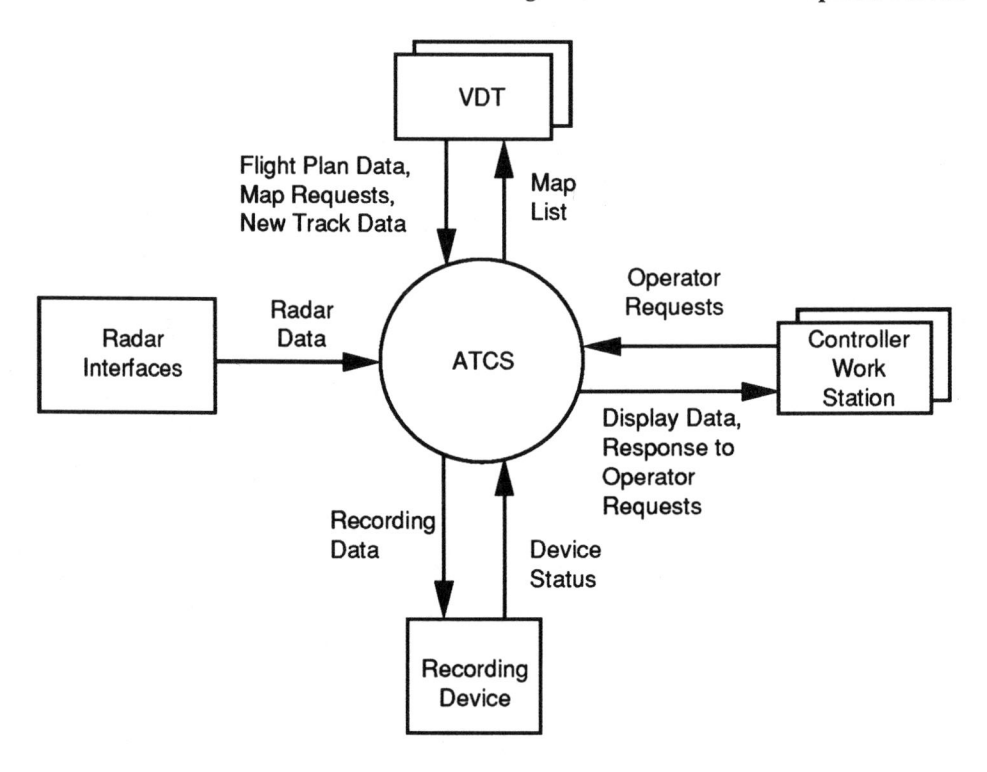

Figure 10-2. ATC context diagram

Some scenarios key on changes of conditions and are roughly analogous to abstract state machines, but other scenarios do not. Temporal performance needs can, at this point, be assigned to each stimulus-response scenario.

Table 10-1. Scenario for Flight Plan Data in an ATC System

Scenario Id: 1	Title: Normal FP Entry
Stimulus	Response
Operator receives FP request	FP is saved
Operator enters FP data	"Acknowledge" is returned to operator
System in NORMAL capacity condition	

10.1.4 Documenting Scenarios

Various forms for documenting scenarios are used, depending on the level of abstraction. The highest level of abstraction describes the set of scenarios and the actors that stimulate those scenarios. An example of this is shown in the scenario diagram in Figure 10-3 for a recycling machine for bottles and cans [JAC92, pp. 155-156]. The actors for the recycling machine are the customers who turn in their cans and bottles and an operator who maintains the machine. The scenarios are illustrated as ovals annotated with the scenario identification.

The scenarios depicted for the recycling machine are explained using a scenario description:

1. **Returning Item.** This scenario is started by a Customer returning bottles and cans. For each item the customer enters into the machine, a count of that particular item is incremented, as well as the daily total for all items received of that type. After all items are returned, the customer presses a button for a detailed receipt of returned items. The information will be prepared and a receipt will be printed as a response to the customer request.

2. **Generate Daily Report.** This scenario is initiated by the operator when he or she wants information regarding daily totals. Daily totals for each type, as well as overall totals for the day, are prepared and printed out. Counters are reset to zero for the start of a new day.

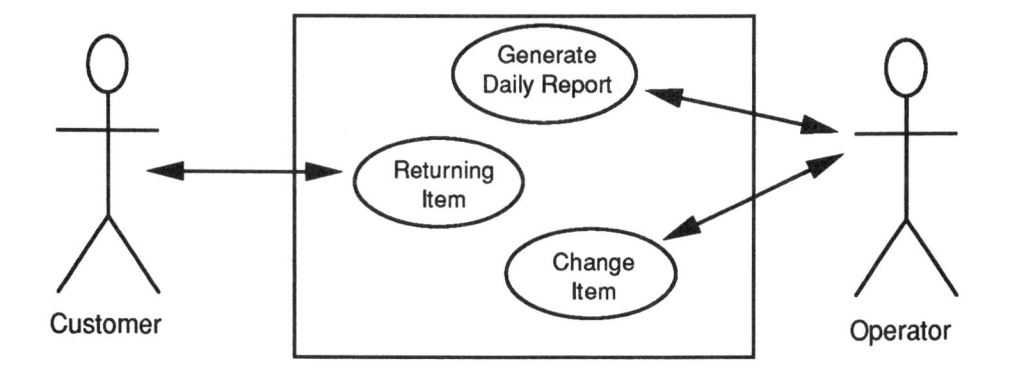

Figure 10-3. Scenario diagram for recycling machine

3. **Change Item.** This scenario is initiated by the operator for system maintenance. The return value, as well as the size of returnable items, can be changed.

The stimulus-response relations that belong to each scenario can be recorded with stimulus-response tables, as was shown above in Table 10-1. Another example for the same ATC system is shown in Table 10-2.

Scenarios are combined to form a "build," i.e., a specific part of the overall system requirements. Each build is given an identifier, and can be illustrated with a scenario sequence diagram, as shown in Figure 10-4. Each shaded rectangle in Figure 10-4 represents a particular scenario, and the ovals depict decision points.

The build structure is used to implement an incremental development approach for large systems, and each completed build is demonstrated to the customer and end user. Builds are also used as a marketing tool to demonstrate system capabilities to potential customers.

Event traces can also be used to describe scenarios, and can show interactions between system objects. An example of a scenario for using a telephone (to call the number 555-1234) is shown in Figure 10-5 [RUM91]. We have only listed events that affect the phone line, since that represents the medium between the caller and callee. Other discussions of the use of event analysis can be found in [MCM84, and SHU92].

Table 10-2. Stimulus-Response for ATC Scenario

Scenario Id: 2 Title: Map Data Request	
Stimulus	Response
Operator receives prompt for map input	Map data is chosen
Operator enters map request	Map data is displayed on console
System in NORMAL mode	

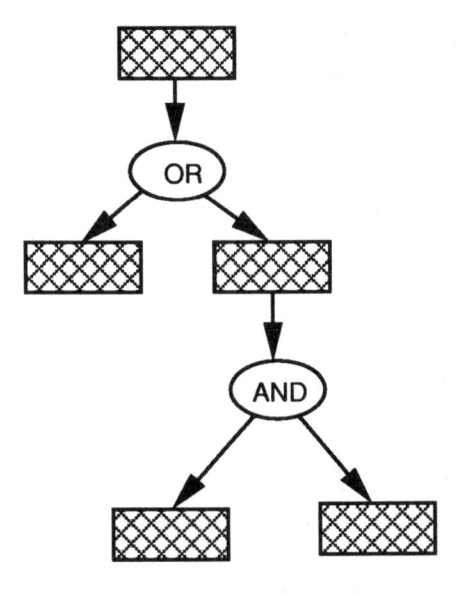

Figure 10-4. Scenario sequence diagram for build X

The events listed in the scenario transmit information between three real-world entities (objects), and an event trace shows how the information flows between the objects.

The event trace for a phone call is depicted in Figure 10-6. Each of the three objects, Caller, Phone Line, and Callee, is shown with a vertical line. Events between the objects are shown with horizontal lines connecting the objects. Time runs from top to bottom, but the relative spacing between horizontal lines is not to scale. These lines can be labeled with specific time increments, if desired. Concurrent events are depicted with events going from the Phone line to both the Caller and Callee at the same instance of time, e.g., ringing tone and phone rings. Note also that events between objects need not alternate, e.g., the Caller dials several digits in succession.

```
Caller lifts receiver
Dial tone begins
Caller dials digit (5)
Dial tone ends
Caller dials digit (5)
Caller dials digit (5)
Caller dials digit (1)
Caller dials digit (2)
Caller dials digit (3)
Caller dials digit (4)
Called phone beings ringing
Ringing tone appears in calling phone
Called party answers
Called phone stops ringing
Ringing tone disappears in calling phone
Phones are connected
Called party hangs up
Phones are disconnected
Caller hangs up
```

Figure 10-5. Scenario for a phone call

As we have seen, the documentation of scenarios takes on many different forms, depending on the level of abstraction and the type of information we wish to convey. Each project will have to decide on the proper set for its development approach.

10.1.5 Scenario-Driven Design

The entire system model is based on the set of scenarios we determine in support of the various "builds" and prototyping efforts. When system changes are required, the appropriate actors and scenarios are remodeled. The system architecture will be controlled by the user requirements. With traceability from requirements to scenarios and objects, changes can be isolated and implemented without having to redesign the entire system. Only particular scenarios and their associated objects will be changed.

Chapter 10 • System Requirements Analysis

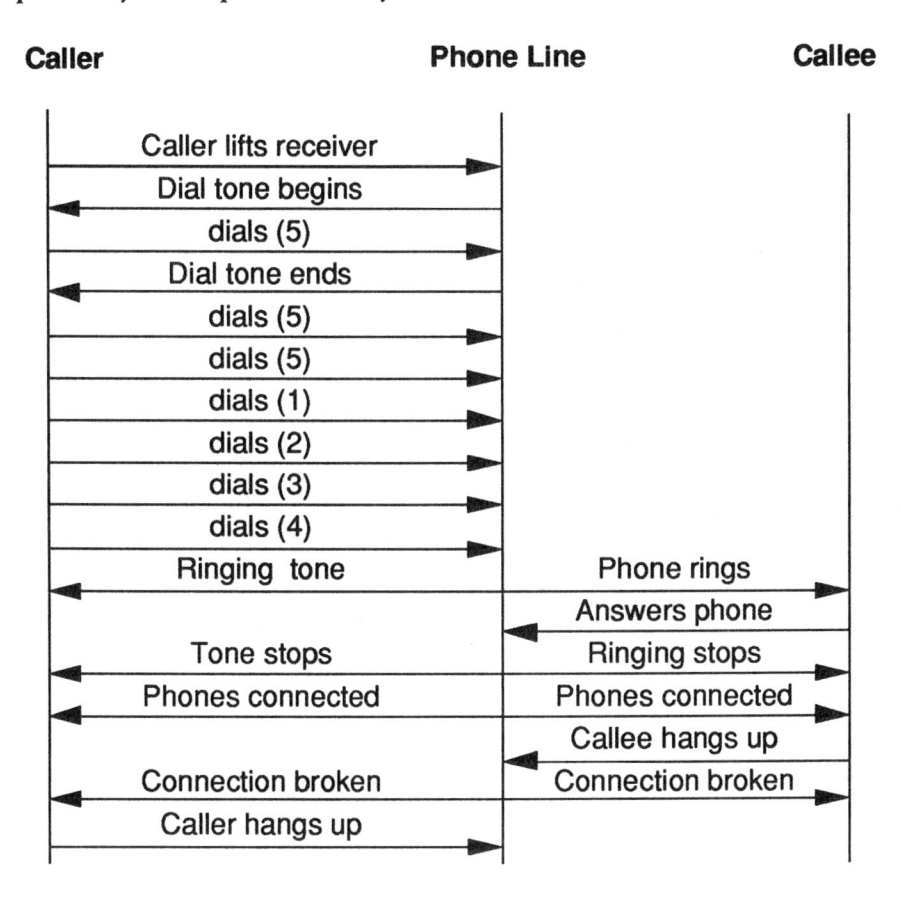

Caller	Phone Line	Callee
Caller lifts receiver →		
← Dial tone begins		
dials (5) →		
← Dial tone ends		
dials (5) →		
dials (5) →		
dials (1) →		
dials (2) →		
dials (3) →		
dials (4) →		
← Ringing tone	Phone rings →	
	← Answers phone	
← Tone stops	Ringing stops →	
← Phones connected	Phones connected →	
	← Callee hangs up	
← Connection broken	Connection broken →	
Caller hangs up →		

Figure 10-6. Event trace for a phone call

A major advantage with this approach is that no special demonstration efforts are required to show the customer or end user a particular feature of the system. One or more scenarios are developed as an entity that represents a well-defined part of the system requirements. This does imply multiple design reviews, rather than a single preliminary and critical design review for the entire system.

Another advantage of a scenario driven approach is that once a set of scenarios has been fully developed (including, of course, a build), it can be used as a marketing tool to demonstrate operational concepts and capabilities to potential customers.

Scenarios are used primarily for systems that include contact with the outside world. It would make no sense, for example, to use a scenario-driven approach for the creation of C++ class libraries. These libraries will be used by other C++ programs, and do not involve an interface with users or external systems.

10.2 OBJECT-ORIENTED ANALYSIS

The real-world objects determined during the domain analysis formed the basis for establishing potential reuse of software, documentation, and subsystems. The domain analysis objects were derived strictly from the system requirements without any concern for a logical structure. These real-world objects will now be refined and transitioned to analysis objects that will form the basis for the analysis model.

The abstract real-world objects we are seeking have a set of attributes and operations associated with them that can form the basis for the creation of design objects. A class can be identified, for example, for Tracks with objects (instances) as External Tracks (in a world coordinate system) and System Tracks (with local (x,y) coordinates). Attributes of Tracks could include track identifier, position, speed, altitude, and heading. Typical operations could be to add, update, drop, extrapolate, and correlate tracks.

The analysis model is used to create a logical structure of the overall system, independent of its actual implementation environment. The structuring activity is aimed at creating a robust and stable specification that can accommodate the inevitable requirements changes that will occur for large systems.

One way to capture the representation of the analysis model is to think of a three dimensional space consisting of presentation, behavior, and information axes [JAC92, p. 134] as shown in Figure 10-7. The presentation axis represents user data that describe external interfaces. The behavior axis includes information on how the system will handle and respond to state changes. The information axis includes data describing the system's internal states.

The analysis model is created by determining objects that align themselves with each of the three axes in the presentation space shown in Figure 10-7. The significance of the three icons shown for user interface, entity, and control objects is explained in the next section.

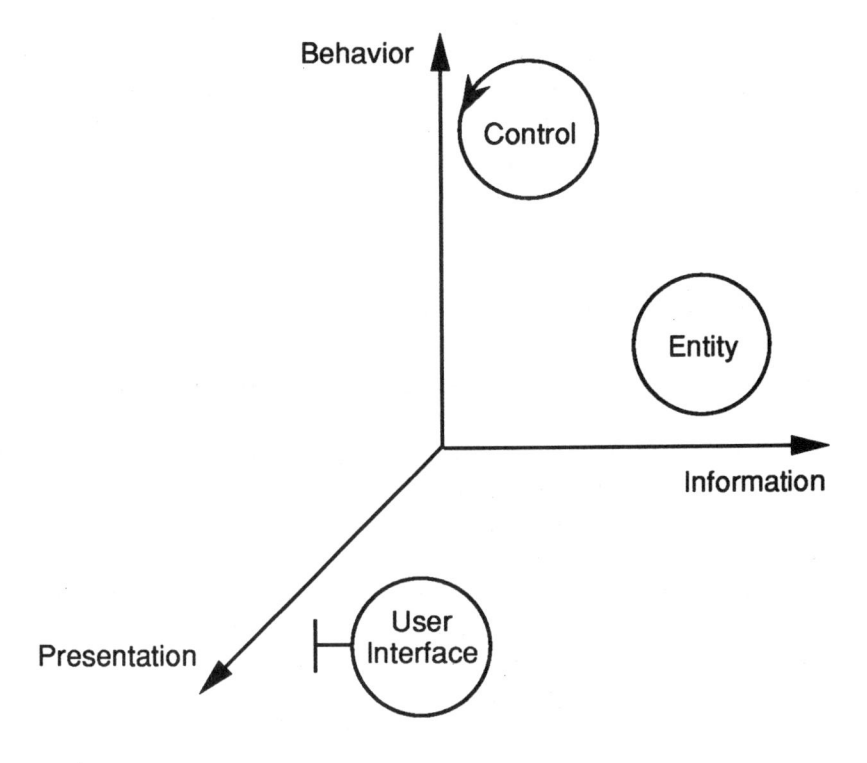

Figure 10-7. Objects in the information space

10.2.1 Object Classification

A classification scheme was suggested in Chapter 9 (see Section 9.3.1) as an initial aid in the determination of real-world objects during the domain analysis. For the current development phase, we will be using an object classification scheme reported by Jacobson et al. [JAC92]. This classification is limited to three object categories related to the information space, and we will transition the domain analysis objects to objects of the new categories.

The objects depicted in this analysis model will be categorized as *entity* objects, *interface* objects, and *control* objects. Entity objects represent the requirements expressed in the real-world objects and are associated with the information axis in the three dimensional presentation space shown in Figure 10-2. Interface objects model information representing the external system interfaces and are aligned with the presentation axis. Control objects represent the handling of short-lived state changes within the system and align themselves with the behavior axis. These three classes of objects are described as follows:

1. **Entity Objects.** Entity objects are derived by refining and transitioning the real-world objects determined during the domain analysis phase. The information associated with these objects should survive a scenario, and is expected to stay in the system for a relatively long time. For an ATC system, for example, this could be objects describing flight data, but not target display data.

2. **Interface Objects.** Interface objects represent information associated with user interfaces or interfaces to external systems. Responses to user commands, such as menus, text, and graphics displayed on a user console, are examples of data that should be placed with interface objects.

3. **Control Objects.** Control objects model information that is neither tied to entity objects, nor interface objects. Typical control objects will get information from entity objects, perform some computation on the data, and return the result to interface objects. An example of a control object for an ATC system, is a coordinate transformation required of the radar data before it is displayed on a controller's console. Many of the control objects will represent derived requirements.

The analysis model we create does not merely consist of the high-level, real-world entities we found in the domain analysis. The high-level objects are refined into interface, entity, and control objects, resulting in a more stable model. When requirements changes occur, they can be localized to individual objects, rather than being distributed across several objects. For large systems, objects of the three categories are combined into subsystems.

10.2.2 Object-Oriented Analysis Methods

We are not concerned here with the use of any particular name-brand OOA method. Methods such as the Object Modeling Technique (OMT), Shlaer-Mellor, or Booch'93 are merely tools for documentation purposes. The focus of creating the analysis model is on scenarios and the structuring of objects to support these scenarios.

Few of the common OOA methods consider the scenario concept, and their respective tools only deal with objects, classes, and relations. The only tool that can currently handle the structuring of objects from scenarios is Objectory

[JAC92]. Any of the common OOA tools can be used for documenting the object structure. The documentation of the scenarios will then have to be done with other drawing tools and word processors.

10.3 THE ANALYSIS MODEL

The purpose of the analysis model is to create the basis for system design. This involves the development of a structuring of the system requirements. The aim of the analysis structure is to be able to handle future requirements changes without having to restructure and/or redocument large portions of the system.

The analysis model is based on the scenario model. Each scenario will have a number of analysis objects of the three types, i.e., the functionality associated with each scenario will be assigned to a number of different objects. Some of the objects will support more than one scenario, and this becomes important for the order in which the objects are developed. The scenarios are partitioned according to the following guidelines [JAC92]:

1. Scenario functions that are directly dependent on the system environment are placed in interface objects. Some of these objects can be transitioned from domain analysis objects categories of Device Interface, External System, User Interface, and Role classes.

2. Scenario functions dealing with storage and manipulation of data that is not dependent on the system environment are placed in entity objects. Some of these objects can be created by refinement and transitioning of domain analysis objects in the Computational and Data Abstraction classes.

3. Scenario functions that are specific to one or a few scenarios, and which do not fit naturally into either interface or entity objects, are placed in control objects. For a simple and small system, there may not be any control objects; an entire analysis structure can be created with interface and entity objects alone.

Since there may not be any control objects for a particular structuring, these objects should be created after objects in the other two categories have been found. Interface and entity objects can be developed in any order. In reality, there will most likely be an iterative process for the creation of objects in these two categories.

After this short introduction to the three categories of objects, we will now look at the relations between scenarios and analysis objects in more detail.

10.3.1 Interface Objects

All the functions of a scenario that are associated with the system environment are placed in interface objects. The actor who initiates a scenario communicates with the system via these objects. The purpose of an interface object is to translate actor commands into system events and to return system responses to the actor.

Interface objects are identified from scenarios by starting with an actor and determining the boundary function between an actor stimulation and a system function. If domain analysis objects are available, objects in the Device Interface, External System, User Interface, and Role categories should translate directly to interface objects for the corresponding scenario function. A third approach is to identify interface objects from a textual scenario description, which is taken directly from the requirements model.

The interface objects identified to support the Return Item scenario of the recycling machine described above are illustrated in Figure 10-8. The objects interfacing with the Customer and Operator actors are Customer Panel, Receipt Printer, Operator Panel, and Alarm Device.

Interface objects may, typically, be composed of other interface objects, as shown in Figure 10-9. This illustrates a containment hierarchy (aggregation) using OMT notation. The significance of the object category has been noted with an I (Interface) in the lower right hand corner, since OMT does not support this type of classification.

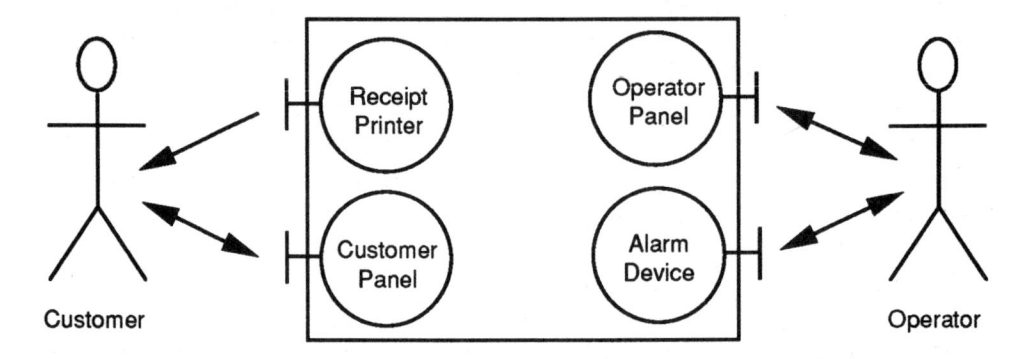

Figure 10-8. Interface objects for the Return Item scenario

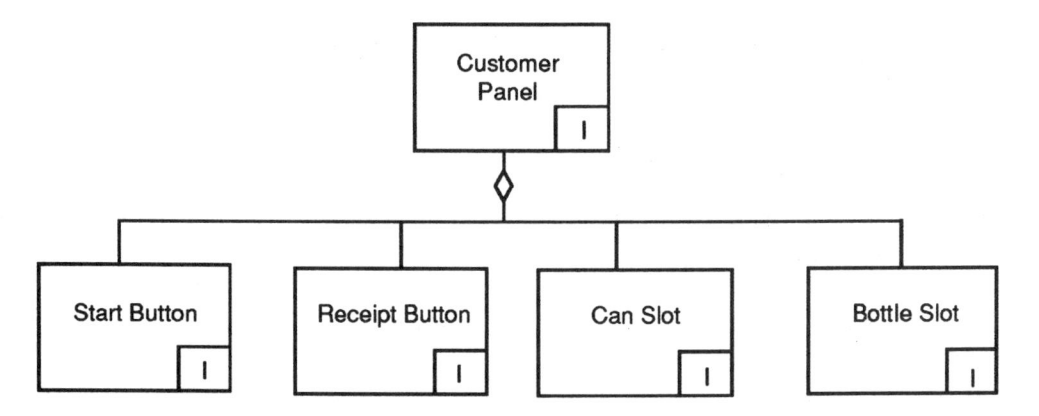

```
                    ┌─────────────┐
                    │  Customer   │
                    │    Panel    │
                    │          I  │
                    └──────◇──────┘
         ┌──────────────┼──────────────┬──────────────┐
┌────────────┐ ┌──────────────┐ ┌────────────┐ ┌────────────┐
│Start Button│ │Receipt Button│ │  Can Slot  │ │Bottle Slot │
│      I     │ │       I      │ │      I     │ │      I     │
└────────────┘ └──────────────┘ └────────────┘ └────────────┘
```

Figure 10-9. Aggregate of the Customer Panel interface objects

As was mentioned earlier, an actor can also be an external system; it is not limited to a human user. When interface objects communicate with other systems, the interface can be described in terms of a communications protocol. The protocol may consist of a standard, e.g., eXternal Data Representation (XDR) for the Remote Procedure Call (RPC) mechanism, or a set of application-unique messages. If the protocol changes, the changes are isolated to the interface objects supporting the protocol functions.

10.3.2 Entity Objects

Entity objects are used to model information that will persist for some time, even after the scenario has completed its sequence of events.

Entity objects can be determined from the scenario descriptions. They can also be identified from the domain analysis objects by transitioning objects in the Computational and Data Abstraction categories.

Entity objects for the Return Item scenario include Deposit Item and Receipt Basis. Deposit Item is associated with information regarding the return of both bottles and cans and their respective sizes and return values. This information is not unique to a single scenario, as a customer can return either bottles or cans of an unknown quantity. The Receipt Basis object is associated with information dealing with the totals of what a customer is returning.

The entity objects for the Returning Item scenario are shown in Figure 10-10. Receipt Basis is shown with an association to Deposit Item, and the latter has derived objects Can and Bottle. (We have used an E to signify an entity object.)

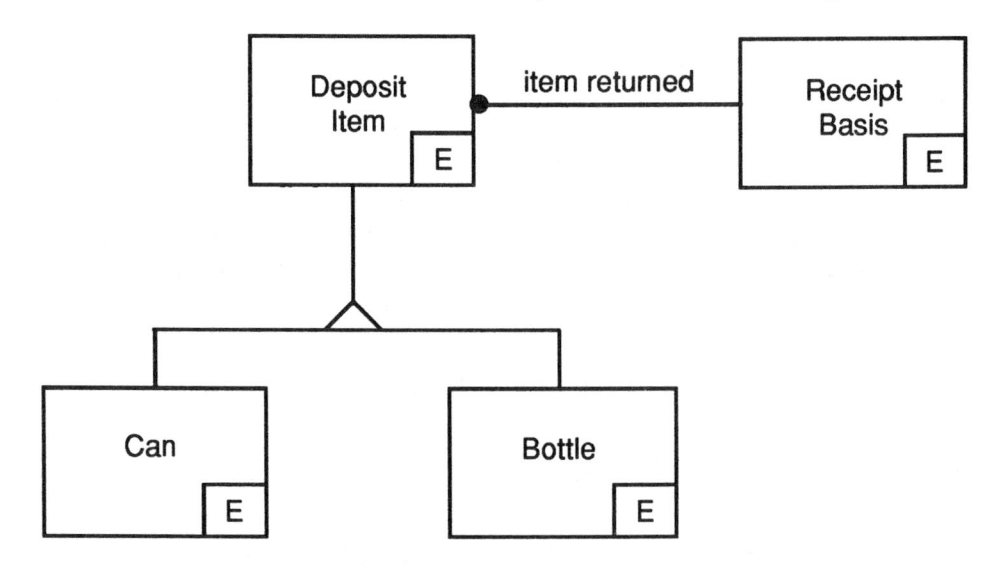

Figure 10-10. Entity objects for the Returning Item scenario

It is likely that similar entity objects will occur in different scenarios. It thus becomes important to analyze the similarities to determine if entity objects with direct reusability can be created. It may sometimes be desirable to slightly expand the functionality of an entity object to create the desired reusability across several scenarios.

10.3.3 Control Objects

Control objects are determined by allocating the remaining functionality that did not fit directly into either interface or entity objects. If all the functionality has been allocated prior to the analysis of the control objects, there simply won't be any control objects. This is the reason why they should be determined after interface and entity objects.

For most large systems, there will always be behavior or state information changes that can be allocated to control objects. The control objects can be considered the glue that holds the interface and entity objects together. Information associated with control objects is of short duration and may, typically, only last during a portion of a scenario, e.g., a coordination transformation of radar data to be displayed.

Control objects are normally found directly from the scenario descriptions. Any functionality associated with system behavior that remains after interface and entity objects have been determined is allocated to control objects. Typical functions placed in control objects are transaction-related behavior, control sequences specific to one or a few scenarios, and functions used to isolate the entity objects from the interface objects.

The control object Deposit Item Receiver is assigned for the Returning Item scenario This object isolates the interface objects Customer Panel and Receipt Printer from the entity objects Deposit Item and Receipt Basis. These relations are further described in the next section.

10.3.4 Combining the Analysis Objects

After all the objects have been identified for a given scenario, their relations are analyzed. The objects for the Returning Item scenario are illustrated in Figure 10-11. This is an event flow diagram used by the OMT method. The object categories are shown in the lower right corner of the rectangle describing each object (C = control, E = entity, I = interface). The Deposit Item Receiver controls the inputs from the Customer Panel and sends a message to Deposit Item that returned items will be arriving. When all the items have been deposited, Deposit Item Receiver gets the totals from Receipt Basis and sends a message to Receipt Printer for the latter to print a receipt.

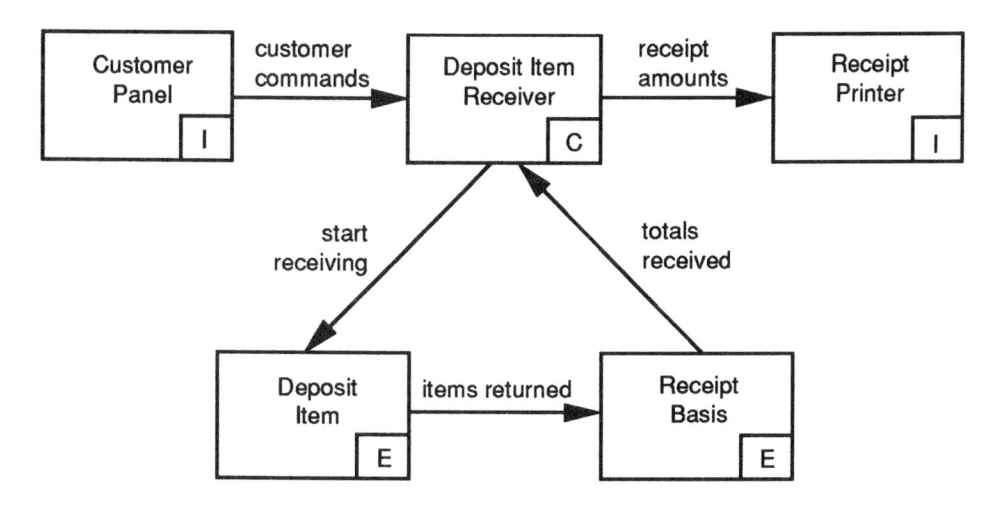

Figure 10-11. Event flow diagram for the Returning Item scenario

10.3.5 Stopping Criteria

One of the controversies associated with OOA is when to stop the analysis. Too much detail may lead directly into the design phase and reduce the logical structure we are striving for. If there is no dividing line between analysis and design, requirements changes may effect a redesign of a significant portion of the system. The logical structure we have seen above is intended to localize any requirements changes to a scenario and associated objects, without affecting the design.

A stopping criterion can simply be that all the scenarios have been identified, objects have been associated with each scenario, and similar objects that may support several scenarios have been analyzed for common functionality.

Very little has been said above about attributes and operations. This has been deliberate and supports the notion about a strict separation between analysis and design. The only significant analysis of attributes and operations associated with objects can be to determine the commonality of objects that may support several scenarios.

10.3.6 Subsystems

Large systems will consist of several scenarios and a large number of objects. The project management of these entities must be simplified by somehow grouping objects into larger units that are referred to as subsystems. These subsystems represent a way of structuring large systems for further development and maintenance.

There is usually a separate development phase called System Design (see Figure 9-1), which deals with the proper partitioning of a large system into subsystems. This has traditionally been done top-down based on functionality, rather than on objects. Some OOA techniques advocate an entirely bottom-up solution to the construction of subsystems. This does not account for the proper allocation of system requirements to hardware and software, distributed issues, and separate development organizations, and is not recommended. Some subsystems may be identified during the domain analysis when reusable entities are determined.

A first attempt at the creation of subsystems can be performed during the analysis phase. Large systems should, however, include a separate (or parallel and iterative) system design phase to determine distributed issues, general fault tolerance requirements, dynamic reconfiguration, reusability, organizational issues, etc. The creation of subsystems for large systems will be described in Chapter 11, System Design.

10.4 HEURISTICS FOR CREATING ANALYSIS OBJECTS

There is no cookbook fashion available for creating analysis objects. Several guidelines were offered above for the creation of analysis objects based on a set of scenarios. For projects electing not to use the scenario approach, or, if other analysis activities have already taken place, here are some additional guidelines for creating objects:

1. **Using Noun Phrases.** One of the earliest accounts of object-oriented development [ABB83] suggested underlining noun phrases in the requirements specification as the basis for determining objects. This will usually produce a lot of irrelevant "objects" for a large project when it is performed by someone who is new to the process. A skilled practitioner, however, will focus on the relevant entities. Suggestions have been made [RUM91, COA91] for challenging the objects determined in this fashion to eliminate objects that may only be attributes or outside the scope of the system to be developed. The OMT method for selecting objects and classes is outlined in the next section.

2. **Entities in Entity Relationship Diagrams (ERDs).** If ERDs are already available, the entities depicted can be transformed directly to analysis objects. The relations between the entities can be transformed to the equivalent associations between the objects.

3. **Data Flow Diagrams (DFDs).** If DFDs have already been drawn, the data stores can be transitioned to objects, and the transforms associated with a particular data store become operations for that object.

4. **Refinement of Domain Analysis Objects.** The real-world objects determined during the domain analysis are coarse-grained, high-level abstractions and can be refined. Some of the domain analysis objects will transition to entity objects; others may become interface or control objects. A single domain analysis object can be decomposed into several analysis objects.

5. **Roles.** Particular roles played by users of the system may be used to uncover classes and objects. The role of a Controller in an ATC system, for example, may be envisioned as a class, with particular instances of a Supervisor, Sector Controller, Trainer, and Trainee.

10.4.1 Identifying Analysis Objects

The guidelines that follow are based on the OMT OOA course notes with some slight modifications [ACC93a]:

1. Underline all noun phrases in the problem statement using the following criteria:
   - begin with the nouns from the problem area
   - use relevance to the problem as the only criterion for selection
   - include physical entities as well as concepts
   - do not try to organize using aggregates or generalization at this time
   - do not try to differentiate between objects and attributes at this time

2. Generate a context diagram:
   - helps to visualize system boundaries
   - choose a descriptive name for the system (we should already have one from the domain analysis activity)
   - scan existing information for interfaces with entities external to the system being developed
   - identify all data being exchanged between the system and each of its external interfaces

3. Modify initial list of objects:
   - initial list may include objects that are external to the system, these should be eliminated from further analysis
   - initial list may be missing important interface objects, these should be added to the list
   - Use the context diagram to guide the selection process
     — eliminate terminators or actors
     — add external data flows

4. Apply real-world knowledge:
   - identify additional objects
   - add additional requirements to the requirements specification

5. Choose names carefully:
   - make names descriptive and unambiguous

- choosing good names takes practice
- establish a naming style guide, e.g., use of singular versus plural nouns

10.4.2 Selecting Classes

The selection of a suitable set of classes takes place after the analysis objects have been identified. The guidelines that follow are also based on the OMT OOA course notes [ACC93a]:

1. Assign the analysis objects to an initial set of classes.
2. Eliminate redundant classes:
   - apply generalization/specialization
   - combine very small subclasses into larger classes
   - two classes that describe the same information are redundant
   - keep the class with the most descriptive name, e.g., Check and Paycheck, for a payroll system, for example, keep Paycheck and eliminate Check
3. Eliminate irrelevant classes:
   - eliminate a class with little or nothing to do with the problem
   - expect a certain amount of subjective judgment to be involved in the discussions
   - a class may be relevant in one context, and not in another. For example, the cost of meals is irrelevant for a restaurant payroll system unless the employees are charged for their own meals by deductions in their pay
4. Eliminate classes that should be attributes:
   - names that describe objects are attributes rather than objects
5. Eliminate classes that are operations:
   - if a name describes an operation that is applied to classes, it is not a class in its own right
6. Eliminate implementation constructs:
   - items that are not part of the real-world should be eliminated, un-

less they represent necessary (implementation independent) derived requirements
- data structures such as "tables" and "queues" are almost always implementations
- a "CPU" may be an acceptable class if we are building a computer system, but not if we are modeling a payroll system

7. Clarify vague classes:

- rename classes that are not specific
- look for class names with a broad (vague) scope
- look for classes with poorly defined boundaries

The identification of objects and selection of classes should be performed by a mixture of domain experts and analysts familiar with object-oriented paradigms. The domain experts will be able to discover missing objects and vague classes. The OOA experts will be able to direct the analysis and discussions regarding suitable decisions of objects, classes, attributes, and operations.

10.4.3 Evaluation of Analysis Objects

The objects identified in this phase have more details associated with them than the ones determined during the domain analysis. There are also additional objects to consider, since we now have entity objects, interface objects, and control objects.

The guidelines listed in the previous sections can be used directly to evaluate the analysis objects and associated classes derived in this activity. A checklist for analysis objects is shown in Figure 10-12, and can be used to document the result of the evaluation.

10.5 REFINEMENTS OF BUILDS AND PROTOTYPES

The initial set of builds and prototypes from the domain analysis may change as scenarios are developed and real-world objects are refined. A set of scenarios will be mapped to a particular build or prototype, as was shown in Figure 10-4. The functionalities of the original builds and prototypes may be altered as the details of the scenarios are determined.

Chapter 10 • System Requirements Analysis

Object Id: _____   **File/Location:** _____

Review Item		Comments
1. Object Category		
2. Completeness		
3. Size		
4. Attributes		
5. Operations		
6. Scenario Id(s)		
7. Level of Detail		
8. Volatility		
9. Implementation Dependencies		
Hardware		
Operating System		
DBMS		
10. Subsystem Candidate		
11. Aggregate Of		
12. Associated With		

Reviewer: _____   Date: _____

    Corrective action required (Yes/No): _____

    Further review required (Yes/No): _____

Corrective action completed, date: _____   Reviewer: _____

    Page _____ of _____

Figure 10-12. Checklist for analysis objects

The development of the identified objects will be prioritized to support the chronological order of the various builds and prototypes. This becomes especially important for objects that are determined to support multiple scenarios.

10.6 RISK AREAS

A significant number of risks are associated with an object-oriented approach to the system requirements analysis phase. These risks should be carefully evaluated for a particular project before the development starts. The larger the project, the larger the risk becomes if this is the first attempt at using object-oriented techniques.

10.6.1 OOA Methods versus a Development Process

The process shown in Figure 9-1 represents the overall strategy for developing large systems. An OOA method is merely a tool to support the requirements analysis phase. Too many practitioners become enamored with the details of "their" method and lose sight of the overall goal of developing large systems. This can lead to a lot of wasted time, with focus on the relative merits of various OOA methods and detracting from the development process.

The particular OOA method to be used should be chosen based on an impartial evaluation of available methods, and should not be based on a practitioner's prior experience with a single method. The purpose and limitations of the use of the method should also be clearly identified to prevent the method from becoming the process. (See recommendations for selecting the "right" method in Chapter 8.)

Current OOA methods make vague attempts at structuring large systems by "clustering" objects into subsystems. No considerations are made in these methods for hardware/software requirements allocation, fault tolerance, or distributed issues. It is important that these topics are adequately covered, preferably as a separate system design activity.

10.6.2 Training

Most software organizations that have built large systems have utilized structured techniques. Substantial training will be required for a successful project implementation using object-oriented techniques. This training must be carefully timed to coincide with the start of this development phase. Otherwise, significant re-training will be necessary.

The use of scenarios is not new to the software development community. Event analysis and thread analysis have been utilized on a number of large projects. The use of scenarios as presented here, however, will require training. The process for identifying scenarios and the documentation using textual descriptions and graphical illustrations should be specific parts of the training. Each project should pick a consistent set of documentation items to be followed.

The most substantial training should be expected for the OOA techniques used to support the scenario approach. This will consist of regular classes as well as on-the-job training via mentoring. Class material should include guidelines for supporting the scenario approach.

Most software organizations do not have certified instructors for teaching OOA courses. This means that the OOA courses will be taught by vendors or consultants who have a monitory stake in the method. It is important that project senior staff members attend the training to keep the focus and scope of the OOA method on the task of supporting the development process.

The impact of increased cost and, potentially, longer schedules because of additional training should be recognized at the start of the project. Statistics on real startup costs on projects switching from a structured approach to object-oriented techniques are hard to come by, but a general consensus in the literature and at software conferences seems to be that the costs are significant.

The benefits of training in OT are the preparation for creating stable structures that can accommodate expected requirements changes, and the potential for reusable systems. An intangible benefit of OT training could be a boost to employee moral with an exposure to state-of-the-art technology. In the age of company restructuring and downsizing, this might be an important aspect of long-term planning.

10.6.3 Notation

The various OOA techniques use different notations for describing the same concepts, and, collectively, the OOA notation is quite different from what is used in structured methods. This creates a significant confusion factor to the novice OT practitioner. Some of these notations can be supported with ordinary drawing tools, e.g., MacDraw, whereas others, e.g., Booch's, are so complex that they require a CASE tool. Some of the CASE vendors (e.g., IDE and Cadre) are working on new versions of their tools to implement several of the

OOA notations. Each of the primary OOA methods (OMT, OOSE, Shlaer-Mellor, Coad-Yourdon, and Booch) is represented by a tool for that method. If we decide to change from one method to another, we have to buy the tool for that method.

The scenario descriptions illustrated above use mostly familiar notations. A project must pick a consistent set for documenting textual and graphical representations of scenarios, stimulus-response, and events. The use of the special icons in Jacobson's method to illustrate the three different object categories can be minimized. This was illustrated above with the adaptation of the OMT notation with an annotation for I, E, or C for interface, entity, or control objects, respectively. The tool Objectory is available for complete support of Jacobson's method and notation, but is not yet well known in the U.S.

A context diagram was recommended above as an aid to determining the actors of the system. This is a familiar notation in structured analysis and does not represent any risk. It is also used in some of the OOA methods. Another structured analysis artifact is the data dictionary. This is also a familiar concept and does not represent any risk in this context.

10.6.4 Analysis versus Design

Some practitioners claim to use OOA, but are really hacking. A significant risk associated with the use of some OOA methods is the "seamless transition" from analysis to design. The exact same notation is used in both OOA and OOD for these methods, with the result that the "what" of the system requirements is lost. What remains is the "how" of the design and a structure that is implementation dependent. Changes in system requirements require a re-design, and entire sections of the documentation need to be redone.

The scenario-driven approach described above is aimed at separating analysis and design with a structure that can handle requirements changes with minimum impact on the products that have already been developed.

Stopping criteria can be effective in delineating between analysis and design. Too much emphasis on the details of attributes and operations, for example, may be a sign that the analysis phase has been transcended.

10.6.5 First Large Project Using OOA

The biggest risk of using OT is facing an organization that is planning to employ an OOA method on a large project for the first time. The startup costs could be significantly higher than for a comparable project using well-known structured methods. Training; development of new guidelines, standards and procedures; new management techniques; and new tools are all significant cost factors. A longer schedule is almost also assured.

The driving forces compelling us to employ OT could be customer demand, promise for higher productivity, and potential for reuse. The first is part of a requirement we have to satisfy. The latter two are desirable results from using new technology. Neither of these two should be expected for the first large project using OT.

One way to mitigate the risk is to carefully choose portions of the requirements for prototyping. This type of prototyping does not only deal with operational concepts, but also verifies the process. The process must be followed completely with regard to methods, tools, management, and documentation. An evaluation must then be made for how well the prototype will scale up for the rest of the project.

10.7 WORK PRODUCTS

A number of products are created as a result of the system requirements analysis activity. Most of them have been referred to above. Here is a summary of the most important products:

1. **Context Diagram.** This is used to identify actors and was shown in Figure 10-2.
2. **Scenario Diagram.** This illustrates the actors and the scenarios and was shown in Figure 10-3.
3. **Scenario Descriptions.** Textual descriptions of scenarios were made in Section 10.1.4. A scenario can be described as a sequence of events and was shown in Figure 10-5. The relations between events and objects are described with an event trace, as shown in Figure 10-6. The response to a stimulus initiated by an actor was documented as a stimulus-response and shown in Tables 10-1 and 10-2.
4. **Scenario Sequence Diagram.** A build consists of a set of scenarios, as shown in Figure 10-4.
5. **Object Diagram.** The relations between actors and the objects that support a given scenario are depicted in an object diagram, as shown in Figure 10-8.
6. **Analysis Objects and their Relations.** The various analysis objects that

support a given scenario and their relations are depicted in the OOA diagrams shown in Figures 10-9, 10-10, and 10-11.

7. **Revised Build and Prototype Plan.** The initial build and prototype plans developed during the domain analysis are revised with regard to functionality, schedules, and prototyping descriptions.

8. **Risk Analysis.** The risk analysis created during the domain analysis phase is revised as a result of the identification of scenarios and prioritization of supporting objects.

9. **Data Dictionary.** The format for this is project dependent and will include attributes associated with objects supporting specific scenarios.

10. **Checklist for Analysis Objects.** This is used in the evaluation of the analysis objects and is illustrated in Figure 10-12 This evaluation has been expanded from the evaluation of real-world objects, since the analysis objects have a different mission (i.e., to support specific scenarios) and may have been derived from the domain analysis objects.

11. **System Requirements Specification.** This document specifies the "what" of the system to be developed. The format and contents depends on who the customer is. A U.S. DoD customer will probably require the System/Segment Specification of DOD-STD-2167A. For a commercial customer, we can usually choose our own contents and format for the description of the system requirements. Some customers have their own specification document which we may have to revise after requirements discussions and negotiations have been completed.

11

System Design

The goal of system design is to allocate the requirements of a large system to hardware and software components. There are two primary activities that take place during this phase. We first partition the set of requirements into subsets that will form the basis for the system architecture, i.e., architecture modules. We then configure the system by allocating the requirements within each module to hardware and software components. There is usually an iterative process between these two substeps: We may have to modify the partitioning to obtain the best possible system architecture, given a set of requirements constraints.

The system design activity starts after the system requirements analysis has been completed. The starting point is a System Requirements Specification and the documentation created during the system requirements analysis.

The transitioning from the system requirements analysis to system design is usually a non-trivial exercise, since there is seldom a single, obvious solution that presents itself to the designers. The steps suggested here are intended to ease this difficult transition.

Sometimes, the transition is made easier by customer documentation that includes a partitioning. This may be the case, for example, if we are building a flight simulator and the customer furnishes system diagrams that contain a number of subsystems or Line Replaceable Units (LRUs) that are connected via buses. The LRUs can then represent subsystems ("black boxes") which we can transform directly to architecture modules. The major task in this case is the configuring step of allocating requirements to the hardware and software of each module (LRU).

The first step in the system design phase is the partitioning activity where a large system is decomposed into smaller entities to reduce the overall complexity, and to allow subsequent development of architectural modules by several teams of developers.

11.1 PARTITIONING

The partitioning process and the concept of a "partition" differ greatly depending on the view of the developers. The method used in the partitioning activity may be purely analytical, using structured methods with data flow diagrams (DFDs), control flow diagrams (CFDs), process specifications (PSPECs), and control specifications (CSPECs) [HAT87], purely intuitive by selecting entire subsystems based on previous experience, or clustering of objects based on an OOA performed during domain analysis or system requirements analysis. The system may also be pre-partitioned by the customer, as suggested above for a set of LRUs connected via buses.

The primary purpose of partitioning is to decompose the requirements of a large real-time system into smaller, manageable units that can be designed as architectural entities by teams of hardware and software engineers. The individual entities will be integrated into a total distributed system that can implement the system requirements and operational conditions specified by the customer. A distributed system is the preferred architectural model for the achievement of flexible, extendible systems that can easily be modified to include new and expanded requirements.

11.1.1 Views

The partitioning activity is viewed differently depending on a developer's background and experience. There are at least three different views perceived of what partitioning is all about:

1. **Subsystem View.** An engineer used to building similar systems for different customers, e.g., flight simulators, may insist that a formal partitioning step is not required. The primary issue to this engineer is what changes will have to be made to existing "black boxes" to satisfy the new set of requirements.

2. **Configuration Items.** Engineers building new and unique systems will most likely hold the traditional view that the partitioning step is intended to create subsets that can form the basis for hardware and soft-

ware configuration items. These configuration items form logical entities (but not necessarily ideal design entities) that can be created and managed by teams of developers.

3. **Product Line View.** Engineers building software-intensive systems as a product line may partition a set of system requirements into subentities that can be implemented as software components with only minimal regard for a hardware architecture. Configuration items will be defined later when a particular system is developed for a given customer. The software components will be used as building blocks for the system architecture of small, medium, and large systems within the same problem domain. A formal partitioning and configuring activity is not required for this approach.

11.1.2 Partitions

A partition is a distinct subset of the requirements of a real-time system and includes the following characteristics:

- it is implemented as software, hardware, or a combination of hardware and software
- it has well-defined and robust interfaces
- it is a reusable entity that can be allocated to different physical nodes (PNs) in the distributed system
- it can be implemented to execute concurrently with other implemented partitions in a distributed configuration
- it communicates with other partitions via message passing only, (shared data may be employed within a partition)

Partitions are normally created during the system design phase and allocated to a hardware element during the configuring activity. We will think of partitions in terms of system requirements, and refer to virtual nodes (VNs) as software elements that implement a certain portion of the system requirements, i.e., a partition may be implemented with one or more VNs.

11.1.3 Partitioning Guidelines

The sections that follow provide a set of guidelines for partitioning a real-time distributed system for each of the views described above.

11.1.3.1 Subsystem View

The baseline for the partitioning step is the System Requirements Specification which will normally include a system context diagram. For the system design phase, we use rounded rectangles, as suggested by Hatley-Pirbhai in [HAT87], to denote architecture modules to differentiate from the circles that represent essential requirements in the system requirements analysis. An example of an architecture context diagram for a Flight Management System (FMS) is shown in Figure 11-1.

A subsystem is sometimes referred to as a "black box" and performs a given function specified in the system requirements. An example of subsystems is illustrated in Figure 11-2 for a flight management system. The Navigation and Guidance subsystems, for example, are implemented as black boxes containing the necessary hardware and software to satisfy the systems requirements for those two functions.

An attempt was made during the domain analysis phase to locate existing subsystems that can be reused and modified for the new system. A performance analysis should be made to determine if the existing hardware can handle the new requirements. If this is the case, it is simply a "small matter of programming" to make the software perform the new or expanded functions. A formal partitioning and configuring activity will not be necessary in this case, and the system design teams can concentrate on perfecting existing products.

If the hardware does not measure up to the new requirements, a redesign of the hardware architecture is necessary. This could include a more powerful CPU, additional or faster memory, or different communication media, e.g., buses.

If a reusable subsystem is not available, a traditional partitioning activity must be performed. The allocation of functionality to subsystems can be accomplished using the Hatley-Pirbhai architecture template and the control and process models (i.e., DFDs, PSPECs, CFDs, and CSPECs).

In a scenario-driven approach (see Chapter 10), the objects supporting scenarios are mapped to subsystems (more about this later).

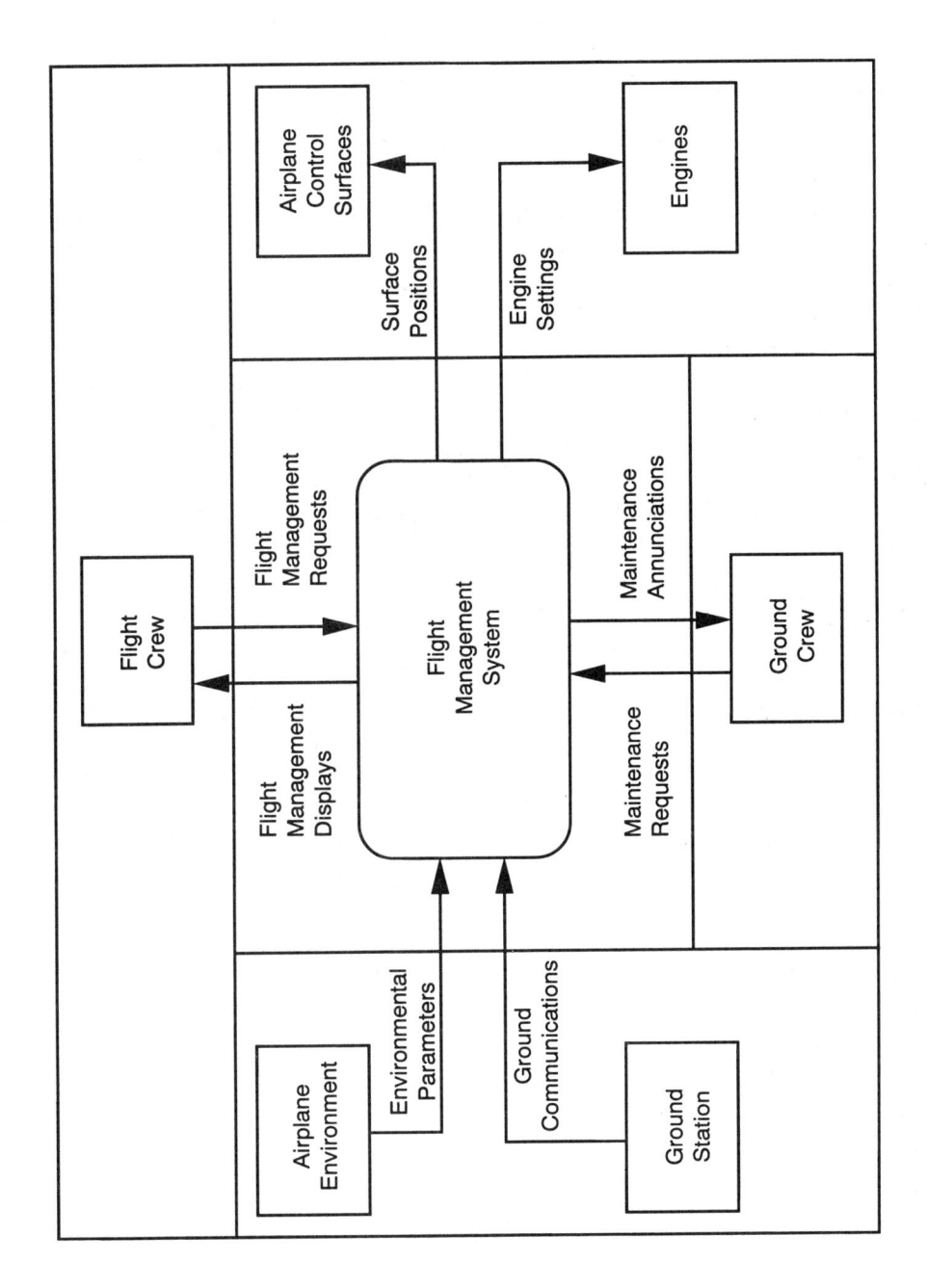

Figure 11-1. FMS architecture context diagram

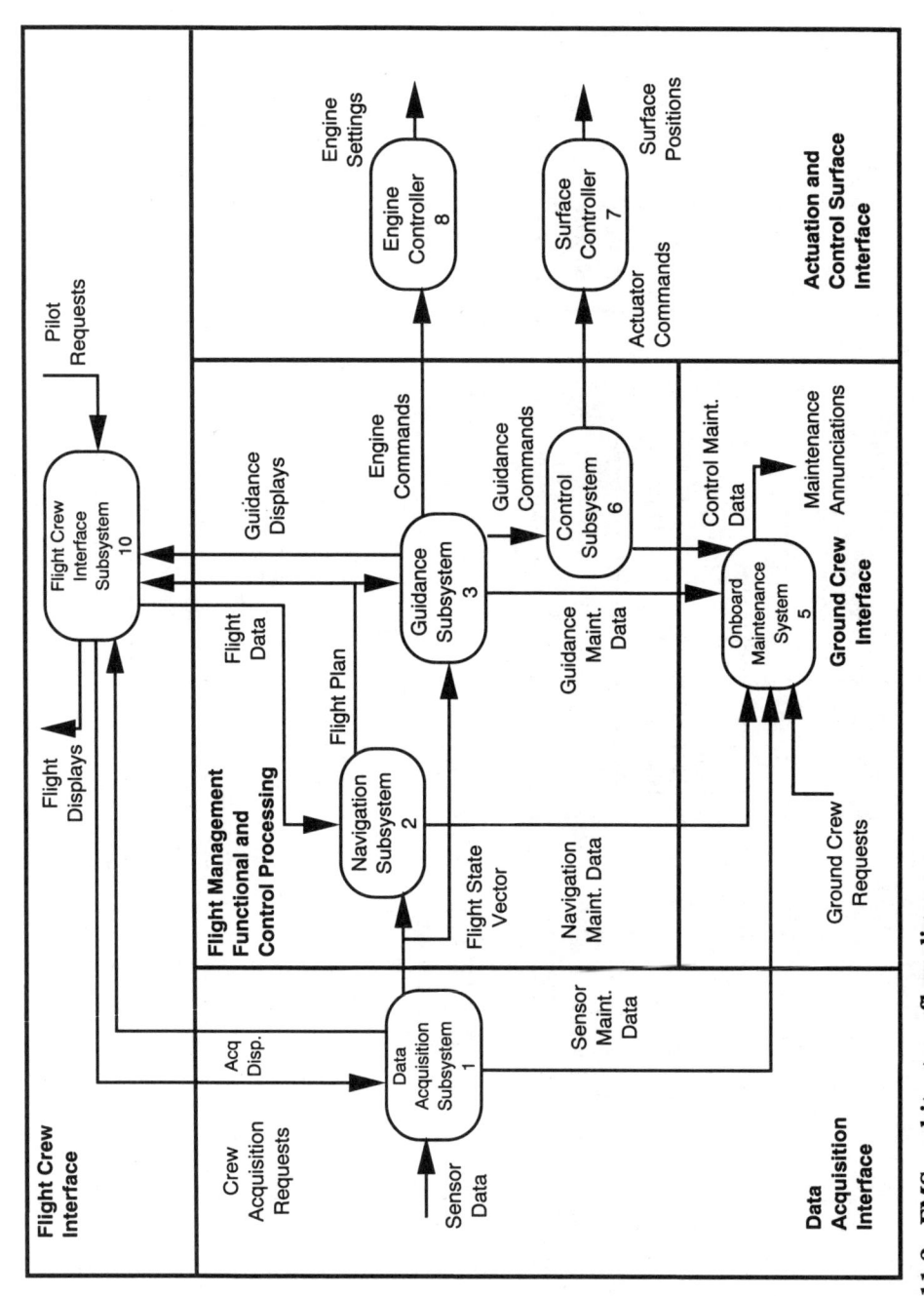

Figure 11-2. FMS architecture flow diagram

11.1.3.2 Configuration Item View

Sometimes a partitioning activity is performed to determine the major software and hardware entities that need to be developed for the system. The objective of this activity is to identify configuration entities that can be created by different development teams, including different subcontractors. We will only consider software entities here, and refer to these entities as software configuration items (SCIs). Here are some guidelines for establishing a set of SCIs:

- SCIs should be determined based on a proper hardware/software functional allocation analysis. This is an iterative process, and a reallocation may result after the SCIs have been selected.
- All the activities of the SCI should be related to a cohesive function, or groups of functions. For an ATC system, for example, SCIs could be Display, Radar Data Processing, Monitor and Control, and Flight Data Processing—independent entities that could reside on different hardware nodes.
- If possible, make each SCI execute on a single hardware node.
- An SCI composed of reusable components may span multiple processors. This will apply to a distributed database application, and where control spans over several large software components, e.g., the monitor and control function of Display and Radar Data Processing.
- The size of an SCI should not be larger than about 100 to 150K source lines of code (SLOCs) or 5 to 10 objects.
- Each SCI must be testable as a stand-alone entity, as well as in cooperation with other SCIs. Clues to look for include scenarios with a threaded operational view, and support for incremental development. In a scenario-driven approach, an SCI may support one or more scenarios.
- An SCI should provide low coupling with clean internal and external interfaces.
- Minimize the number of SCIs to minimize the number of documents required.
- Create the SCIs first, then decide on subcontractor splits. Don't pick subcontractors first and allocate "SCIs" to them arbitrarily, based on a loose functional allocation.

A subsystem will generally be considered a node in a distributed system. Each node will consist of one or more SCIs and the hardware entities necessary to support the performance requirements associated with the functionality of the SCIs.

11.1.3.3 Product Line View

The creation of a product line of reusable systems implies a different development strategy regarding the system design phase. The software will be developed to be reused in small, medium, and large systems within the same problem domain. A single hardware architecture for all these systems cannot be determined by the traditional partitioning/configuring process. The hardware architecture will evolve to be flexible and expandable for future system requirements. The software elements will be developed as independent, distributable entities, and the most critical factor for this approach is the creation of an efficient interprocess communication (IPC) mechanism.

A formal partitioning/configuring step is not performed for this approach, and the software is developed independently of the hardware architecture. This may include additional requirements for the IPC design. These requirements may include the handling of communications for interprocess as well as inter-processor transfers, and communications in a heterogeneous hardware environment.

11.1.4 Work Products of Partitioning

The products created during the partitioning activity include:

- architecture context diagram (ACD)
- architecture flow diagrams (AFD)
- architecture interconnect diagrams (AID)
- architecture interconnect specification
- architecture module specification
- architecture dictionary
- system design document
- message description document

An ACD and AFD were shown above for a Flight Management System. An AID for the FMS is shown in Figure 11-3.

The work products listed above, which are associated with the system architecture, are all derived from using the Hatley-Pirbhai method [HAT87], independent of any object orientation. We will discuss the effect of the scenario-driven approach and objects later.

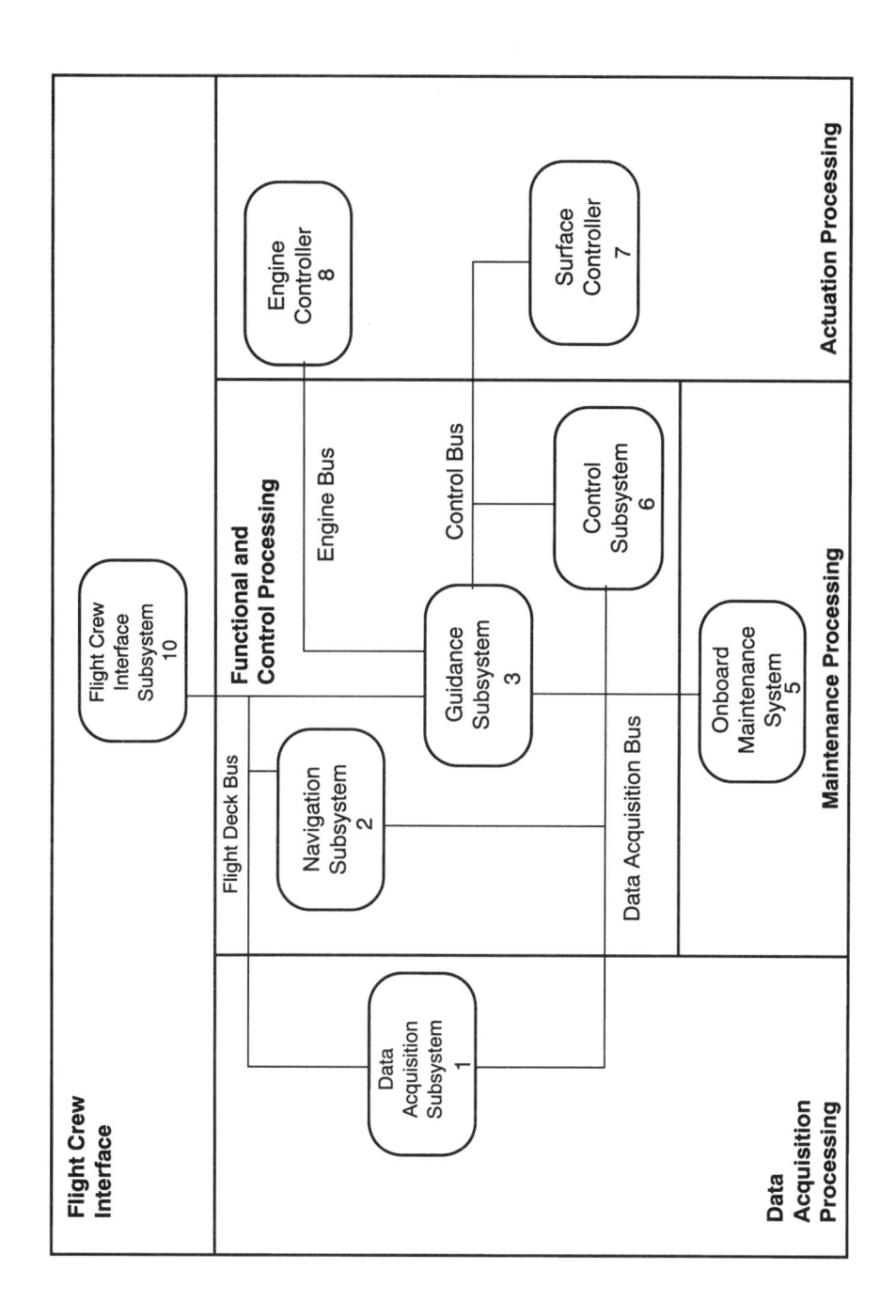

Figure 11-3. FMS architecture interconnect diagram

11.1.4.1 Architecture Interconnect Specification

There is no fixed format for an architecture interconnect specification, but here is a suggestion for the kind of information that should be included for the data acquisition bus shown in Figure 11-3:

Data Acquisition Bus

> This bus carries a 32-bit serial signal with the first 6 bits specifying the contents of the remaining bits.
>
> The impedance is 75 ohms, and the operating voltage is between +5 and -5 volts.
>
> The required transfer rate is 4 Mbps
>
> Duty cycle . . .
>
> Synch pattern . . .
>
> Parity . . .

11.1.4.2 Architecture Module Specification

There is also no fixed format for the architecture module specification. Information to be specified for the Data Acquisition Subsystem (DAS), for example, may include the following:

Description

> DAS has been allocated the requirements necessary to interface with all the sensors.

Architecture Requirements

> DAS shall be built using M68030 chips.

Requirements Trace

> DAS is allocated the following system requirements:
>
> 3.1, 3.3, 3.7, and 4.2
>
> (For a scenario-driven approach, we would list the objects associated with a given scenario.)

11.1.4.3 Architecture Dictionary

An architecture dictionary is used to specify data and control elements flowing between architecture modules, and between architecture modules and external entities. This dictionary also shows the allocation of data and control flows to individual architecture modules.

The architecture dictionary is created as an enhancement to the requirements dictionary by adding columns for originating module, destination module, and channel description. An example of a partial architecture dictionary for an Automobile Management System [HAT87, Figure 19-8] is shown in Figure 11-4. In the Type column, a "C" indicates a control element and "D" a data element.

11.1.4.4 System Design Document

The format for a system design document depends on whether or not a formal specification is required. Under DOD-STD-2167A, for example, there is a specific Data Item Description (DID, DI-CMAN-80534) which lays out the format down to the paragraph numbering level. For non-military projects this DID can be used as a guide for the kind of material that should be included and how to organize it.

Name	Composed of	Type	Origin Module	Destination Module	Channel
Activate	\Driver's cruise control activate command\ 2 Values: On, Off	C	Driver Interface	Automobile Management Computer	Driver Interface Bus
Braking	\Input signal indicating brake applied\ 2 values: On, Off	C	Brake Interface	Automobile Management Computer	Brake Bus
Desired Speed	\Desired speed cruise control is to maintain\ Units: Miles per hour	D	Automobile Management Computer		
Fuel Quantity	\Entered value of fill-up fuel quantity\ Units: Gallons Range: 0-18 gallons	D	Driver Interface	Automobile Management Computer	Driver Interface Bus
Throttle Position	\Output signal driving throttle position\ Units: Volts Range: 0-8 volts	D	Automobile	Throttle Management Interface Computer	Throttle Bus

Figure 11-4. Partial architecture dictionary

11.1.4.5 Message Description Document

A message description document (MDD) can be used to augment the architecture dictionary by specifying the contents of messages used in a message-driven system, e.g., an air traffic control system (ATC). The MDD can also be used as a baseline for determining event-driven scenarios for the development of prototypes and a build-strategy for an incremental approach. In that case this document should be created during the system requirements analysis as the scenarios are determined. A partial table of contents include:

1. Scope
2. Message Design
   - 2.1 Message Identification
   - 2.2 Message Type
   - 2.3 Message Description
3. Message Operational Sequence
   - 3.1 Message to Module Mapping
   - 3.2 Message Utilization
4. System Thread Models
5. Referenced Documents

The format for the message design can be taken from existing message type specifications, i.e., Ada definitions packages or C/C++ .h files for groups of related messages.

The Message Operational Sequence section maps each message to its functional module. The module mapping will be to an architecture module during system design, and to a software module during the software design phase. The message flow through the system for each message is described with a source and destination module, and the type of event or condition that will trigger the message.

The system thread model is used to describe the operational sequence model for a prototype or build-structure. The same message may appear in different threads, and complete threads will represent the scenario for an individual prototype or build-structure.

11.2 CONFIGURING

The system design phase consists of the decomposition of a large system into partitions that can execute as independent entities in a distributed configuration. The configuring step is performed in close concert with the partitioning. During the configuring step, we allocate the requirements within each partition to hardware and software. An iterative approach between the partitioning and configuring steps is anticipated, since it is possible that the requirements allocation will suggest a more effective partitioning than the initial attempt.

The completion of the configuring step represents the logical conclusion of system design, allowing the hardware and software components to be designed and implemented by separate teams. Systems and hardware engineers will then complete the hardware architecture, whereas the software engineers will start the software requirements analysis for each software component.

11.2.1 Functional Allocation

The functional allocation of system requirements to hardware and software is a very important design decision for a large system. This step serves to reconcile the concurrent engineering view of systems and software designers. If any software design decisions were made during the partitioning step, these decisions are revisited now to finalize the hardware and software components. Likewise, hardware decisions made without consideration for software issues are evaluated during this step.

Distributed solutions are fundamental to modern, large real-time systems. Distributed issues for hardware and software components design are resolved during the configuring step. The architecture modules determined during the partitioning phase, and reconfirmed or reallocated here, are mapped to a number of physical nodes (PNs), where each PN will consist of one or more CPUs, required local memory, and interconnecting media. Global memory and hardware devices are also part of the distributed hardware architecture solution. Associated architecture design decisions considered during this phase include:

- the total number of processors in the system
- expansion capabilities

- processor interfaces
- processor intercommunication mechanism
- location and protection of databases
- error detection, reporting, and recovery

Distributed issues related to software design include:

- interprocess communication mechanism
- static reconfiguration (startup, restart)
- dynamic reconfiguration (partial functionality, switch-over, hot stand-by)
- local and shared data
- distributed databases
- error detection, reporting, and recovery

The allocation of system requirements can be made to hardware only, a combination of hardware and software components, or software only (will need a CPU to execute). How this allocation is actually made is highly system dependent. A time-critical, embedded system may have a high ratio of requirements allocated to hardware, whereas a data-intensive system is likely to have a large ratio of the system requirements allocated to software.

11.2.2 Using Structured Methods

The basic method for the configuring step is to use the same Hatley-Pirbhai (H-P) architecture templates as we used for the partitioning step. The DFDs and CFDs for each architecture module are enhanced to determine the split between hardware and software functions. An example of the use of the architecture template for the requirements of the Patient Health Monitoring System (PHMS) is shown in Figure 11-5. The asterisks in this figure are used as on-page connectors to avoid crossing of data flow lines. The corresponding AFD for the PHMS subsystems is shown in Figure 11-6.

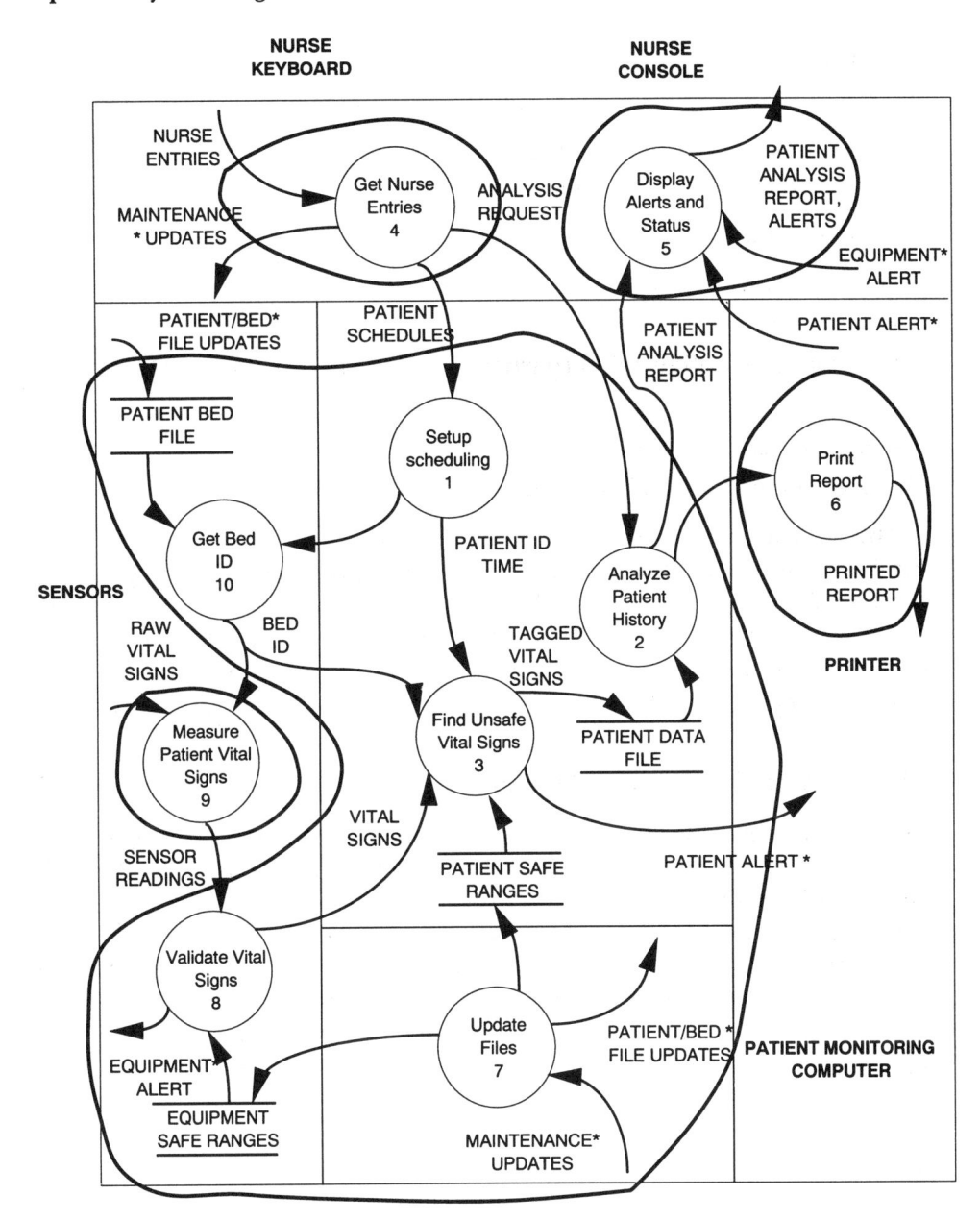

Figure 11-5. Allocated requirements for PHMS

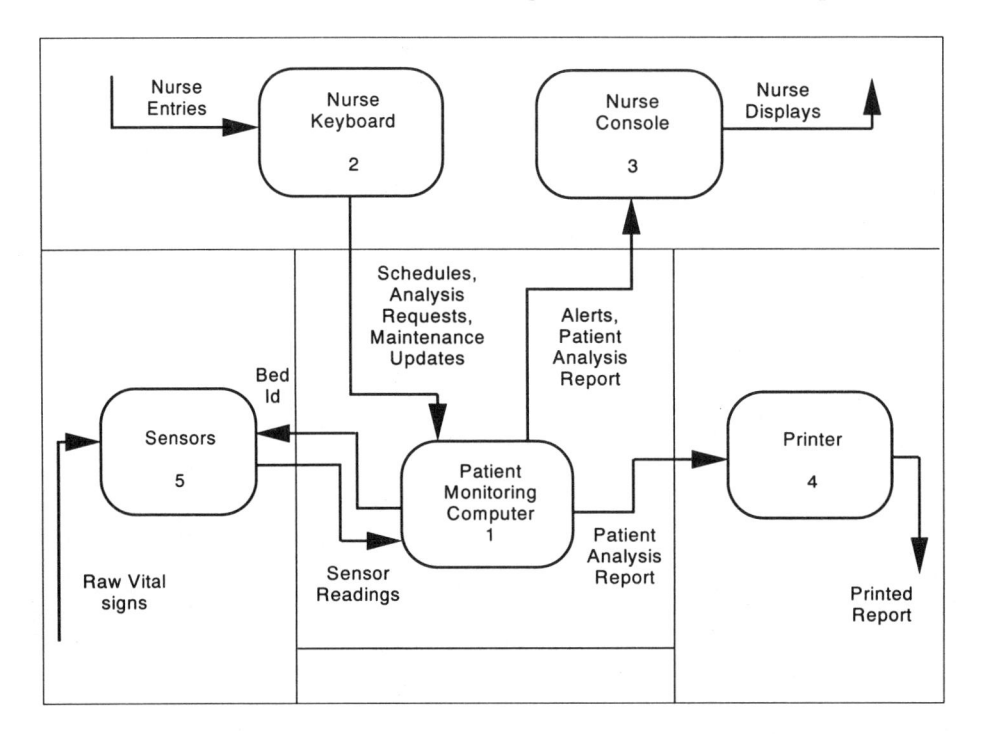

Figure 11-6. AFD for the PHMS

An example of the allocation of requirements to software is illustrated in Figure 11-7 for the Patient Monitoring Computer (PMC) subsystem. This will provide the starting point for the software requirements analysis of the PMC architecture module (subsystem).

Note the renumbering of transforms in Figure 11-7, corresponding to the PMC as architecture module number 1, Analyze Patient History, for example, is now numbered 1.3, compared to number 2 for the original transform in Figure 11-5. This type of renumbering is highly recommended, since additional transforms can be added without affecting the numbering of transforms in the other architecture modules.

It is important that we provide a trace from each new design decision back to the original requirements. The traceability matrix shown in Table 11-1 includes the original transform number under the Requirements Model column and the new numbers in the corresponding Architecture Module column.

Chapter 11 • System Design

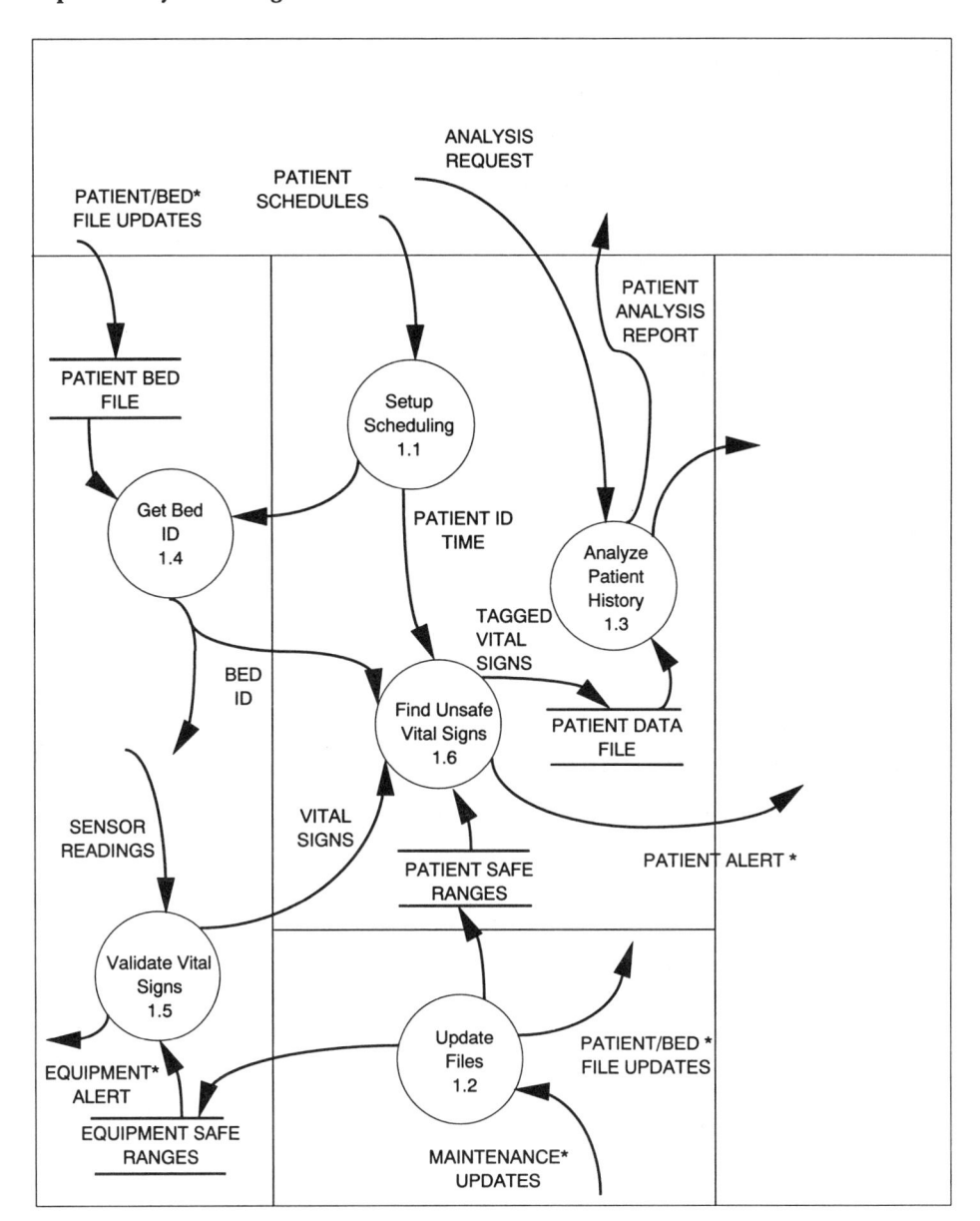

Figure 11-7. Requirements allocated to PMS

Table 11-1. PHMS Traceability Matrix

Architecture Modules / Requirements Model	NURSE KEYBOARD 2	NURSE CONSOLE 3	PATIENT MONITORING COMPUTER 1	PRINTER 4	SENSORS 5
Setup Scheduling 1			X(1.1)		
Find Unsafe Vital Signs 2			X(1.6)		
Analyze Patient History 3			X(1.3)		
Measure Vital Signs 9					X
Print Report 6				X	
Get Nurse Entries 4	X				
Get Bed ID 10			X(1.4)		
Display Alerts and Status 5		X			
Validate Vital Signs 8			X(1.5)		
Update Files 7			X(1.2)		
Patient Data File			X		
Patient Safe Ranges			X		
Patient Bed File			X		

The criteria used in determining the allocation between hardware and software include:

- performance issues

- interfacing requirements
- maintenance requirements
- ease of testing
- reusability
- reliability
- availability
- cost and schedule

11.2.3 Hardware Architecture

The hardware architecture is specified in terms of processors, memory, interconnections (buses, LANs, and physical connections), and a physical node description. The H-P method uses the architecture interconnect diagram (AID) to describe the architecture modules and their interfaces. A hardware architecture diagram is shown in Figure 11-8 for an ATC system. Physical nodes in this system include dual radar data processors (RDPs), flight data processors (FDPs), multiple graphical user interface (GUI) units, and training positions. Interconnections are shown as dual LANs (LAN 1 and LAN 2).

The major hardware architecture considerations of growth, expansion, and adaptability include:

- faster response
- additional functionality
- reconfiguration of reusable elements for the same problem domain for small, medium, and large systems
- hardware/software tradeoffs
- hardware upgrade path

Considerations for fault tolerance include:

- redundant processor (see ATC example) or memory
- redundant LANs (see ATC example)
- reconfiguration
    — reduced functional capability
    — error detection, reporting, and recovery
    — master/slave software control
    — load balancing
    — manual versus automatic reconfiguration

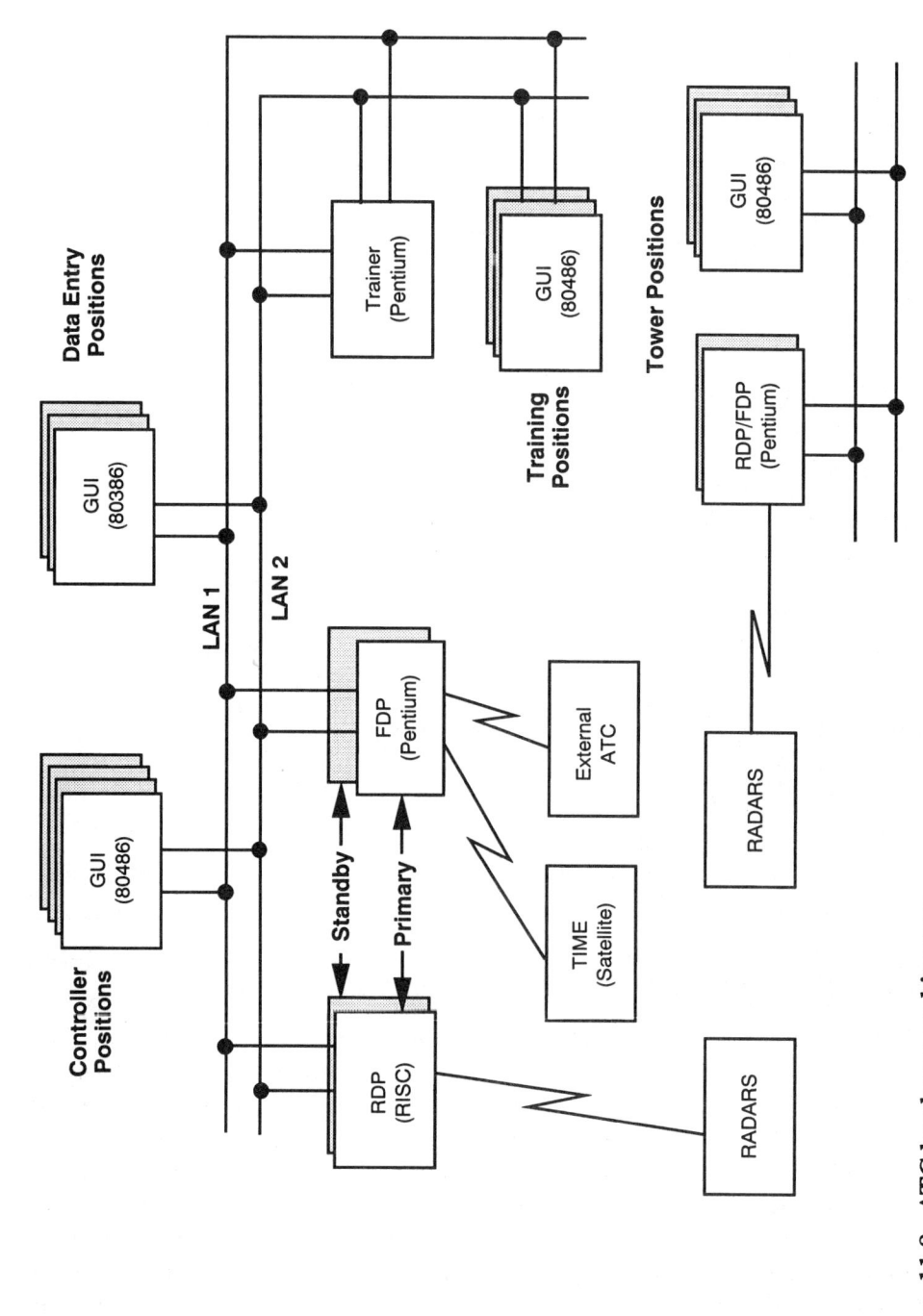

Figure 11-8. ATC hardware architecture

The hardware architecture diagram does not depict the system partitioning into architecture modules. The architecture modules shown in AIDs must be mapped to the physical nodes depicted in the hardware architecture diagram.

11.2.4 Work Products of Configuring

The primary work products from the system design step include:

- hardware architecture specification
  - hardware nodes (CPU, memory, interfaces)
  - network architecture
  - I/O devices
  - hardware architecture diagrams
- final requirements allocation
  - DFDs, PSPECs
  - CFDs, CSPECs
  - architecture module specifications and diagrams
- mapping of architecture modules to physical nodes
- specification of derived requirements
- hardware and software design constraints
- traceability matrix to system requirements
- final version of the system design document

11.2.5 Subsystems and Object-Oriented Methods

Almost all of the OOA approaches create subsystems by "clustering" of objects. This is a bottom-up activity performed after all the analysis objects have been determined. No specific treatment is made of requirements allocation to hardware and software, as is done in the Hatley-Pirbhai approach.

The OOA methods that consider the creation of subsystems use their class/object notation to describe architecture modules. The advantage is that the same tool can be used. The disadvantages are that the same notation is used for entirely different concepts, and that the tool does not distinguish between architectural entities and analysis objects. The H-P method with different notation (rounded rectangles for architecture modules) clearly distinguishes the architectural elements and their interfaces from the process structure. The OOA methods use their notations for associations and links to depict architecture connectivity.

Using the same OOA notation for the system requirements analysis, system design, and software requirements analysis can be confusing to our customers, who may not be familiar with our development approach. The architecture notation of H-P is preferred over any of the OOA notations.

CASE tools for OOA methods are immature and do not support the overall development process. These tools merely focus on the notation and description of classes, objects, attributes, operations, and associations that apply to that particular method. CASE tools for structured approaches are more mature and cover most of the development process. Many of the CASE vendors (e.g., Cadre and IDE) are currently integrating OOA/OOD methods with their development tools for structured approaches that can be used for the subsystem views.

11.2.6 Subsystems and the Scenario Driven Approach

The scenario-driven approach (OOSE) described in [JAC92] (see Chapters 7 and 10) includes some guidelines for associating scenarios, objects, and subsystems:

1. **System Changes.** The most important criterion for the subsystem division is predicting what the system changes will look like. A subsystem should preferably be coupled to only one actor, since changes are usually caused by an actor.

2. **Functionality.** The division into subsystems should also be based on system functionality. Objects with a strong functional coupling should be placed in the same subsystem. Here are some heuristics for determining the functional coupling of objects:

   - Will changes of one object lead to changes in other objects?
   - Do related objects communicate with the same actor?
   - Are two related objects dependent on a third object, such as an interface or entity object?
   - Does one object perform several operations on the other?

3. **Communication.** Subsystems should be created to minimize the communication required between the different subsystems. This will represent a weak coupling between subsystems. One approach is to first

place a control object in a subsystem, and then add strongly coupled interface and entity objects. This collection of control, interface, and entity objects will thus constitute a subsystem.

4. **Actors.** One way to test the feasibility of the subsystem division is to note how many actors are dependent on a certain subsystem. The ideal situation is to have a single actor associated with each subsystem. This is not always realistic, and a goal is to minimize the number of actors that are dependent on a given subsystem.

5. **Productization.** One view of a subsystem is that it represents the smallest entity a customer may want to buy for a system. The customer is offered either all of the subsystem or nothing as an optional entity. This means that the subsystem is identified with a product number in the sales catalog and treated as a system plug-in component.

The heuristics described for determining subsystems using the scenario-driven approach can be used as a complement to the H-P method and will then provide an additional test for the subsystem division. These heuristics can also be used without the H-P approach. Subsystems are then depicted with rounded rectangles, just as in the H-P notation, with requirements traced to control, interface, and entity objects instead of the H-P processes.

11.3 SUMMARY

The configuring step is highly iterative with the previous partitioning activity. The allocation of system requirements to hardware and software is a major design activity for large, distributed systems and serves to reconcile a concurrent engineering view.

The completion of the configuring step represents the logical conclusion of system design with the specification of a number of hardware and software components. This allows the hardware and software components to be designed and implemented by separate teams. Systems and hardware engineers will then complete the hardware architecture, and the software engineers will start the software requirements analysis for each software component.

The H-P notation for subsystems is preferred over the OOA notation for the illustration of system architecture elements. Using the OT notation of classes, objects, links, and associations can be confusing, since the same notation is used to describe OOA and OOD models and views.

The structured H-P method and the heuristics of the scenario-driven approach can be used as complementary approaches for determining subsystems. The scenario-driven approach can also be used without H-P for determining subsystems.

12

Software Requirements Analysis

The software requirements analysis phase starts after the system design has been completed, i.e., after the overall system has been decomposed into a number of subsystems. The system requirements have been allocated to hardware and software, and we are now ready to analyze the requirements associated with each major software component or subsystem.

This phase may also be started directly after the system requirements phase if we are developing a software-intensive system. This is likely to be the case in the development of reusable software components, e.g., for an air traffic control system, where there is no specific system design phase until a system is constructed, based on a set of requirements for a particular customer. The reusable components will then be customized for a particular hardware configuration.

For software-only systems, e.g., a C++ class library, the system requirements analysis and system design phases will be skipped, and the software requirements analysis follows directly after the domain analysis.

The primary difference between the system requirements analysis and the software requirements analysis is that we are now focusing on the requirements of individual software components rather than the entire system.

The focus of this chapter is on the use of OOA models to refine real-world entities defined during the domain and system requirements analyses, to decompose and refine subsystems, or to define abstract classes and objects if the other two phases have not been performed. The OOA classes and objects developed here form the basis for transitioning these elements into design entities.

12.1 MODELS

The focus of the software requirements analysis is to create models that can serve as transitioning vehicles from analysis to software design. With a structured approach, real-time structured analysis (RTSA) is used to create a behavior model that can serve as a transitioning tool for process abstraction. Data flow and control flow diagram (DFD/CFD) models are combined with a set of process selection rules to determine the concurrent elements of the subsystem. The resulting concurrency model represents the software architecture that can be implemented with a particular programming language. The primary references for RTSA are Hatley-Pirbhai [HAT87], Ward-Mellor [WAR85], and Shumate-Keller [SHU92]. Examples of the Hatley-Pirbhai notation are shown in Figure 12-1 for an architecture level context diagram for a patient monitoring computer (PMC), and the corresponding DFD is shown in Figure 12-2.

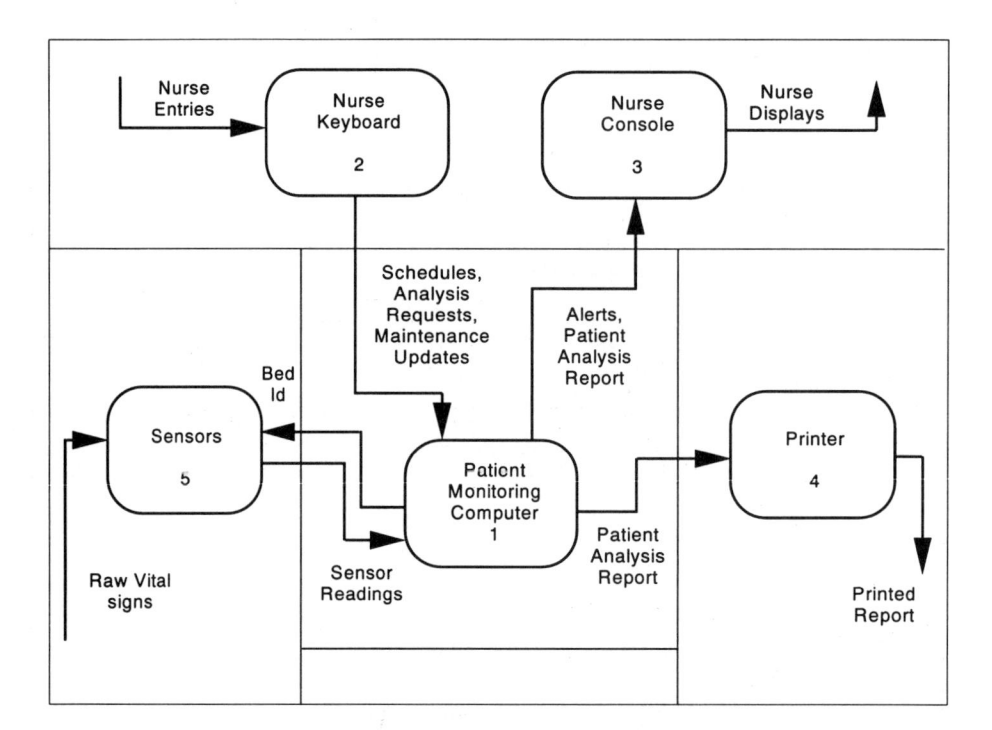

Figure 12-1. PMC architecture module context diagram

Chapter 12 • Software Requirements Analysis

Examples of a more generic notation are shown in Figure 12-3 for a robot controller architecture module context diagram, and for the architecture

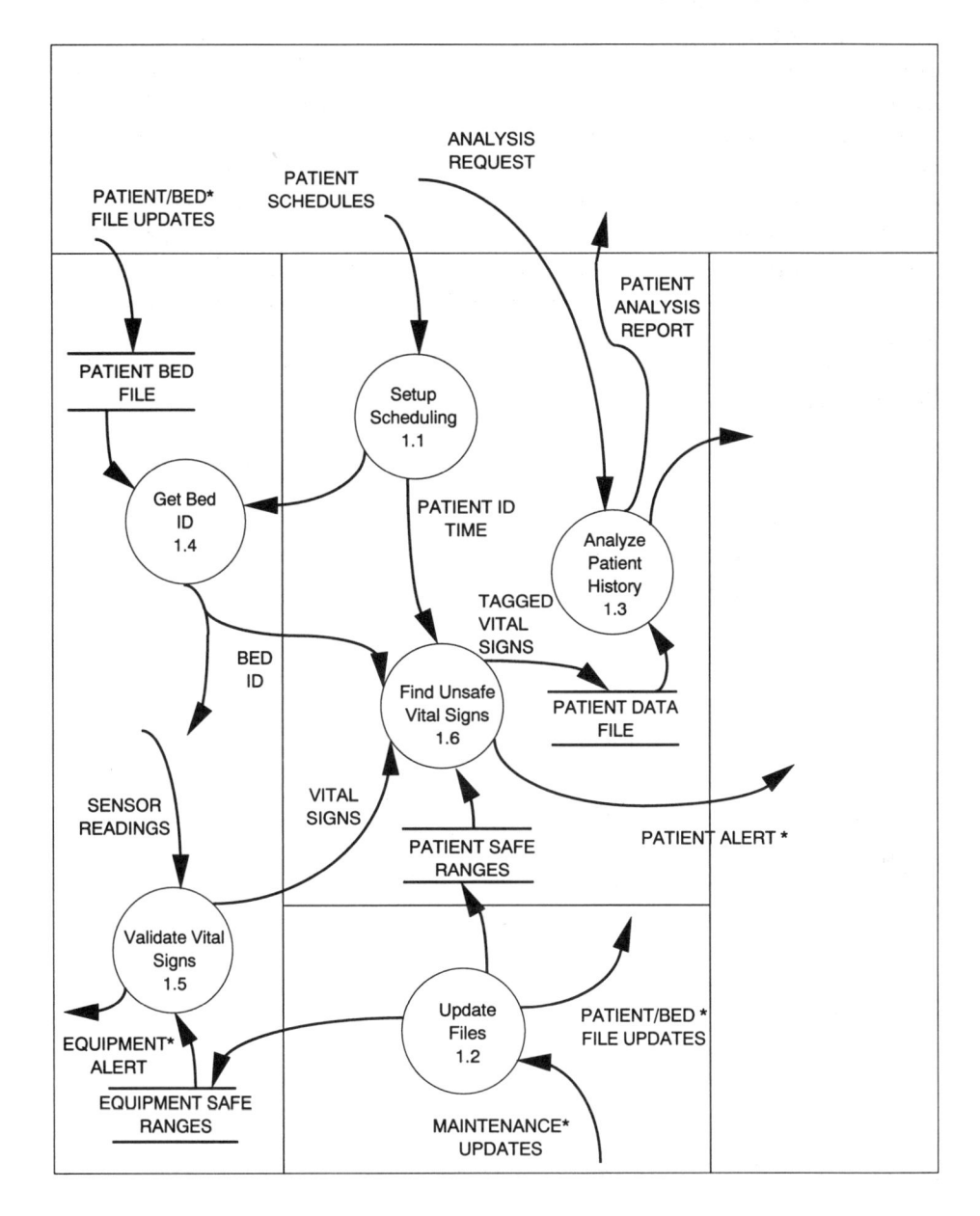

Figure 12-2. DFD for PMC architecture module

components in the architecture flow diagram in Figure 12-4. The entities shown in Figure 12-4 represent the major real-world entities of a robot controller system, and can be used as the starting point for the software requirements analysis, regardless of whether we use RTSA or OOA.

An information model can be added to get a better understanding of the primary data areas using an entity-relationship approach. This may already have been done during the domain analysis (if there was one) or during the system requirements analysis phase. An example of the notation used with ERDs is shown in Figure 12-5 for data elements of a simplified air traffic control (ATC) system.

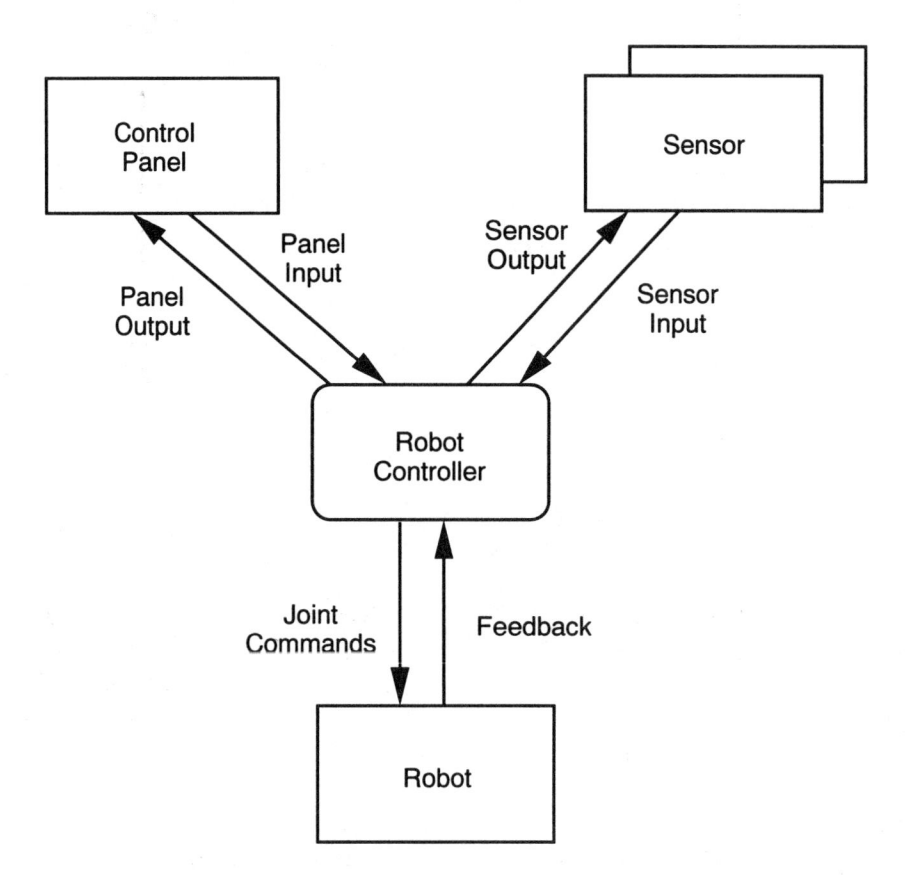

Figure 12-3. Robot controller architecture module context diagram

Chapter 12 • Software Requirements Analysis

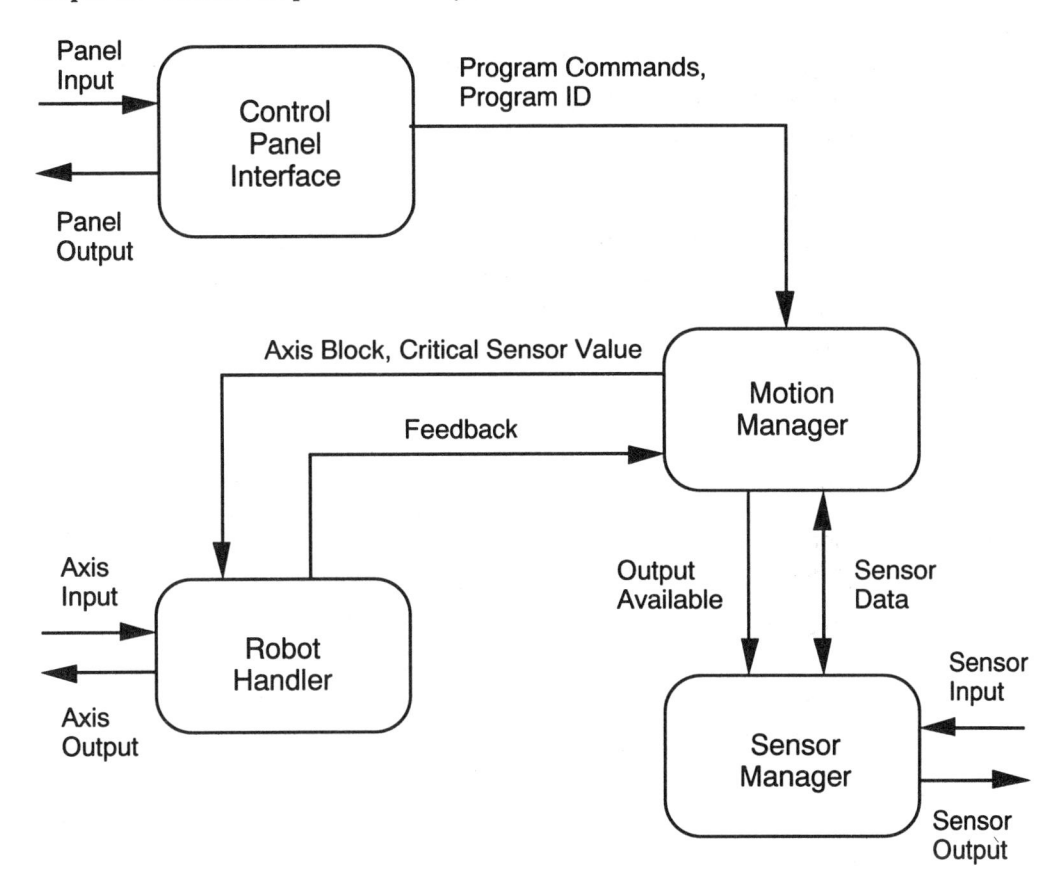

Figure 12-4. Robot controller architecture module flow diagram

The use of ERDs can be especially useful for data-intensive systems where derived requirements become important elements of the object model. Of the entities shown in Figure 12-5, Correlation Data is an example of a derived entity that is not likely to be listed in the system requirements specification. This entity will be used to correlate radar data with flight plan data to create a possible "target." We can thus use ERDs as an aid to determine objects. The ERDs are saved as backup documentation and are not part of the object model view. When entities from an ERD are supplemented with operations and attributes, they can be added to the other real-world objects obtained from the system requirements document.

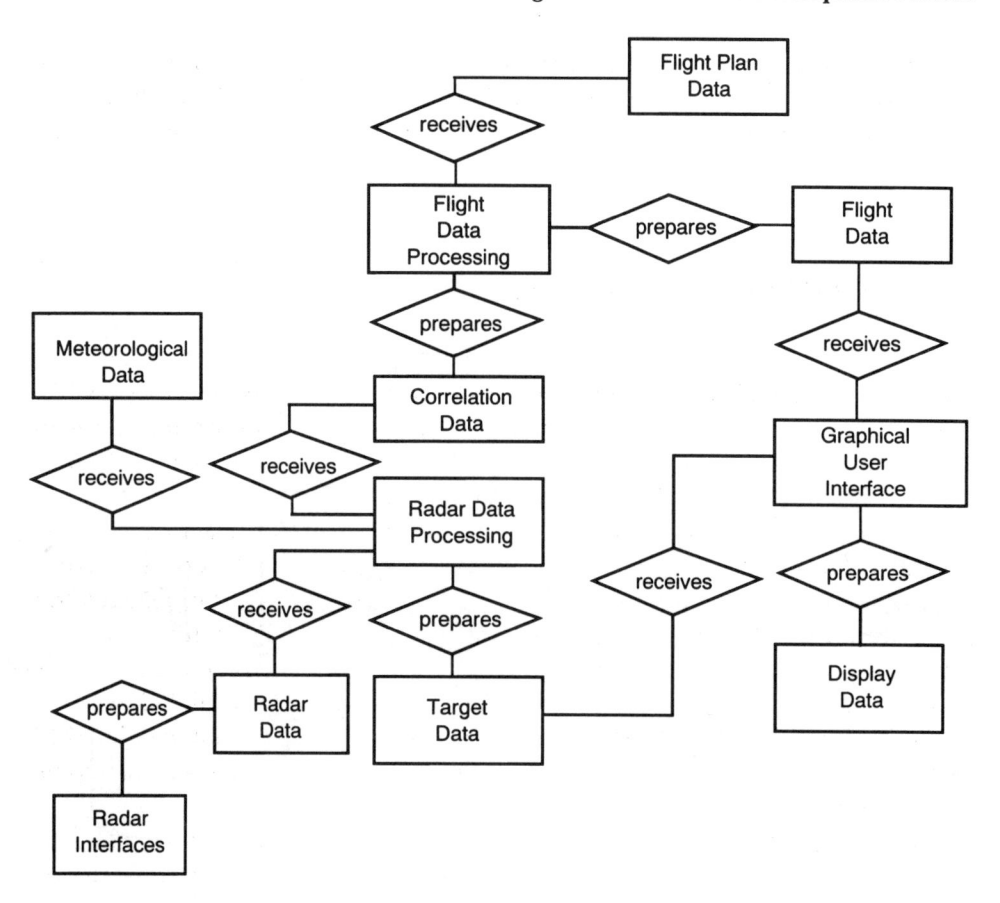

Figure 12-5. ERD for an ATC system

Object-oriented models are used to help us produce reusable components by creating real-world classes and objects. The RTSA and OOA models can be used together and can complement each other, with RTSA providing the necessary link between real-time requirements and design, and OOA supporting reusability concepts.

It is important to note that OOA is not required for implementing a design using object-oriented design (OOD). A perfectly acceptable OOD structure can be obtained from the RTSA activity. The creation of OOD entities is primarily dependent on which OOD paradigms the programming language can support—not on whether or not OOA was used. OOD features can be built into a software solution via a set of design guidelines irrespective of whether or not OOA has been performed.

The focus of this chapter is on the use of OOA models on individual subsystems or major real-world entities, such as the robot controller architecture elements shown in Figure 12-4 and the data-intensive ATC system shown in Figure 12-5.

12.2 OBJECT-ORIENTED ANALYSIS

The OOA models used during the *software* requirements analysis phase are the same as those used during the *system* requirements analysis. The only difference in the use of the models is that we are now focusing on the requirements of individual software components rather than the entire system: A large system has already been decomposed into subsystems.

One of the activities of OOA is the identification of abstract classes and objects that can form the basis for design objects. The objects represent components of larger real-world entities, e.g., aircraft engine, flight simulator navigation, or robot motion manager. Objects are considered instances of a class of a particular category. Associated with each class is a set of operations and attributes that are inherited by each object belonging to that class.

The primary benefit of OOA is an early focus on functional entities that can later be implemented as reusable software components with a particular programming language.

The steps performed during this phase are extensions and refinements of the domain analysis, system requirements analysis, and system design (all of these may not have been performed) and include:

- creating scenarios
- identifying classes and objects
- identifying attributes and operations
- preparing object views
- data modeling
- class/object evaluation

12.3 CREATING SCENARIOS

The creation of scenarios is a refinement of the scenario description performed during the domain analysis and the system requirements analysis.

More details are added as we gain a better understanding of the requirements.

The same guidelines for scenario preparation are used in this phase as were outlined in Section 10.1 of Chapter 10.

12.4 IDENTIFYING CLASSES AND OBJECTS

The creation of classes and objects is the activity of identifying high-level abstractions of real-world entities. Once we have found these entities, we associate them with operations and attributes. The starting point for the identification is a Software Requirements Specification (SRS), which was prepared during the system requirements analysis for the current subsystem. If an SRS is not yet available, we have to use the documentation for the system specifications allocated to the current subsystem.

The classes we create and refine during this phase will be transitioned to design entities during OOD for an implementation with C++ during OOP.

For the identification of classes and objects, we have already recommended two different categories of classes: (1) a functional category based on the real-world key abstractions of the system requirements, and (2) categories for entity, interface, and control objects [JAC92].

The following set of class categories can be used as a guideline in the creation of classes from the system functional requirements (this classification may already have been used during the domain analysis and/or the system requirements analysis):

1. **Device Interface Class.** Most of our systems will interface directly with hardware devices (e.g., radars, ATMs, and printers), and provides a readily identifiable class category (we are distinguishing these devices from user interface devices).

2. **External System Class.** This is an appropriate category for those systems that interface with similar external systems, e.g., an ATC center receiving a handover message from another center, or a banking system receiving information from a credit clearing institution.

3. **User Interface Class.** Most of our systems interface with users via a keyboard or graphical device. This may be subdivided into separate categories for each type of user interface device, e.g., keyboard, mouse, and lightpen.

4. **Computational Class.** This category is appropriate for systems that include significant computations to support the system requirements.

Examples of this category include coordinate conversions for robot control and ATC systems, and the calculation of compound interest for a savings institution system.

5. **Role Class.** This category can be used where a person is an important part of the operational system. A Controller in an ATC or air defense system, for example, can take on the role of Supervisor, Trainer, Trainee, Approach Controller, or Tower Controller. In a banking system, a teller is one of the important roles.

6. **Data Abstraction Classes.** Classes in this category may not readily appear in the system requirements, but will become evident if we are employing data modeling as part of our development strategy. Entity relationship diagrams (ERDs), for example, may be used during the domain analysis. The major data entities in the ERDs are real-world objects, and we can sometimes collect similar entities into data abstraction classes. Examples of data entities include radar and weather data for an ATC system, and user accounts for a banking system.

This set of class categories can be used during OOA to determine real-world abstractions from the software requirements for a given subsystem. The class categories are only used as a guide for finding objects, and for grouping common objects. Real-world abstractions rarely appear as classes.

Additional objects can be determined using the classification based on scenarios:

1. **Entity Objects.** Entity objects are derived by refining and transitioning the real-world objects determined during the domain analysis phase. The information associated with these objects should survive a scenario and is expected to stay in the system for a relatively long time. For an ATC system, for example, this could be objects describing flight data, but not target display data.

2. **Interface Objects.** Interface objects represent information associated with user interfaces, or interfaces to external systems. Responses to user commands, such as menus, text, and graphics displayed on a user console, are examples of data that should be placed with interface objects.

3. **Control Objects.** Control objects model information that is neither tied to entity objects, nor interface objects. Typical control objects will get information from entity objects, perform some computation on the data, and return the result to interface objects. An example of a

control object for an ATC system, is a coordinate transformation required of the radar data before it is displayed on a controller's console. Many of the control objects will represent derived requirements.

The analysis model we create does not merely consist of the high-level, real-world entities we found in the domain analysis or system requirements analysis. The high-level objects are refined into interface, entity, and control objects, resulting in a more stable model. When requirements changes occur, they can be localized to individual objects, rather than being distributed across several objects.

The use of the second classification scheme is more appropriate for a subsystem that includes user interfaces or interfaces with external systems (including other subsystems). Interface objects can be used for an interprocessor communication (IPC) mechanism between subsystems, for example, and control objects can be modeled as agents to handle the receipt of incoming and preparation of outgoing messages on different processors.

12.5 IDENTIFYING ATTRIBUTES AND OPERATIONS

Attributes are the data values associated with a class. This includes the state values of class instances, as well as constant data values for an instance. Operations are the services that set and manipulate the values of the attributes. A class interface is represented by the set of visible operations that clients can invoke to examine values and to change the behavior of class instances.

Attributes can be identified by determining the data values necessary to describe the static and dynamic properties of class instances. For the Account class shown in Figure 12-6, for example, the static values are Name and Account Number. Dynamic values include Address, Balance, and Beneficiary.

Attributes should be carefully scrutinized with regard to their content. A complex attribute may contain several data elements, and could really be an instance of a to-be-determined class.

Operations can be determined by examining the set of services that is required to affect the behavior of a class instance. For the Account class in Figure 12-6, operations include Open, Close, Add, Withdraw, and Transfer.

The proper determinations of attributes and operations require problem domain expertise. The software requirements document will provide some of the operations via verb phrases, but a complete set will only be obtained by

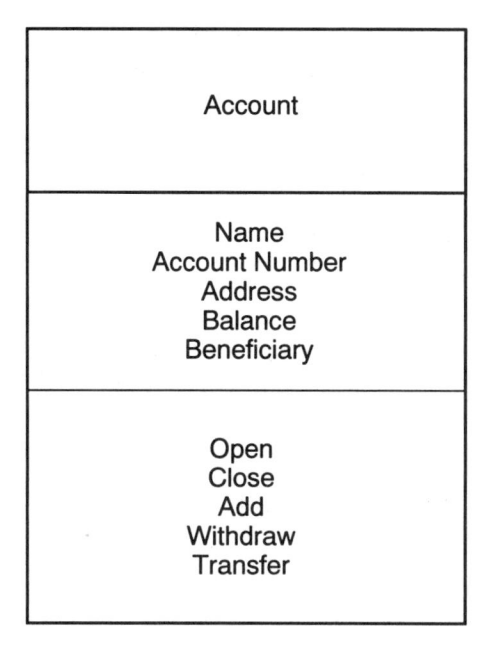

```
┌─────────────────────────────┐
│          Account            │
├─────────────────────────────┤
│           Name              │
│       Account Number        │
│          Address            │
│          Balance            │
│        Beneficiary          │
├─────────────────────────────┤
│           Open              │
│           Close             │
│            Add              │
│         Withdraw            │
│          Transfer           │
└─────────────────────────────┘
```

Figure 12-6. Class attributes and operations

knowing the problem domain. This is especially true for a large subsystem, where many of the requirements are hidden in large abstractions.

12.6 PREPARING OBJECT VIEWS

An object model is prepared by determining the associations between the various real-world objects that represent the key abstractions of the problem domain. An example of an object model for the ATM application is shown in Figure 12-7. This view describes the major abstractions and their relationships. One or more of these abstractions represent a software configuration item (SCI). The ATM Machine and ATM Card, for example, can be the ATM SCI (module).

Inheritance relations are not shown in Figure 12-7, and should be developed during OOD. Inheritance does not represent the view of a real-time abstraction and belongs to the design activity.

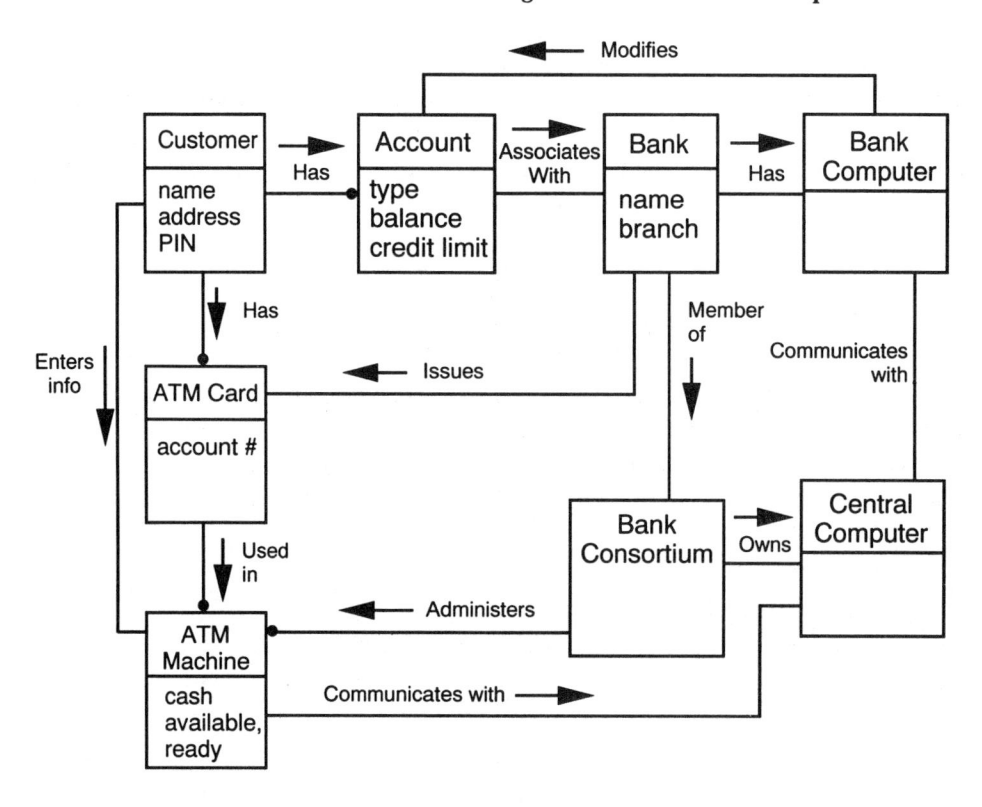

Figure 12-7. Object model of ATM application

Aggregation relations may also be postponed to the OOD phase, but sometimes these relations are available in the requirements specification and can thus be included in the OOA object model.

12.7 DATA MODELING

There is a close relationship between the entities determined during information modeling and the creation of abstract classes and object. The entities shown in ERDs correspond directly to real-world objects. These entities may have attributes associated with them, but normally not any operations. By adding a set of operations to the entities described on ERDs, we have the equivalent of OOA objects. If we add a set operations to the entities shown in ERDs, we have a one-to-one mapping with the objects identified during OOA.

Software development organizations that are currently using ERDs can use data modeling as a complement to the determination of real-world abstractions by adding rules for the identification of operations. CRC cards can supplement data modeling to provide the required operations associated with a class.

12.8 CLASS/OBJECT EVALUATION

It is important that the classes and objects defined in this phase be carefully evaluated for properties such as completeness, size, level of detail, and associated attributes and operations. A slightly modified version of the checklist used for the system requirements analysis is shown in Figure 12-8.

12.9 WORK PRODUCTS

The primary work products created during the OOA activity are static descriptions and views of classes and objects. An example of a specification for a Track Store class is the following:

Name: Track Store
Abstraction: Data abstraction class that defines track data attributes and operations.
Hidden Information: Hides the internal representation of a track (or target).
Anticipated Changes: Additional attributes and operations may be required. Data now envisioned to be in the Track File object may be included here.

Attributes:	Track Id	Track Status	Squawk
	Speed	Heading	Altitude
Operations:	Initiate a track	Drop a track	Add a track
	Read a track	Read all tracks	Update a track
	Correlate tracks	Extrapolate tracks	Correct Mode C

Usage Constraints: None
Undesired Events: Track Store empty, Track Store full. Unable to access group of tracks within requested region.
Effects: Track positions are extrapolated if no new position data received in *adaptable* seconds.

Object Id: _____ File/Location: _____

Review Item		Comments
1. Object Category		
2. Completeness		
3. Size		
4. Attributes		
5. Operations		
6. Scenario Id(s)		
7. Level of Detail		
8. Volatility		
9. Implementation Dependencies		
Hardware		
Operating System		
DBMS		
10. Subsystem Candidate		
11. Aggregate Of		
12. Associated With		

Reviewer: _____ Date: _____

    Corrective action required (Yes/No): _____

    Further review required (Yes/No): _____

Corrective action completed, date: _____ Reviewer: _____

Page ____ of ____

Figure 12-8. Checklist for analysis objects

Traceability: Radar Data Processing.
            Data Transformations
                Manage Track Data
                    Correct Mode C Altitude
                    Correlate Track
                    Update Track
                    Add New Track
                    Drop Track
                    Extrapolate Tracks
            Data Stores
                Track Store
                Track File
Objects: Track Store Monitor, Track File Monitor.

Another product created during OOA is a mapping of objects to ERD entities, as shown in Table 12-1 (see Figure 12-5). A traceability matrix should also be produced to map the real-world objects to the system or software requirements. The data abstraction objects arriving from derived requirements do not have traceability to the original requirements.

Table 12-1. Mapping of Objects and ERD Entities

Object Abstractions	ERD Entities
Radar Interfaces Module	Radar Interfaces, Radar Data
External Interfaces	(not shown on ERD)
Weather Data Manager	Radar Data
Flight Plan Manager	Flight Plan Data, Flight Data
Meteorological Data Manager	Meteorological Data
Track File Monitor	Target Data
Pairing Module	Correlation Data
Conflicts Module	Radar Data Processing
Track Number Manager	Radar Data Processing
Console Data Manager	Graphical User Interface
Display Data Module	Display Data
Recording Data Module	(not shown on ERD)

A summary of OOA work products includes:

- object models
- ERDs (if used)
- class/object descriptions
- mapping of objects and ERD entities (if ERDs are used)
- event trace diagrams for each scenario
- CRC cards (if used)
- data dictionary
- traceability matrix

12.10 SUMMARY

The software requirements analysis phase uses OOA to determine real-world abstractions for a subsystem or for a small system that is not partitioned into subsystems.

Objects are determined using a functional class category scheme based on system requirements and a scenario-based classification.

Attributes and operations are identified by determining the state values representing an object and the services necessary to examine and manipulate these values.

An object model is created to show the major real-world abstractions and their relations. Inheritance is not included in this view. Aggregation is sometimes given in the software requirements and can be included in the object model. Otherwise, it is postponed with the inheritance relations until the design phase.

ERDs and CRC cards can be used as aids in the determination of real-world abstractions.

A checklist was developed as an aid to class/object evaluations.

13

Software Design

The OOD activity is concerned with the creation of architectural components and their interfaces. An initial set of OOD elements is obtained by transitioning OOA entities to design entities. Additional classes and objects will have to be developed to complete a software design that will meet performance and reliability requirements.

For large real-time systems, the transitioning from OOA to OOD includes the determination of a set of concurrent elements that will represent a model of a process architecture for parallel execution. The transitioning activity also includes the determination of a suitable message-passing scheme for distributed architectures.

An important design consideration for robust and reusable software is the incorporation of fault tolerance. This can be implemented with an exception handling strategy, rather than simply error handling.

The objectives of this chapter are to:

- describe the transitioning from OOA to OOD entities
- describe process abstraction for concurrent elements
- summarize the OOD activity and associated products
- outline a strategy for exception handling
- provide a list of design evaluation criteria

13.1 TRANSITIONING FROM THE ANALYSIS PHASE

The design phase normally follows the software requirements analysis phase, and the first activity is to transition OOA entities to design entities. The objective of the analysis phase is to establish an accurate model of the system requirements of the problem domain. The design phase maps requirements to design entities that can be implemented as one or more programs that will perform the required tasks.

The transitioning activity is the first substep of the overall design phase shown in Figure 13-1. The key abstractions created in the earlier phases must somehow be mapped to concurrent elements as logical processes, and to design objects that will form the basis for a software architecture. If an application is to be implemented as a single-thread program, the process structuring substep can be skipped, and analysis entities are mapped directly to design entities.

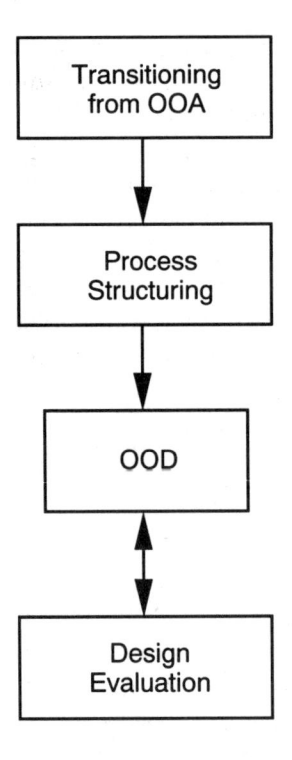

Figure 13-1. Substeps of the design phase

Transitioning can be performed using the objects allocated to the software requirements in subsystems. Each object is a potential process or software module. We use the process selection rules listed below to cluster objects into a set of suitable processes.

If we have a set of analysis objects that comprise the requirements of a single-thread program, without regard for concurrency, the following set of transitioning rules can be applied:

- classes and objects => classes
- attributes => data members
- operations => member functions (methods)
- relationships => inheritance, aggregation, and using
- events => architecture class
- state transitions => architecture class
- state actions => member functions (state dependent)

One of the biggest issues regarding the line between analysis and design is when inheritance should be included. Our approach is to leave inheritance out of the analysis phase, and to transition the class/object relationships derived in the analysis phase to inheritance and aggregation in the design phase. The ATM object model shown in Figure 13-2 is developed using OOA. The structuring of the ATM machine using aggregation and inheritance is done with OOD (see Figure 13-3).

After the transitioning of analysis elements to design elements, we continue to refine the initial, rough design. The process structuring activity creates a framework for a concurrency model, and OOD paradigms are applied to produce a software architecture.

13.2 PROCESS STRUCTURING

The word "process" is used here as an abstraction of an entity that will be implemented as a software module that will execute concurrently with other processes, e.g., Unix processes. Note that we are overloading the word "process" from the meaning used in software development "process."

In decomposing a large real-time system we use process abstraction to model the concurrent elements. The processes we create may include concurrent processes that communicate through shared data or message passing, and distributed processes that only communicate through message passing.

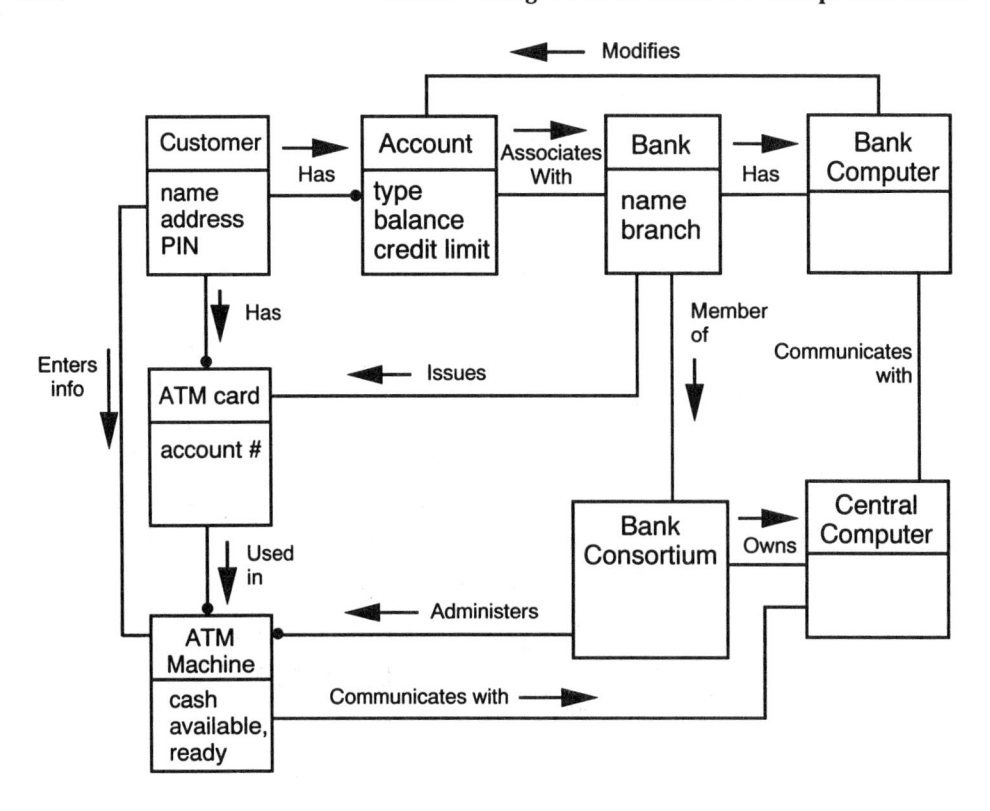

Figure 13-2. Object model of ATM application

When we use process abstraction in our design, it is necessary that the set of cooperating sequential (single-thread) processes satisfy two conditions [BEN82, FOR85]:

1. **Safety.** Each process must perform correctly - independently of the other processes in a static domain. An example of this condition includes the requirement of mutual exclusion for shared data and resources. Without mutual exclusion, data values used by one process could be corrupted by another process through interleaving of instructions, and the first process would no longer be performing correctly. Safety properties can be thought of as related to partial correctness for sequential programs. These properties are relatively easy to determine, since they are usually implemented as a direct result of the stated requirements.

```
                    ┌──────────┐
                    │   ATM    │
                    │ Machine  │
                    ├──────────┤
                    │  cash    │
                    │available,│
                    │  ready   │
                    └──────────┘
```

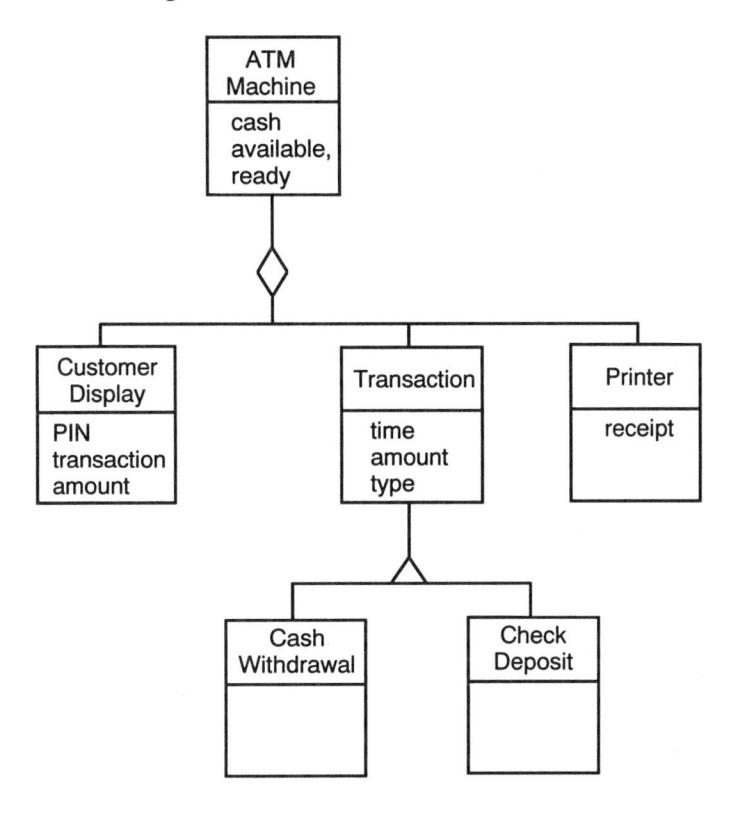

Figure 13-3. Inheritance and aggregation model

2. **Liveness.** This condition deals with dynamic properties and can be compared to total correctness for sequential systems. When a producer sends data to a consumer, the consumer will eventually consume it. When a process is ready to execute a critical section (e.g., a protected section of code), it is eventually allowed to do so. The liveness property is more difficult to determine than the safety property because we are dealing with dynamic events. Our process abstractions may include subtle design errors that can lead to deadlock or starvation [DIJ68, BEN82]. These errors may be extremely difficult to detect because they are usually not reproducible, and we are dealing with a dynamic environment that is constantly changing.

An example of process abstraction is shown in Figure 13-4, where each process (depicted as a parallelogram) is a virtual machine representing a

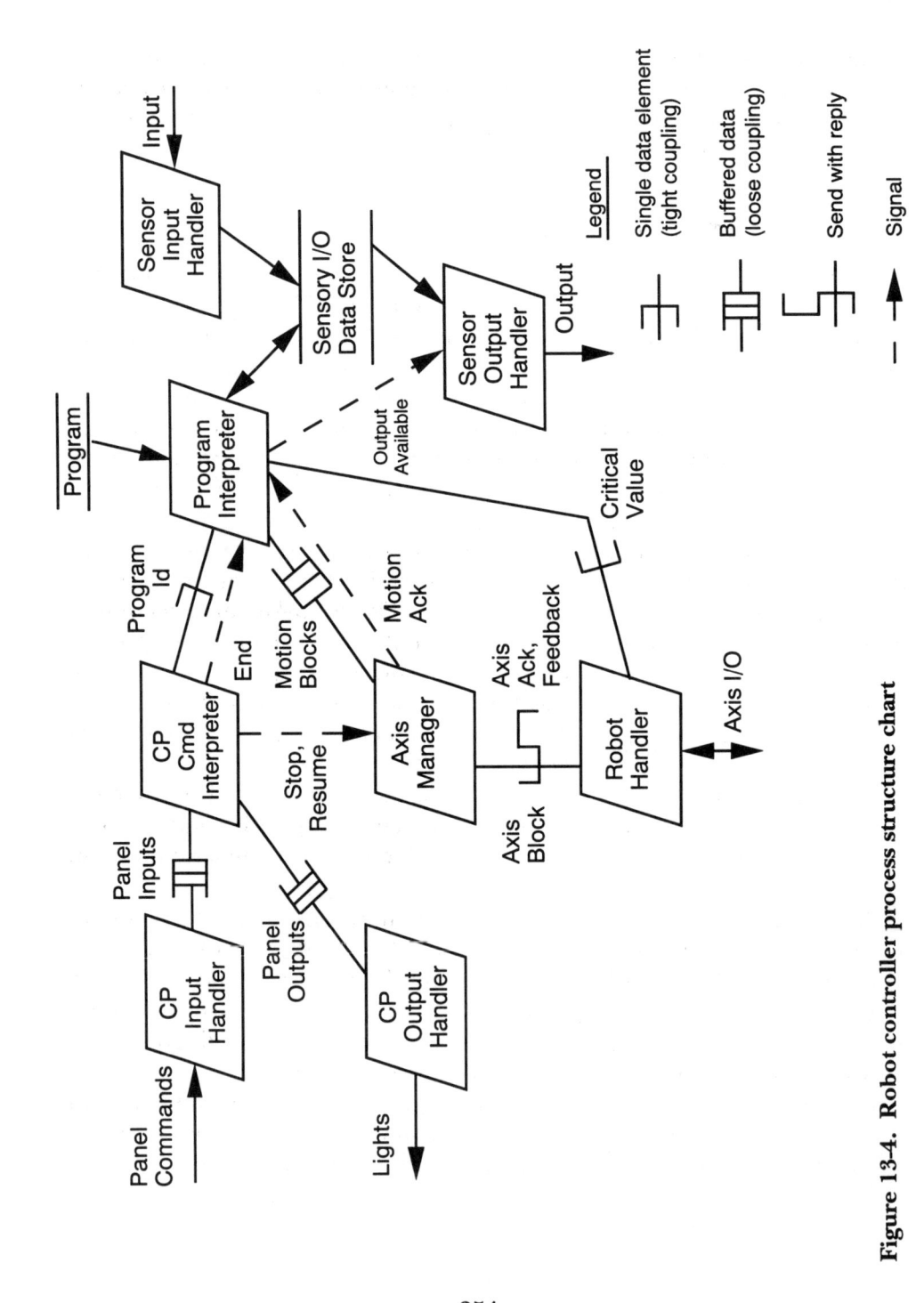

Figure 13-4. Robot controller process structure chart

parallel element of the model solution for a robot controller system. The decomposition of the real-time system into the set of abstract processes shown in this figure is not a simple, intuitive procedure, and guidelines for this partitioning are provided in the sections that follow.

13.2.1 Concurrent Elements

Concurrent entities occur in two different contexts: (1) *real* concurrency in a distributed environment that includes a number of independent processing elements, i.e., hardware nodes; and (2) *apparent* concurrency with multiple processes (tasks) competing for the use of the same CPU.

Distributed solutions have architectures that include two or more physical nodes, and modules residing in different nodes communicate via message passing. An example of a distributed system is shown in Figure 13-5. Each processing element (PE) will have its own local memory, and the PEs may have shared memory across a network or bus.

For large systems, each hardware node can be considered a subsystem, and there is no task scheduling required for tasks residing in the different nodes.

The apparent concurrency model shown in Figure 13-4 includes a number of processes that are treated as schedulable entities by the operating system. The parallelograms are the tasks, and the connecting lines represent the message passing between the tasks. Both data and events can be interchanged between the tasks, and interrupts can be accepted as input from an external system.

Two basic mechanisms are used to manage a set of processes: (1) a preemptive strategy based on readiness for execution and task priority; and (2) time-slicing, where each task is allocated a fixed amount of time in a round-robin fashion.

Some systems employ a non-preemptable multi-threading strategy, where a program is allowed to complete a thread of execution. This is used, for example, in MS Windows applications. Each Windows program is continuously polling for messages in its message queue, and is allowed to complete a series of messages that are waiting. The operating system decides the order in which programs will get access to their message queues.

Most large systems will be implemented as a hybrid of real and apparent concurrency: real concurrency between each node, and apparent concurrency among tasks or programs competing for CPUs within each node.

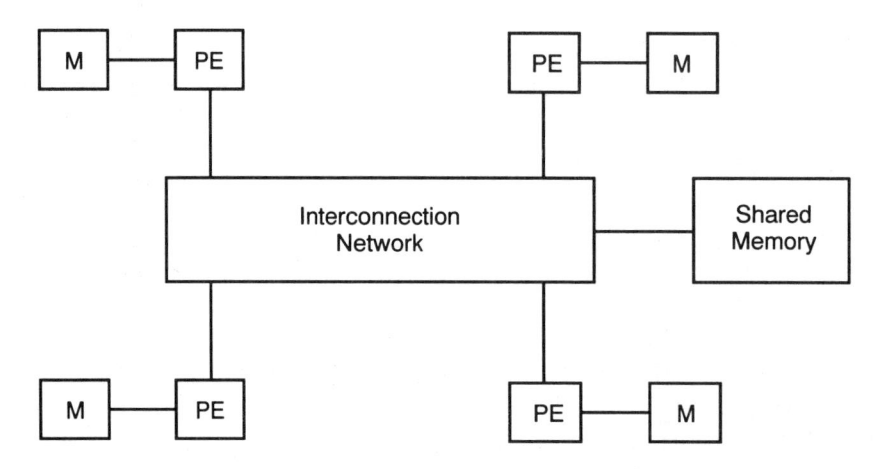

Figure 13-5. Distributed processing elements

A successful implementation of apparent concurrency is dependent on services for task scheduling, dispatching, synchronization, and communication. A mutual exclusion mechanism is required for managing shared resources. Communication among distributed elements requires an efficient interprocess communication (IPC) mechanism, e.g., remote procedure calls (RPC).

13.2.2 Process Selection

The identification of a set of processes originates with the objects derived during the software requirements analysis phase. This usually involves a large number of objects, and a clustering effort must be performed to provide a suitable process architecture. Simply transitioning each independent object to a corresponding process would involve too many tasks and an unacceptable run-time overhead.

The initial set of independent objects is combined into processes using the following process selection rules [GOM84, NIE88, NIE92, BOO93]:

1. **External Devices.** These devices normally run at widely differing speeds and usually require a separate process for each device or channel. These processes should be designed as simple device drivers with a minimum of executable instructions.

2. **Functional Cohesion.** Objects with closely related functionality can be combined into a single process if this will reduce the expected run-

time overhead compared to having each object as a separate process. The implementation of the set of objects as separate modules within the single process will contribute to functional cohesion (highly desirable) within each module as well as within the process.

3. **Time-Critical Functions.** Certain functional requirements must be performed within critical time limits, and this implies a separate (high priority) process for such functions.

4. **Periodic Functions.** An object including a periodic function should be implemented as a separate process that is activated at the proper time intervals. Objects that include different periodicities should not be combined into a single process, because it would quite likely be difficult to program more than one periodic function within the suspend/resume conditions of the process. If periodic tasks compete for the use of a processor, they can be specified with a high priority to ensure a minimum latency for the expiration of the period.

5. **Computational Requirements.** Objects that are not time critical (and often computationally intensive) can be designed as background processes (low priority) that will consume spare CPU cycles.

6. **Temporal Cohesion.** Objects that perform certain functions during the same time period, or immediately following certain events, can be combined into a single process.

7. **Database Functions.** Objects that need access to a shared database can be collected in a single process with mutual exclusion for the access mechanism and the structure of the hidden database. This is the concept of a monitor [HOA74, NIE88], and can be implemented in C++ with visible member functions that specify the access routines.

8. **Asynchronous Functions.** Objects (other than the external device drivers mentioned in 1 above) that appear independently and sporadically throughout the operation of the system should be separate processes. Examples of this type of object include (1) data recording, which is activated and terminated at irregular intervals by an operator; and (2) an alert function, which manages the queuing and display of alerts as they are received from the various processes.

9. **Minimizing Communication.** The combination of objects into processes should be made such that the overall communication between the processes is minimized. When the processes are later distributed among a set of processors, this design consideration will result in a lower overall remote communication latency for the system.

10. **Minimizing Total Number of Processes.** Every effort should be made to keep the number of processes to a minimum. There is a significant amount of run-time overhead associated with each process in the form of context switching, scheduling, and dispatching. Too many processes can eat up valuable run-time resources.

The multiprocessing model is determined using available scenarios and active, independent objects. Each process represents a schedulable entity that performs a portion of the system requirements. Additional processes may have to be added as agents to act as intermediaries between active and control tasks.

13.2.3 Message Passing

We will modify Booch's classification of message passing [BOO91], which covers both sequential and multiprocessing environments:

1. **Simple.** This applies to a sequential system and implies simple procedural calls. Data can flow in both directions.
2. **Synchronous.** When two processes (e.g., two Unix processes) need to communicate, they must be synchronized. This is usually implemented with a blocking mechanism, such as a semaphore. Both tasks are willing to wait "forever" for the rendezvous to take place. Parameter passing can take place just as for procedure calls.
3. **Conditional.** If the called process is not immediately available for synchronization, the caller executes an optional sequence of instructions rather than wait.
4. **Timeout.** The caller is willing to wait for synchronization for a specified time only. At the expiration of the timeout, the caller executes an optional sequence of statements. This can also be implemented within the called process.
5. **Asynchronous.** The caller does not wait for synchronization with another process. The data to be passed is simply deposited by the producer, and the consumer process will receive the data via an intermediary. The intermediary mechanism can, for example, be implemented as a mailbox, or by including a buffer process (agent) between the producer and consumer.

The particular message passing mechanism used will be determined by the desired coupling between a producer/consumer pair.

13.2.4 Distributed Systems Issues

The distribution issue was first addressed during the system design phase as we were allocating system requirements to hardware and software components. This section is concerned with suitable design approaches that may be used to profit from maximum reuse of software components that can be distributed among processors without a major redesign effort. The recommended approach is to employ standard communication protocols and models that are publicly available, and to avoid proprietary approaches.

One of the major design issues in a distributed real-time system is how well the details of the communication mechanism can be hidden from the application modules. If a high degree of reusability is to be realized in such a system, it is imperative that module interfaces be carefully constructed to allow redistribution of major application functions to different processors. In a large ATC system, for example, the modules performing the flight data processing and tracking functions could reside on separate processors. In a smaller system, however, these same functions may have reduced functionality and may reside in the same processor.

An additional dimension has been added to the design complexity by the distribution requirements. The programming objects that are deemed to be distributable should not have direct knowledge of other processes within their local processor, or of processes residing on the other processors in the distributed system. If all interprocess communication is hidden from the programming objects that make up the application packages, these packages can be distributed among processors without major rippling effects throughout the system.

A distributed system can be implemented with shared data as the communication mechanism between application modules. This can lead to major problems, however, and message passing is the preferred method of transferring data in a distributed system. If shared data is used, it must be protected with a locking mechanism to provide data integrity via mutually exclusive access by concurrent elements. Another problem is that data representations are different for heterogeneous processors. Data transformations will have to be provided at the application level, and will reduce the level of reusability that can be accomplished with message passing. In the latter case, data transformations can be implemented in a lower layer and made transparent to the application modules. The major advantage of using shared data is higher efficiency, if care is taken to avoid repeated copying of the data elements.

Regardless of the communication mechanism chosen, every effort must be made to minimize the amount of data transformation taking place. There should be no transformations made for data passed between homogeneous processors in a heterogeneous system.

A significant design issue is the choice (or combination) of point to point, broadcast, and multicast communication. This choice is dependent on the security of the system. The use of point to point connection will guarantee delivery of a message, but uses lots of resources and may be slow, since either a synchronized blocking mechanism or an acknowledgment scheme must be employed. Broadcast (or connectionless) communication does not guarantee delivery, but uses the least amount of resources. Multicast communication increases the complexity of the solution, since multiple destinations can be specified, but it may be a requirement of the system.

The most important piece in implementing reusable software structures is an efficient interprocess(or) communication (IPC) mechanism. The IPC is the important "glue" for reusable software components. For a more detailed discussion of distributed issues, see [NIE90 and NIE92].

13.2.5 Interprocess Communication (IPC) Mechanisms

To enhance the opportunity for reuse of software components, the communications considerations should include *interprocess* communication as well as *interprocessor* data exchanges. This will permit a looser module coupling, if any of the components are reconfigured to another processor in a system restart. This is illustrated in Figure 13-6, where the IPC mechanism is shown as an interface both within and between the processors.

To achieve transparency of the interprocess communication mechanism, the predominant design paradigm is to create the software modules in layers and to use standard protocols. The layering will provide a degree of information hiding where a complete layer can be replaced and only affect the layer above. It is highly recommended that only publicly available protocols be used

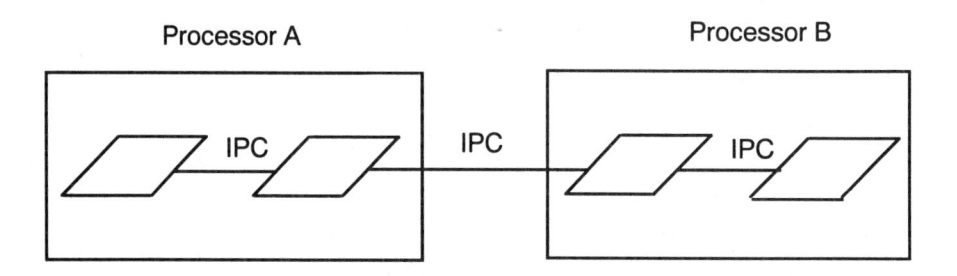

Figure 13-6. Interprocess(or) communication mechanism

to avoid becoming locked into certain vendors' implementations. These choices may, for example, include the Open System Interconnect (OSI) or Transmission Control Protocol/Internet Protocol (TCP/IP). An example of protocol layering is shown in Figure 13-7 for the OSI and a DoD protocol. If we choose the OSI model, the software modules will have specific interfaces between each layer, and the modules in each layer will only need to support the functionality of their respective layer. The OSI model implements all seven layers, whereas the DoD protocol only uses four of the seven.

The overall design objective of an IPC implementation is to insulate the application software from the details of the communication mechanism. This will provide for a portable solution, and will also allow improvements in the IPC implementation without affecting the design of the majority of the application modules. The most promising approach for achieving the design objective is to create layers of software services. The fewer layers the application software has to interface with, the less the impact on the application software when changes in the IPC mechanism are made.

IPC approaches with decreasing levels of coupling between the application modules and the IPC layers can be implemented as: (1) direct calls to low-level communication primitives and (2) message passing. Another choice is to use the remote procedure call (RPC) mechanism described in [SUN86, NIE92, and NIE90].

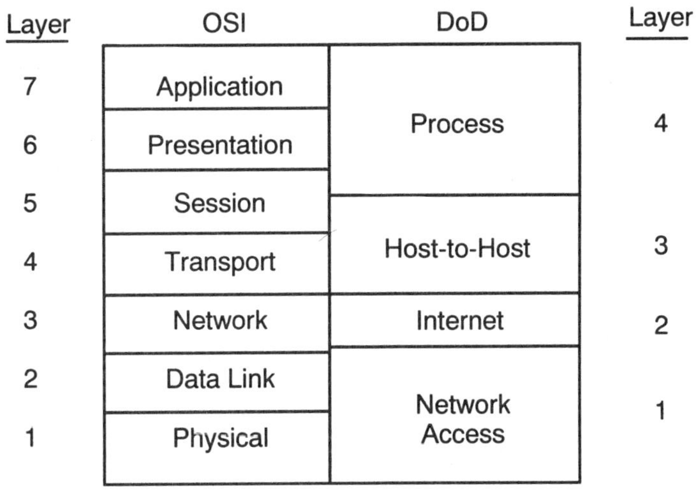

Layer	OSI	DoD	Layer
7	Application	Process	4
6	Presentation		
5	Session	Host-to-Host	3
4	Transport		
3	Network	Internet	2
2	Data Link	Network Access	1
1	Physical		

Figure 13-7. Protocol layering

The determination of a process structure and an IPC mechanism are extremely important design considerations, and should be performed before the primary OOD activity begins. If concerns for concurrency and message passing in a distributed architecture are postponed until after the OOD activity, major redesign may have to be performed.

13.3 OBJECT-ORIENTED DESIGN

The OOD activity is concerned with the creation of architectural components and their interfaces. The design of these interfaces may lead to additional classes and objects (i.e., in addition to the classes and objects transitioned from OOA entities), which are necessary to complete a software design that will meet performance and reliability requirements.

The high-level abstractions of OOA include object models and their interfaces, as shown in Figure 13-2. A major OT paradigm added during OOD is the proper use of inheritance and aggregation, as shown in Figure 13-3.

The primary effort of OOD is the creation of a class/object architecture that can be implemented during the OOP phase using the features of C++. Classes transitioned from the analysis phase are examined to make sure that the attributes and operations satisfy our design guidelines, e.g., that a full set of operations has been defined for each class. Visibility issues are settled during OOD, and the level of encapsulation and data hiding is determined. Each class is developed as an encapsulated object, as shown in Figure 13-8.

The software architecture includes the relations between the classes and is shown in the software module architecture diagram in Figure 13-9. The class icons shown in this figure can be annotated with the names of the class operations, but then the diagram gets more complex and harder to read.

13.4 OOD PRODUCTS

The primary product of the process structuring step is the process structure chart and a description of the processes and their interfaces. A description of the IPC mechanism should be included, with a rationale for the particular choice. IPC documentation should include any restrictions imposed, e.g., connectionless versus connection-oriented, message length, use of shared data, allocation of buffer space for message queuing, use of message identifications, etc.

OOD products include all the documentation related to the design structuring :

- refined object models
- inheritance and aggregation models
- module architecture diagram
- event trace diagrams for each scenario
- STDs at the object level
- descriptions of classes and objects
- CRC cards
- expanded data dictionary

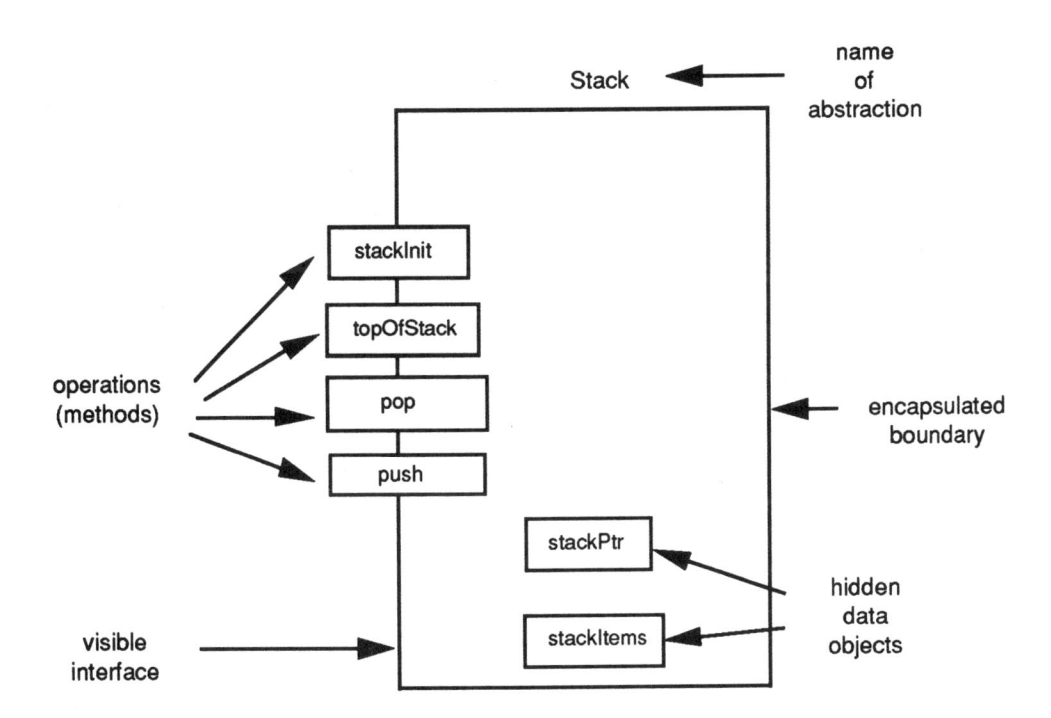

Figure 13-8. Encapsulated class object

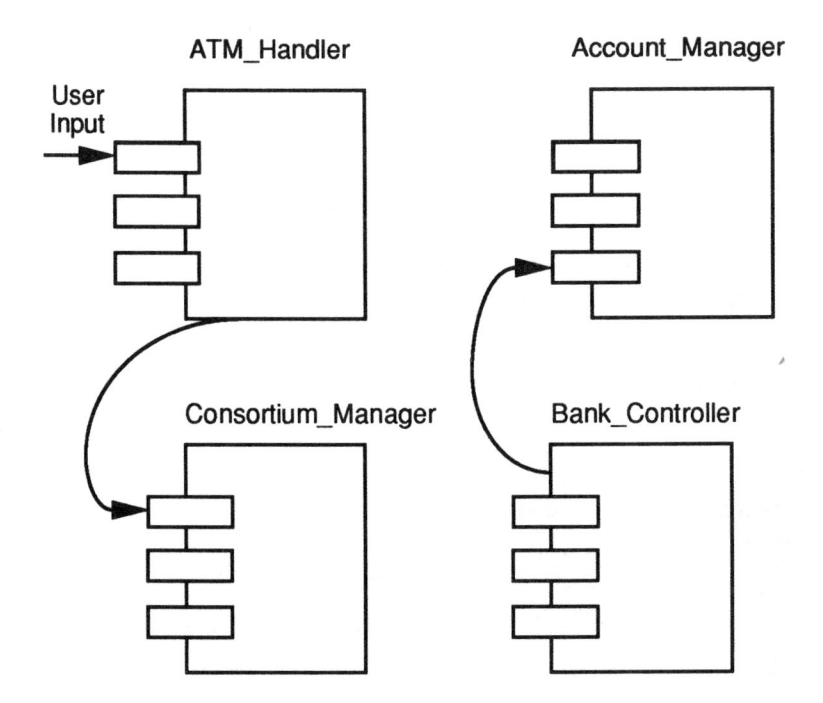

Figure 13-9. Module architecture diagram for ATM application

13.5 EXCEPTION HANDLING

Error handling can be included in the design with several different mechanisms:

- simply ignoring the error
- returning an error status
- setting a shared error variable
- using library routines (e.g., assert())
- creating user-defined error handling routines

Exception handling has a broader scope than error handling and is a major design element in the production of robust, reusable code that includes fault tolerance considerations.

13.5.1 Exception Handling Categories

The following exception handling categories are recommended as part of a general software fault tolerance mechanism:

1. **Anticipated Exceptional Conditions.** This category applies to exceptions that may result from a (rare) condition that should not terminate our program. For example, if we are assigning a sequential set of numbers as "handles," we may eventually get an overflow exception, depending upon how long a particular program is running. We can use an exception handler to re-initialize the set of handlers.

2. **Protection of Server Software.** Erroneous or inconsistent input data is detected in a software module that is called upon to perform a particular service. The server can't repair the input data and raises an exception that is returned to the caller. It is up to the caller to remedy the situation. An example in this category includes software that converts an ASCII string to its integer equivalent. An erroneous or inconsistent input string will cause an exception to be raised and returned to the caller for handling.

3. **Reporting of Hardware Failures.** Hardware devices are usually rated for an effective life of a certain number of hours measured as mean time between failures (MTBF). We would like to be able to detect when a device fails, and can raise an exception when a device does not respond within a given amount of (programming-dependent) time.

4. **Reporting of Unanticipated Errors (Bugs).** Bugs are common in delivered software products and should be detected and reported. Whereas exceptions for the three categories listed above will have explicit names, there is no name for an exception resulting from a bug other than "others" or "bug." This type of exception is always raised by the run-time system and should be captured as close as possible to the point at which it is raised.

13.5.2 Design Strategy

The general strategy for using exception handling is to design a protection mechanism as a part of the overall system. This is considered a defensive programming practice and supports fault tolerance. How far we want the system to continue to execute after an exception is detected, depends on the particular exception that is raised. In some cases we just report the detection in a log and continue execution. In other cases, we report the exception as a fault and quit execution.

One of the most important design issues is where an exception should be handled. A general guideline is that an exception should be handled as close to its detection as possible. In the case of protecting server software, however, the burden is usually placed on the client (caller), and the exception is passed back to the caller. This would be the case, as in our example above, where a client is calling a server to convert an ASCII string to the corresponding integer value. If the call is made with incorrect input data, there is nothing the server can do to fix up the wrong input, and the exception detecting the error is passed back to the caller. It is then up to the caller to decide whether the data can be corrected and resubmitted, or if execution should end.

The chosen exception handling mechanism determined during the design phase should match the features that are supported by the programming language. It is also important that the use of these features does not incur a substantial amount of run-time overhead. C++ does include such a mechanism, which is now available in several programming language implementations. The use of exceptions for C++ will be pursued further in Chapters 17 and 21.

13.6 DESIGN EVALUATION

Designs for reusable systems should not be made in isolation by a single person. Every system design intended for reuse should be evaluated, regardless of size. Even a class library design for a limited range of domain functionality should be subjected to a design evaluation.

The sections that follow provide an outline of a design evaluation strategy, and the rules that can be applied to perform the evaluation.

13.6.1 Design Reviews

Design reviews can come in two flavors: formal and informal. Formal design reviews are usually defined as a part of a customer interaction for the development of large systems. The completion of a successful formal design review may determine a payment of a portion of the customer contract and is thus extremely important.

A formal design review is attended by representatives of the customer and will usually include presentations using design materials. The purpose of this review is to convince a customer that our design can be implemented with the reliability and performance requirements specified. A single design review can be scheduled to cover all of the requirements. A more likely scenario is a sequence of smaller design reviews that will cover the requirements for a specific "build." Formal design reviews may last for several days, depending on the size of the requirements covered.

Informal design reviews should be held regularly and continuously throughout the design phase. This applies to all types of software developments, regardless of system size and whether or not a customer is involved. These reviews are held internally, without customer attendance. Design material is reviewed by peers and senior designers to make sure the design effort is heading in the right direction. An informal design review will typically last a few hours and is scheduled for weekly or bi-weekly meetings.

13.6.2 Process Structure

The following characteristics are evaluated to determine if the composition of processes has been properly accomplished:

1. **Number of Processes.** The use of multiple processes incurs a certain amount of overhead for each process in the system. The more processes introduced, the higher the overhead. The system should be scrutinized to determine if the number of processes representing the solution is acceptable, based on the associated run-time overhead.

2. **Process Interactions.** Process interactions are evaluated in terms of appropriate caller/called decisions and the passing of parameters.

3. **Cyclic Process Dependencies.** Any cyclic process dependencies must be carefully scrutinized. If this is in correspondence with the problem specification, and the solution is correct, the design will be acceptable. Otherwise, a redesign will have to be performed using the scheduling capabilities available with the run-time support.

4. **Polling.** If polling is associated with "busy wait" [GEH84], it is probably not acceptable in the design and will have to be redesigned.

5. **Shared Data and Mutual Exclusion.** If shared data is used, mutual exclusion must be incorporated into the design to preserve data integrity. Data shared between processes should preferably be protected by a monitor process.

13.6.3 Class Structure

A class should encapsulate a single abstraction and reflect a well-defined set of requirements. Class evaluations include how well a particular class fits in a hierarchy, and its set of operations and attributes:

1. **Class Category.** Each class should be a member of the classifications listed in Chapter 8. If it is not, the class is inappropriate or a new classification must be added.

2. **Encapsulation and Level of Abstraction.** Each class should encapsulate a single abstraction. If the level of abstraction is too high, the class must be decomposed into two or more smaller classes.

3. **Inheritance.** A class derived from a base class must satisfy the is-a relationship. If it doesn't, the class must be redesigned as an independent class, or with a has-a relationship, if appropriate.

4. **Aggregation.** If aggregation is used with the class, the component must satisfy the has-a (or whole-part) relationship.

5. **Operations.** The operations associated with a class must form a complete set for the encapsulated abstraction. Complementary operations should be added where appropriate, e.g., add/delete, paint/clear, etc.

6. **Attributes.** The chosen attributes must be data elements associated with instances of the class and must be directly related to the encapsulated abstraction. Large attributes, or attributes with only a loose coupling to the abstraction, may have to be redesigned as additional classes.

13.6.4 Class Interfaces

The interface of a class reflects the client view of that class, i.e., how a client can use the services of the class. This includes the available operations and the level of information hiding. A different view is whether or not the class can perform as a base class to derived classes. Class interface criteria include the following:

1. **Information Hiding.** The operations available to clients should be visible (will be implemented in C++ as *public*), and data elements should be hidden (will be implemented in C++ as *private*).

2. **Operations.** The operations can be evaluated in terms of the following categories:

    - *Manager Functions.* These member functions include management

of initialization, assignment, type conversion, and memory management. (C++ constructors and destructors are included in this category, but will be added during OOP.) Manager functions are usually visible to clients.
- *Implementor Functions.* Functions in this category manipulate the objects created from the class, and represent a portion of the "contract" interface for the class, and are thus visible to the clients.
- *Helping Functions.* Functions in this category perform auxiliary tasks needed by the other member functions. In their strict support role, they are usually hidden and not available to clients of the class.
- *Access Functions.* Since our designs are heavily based on encapsulation and information hiding, we create access functions to provide information about the hidden data members. These functions differ from Implementor Functions by merely peeking at the values, rather than changing them. This set of functions constitutes the other part of the contract interface to clients of the class.

2. **Base Class Features.** The design of a class should anticipate whether or not the class will be a base class for an inheritance hierarchy. The operations included should represent a set of common operations that can be used by derived classes that are specializations of the base class.

13.6.5 Use of Inheritance

The inheritance structure should not be deep, and there should not be a single root class from which all subclasses are derived. The is-a relation must be satisfied for all subclasses, and any use of a subclass that is really a part of an aggregation must be flagged. Parent classes should be stable, with a well-defined set of operations that can be either reused or overridden.

The class hierarchy should be shallow to prevent inordinate amounts of testing of the subclasses. If a change is made to a parent class of a deep hierarchy, significant regression testing will be required of all subclasses to uncover all adverse effects. The recommended maximum level of layers in a class hierarchy is three (at least for the first few projects using OOD/OOP). If the level is higher, the designer(s) should be made to explain the advantages of the deep structure.

If multiple inheritance is used, the designers must explain this design decision and defend its use over single inheritance. The use of multiple inheritance should be avoided for a first-time project. One recommendation is to only include this feature on the fourth object-oriented project attempted by a software development organization [RAC94]:

- The first project will be used to understand a limited set of object-oriented paradigms using a prototyping experiment.
- The second project will include the paradigms management wouldn't allow on the first project.
- The third project will include the "kitchen sink" of OT approaches used for a large development, and will totally overwhelm the developers.

The major problem with multiple inheritance is the close coupling between derived class structures and the amount of redesign and testing required when any of the parent classes are changed.

Significant efforts should be undertaken by members other than the design team to evaluate the inheritance hierarchies. A tendency among designers and programmers may be to skimp on the design effort and simply "reuse" a parent class to create a derived class during the coding phase, even if the inheritance relation is not appropriate.

13.6.6 Use of Exceptions

The proper use of exceptions should be evaluated in terms of the exception taxonomy listed in Section 13.5. The general usage of exception handling will typically be specified during top-level design, and evaluated during detailed design. The following uses are accepted:

1. **Anticipated Exceptional Conditions.** Applies to (rare) conditions that are expected to occur during the normal execution of the program.
2. **Protection of Server Software.** Exceptions are raised to protect general purpose software from misuse.
3. **Reporting of Hardware Failures.** Exceptions are used to implement a fault tolerant system that includes hardware failures.
4. **Reporting of Unanticipated Errors (Bugs).** Exceptions in this category are used to detect and report bugs.

The evaluators should make sure that exceptions have not been used for program control, and that unnecessary exceptions have been eliminated. In general, an exception should be handled as close as possible to the point where it is raised.

13.7 SUMMARY

An initial set of design entities is obtained by transitioning OOA abstractions to OOD elements. This initial set represents the problem domain requirements. Additional classes and objects are obtained by determining the classes and objects that are necessary for completing a software architecture which can be implemented with the specified performance and reliability requirements.

A process structure that models a set of concurrent elements is created for real-time systems. Process selection rules are used to determine a set of processes with minimum run-time overhead. An IPC mechanism is determined early in the design phase for distributed systems.

Inheritance and aggregation relations are added to the OOA object model during OOD.

Encapsulated class objects are created for each major abstraction. Class interfaces include attributes and operations.

An exception handling strategy is incorporated into the overall design and is based on a classification of exceptions.

A set of design evaluation criteria is specified and can be used during informal design reviews and in preparation for formal design reviews.

14

Implementation

The implementation phase is the last step in the development process. The software architecture derived from a set of software requirements is created by using the features of the chosen programming language. An implementation can be for an entire application, but is usually performed in an incremental fashion for a "build" that corresponds to a well-defined portion of the requirements.

The implementation includes the programming activity, aided by a testing strategy for discovering bugs. One of the important tools of this phase is a symbolic debugger that can be tailored for a given test script with breakpoints to examine a stationary slice of the running program.

14.1 TRANSITIONING FROM DESIGN

The design entities created during OOD will now be implemented using C++ constructs. Design decisions made in the design phase will be implemented directly using appropriate constructs or by making use of available language features. Transitioning from design entities to programming entities includes:

- classes   =>   C++ classes
- operations   =>   member functions
- attributes   =>   data members
- Information hiding   =>   *private* and *protected* segments in the class interface

- relaxation of data hiding => using *friend* construct
- inheritance hierarchy => using inheritance constructs
- aggregation => declaring data members as objects of other classes
- modularity => separate header and source files
- exception handling => C++ exception constructs or *assert ()*

The transitioning step will provide the initial set of elements to be programmed. The need for additional programming entities is usually discovered during the programming activity, and an iteration will then take place between design and implementation.

14.2 PROGRAMMING

The programming activity includes the implementation of classes, objects, and a hierarchical software structure for maximum reuse.

C++ supports OOP with constructs for the implementation of inheritance and run-time support for polymorphism. Since C++ has been derived from C as a superset, a hybrid strategy is employed with a mix of procedural, modular, and object-oriented programming.

The classes transitioned from design objects are implemented as abstract data types, encapsulated as C++ classes. The level of information hiding was determined during the design phase and is implemented with *public, protected,* and *private* program segments.

Some of the ADTs, e.g., queues and stacks, are implemented using templates to maximize code reuse for data structures that only differ by type.

The inheritance hierarchies are implemented directly using the C++ OOP features, i.e., constructs for the creation of base classes and derived classes.

Aggregation relationships are implemented by declaring C++ data members as objects of classes that are components in a has-a (or whole-part) hierarchy.

The member functions associated with the transitioned design entities must be scrutinized for completeness. The creation of constructors and destructors, for example, is a programming activity and will be performed during this phase.

Modular programming is employed to provide reuse and ease of maintenance. A file structure must be prepared to minimize compilation during development, as well as when the inevitable requirements changes are specified. This is usually performed in C++ with the use of header files for the specification of interfaces, i.e., what is visible to a client. C++ source code is placed in different files. This separation of specification from implementation supports an incremental compilation strategy. If the interfaces do not change, the client software does not have to be recompiled.

The details of C++ programming will be covered in Part V; we are only providing an outline of the programming step here, as the last phase in the overall software development process.

14.3 EXCEPTION HANDLING

The detection and reporting of exceptional run-time events is an important implementation issue, and may have an effect on run-time performance. The design strategy for fault tolerance was determined during the design phase. The implementation of the design can be performed by the following methods:

- using the C *assert()* function
- using the built-in C++ exception handling
- mixing the two methods

The primary purpose of including an exception handling mechanism is to provide robust code that includes a level of fault detection and reporting. The built-in C++ exception handling is now available with major development systems. Its use will cost us some run-time overhead, but that is not unreasonable, since letting an exceptional condition propagate unchecked, will probably result in a fatal error anyway.

Programming with the C++ exception handling constructs is demonstrated in Chapter 21.

14.4 TESTING

The test effort is determined by the scenario that is being implemented. The tread analysis is used to write test scripts, including input stimuli and expected results. The tests performed will only cover a portion of the total number of possible paths through all the software modules. It is simply not feasible to check all of the millions of paths that may be exercised in a large program.

Test scripts should be prepared for all of the expected user interfaces with the system. It is important to test individual classes (component testing) before they are used in an application program (integration testing). By testing the individual classes first, we can reduce the overall testing time by isolating errors to the remaining software modules.

Even though software testing is performed during the programming activity, it should be planned during the design activity. Test scripts can actually be written as soon as scenarios have been developed, i.e., during the analysis phase.

The exception handling mechanism determined during the design phase can be used as part of the testing effort. Handlers to control the raising of unknown exceptions (bugs) can be placed in every new function that is being tested. These handlers can be removed before the application software is shipped to the customer. Leaving them in the code will cause overhead in the number of machine instructions and probably some run-time overhead.

There is no magic formula for when and how much testing should be performed. The old adage that testing only proves that bugs exist, but does not eliminate them all still exists. Software testing should be started early and performed on all new code.

Imported class libraries must be tested thoroughly with the application software at least once, unless the libraries have been developed in-house with a rigorous testing activity that has been documented. Vendor class libraries must be tested carefully to ensure that all of our design paradigms can be implemented. This is especially true for library structures that include inheritance [JAC92, p. 82, and PER90]. A member function at a lower level in the hierarchy may behave differently than the same function in a base class. Testing member functions only in a base class may not uncover unexpected conditions related to polymorphism.

14.5 DEBUGGING

The activity of debugging has been described as a process of directing a programmer's attention to an error so it can be fixed [CLA93]. A debugger is usually a tool that can assist us in the debugging process by allowing us to examine a stationary slice of the running program.

The debugging effort is thus a sequence of steps including testing, inspection, fixing the code segment that contains the bug, and retesting (after recompilation and relinking). The debugging phase is done during the testing effort and is necessary to uncover as many software errors (bugs) as possible.

The use of debuggers is nothing new to C programmers, but C++ programs provide a special challenge with many of the new language features that are difficult to discern during run-time. Examples of these complications include function overloading and name mangling, creation of objects by constructors in inheritance and aggregation hierarchies, and temporary values and objects associated with abstract data types.

A successful implementation of complex C++ programs is highly dependent on a good debugger to help untangle the subtleties inherent in an object-oriented program. Good debuggers are now available for several of the major C++ development systems, such as Microsoft Visual C++, Borland C++, and SunPro WorkShop.

14.6 SUMMARY

The first step in the implementation phase is to transition design entities such as class, operations, and attributes into the equivalent C++ programming entities of classes, member functions, and data members. Additional, required programming entities are usually discovered during the programming step, and are added to the design entities.

Inheritance hierarchies are implemented in C++ using the appropriate constructs. Aggregation hierarchies are implemented by declaring data members as objects of the classes in the has-a relationship.

Modularity is implemented by separating class specifications and implementations into header files and source files, respectively. This is accomplished in C++ by convention, rather than by a compiler requirement.

Testing is based on the scenarios developed for a particular "build" or prototype being implemented. Imported class libraries must be tested carefully. This is especially important for inheritance hierarchies.

Debugging tools are required as an aid during testing to manage the additional complexity of hierarchical levels and the creation of objects by several constructors. Other complexities include name mangling of overloaded member functions and determining which object is referenced via polymorphism.

P A R T   IV

Object-Oriented Design for C++

C++ has established itself as a major force for the implementation of a wide array of different application domains. Complete software development systems are available for workstations running Unix, Macintoshes, PCs running DOS and Windows, and mainframes. C++ is a fully object-oriented programming language and is well suited for implementations of object-oriented designs.

The design phase is based on the products created during the analysis phase. During the transitioning step, we use a set of rules to transfer the analysis products to design entities. This step is largely language independent. The models of abstract classes and objects created during the analysis phase are reused as design models, but now with a view towards implementation; analysis products are used to document system requirements.

Since C++ is an object-oriented programming language, the transitioned classes and objects will be implemented during the OOP phase with C++ language constructs. Most of the design phase is concerned with the creation of the required set of classes and their interfaces. The classes and objects transitioned from analysis products will reflect design entities for the system requirements. These design entities will not be sufficient for a complete design, however; and additional classes will be required to support an architecture that can be implemented using C++.

Many application domains exhibit natural concurrency and will benefit from an implementation that employs a tasking structure. The design is simplified, and a concurrent model can be more efficient than a sequential implementation. This step is referred to as process structuring and includes the selection of concurrent elements, and the determination of an interprocess communication (IPC) mechanism.

15

Why Use C++?

C++ is emerging as the major programming language of choice for implementing object-oriented features for a wide variety of applications. These applications include science and engineering, industrial and manufacturing, business, and robotics systems. Other programming languages used for these same applications are C and Ada. The only other object-oriented programming language considered a rival for C++ is Smalltalk. Its use tends to be focused on simulation and artificial intelligence applications and is of less interest here.

The objective of this chapter is to first give a brief overview of some of the popular programming languages that support object-oriented features, and their level of object-orientedness. We will then discuss the benefits and potential problems with using C++. A discussion of reusability issues will focus on the reuse that can be realized by using C++.

15.1 OBJECT-ORIENTED LANGUAGES

Programming languages that are considered "object-oriented" include C++, Eiffel, Lisp, Prolog, Simula, and Smalltalk. By object-oriented, we mean that these programming languages have constructs that provide direct *support* for object-oriented features. Other programming languages, e.g., Ada and C, may *enable* us to implement some object-oriented features by using certain programming techniques, but they are not considered object-oriented [STR91, p. 14].

The primary programming languages currently used for real-time systems are C and Ada. Ada was designed specifically for the implementation of real-time systems. Although Ada may not satisfy all the major properties of an object-oriented programming language (e.g., inheritance and dynamic binding), it does supports an object-oriented design approach and is usually referred to as an "object-based" language [WEG87].

15.1.1 Object-Orientedness

A taxonomy of degrees of object-orientedness for programming languages has been created by Wegner [WEG87, pp. 508-10]. The classifications include object-based, class-based, and fully object-oriented:

1. **Object-Based.** A programming language is object-based if its syntax and semantics support the creation of objects having the properties described in Chapter 5.
2. **Class-Based.** If a programming language is object-based and, in addition, supports the creation of classes, it is considered class-based, with the definition of classes as described in Chapter 5.
3. **Object-Oriented.** A fully object-oriented programming language is a class-based language that also supports inheritance. This is implemented by deriving subclasses from one (single inheritance) or more (multiple inheritance) superclasses.

This taxonomy of object-orientedness provides a strict definition for those object-oriented programming languages. It is thus not sufficient for an object-oriented programming language to support the creation of objects; constructs must be available for the creation of classes with support for inheritance as a class property.

The taxonomy of object-orientedness is illustrated graphically in Figure 15-1. C++ supports the construction of objects and classes with inheritance and is fully object-oriented. Ada, on the other hand, supports the creation of objects as abstract data types using packages and is thus object-based. An Ada package is not a type definition like the C++ class, and Ada is thus neither class-based nor object-oriented, but only object-based. (Reasons for selecting Ada on large systems have recently been reported in IEEE's *Computer* [STE94, p. 49].)

15.1.2 Desired Programming Language Features

Aside from the obvious desired feature of being object-oriented, other programming language features are also important for the implementation of the kind of applications we are considering in this book. These additional features include:

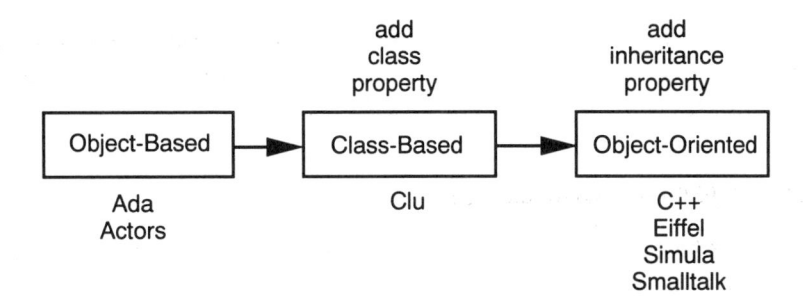

```
                    add                    add
                   class                inheritance
                 property                 property
 ┌──────────────┐        ┌──────────────┐        ┌──────────────┐
 │ Object-Based │───────▶│ Class-Based  │───────▶│Object-Oriented│
 └──────────────┘        └──────────────┘        └──────────────┘
       Ada                    Clu                      C++
     Actors                                           Eiffel
                                                     Simula
                                                    Smalltalk
```

Figure 15-1. Object-orientedness of programming languages

1. **Strong Typing.** This property greatly supports the software development effort. Programming errors related to the number of parameters, parameter types, and module interfaces are detected during the design and implementation phases, rather than at run-time.
2. **Encapsulation.** It is highly desirable that the language support information hiding with separate specification and implementation parts. This can provide a loosely coupled design that is easily tailored for different hardware architectures. Encapsulation is usually a guaranteed feature of object-oriented languages.
3. **Incremental Compilation.** This is a great benefit in the development of large systems where portions of the system are created and implemented in a piecemeal fashion. This also complements the strong typing feature with support of separate specification and implementation parts.
4. **Genericity.** Parameter-typed templates for classes and operations support a high degree of reusability. The generic elements are prestored templates with formal parameters that are instantiated with actual parameters to create instances of modules to be compiled, and later linked and executed.
5. **Message Passing.** It is highly desirable that the language support bidirectional message passing between modules. This provides for loosely coupled modules and flexible designs. It is also desirable to be able to pass signals between modules, without actually passing any data elements.
6. **Shared Data.** It is desirable that modules be able to communicate via shared memory, in addition to message passing. This is important in

allowing multiple objects from the same class to interface with common data elements. This may also be required in those systems where message passing is deemed to be too inefficient.

7. **Polymorphism.** It is highly desirable that program elements be allowed to refer to an object name that may belong to different classes that are derived from a superclass. Operations can be used to manipulate objects of different types at execution time without reprogramming these methods. Polymorphism is usually implemented in tandem with inheritance.

8. **Exception Handling.** It is highly desirable that exceptional conditions be detected, reported, and handled using language constructs. This can greatly add to the support of software fault tolerance as a general design strategy that can be implemented efficiently.

9. **Concurrency.** The applications we are targeting with our OT approach include real-time systems, and it is desirable that the language support the creation of operating system independent processes. This can simplify the porting of a real-time system from one platform to another. Desired run-time support includes capabilities for process management, such as activation, scheduling, queuing, prioritization, preemption, and termination. It also includes features for process synchronization and communication.

Currently available programming languages do not satisfy all of the desired features listed above. In general, the object-oriented languages do not have concurrency features, and real-time languages such as Ada, are not object-oriented. C++ is classified as object-oriented, but does not have concurrency features built into the language constructs. To build concurrent elements with C++ requires an interface to an executive that can handle the required tasking control and coordination functions.

15.2 BENEFITS OF C++

Object-oriented programming implies that we are using a programming language that supports OT paradigms with language constructs. C++ does support all of the OT paradigms outlined in Part II. It also supports all of the desired programming features outlined above, except concurrency.

If we are to take advantage of the C++ features, development systems must be available, including linkers, browsers, debuggers, and efficient run-time systems. Several excellent C++ development systems are available for PCs, Macintoshes, and Unix workstations to make the development of large systems a reality.

C++ is a superset of C and provides a natural progression from a procedural to an object-oriented programming language. This lowers the learning curve compared to, for example, going from C to Smalltalk. All of the C++ syntax that does not deal with object-oriented features are inherited from ANSI Standard C. C programmers can thus focus on the new features and their semantics, and migrate to full C++ at a comfortable pace.

C++ is strongly typed, and the compiler checks for the correct use of function parameter types and the number of parameters. Separate declaration files (header files) for interface definitions and implementation files (source files) can be used for the development. The compiler checks for consistent function invocations between the corresponding files.

The C++ class construct and overloaded operators support the construction of concrete data types [COP92, p. 37]. These are user-defined types that can be used exactly as built-in types such as *int* and *float*. Instances (objects) are created from a class type, and operators such as "+" and "[ ]" can be used with these objects, i.e., there is a uniform style for all of the types used within a program.

C++ is linkage compatible with C and other languages, e.g., Fortran. This linkage is accomplished via a mechanism that is specified in the reference manual [ELL90, p. 116]. C++ is especially beneficial to applications that use GUIs that are written in C, e.g., MS Windows and the X Window System. The interface functions can be called directly from a C++ application, or some or all of the GUI functionality can be encapsulated in C++ class libraries (see Chapter 22 for examples).

The linkage mechanism to C provides support for an incremental development strategy where all new code and selected legacy code for a given application is written in C++. The program links the new code with the remaining legacy code in C to create the new application. Additional C legacy code can be rewritten for each increment of new C++ update code until the entire application has been transferred to C++.

15.3 POTENTIAL PROBLEMS WITH C++

Novice designers and programmers using C++ on their first project may attempt to use the object-oriented features with only a limited understanding of their implications. This may result in intricate and convoluted structures that will be difficult to test and debug.

The implementation of object-oriented programming features requires elaborate development facilities for compilation, linking, and debugging. This is partially due to the implementation of inheritance and function overloading. Lack of browsers and symbolic debuggers on a particular development platform can significantly increase the testing and debugging effort compared to development systems that are used with traditional techniques.

A significant training effort should be expected for educating the development staff in OT paradigms and C++ programming. Moving a development effort from another programming language, even C, to C++ requires a well planned strategy and a definite commitment from management.

Applications reusing existing C code and libraries are likely to have mixed programming styles and paradigms: a fairly cryptic C style for the procedural oriented portions, and a more readable C++ style for the object-oriented parts. Maintaining these applications could be more difficult than either straight C or C++ applications.

15.4 SUMMARY

C++ is a fully object-oriented programming language compatible with C. Classes and objects created as design entities can be implemented directly, using C++ language constructs. C++ code can be linked with existing C code for maximum reuse of an application's legacy code and existing C libraries. C++ development systems are available for all the major development platforms in current use.

Potential problems with using C++ include a significant training effort, convoluted designs by novices trying to implement multiple inheritance, and lengthy debugging sessions.

16

Transitioning from Analysis to Design

The objective of this chapter is to describe how we move from the OOA phase to the OOD phase. A number of OOA products used in modeling classes, objects, and their interfaces can be reused in the OOD phase with some guidelines for an orderly transition. We start this chapter with an outline of our overall design goals.

16.1 DESIGN GOALS

As we transition from analysis to design, it is important to keep in mind the overall design goals we would like to achieve:

1. **Reusability.** The OOA products we created during the analysis phase can, hopefully, be used in the design phase to reduce the development time. This applies, in particular, to the various modeling views used to describe classes and objects and their interfaces.

2. **Portability.** We expect to field our software products on multiple platforms, e.g., Pentium, PowerPC, Alpha, and RISC-based machines. This is also important for evolving operating systems, e.g., Windows 3.1, Windows 4.x, and Windows NT. How we design the class interfaces and what type of information we hide may have a profound impact on the portability of the final product.

3. **Full Functionality.** The design should include all the functionality expected for the delivered product. Add-on functionality may result in a patchwork development approach and a configuration nightmare.

4. **Maintenance.** It has often been said that a software system is obsolete the day it is fielded, and application upgrades have become a normal part of software development. The design should anticipate a number of expected upgrades and provide for ease of extending the features of the product.

5. **Exception Handling.** A strategy for creating a uniform exception handling mechanism should be specified as part of the design approach. Such a mechanism is specified for C++ [ELL90, p. 353] and should be used whenever the compiler and run-time system implement this feature.

These design goals are general and apply to most applications we will be designing and implementing. More specific design goals may be required, e.g., for class interfaces if we are designing a class library.

16.2 OOA PRODUCTS

The products created during the analysis include:

- classes and objects
- object models
- attributes associated with classes
- operations associated with classes
- state transition diagrams (STDs)
- event trace diagrams
- event flow diagram
- scenarios
- data dictionary
- requirements trace

Many of these OOA products can be transitioned and reused in the structuring of the architectural design to support the various OOD modeling views.

16.3 OOD MODELING VIEWS

The modeling views used to create the complete design include:

- object model
- module architecture model
- STDs
- process structure chart
- hardware architecture diagram

The transitioning from analysis entities to design entities is far from intuitive, and the more rules we can specify, the easier the transition becomes.

16.4 TRANSITIONING RULES

Here is a list of rules that will support an orderly transition from the OOA to the initial OOD phase:

1. **Abstract Analysis Classes.** The abstract classes we created during the domain analysis and/or during the requirements analysis phase are made into C++ classes.
2. **Operations.** The operations identified with the abstract classes are made into member functions for the corresponding C++ classes.
3. **Attributes.** The attributes associated with the abstract classes are made into data members for the corresponding C++ classes.
4. **Class Hierarchies.** The decomposition hierarchies used for the abstract classes are transitioned to C++ classes using inheritance and aggregation relations.
5. **Class Relations.** "Using" relations are created by referencing other objects from within the class that needs the objects.
6. **STDs.** Transfer each STD to a corresponding C++ base "state" class, with a derived class for each state [FAI93]. An STD for three states X, Y, and Z and two events E1 and E2 is shown in Figure 16-1. The corresponding C++ class hierarchy is shown in Figure 16-2.
7. **Scenarios and entity Objects.** Abstract objects within a given scenario are transferred as entity objects.

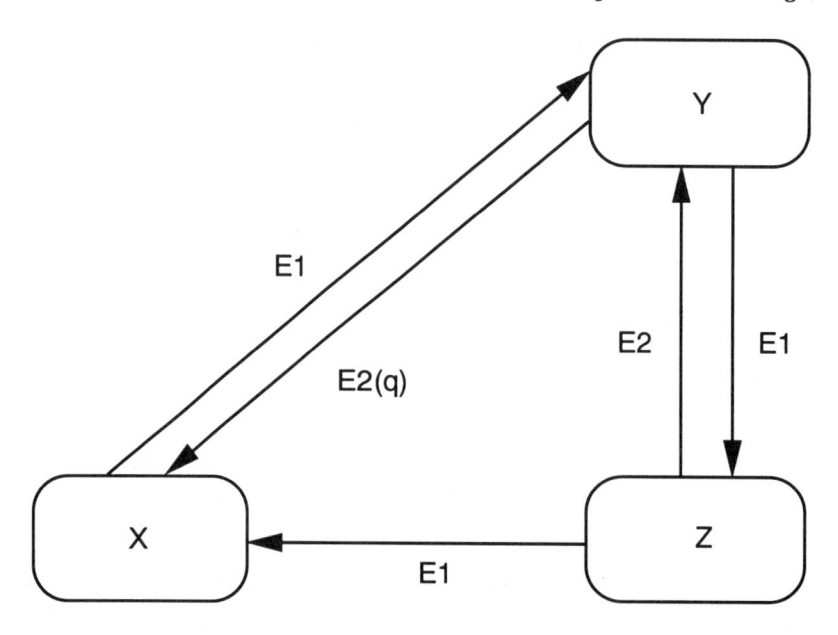

Figure 16-1. State transition diagram

8. **Object Flow Model.** Transfer each object in the object flow model to a potential subsystem (independent of C++). This can be the starting point for system design.
9. **Event Trace Diagram.** Transfer events to messages passed between objects (perhaps subsystems).

A careful analysis should be made of the transferred attributes to make sure they are, indeed, suitable data members. The attributes defined during the analysis phase are sometimes coarse grained, and can be further decomposed into additional member functions and data members.

This list is by no means exhaustive and is intended as a "living" document. Additional rules can be added as a result of "lessons learned" as the project staff gains experience with this step.

The transitioning between analysis and design will only provide some of the required design entities; primarily those associated with the system requirements. A large part of the design phase will be spent on discovering additional classes required for implementing the system, and on determining the proper interfaces between the classes.

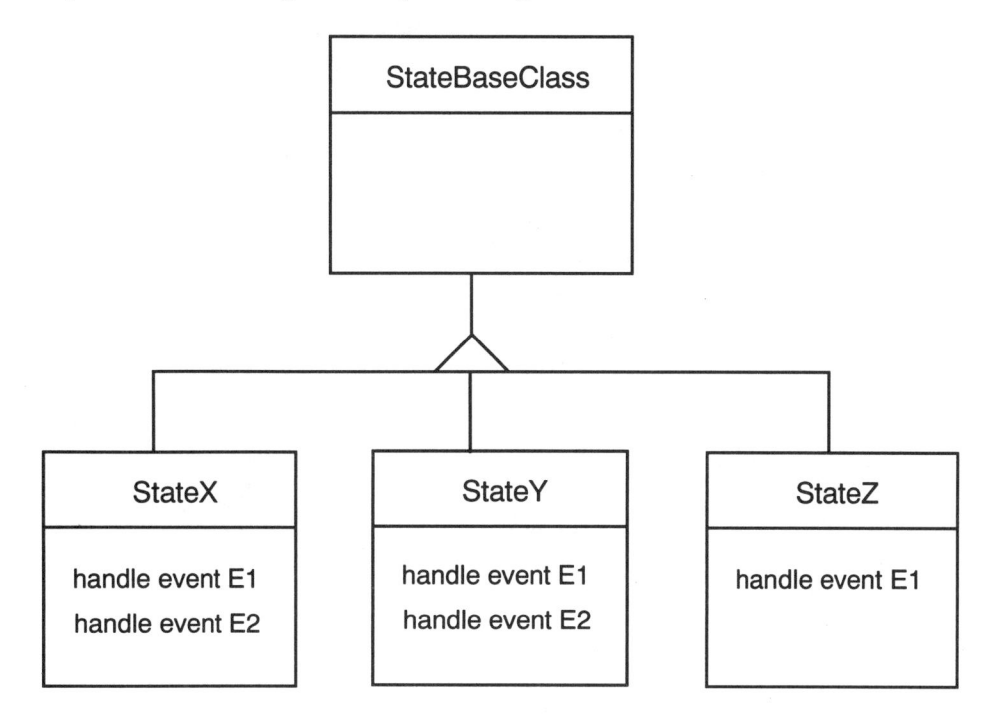

```
                    ┌─────────────────┐
                    │  StateBaseClass │
                    │                 │
                    └─────────────────┘
                             △
            ┌────────────────┼────────────────┐
   ┌─────────────┐   ┌─────────────────┐  ┌─────────────┐
   │   StateX    │   │     StateY      │  │   StateZ    │
   │handle event E1│ │handle event E1  │  │handle event E1│
   │handle event E2│ │handle event E2  │  │             │
   └─────────────┘   └─────────────────┘  └─────────────┘
```

Figure 16-2. Class design for STD

16.5 REUSABILITY ISSUES

An abstract class and object model can be reused to create the equivalent design model. Scenarios developed during the analysis phase are used to identify interface and control objects, in addition to the entity objects that are transitioned directly.

Hierarchical decompositions developed during the analysis phase are reused directly and designed with C++ inheritance and aggregation structures. Inheritance is supported by C++ constructs, whereas aggregation is accomplished by having data members of other classes as the components.

The requirements trace started during the analysis phase is expanded in the design phase to include C++ class names for the corresponding system requirement. The data dictionary is also expanded as new classes are developed during the design phase.

17

Designing Classes

Most of the design work associated with systems to be implemented with a procedural language such as C is primarily concerned with the creation of data structures and corresponding operations. Designing for C++ implementations is primarily concerned with the creation of classes. Most of these classes will represent an encapsulation of a key abstraction that can be traced back to the user requirements. Other classes needed to implement a system are created to provide clean interfaces (i.e., loose coupling) between software modules or for controlling concurrent elements.

The activity of designing C++ programs that involves classes can be viewed from two different perspectives [HEI94]: (1) class users; and (2) class providers. Design decisions will differ for these two notions. As a class user, we focus on the interface and whether to incorporate the class as a component, a base class, or with a using relation. As a class provider, we have to anticipate how the class will be used and provide the necessary interface and level of data hiding.

One of the most important object-oriented features of C++ as a programming language is the direct support of classes and class instances, i.e., objects. This feature provides a great opportunity for developing reusable and extendible software for a wide variety of applications.

The primary objective of this chapter is to discuss design decisions that affect the creation of proper classes. By "proper" in this context, we mean efficient, easy to understand, easy to use, at the right level of abstraction, and highly reusable.

17.1 CLASS DESIGN

The users of a particular C++ class can be considered to be two different clients [BOO93, p. 333]: (1) clients that declare instances of a class and manipulate those instances within their program; and (2) clients that use a base class to derive subclasses.

Design decisions regarding class interfaces will differ depending upon the type of clients that will be using the class. Class interfaces for the first type can be made with complete data hiding. For the second type, the data hiding must be relaxed, and careful considerations must be made regarding which member functions should be allowed to be redefined (overridden) in the derived classes. The C++ aspects of these considerations are discussed in Chapter 20.

After the analysis work has been completed to establish the need for a set of classes or class libraries to support a particular application, or a set of applications, the classes have to be designed. The construction of classes requires a significant amount of design work before the classes are actually coded. This includes a determination of whether to design the classes from scratch or buy a class library from an outside vendor. A design evaluation of the potential products will then become a part of the design effort.

The activities of class design include a buy/develop decision, the determination of a proper class hierarchy, the user interfaces to be provided in a client/server relationship, and the level of information hiding

17.1.1 Design Decisions

Initial design decisions include whether we are to design individual classes or a collection of classes to provide a class library. Here are some guidelines for making the initial design decisions about a class library:

1. **Reusable Functionality.** Determine the various areas of reusable functionality for the current application and for expected future, similar applications. The abstract real-world classes and objects identified in the domain analysis can be used as a starting point here. A refinement of the abstractions will reveal finer-grained classes and objects that can serve as the discriminators for the class boundaries.

2. **Foundation Classes.** Determine the need and desirability for foundation classes. These are high-level classes that can support a wide variety of applications. Many of the C++ compiler vendors supply a set of these,

e.g., the Microsoft Foundation Classes (MFC) from Microsoft and Symantec, and the ObjectWindows Library (OWL) from Borland can be used for PC Windows applications implemented with C++. If a set of foundation classes already exists, it is important to identify its structure and ascertain that the structure is satisfactory for the application(s) being considered. A hierarchy based purely on inheritance, for example, may not be acceptable if the application classes require a mixture of inheritance and composition.

3. **Buy versus Develop.** Aside from the C++ foundation classes mentioned above, a number of vendors offer C++ class libraries. Examples of these include libraries for string and character manipulation, B-tree operations for keyed access of disk records, tasking libraries for real-time systems, and mathematical functions.

If we are developing individual classes as part of a class library, or independent classes for a given application, the focus is on providing the proper interfaces and class structure:

1. **User Interfaces.** The level of abstraction and the class operations provided must be carefully determined. Each class interface will hide the underlying implementation details, and will thus correspond to a certain level of abstraction. If this level is too high, the implementers may have to develop a number of new classes, and may ignore the classes intended for reuse. If the level is too low, the implementers may decide to add higher-level classes, most likely with added overall complexity. An example of reducing the level of encapsulation is the use of *friend* classes and functions to allow external classes and functions access to hidden data.

2. **General Structure.** The overall class structure must be carefully thought out. It may be tempting to simply create a multi-level hierarchy anticipating the support of C++'s built-in inheritance mechanism. Large software systems employing object-oriented features are created using both inheritance and composition, and the latter paradigm must be accounted for in the reusable classes provided.

The design of classes is the single most important activity during the last part of the OOD phase. This is sometimes referred to as detailed design, and takes place after the transitioning of analysis entities to design entities.

17.1.2 Class Construction

After we have made the decision to create a set of classes in-house (rather than buying from an outside vendor), the classes and class libraries have to be constructed. Here are some guidelines for the steps required in the construction of classes:

1. **Create an Interface.** This involves the creation of a shell which includes a set of operations (C++ member functions) that provide access to the domain specific data abstractions (C++ data members).

2. **Shield Users from Implementation Details.** The level of access must provide the right mix of information hiding and access to the required data abstractions. Choices include completely hidden (private), visibility to derived classes (protected), completely visible (public), and special visibility privileges (friend).

3. **Maximize Reuse.** Include a complete set of operations for the domain application. Also, anticipate the use of the class by other applications by including a complete set of operations for the class. For example, if Add is a required function, include the complement function Subtract or Delete.

4. **Abstract Away Entire Program Concepts.** Attempt to replace commonly used programming concepts by including corresponding operations in the class interface. An example of such a common programming concept is the message loop used by Windows programmers to get the next message (event), translate the message, and dispatch the translated message for execution. This can be abstracted by a single C++ member function MessageLoop() [POR93, p. 85].

5. **Use Meaningful Names for Abstractions.** The operations created in the visible interface should have names that the users can readily identify. For the example above, every Windows programmer will associate the name MessageLoop with the message loop programming concept.

6. **Provide Adequate Documentation.** To make the classes easy to use, the abstractions included in the interface must be well documented.

7. **Think about Efficiency.** The creation of a class hierarchy produces an additional programming layer that is implemented with multiple calls at run-time. There should be no significant additional run-time overhead associated with the extra calls. (See the discussion of performance issues in Chapter 19.)

Stroustrup [STR91, p. 153] summarizes a "good" class as a class with a small and well-defined set of operations. A class can be considered a "black box" whose objects and data abstractions can only be manipulated via the operations.

After having decided on the set of steps to be used in the construction of the classes, we focus on what to provide for the class interfaces.

17.2 CLASS INTERFACES

Every class we construct will consist of two types of interfaces: one for the users of the class, and one for the implementation. The design decisions to be made for these interfaces and how they are documented depend on their intended purpose. A class that is a pure server without any hierarchy only needs to provide documentation for the visible user interface. A class designed for inheritance, however, must include documentation for the implementation (this will be made clear in Chapter 19).

The class interface refers to the visibility of operations (C++ member functions) associated with instances of the class and the level of data hiding provided for attributes of the class (C++ data members).

The classes we obtained from the transitioning phase (see Chapter 16) are now scrutinized to provide the final design. The member functions created from the operations associated with the abstract classes are usually not sufficient for complete C++ classes. The existing functions are divided into functional groups, and additional member functions are added to complete the design. The recommended functional groups are [LIP91, p. 223]:

1. **Manager Functions.** These member functions include management of initialization, assignment, type conversion, and memory management. Constructors and destructors are included in this category.

2. **Implementor Functions.** Functions in this category manipulate the objects created from the class, and represent a portion of the "contract" interface for the class.

3. **Helping Functions.** Functions in this category perform auxiliary tasks needed by the other member functions. In their strict support role, they are usually hidden and not available to clients of the class.

4. **Access Functions.** Since our designs are heavily based on encapsulation and information hiding, we create access functions to provide information about the hidden data members. This set of functions constitutes the other part of the contract interface to clients of the class.

An example of a C++ skeleton class interface that encapsulates an abstraction for sending and receiving messages in a communication system is the following:

```
struct date {
  int month;
  int day;
  int year;
};

class Message {
public:
  void Message (...); // constructor
  void ~Message (); // destructor
  void Send (...); // send message
  void Retrieve (...); // retrieve message
  void Delete (...); // delete message from buffer
  ...
private:
  date* timeTag; // time tag
  char* source;  // sender
  char* dest;    // receiver
  char* text;    // message text
};
```

The encapsulation of the Message abstraction includes private (hidden) data members required for each object, and a public interface for the member functions that can operate on Message objects.

To maximize the potential for reusability, the set of operations proposed for the class should be scrutinized in terms of the four groups of operations listed previously in this section. The Message class includes manager, implementor, and access functions. Additional member functions could be RetrieveNext, RetrieveAll, RetrieveHiPriority, etc.

An analysis of the member functions is highly recommended, and should include design reviews to ensure a complete design and a suitable class interface for potential derived types. Design guidelines for creating C++ class interfaces will be presented in Chapter 20.

17.3 CLASS ARCHITECTURE

The class architecture refers to the design of class relationships, such as aggregation, inheritance, and using. The class designer is faced with difficult decisions of how to choose among these relationships.

A system built with deep hierarchical inheritance layers has a straightforward structure, but may become a nightmare to debug because of the multiple levels of constructors and the difficulty in determining the origin of objects. Using inheritance blindly will usually lead to a class architecture that is convoluted and far from "real-world." On the other hand, a carefully constructed inheritance hierarchy can take advantage of the built-in polymorphism and greatly simplify the coding task.

Aggregation is used to implement an object decomposition, and should be used where the has-a (or whole-part) relation holds. This is implemented in C++ by having data members as objects of other classes (the component classes).

Using relations are employed when a class object needs to send a message to an object of another class that is not related by either the has-a or is-a relations. This is implemented in C++ by making a call to a member function of the unrelated object.

A general strategy is to have member functions in the class interface abstract away normal event handling that involves tedious and repeatable programming features. An example includes replacing the message handling inside a Windows application implemented in C. This involves massive case statements (switch statements) that handle the various Windows messages. An example of such a message is the WM_PAINT message, which is used to redraw a portion of a window. In C++, we will typically replace this by a member function PaintWindow, which is a member of a Redraw class.

The determination of the proper class architecture is part of the design phase. Skeleton C++ class interfaces can be constructed as "pseudocode" to document the architecture for design reviews. The details of the architecture will be completed during the OOP phase (see Chapter 19).

17.3.1 Inheritance

The inheritance relationship should only be used where there is a true is-a relationship, i.e., where a derived class is a special case of the parent class. This implies the generalization/specialization paradigm. The general Message class, for example, can be used to derive specialized classes for LocalMessage and ExternalMessage. Both of these two derived classes satisfy the is-a condition since they are, indeed, message classes with special characteristics:

```
class LocalMessage : public Message {//derived class
public:
  // unique member functions here
private:
  // unique data members here
};


class ExternalMessage : public Message {
                                        // derived class
public:
  // unique member functions here
private:
  // unique data members here
};
```

17.3.2 Aggregation

The use of class inheritance in not appropriate for parts of a system that satisfy the whole-part or has-a relationship. In this case, we should be using aggregation instead of inheritance. Aggregation is used to decompose a large element into smaller components. When designing classes, an aggregate class is defined by using components as instances of other classes. An example of aggregation for an Airplane class is the following:

```
class Airplane {
public:
  ...
private:
  Engine rearEngine;
  Engine lwingEngine;
  Engine rwingEngine;
  Navigation GPS;
};
```

The attributes rearEngine, lwingEngine, rwingEngine, and GPS are all components of an airplane. From the view of the Airplane class, these attributes satisfy the has-a relationship. Similarly, viewed from the components, it is clear that they do not satisfy the is-a relationship of subclasses, e.g., a rearEngine is not an Airplane.

17.3.3 Using

When designing classes, we may discover that we need a relationship that is neither inheritance nor aggregation. If a class structure does not seem to fit in either of the two hierarchies, we try a using relationship. This is where the class needs to refer to other classes as types. The classes referred to are not part of the class by either an is-a or has-a relation, but are independent entities. The references to these classes may be appropriate in the class specification or implementation as an object declaration or a parameter type. Here is an example of an ATM class referring to the class Account in its implementation:

```
extern class Account;
class ATM {
  ...
  float Balance (const char* accountNo);
  ...
};

...
float ATM::Balance (const char* accountNo) {
  ...
  return Account::GetBalance (accountNo);  // using
}
```

Our ATM class includes a member function Balance, which calls the member function GetBalance in the Account class. The Account class is not related to the ATM class by either inheritance or aggregation. The ATM class is a client of the Account server class.

To achieve an appropriate architecture of a set of classes for a particular domain is a difficult task. The kind of design decisions listed here must be carefully considered, with suitable trade-offs made to get the structure that will afford the highest level of reusability. Specific examples and design guidelines for C++ will be presented in Chapter 19.

17.4 EXCEPTION HANDLING

Exception handling can be designed into a system for dealing with a number of run-time execution situations. At one extreme, we can decide to only address error handling. At another extreme, we can use exception handling as a programming control mechanism, e.g., a substitute for a "goto" mechanism. We do not advocate either of these two extremes here, and recommend that exception handling should be designed to handle anticipated exceptional conditions, protection of server software, reporting of hardware failures, and reporting of unanticipated errors (bugs).

17.4.1 Exception Handling Categories

The following exception handling categories used to implement a software fault tolerance mechanism in C++ programs were described in Chapter 13:

- anticipated exceptional conditions
- protection of server software
- reporting of hardware failures
- reporting of unanticipated errors (bugs)

Examples of how we can implement exception handling for each of these four categories are given in Chapter 21.

17.4.2 Design Strategy

The general strategy for using exception handling is to design a protection mechanism as a part of the overall system. This is considered a defensive programming practice and supports fault tolerance. How far we want the system to continue to execute after an exception is detected, depends on the particular exception that is raised. In some cases we just report the detection in a log and continue execution. In other cases we report the exception as a fault and quit execution.

The implementation of an exception-handling design is dependent on the support provided by the programming language. The traditional mechanism employed by C programmers is to use the *assert()* function (or macro) specified in the C Standard *assert.h* file. For C++, we will be using the exception handling mechanism supported directly with language constructs, as shown in Chapters 19 and 21.

The use of exceptions demands a uniform design strategy. Exceptions can be designed as classes or objects, or a combination of the two [KOE90]. Using classes will allow us to group exceptions and to create derived classes representing subgroupings.

The general exception handling strategy is determined during the design phase and implemented using C++ constructs during the OOP phase. The design should anticipate the C++ implementation for an easy transitioning between OOD and OOP, i.e., the detailed design of the exception handling mechanism is technology-dependent.

17.4.3 Implementation and Performance Issues

It is implicitly assumed here that a run-time mechanism is available for propagating an exception from its point of detection to a handler, and that the propagation mechanism is deterministic. C++ supports such a mechanism and includes semantics for a deterministic propagation path.

Another basic assumption is that the run-time exception handling mechanism can be implemented efficiently without significant run-time penalties for our systems. In general, we would like to get a guarantee from the C++ vendors that implement the exception handling that only a minimal run-time overhead will affect our systems when exceptions are not raised, propagated, and handled. We would also like the exception handling mechanism to be as efficient as possible when we use it. How well C++ exception handling is implemented is not yet known, since it is only recently that major C++ compilation systems have fully supported the exception handling mechanism specified in the reference manual [ELL90, p. 353].

17.5 CLASS LIBRARIES

The creation of class libraries did not start with C++. Fortran and C libraries (e.g., mathematics and I/O libraries) have been in use for more than two decades. Fortran libraries are based on collections of subroutines and functions, and C libraries are based on collections of functions and associated data structures. A typical C++ library takes advantage of the programming language constructs, and includes encapsulated class structures, templates, and inheritance relations

The creation of class libraries provides a level of reusability above single classes. These libraries contain a number of C++ classes that can be used by programs which require services for certain categories of operations, e.g., sort functions, statistical analysis, data persistence within a database, or matrix manipulations. The construction of truly reusable class libraries involves a number of design trade-offs, and careful use of the language features that directly support library creation.

17.5.1 Design Trade-Offs

Stroustrup has suggested several design trade-offs that should be considered by C++ class library builders [STR93]:

1. **Ease of Use.** For a class library to be easy to use, adequate documentation for features and access to available operations must be available. The operations should include a complete set of functions for the intended client application programs.

2. **Library Extensions by Users.** Extending existing class libraries requires the source code to those libraries; an important consideration in deciding whether to buy from a vendor or develop class libraries in-house. A class library that is built around a deeply nested inheritance hierarchy will be difficult to modify, and should be avoided.

3. **Run-time Efficiency.** The run-time efficiency of class libraries can only be determined after the libraries have been coded. Evaluating class libraries from vendors will include an examination of available benchmarks, but this is no substitute for running dummy applications on the target system. Benchmark results from vendors are often based on best-case conditions and suped-up hardware, and may not reflect the actual running conditions of the system to be built.

4. **"Universal" Base Classes.** One tendency of the makers of class libraries has been to anchor the library with a base object class (metaclass) that includes common functions such as input, printing, object comparisons, and object management. This kind of top-level class violates the is-a inheritance paradigm, and adds to the complexity of the class hierarchy. Current thinking on class library structures favors simpler hierarchies with fewer levels. This can be accomplished with a combination of *using* and *aggregation* relations rather than strict inheritance hierarchies. Examples of this simplification include the latest Microsoft Foundation Class (MFC), version 2.5, and Borland's ObjectWindows Library (OWL), version 2.0.

5. **Combining Class Libraries.** The reuse of an application program can

be maximized by using multiple class libraries. To provide ease of use, the fundamental paradigms should be implemented with the same mechanisms. These paradigms may include encapsulation and level of data hiding, exception handling, use of templates, and the hierarchical structure. The use of universal base classes that include the same functionality, for example, will cause additional complexity that may confuse the library users.

6. **Error Handling.** A uniform error handling strategy should be designed for every class library. This can be implemented with the built-in exception handling mechanism available in C++.

7. **Minimizing Recompilation.** The use of a class library should not cause a large amount of recompilation when the application program is being implemented. The structuring of the library should include separation of specification and implementation into different files, e.g., specifications in header files and bodies in source files.

Significant design reviews should be conducted before the programming phase is started. These design trade-offs can be used to evaluate the design of an existing library or a new library to be built in-house. The potential for a considerable code reuse is highly dependent on how well the planned class libraries will match with the requirements and the design of the applications using the libraries.

17.5.2 Language Features

There are a number of programming language features that support the creation of C++ class libraries. These features include:

1. **Encapsulation and Information Hiding.** The class mechanism provides direct support for this paradigm. The level of user access to member functions and data members can be specified with the private, protected, public, and friend constructs.

2. **Inheritance.** C++ provides constructs for the creation of derived classes from one or more parent classes.

3. **Exception Handling.** A uniform error handling mechanism can be designed using the built-in exception handling.

4. **Templates.** Multiple types can be applied to functions and classes using the template structures. This provides yet another level of reuse by expanding major structures from a single type to a set of types.

5. **Strong Typing.** C++ provides compile-time checking that should be utilized. The type system should be followed, and the use of void* and explicit casts should be avoided [STR93]. Compile-time mechanisms are preferred over run-time equivalents, and will result in a more robust application program.

The creation of a class library should carefully consider the design trade-offs listed above, and should use the available language features that directly support class constructions. Every class library should be constructed to anticipate user requirements, and the inevitable future extensions that will follow.

17.6 FRAMEWORKS

Frameworks include collections of C++ classes that can be used by programs within an application domain, e.g., a framework for MS Windows or X Window System applications, or air traffic control systems. C++ frameworks will usually contain a number of class libraries, and can be considered the ultimate in design and code reuse when building new application programs.

Each framework may contain clusters of related classes that simplify the user navigation across the many classes [BOO93, p. 336]. Examples of class clusters include queues and lists, GUIs, and communications libraries. Taken together, the set of clusters, i.e., the framework, can support a complete application domain. Each cluster may contain a set of classes that are related by inheritance, but there is usually no inheritance between clusters. There should also not be a common base class anchoring different clusters of classes.

There is no single way to design an application using a framework, since a framework is created to support a wide variety of applications within a given problem domain. Since there are an infinite number of ways to create an application within a given application domain, each application program must pick and choose from the available classes. All of the classes are rarely used by any one application. A careful design phase must be undertaken to obtain a robust application using the available class features.

17.7 EVALUATION OF CLASS DESIGN

An evaluation of a vendor's class library structure is especially important as an input to a buy-or-develop decision. The inheritance structure should not be deep, and there should not be a single root class from which all subclasses are derived. If we decide to buy a class library, there will always be newer versions that will have to be integrated with our software in the future. The simpler the structure of the purchased library, the less effort will be required for the integration of future versions. Any application program that is dependent on multiple inheritance is more complex than one that depends on only single inheritance.

It is preferable that the source code be supplied with a class library. If a vendor should go out of business or simply not support the library anymore, we can then always make the necessary revisions ourselves.

The class interfaces should be well documented and contain a complete set of operations that reflects the functionality of the problem domain.

One suggestion for attempting to minimize the effect of vendor class library revisions has been made by Racko [RAC94]. The code we are developing can be organized into categories such as:

- input/output (including user interface)
- data transformation (reflect the functional requirements)
- control and coordination

The code corresponding to these categories is kept in different source files. The vendor's classes are partitioned in a similar fashion, and we attempt to determine which of the classes are most likely to be revised by the vendor. The code we develop can be made to depend most heavily on the vendor classes we consider most stable. Information regarding potential revisions may also be available from the vendors, since they usually have long term plans for their development strategies.

17.8 CLASS MANAGEMENT

In the previous sections that deal with classes and collections of classes, we have made the tacit assumption that the contents of a class library are easy to find and integrate with our application program. This assumption ignores the fact that for class libraries to be useful, they must be carefully managed [GIB90].

To take advantage of the potential reuse of existing classes and class libraries, appropriate tools must be available, e.g., for querying and browsing, searching by topic, and pointing to relevant documentation. The documentation must include guidance for how to use the library and information regarding class structuring, e.g., inheritance, and aggregation relations. New features must be carefully implemented and documented in a new version, employing version control.

Here is a collection of some of the features that are necessary for managing class libraries and providing a high level of reuse:

1. **Documentation.** Necessary documentation includes a programmer's manual that describes the contents of each library, and how to access the various parts of the library. Model descriptions will include graphical and textual descriptions of class dependencies and design paradigms used, e.g., single and multiple inheritance, aggregation, using relations, etc. The documentation can be maintained in hard copy form or on electronic media, e.g., CD-ROM.

2. **Quality Control.** Every class library developed should be subjected to formal and informal design reviews. This can be controlled for class libraries developed in-house by making quality control part of the development process. To evaluate the quality of vendor products, we can use checklists to ensure consistent naming conventions, proper access levels and degree of information hiding, and use of decomposition paradigms.

3. **Browsing Capabilities.** A GUI should accompany the class library and provide support for browsing through the library contents. The browser should include facilities for copying library files and directories into user areas.

4. **Version Control.** Any class library intended for reuse must be placed under strict configuration control. Changes to a library should only be allowed via a check-in/check-out mechanism on an interim version that is not yet being distributed. Any distribution of class libraries must only be made from a single repository with a frozen version number. New versions are only allowed after quality control has been completed and the new version is officially blessed.

5. **Packaging.** The packaging of a reusable class library includes binary and/or source files, documentation, browsers, etc. Source files are preferred over binaries, and provide a more flexible implementation strategy for multiple platforms. Source files should be separated according to specification and implementation to support a minimization of recompilation. Special attention should be given to inline functions placed in header files. This may drastically increase the amount of recompilation required when changes are made in source files that

access these functions. Inline functions should usually be placed in separate source files.

Proper management of class libraries is the single most important issue for attaining the high potential of reuse that is possible with these libraries. If the components of a class library are difficult to find and access, users are going to ignore the "reusable" entities and simply create their own classes. The preferred method of finding and accessing a reusable library is via a GUI, which makes it easy to navigate among the myriad of components.

Version control must be strictly adhered to, and each new version must be adequately documented regarding new and modified features.

17.9 REAL-TIME ISSUES

C and C++ are used in the implementation of real-time systems, but these programming languages do not include constructs for real-time features. Ada, for example, has language constructs for the creation of tasks, task priorities, preemption, task synchronization, interrupt handling, critical sections, and time-outs. The Ada elaboration process creates tasks (similar to the C++ constructor mechanism), and the run-time system manages preemption, task scheduling and dispatching, critical sections, and time-outs.

Real-time programs developed in C and C++ must either use low-level functions provided by the operating system or the services included in real-time libraries. Several real-time C++ libraries are now available, and using these libraries is the preferred method for C++ programs. Using the operating system low-level functions creates a strong coupling to the operating system, and makes debugging and program modification more difficult.

C++ real-time libraries include the AT&T C++ Task Library [SHO87] that is primarily Unix oriented, and the DDC-I, Inc., C++ RTOS library [DDC94], for use with DOS/Windows systems. These libraries provide interfaces for multi-threaded C++ programs.

18

C++ Concurrency Support

We noted in Chapter 13 that the design of large real-time systems includes the determination of a set of concurrent elements that will represent a model of a process architecture for parallel execution.

Support for concurrency can be placed in two major categories: (1) programming language syntax and semantics and (2) use of tasking libraries. In this chapter, we describe the support that exists for implementing concurrency in C++ programs for these two categories.

18.1 PROGRAMMING LANGUAGES

Some programming languages, such as Ada, have explicit built-in support for the creation and management of tasks. C++, as defined in the reference manual [ELL90], has no support for the creation or management of concurrent C++ programs. If we are going to use the standard C++ language, we have to rely on the other category of concurrency support.

Several programming languages have been derived from C++ and added concurrency support. These languages fall in two basic categories [ARJ94]: concurrency is implicit or concurrency is explicit.

The creation of concurrent elements, a synchronization mechanism, and mutual exclusion are all implicitly encapsulated with an object or the class definition for languages in the first category. For languages in the second category, concurrency creation and management is explicit at the user-interface level. Some of the implicit languages include ACT++ [KAF90], CHARM++ [KAL93], and Mentat [GRI92]. Examples of the languages in the explicit category include Concurrent C++ [GEH88a] and Extended C++ [SEL90].

Concurrent C++ is based on Concurrent C [GEH88b], where a concurrent C program consists of a set of sequential processes that execute in parallel. The processes interact via transactions that can be synchronous or asynchronous. Synchronous transactions use the extended rendezvous concept (as is used in Ada). Two processes enter a rendezvous by synchronizing their activities and exchanging bi-directional messages. At the end of the rendezvous, both processes continue their separate execution paths.

The asynchronous mechanism lets a caller post its message and continue with its execution without waiting for either a rendezvous or a reply. The message passing direction for an asynchronous transaction is strictly unidirectional: from the caller to the called process.

The following example of a concurrent C program is taken from [GEH88b, p. 192], and illustrates the classical producer-consumer paradigm shown in Figure 18-1.

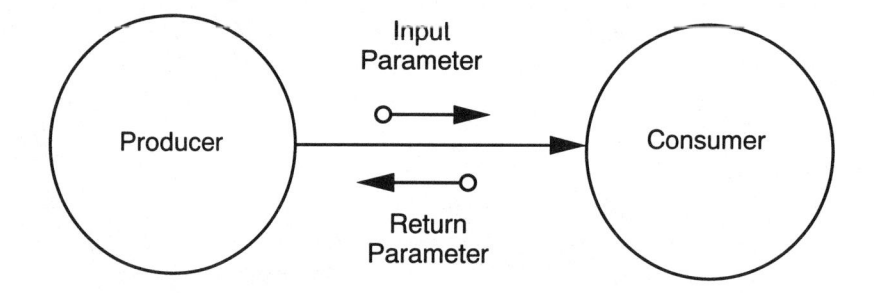

```
#include "concurrc.h"
#include <stdio.h>
#include <ctype.h>

process spec consumer () {
  trans void send (int); //synch send with blocking
};

process spec producer (process consumer);
                    // client of consumer
                    // no transaction here
```

Figure 18-1. Producer-consumer paradigm

```
process body producer (cons) {
  int c;
  do {
    cons.send (c = getchar ());// send c to consumer
  } while (c != EOF);
}

process body consumer () {
  int ch;
  for (;;) {
    accept send (c) // start rendezvous
      ch = c;       // end rendezvous
      if (ch == EOF)
        break;
      if (islower (ch))
        putchar (toupper (ch));
      else
        putchar (ch);
  }
}

main () {
  create producer (create consumer ());
                  // create producer & consumer
}
```

Two independent processes are created in main. The consumer is waiting at the accept *send ()* for a rendezvous with a potential producer. The producer uses the *cons* object to send a character from standard input to the consumer (cons.send(c = getchar ());). The producer is blocked while the consumer is accepting the character in the rendezvous (ch = c;).

The coding example shown above is for synchronous transactions between the producer and the consumer. Concurrent C supports asynchronous transactions via the async construct:

```
process spec consumer () {
  trans async send (int); //asynch send w/o blocking
};
```

The primary benefit of using language constructs, as shown above for the Concurrent C program, is that the concurrent model is expressed directly within the program. It is relatively straightforward to test and debug concurrent programs with a programming language that has concurrent syntax features and deterministic semantic rules. The primary drawback to using concurrent C/C++ languages is that the concurrency features are not part of C++, and thus are not standardized. There is also the possibility of limited or no support for the language, since many of the C/C++ derivatives are experimental languages.

18.2 C++ LIBRARIES

A library of tasking primitives is used in the absence of language support. This approach is usually preferred for commercial software developments over using a specialized concurrent language without any links to an ANSI or ISO standardization committee.

An example of such a library is the AT&T C++ Task Library. This library supports the creation and control of lightweight processes using coroutines [HAN90, p. 395], and [COP92, p. 378]. The interface is specified in the <task.h> header file and contains several classes for multitasking support:

- *Tasks (class task)*. Objects of this class (and derived classes) represent the active system resources, and behave as if they had their own program counter and are running in their separate CPU. The constructor of a task class acts as a main() routine. The constructor is given control and executes until it performs a task::wait(), task::sleep(), or task::resultis(). A task object has its own private data and its own center of control. This class is derived from the class sched (see next paragraph).

- *Scheduled Objects (class sched)*. Member functions include services for checking the state of a task (idle, running or runnable, or finished), manipulating a simulated clock, canceling a task, and checking on the result of a task.

- *Timers (class timer)*. Objects of this class are special tasks which delay for a certain amount of simulated time. This class is derived from the class sched.

- *Queues (classes qhead, qtail, and oqueue)*. Tasks communicate with each other via FIFO queues. A client will use qhead::get() to retrieve an item from a queue, and qtail::put() to store an item in the queue. Since both

qhead and qtail are derived from class objects (see below), tasks can block on a queue's head while waiting for data to be supplied.
- *Objects (class object).* This is the base class for all the other classes listed above. The state of instances of this class can be either *pending* or *ready*, and is used by the central scheduling system to determine if an object is available for execution.

The low-level features required to implement a multitasking system are machine dependent, and thus are not portable. These features should be well documented to ease the reprogramming necessary to port the system to another platform.

Other C++ libraries with tasking support do exist. Examples include ABC++ [ARJ93], EPT/C++ [ENC88], and RTC++ [ISH92]. A summary article discussing the features and merits of concurrency libraries and languages can be found in [ARJ94].

The primary benefit of using a library for C++ concurrency support is that if the vendor supplying the library should vanish, we can maintain and extend the library ourselves (assuming we have the source code, of course).

A major drawback to this approach is that the concurrency model must be implemented using existing tasking features, such as classes and member functions. All tasks and task primitives must be created within our program without the benefit of programming language syntax and semantics.

The trade-offs between using a library or a non-standardized C++ language extension favor the former. It will be easier to maintain and port concurrent systems across platforms by replacing the low-level, machine-dependent features, than to rely on vendors to prepare language extensions for multiple machine architectures.

18.3 SUMMARY

Two primary mechanisms are available for C++ concurrency support: language support and library support.

Special programming languages have been derived from C++ to provide concurrency support. These languages are not standardized and should only be used for experimentation or research. Commercial software developments should use a task library to provide the required tasking primitives.

PART V

Object-Oriented Programming with C++

In Part V, we focus on how to implement our design structures with C++. The primary goal of our implementation effort is to create software that includes the following features:

- *Reusable.* The software must be highly reusable for a particular application domain. This is supported using the OOP constructs available in C++, and by creating a modular software structure using separate specification and implementation files.
- *Efficient.* The applications must be implemented without significant extra overhead compared to the same applications using non-OOP techniques. The use of *inline* functions can eliminate most of the overhead associated with multiple function calls.
- *Robust.* Applications using our programming techniques should be robust and permit a certain level of fault tolerance. This is supported with the use of exception handling, which goes significantly beyond mere error reporting.
- *Ease of Maintenance.* Applications must be easy to maintain and extend. This is supported by creating C++ class structures that are not too deep or convoluted in terms of class relationships. Multiple inheritance should only be used where there is a clear "is-a" relation to more than one class.
- *Ease of Use.* There must be a one-to-one relationship between domain

abstractions and the corresponding encapsulated C++ program entities. This is supported by providing the proper level of information hiding and by making the encapsulated entities well documented. The file structure must be organized to allow for incremental compilation.

After describing the implementation of object-oriented features in C++, we focus on the creation of class interfaces. These interfaces provide a certain level of information hiding for user access, as well as a preparation for the derivation of child classes from base classes.

Software fault tolerance is described in terms of exception handling using available C++ constructs and semantics.

Part V concludes with a set of recommendations for how we can construct a C++ library to support Windows applications. This demonstrates the implementation of many of the OT paradigms described in earlier chapters.

19

Implementing Object-Oriented Features in C++

In this chapter, we will demonstrate how object-oriented features can be implemented in C++. This programming language supports almost all of the object-oriented design paradigms discussed in earlier chapters with suitable language constructs, i.e., C++ *supports* these paradigms directly; it does not merely *enable* us to create object-oriented entities.

Before we dive into the details of C++ implementations, it is important to describe the transitioning phase between design and implementation. A proper design should be performed for every software product that is expected to be used by a set of customers. This is especially important when choosing among the three major class relationships of *inheritance, aggregation,* and *using*. The class design forms the basis for the ensuing implementation, but first we need some guidelines for the elusive transitioning.

19.1 TRANSITIONING FROM DESIGN TO PROGRAMMING

The transitioning period is used to transform our design goals and models, and to get us to the start of the implementation phase. Some of the goals we wish to achieve with object-oriented design and programming include the following:

- Create programs that accurately model real-world objects. This will provide our customers with products that are easy to use, and will make maintenance and extensions easier to implement.
- Create programs that are robust. The design phase should be thorough enough that we can avoid wasting implementations of models that will not function properly, or that will be riddled with bugs after the product is delivered.
- Create programs that are easy to understand. This will support ease of maintenance of existing products and extendibility for future products.

The underlying assumption for the transitioning is that considerable thought has been given to the design, and that design documentation in the form of graphical models and textual descriptions does exist. Recommendations from previous chapters include separate development phases for analysis and design and, in particular, that a domain analysis be performed for a new product line. The transitioning effort depends upon how well the earlier phases have been documented.

Here are some guidelines for the transitioning phase, assuming that adequate design documentation exists:

1. **Transform Real-World Classes into C++ Classes.** Each real-world class identified during the domain analysis and refined during the system analysis and design phases will be implemented as a C++ class.
2. **Transform Class Attributes to C++ Data Members.** Attributes associated with the various classes will be implemented as C++ data members to provide the necessary state model for each object.
3. **Transform Class Operations to C++ Member Functions.** Operations associated with the various classes will be implemented as C++ member functions to provide the necessary interface to each class. The member functions transformed from OOA/OOD classes are classified as implementers, i.e., they implement the operations required by the clients of the class. This will usually not provide a complete set of class member functions as we strive to maximize reusability. The guidelines that follow expand on this issue.
4. **Add Class Manager Functions.** C++ class instances are created with one or more *constructors*. The proper implementations of these may involve overloaded operators (e.g., an assignment operator) and conversion operators. C++ objects must be destroyed properly when they are no longer needed. This is the job of a *destructor*. The implementation of constructors and destructors is covered later in this chapter.

5. **Add Access Functions.** These are functions that can only access the data members and return information about them. They cannot modify the values of data members. An iterator is a special case of an access function that can traverse a list, queue, tree, etc., and return information about an element in that structure. Access functions are usually made public.

6. **Add Helper Functions.** These are functions required by the other member functions to accomplish their job. Helper functions are not available to the clients, and are made private.

7. **Transform Exception Handling.** Error messages and exceptional conditions that occur within any of the class member functions must be reported to clients of the class, and must be properly documented. This must be done as a part of the class implementation and not simply added as an afterthought. The choice of whether to use a traditional C error/signal mechanism or the built-in C++ exception handling is up to the implementors. This is an extremely important part of the implementation and must be carefully designed and documented. Exception handling in C++ is discussed later in this chapter, with more detail provided in a Chapter 21.

8. **Consider the Class Interface.** As the elements of a class are determined, their visibility to a client or derived classes must be carefully considered. The use of public, protected, private, virtual, and friend are discussed in the next chapter.

The transitioning step will provide the initial set of C++ program elements. The need for additional C++ entities is usually discovered during the programming activity and may have an effect on our design, which will then have to be modified.

19.2 TYPES AND CLASSES IN C++

C++ is a strongly typed language and fully object-oriented, i.e., classes are types, and inheritance and polymorphism are both supported. The significance of the strong typing and classes-as-types concept is that user-defined types can be created and treated just like built-in types such as int, float, and double. Static and dynamic instances can be created from the various classes, and these instances are subjected to the strong type checking.

The encapsulation mechanism of classes enables us to create abstract data types (ADTs), i.e., a data abstraction and its operations is implemented within the class. A class specification provides the interface to clients of the class. The data abstraction itself is hidden and can only be accessed via the visible operations. The implementation of the ADT is hidden from the interface provided to its clients. Here is an example of an ADT for a Screen abstraction:

```
class Screen {
public:
  Screen ();
  ~Screen ();
  void home (); // position cursor at "home"
  char get (); // return char at cursor
  char get (int, int);  // return screen char
  void move (int, int);  // move cursor to (x, y)
  void dumpImage ();  // dump image of screen
  . .
private:
  short height,  width;
  char  *cursor, *screen;
};
```

The data members that determine the state values of Screen objects are hidden in the private part. The client interface for manipulating Screen objects is specified in the public part.

The combination of ADTs as classes, overloading of operators, and classes as types gives rise to the concept of concrete data types. This combination lets the compiler treat a class just as a built-in type. Concrete data types differ from ADTs by their canonical form [COP92, p. 37], i.e., they include the necessary semantics to allow the compiler to treat them just as built-in types. Here is a partial example of a concrete data type for a vector abstraction:

```
class Vector {
public:
  Vector (int); // constructor
  Vector (const Vector&);  // initialization;
  ~Vector ( ); // destructor
  int&  operator[] (int index);
                             // subscript operator
  vector& operator= (const Vector&); // assignment
```

```
  vector operator+ (const Vector&);
                                      // addition
  vector operator- (const Vector&);
                                      // subtraction
  int& operator* (const Vector&, const Vector&);
                                      // multiplication
private:
  int vn; // number of elements in vector
  int* v; // pointer to integer vector
};
```

The primary difference between the implementation of an ADT and a concrete abstraction is the addition of the overloaded operators for the latter abstraction. These operators provide for vector manipulations just as for built-in numeric types of ints and floats. Vectors can be added and subtracted, and arrays of vectors can be manipulated via the index operator.

It is clearly more work to produce concrete types than ADTs, but once they have been created, they can be used just like numeric types. This provides a higher level of reusability than the more abstract ADTs.

It is highly recommended that concrete data types be developed for classes that are expected to support a high level of reuse, especially among different applications. A class that is expected to have a limited role in an application, and that will not be reused across applications, may be developed as a "simple" ADT for the given application. A mathematics library should be developed as a collection of concrete types to provide manipulations as close to the mathematical notation as possible, e.g., for vector and matrix manipulations.

19.3 USING *STRUCTS* VERSUS CLASSES

C uses structs extensively for the creation of data structures. The OT equivalent construct in C++ is a class which encapsulates a data structure and the operations that act on instances declared from the class type. C-type structs can also be used in C++, including the declaration of operations within a struct. All data members of a struct are public by default, and inheritance is not allowed.

There are times when we don't need to create either abstract or concrete data types. If we discover a collection of related data elements without any associated intrinsic behavior, the elements can be collected inside a record using the *struct* construct. In this case, there is no encapsulation of a real-world abstraction or design entity. The record is simply an aggregate collection of data elements.

An example of a simple data structure is a singly-linked list with nodes linked in only one direction. If we decide that this is the only link structure required for our application, and that there is no need for data hiding, the simple structure could be implemented as follows:

```
struct intNode { // node for an integer
  int      data; // data element
  intNode* next; // pointer to next node
};

int main () {
  intNode i, j, k; //
  i.data = 7;
  i.next = &j;

  j.data = 0;
  j.next = &k;

  k.data = 11;
  k.next = NULL;

...
  return 0;
}
```

A major problem with the use of this type of simple data structure is its limited reusability. The singly-linked list above is only usable for integers, and will have to be recoded for linking other data types.

Another example of when we may want to create a struct, is a Windows application that combines data elements to register and create a Windows class [DIL92, p. 50]:

```
struct CREATEWINCLASS {
  WNDCLASS  wndclass;
  LSTR      wincaption;
  DWORD     winstyle;
  DWORD     exstyle;
```

Chapter 19 • Implementing Object-Oriented Features in C++

```
    RECT      winpos;
    HWND      parent;
    HMENU     hmenu;
    HINSTANCE hinstance;
    UINT      wParam;
    LONG      lParam;
};
```

This type can be used by the object(s) that register and create the original window. Operations on the window object are all included in the classes that encapsulate the window.

Note the difference in syntax between C and C++ structs: The name following the struct keyword in C++ signifies the name of a type, and objects can be declared of this type using the same syntax as we use for the predefined types :

```
CREATEWINCLASS newWinClass;
                    // declare the object newClass
```

If we create classes to replace the functionality of existing structs, the size of the new class instances should correspond to the size and elements in the associated struct. This will allow us to use older code and cast between the old structs and the new class instances. For Windows applications, for example, if we create a class dealing with points in a window [DIL92, p.13], the structure should correspond to the POINT structure already available in *windows.h*:

```
class WPoint {
public:
  WPoint (...);
  set (...);
  // other member functions here
private:
  int x, y;
};
```

The declaration from *windows.h* includes:

```
typedef struct tagPOINT {
  int x;
  int y;
} POINT;
```

A Windows application can now be using types from both the API and the custom class library by appropriate casting:

```
WPoint pt; // from custom library
...
ScreenToClient (hwnd, (POINT)&pt);
                    // cast 'pt' to API POINT type
...
```

The size of the custom object 'pt' is exactly the same size as any API object of type POINT; the additional member functions declared in the class *WPoint* do not affect the size of the object declared as an instance of the class *WPoint*. The casting from the custom object to an API object will use the correct data structure inside the API function *ScreenToClient()*.

The data abstractions transitioned from the design phase will usually represent encapsulated objects that we will implement as ADTs or concrete types using C++ classes. Simple data structures that could be implemented with *structs* will typically be discovered as we are programming the major design abstractions.

19.4 INHERITANCE

C++ provides language constructs for the implementation of the is-a or generalization/specialization paradigm. A general *Message* class, for example, can be specified as follows:

```
struct date {
  int month;
  int day;
  int year;
};

class Message {
public:
  Message (...);   // constructor
  virtual ~Message ();    // destructor
  virtual void Send (...);     // send message
  virtual void Retrieve (...); // retrieve message
```

```
    virtual void Delete (...);
                     // delete message from buffer
  ...
protected:
  date* timeTag; // time tag
  char* source;  // sender
  char* dest;    // receiver
  char* text;    // message text
};
```

Note that the keyword *protected* is used to lessen the level of information hiding to allow anticipated derived classes access to the private data members. Clients of this class can still only access the public data members; the protected segment only affects the derived classes.

A specialization of derived classes for encapsulating local and external messages can be specified as follows:

```
class LocalMessage : public Message {
                               // derived class
public:
  // unique member functions here
private:
  // unique data members here
};

class ExternalMessage : public Message {
                               // derived class
public:
  // unique member functions here
private:
  // unique data members here
};
```

An important design decision when using inheritance, is the consideration for declaring virtual member functions in the base class, and for providing protected level of information hiding rather than private. This provides direct support for polymorphism and overriding of member functions in C++.

An initial design guideline is to make all member functions in the base class virtual while the hierarchy is being developed. This will allow these member functions to be overridden in the derived classes. If it is decided that some of the member functions in the base class should not be overridden in the derived classes, the virtual description is removed before the class is released for reuse.

Member functions that are unique to a derived class should not be overridden from a base member function, but should be added to the derived class with a unique name. This will preclude the creation of artificial polymorphism which is likely to become confusing during testing and debugging.

Inheritance hierarchies should be developed using public inheritance to provide users of the derived class access to the public and protected members of the base class.

Private inheritance should only be used when the inheritance is an implementation detail [MUR93, p. 90]. Users of the derived class have no access to the public and protected members of the base class. Changing the specification of the class *LocalMessage* from public to private inheritance:

```
class LocalMessage : private Message {
                                       // derived class
public:
  // unique member functions
  // Message::Send () is not overridden here
private:
  // unique data members
};

int main () {
  LocalMessage msg1 (...);
  ...
  msg1.Send (...);
              // compiler error, trying to access
              // the now private Message::Send ()
  ...
  return 0;
}
```

Inheritance should never be used just because it may be convenient to "derive" properties from an existing class, and thus save a little coding. Inheritance should only be used for a true is-a relationship. Private inheritance should be avoided except when we have to override a base member function that is required for the implementation of the derived class.

The use of virtual classes and member functions is discussed in further detail in Chapter 20.

19.5 AGGREGATION

Aggregation is used to model the whole-part paradigm and can be described by the has-a relationship. For example, an airplane has a fuselage, wings, engines, landing gear, etc. An easy test for describing these components in a whole-part or has-a relationship is to try the inheritance relation of is-a. It is quite clear that an engine is not a specialization of an airplane, and an inheritance relation would thus be an incorrect representation for this airplane hierarchy. As we discussed in Chapter 5, the term aggregation is synonymous with the terms composition, containment, and embedding.

The way we can implement a hierarchy that models aggregation in C++, is to declare data members of the top level class as instances of classes that represent the parts of the aggregation. For an airplane, for example, this could be done with the following classes:

```
class Engine { ... };
class Wing { ... };
class Fuselage { ... };
class LandingGear { ... };
...
class Airplane {
public:
  Airplane (); // and other constructors
  virtual ~Airplane ();
  // other visible member functions
protected:
  // members used by derived functions here
private:
  Engine engine;       // component
  Wing leftWing;
  Wing rightWing;
  Fuselage fuselage;
  LandingGear landingGear;
  ...
};
```

In this example, the Airplane class is at the top level of the hierarchy, and is layered above the component classes Engine, Wing, Fuselage, and LandingGear, for which we have declared data members.

The aggregation relation can be viewed as a client/server mechanism with the aggregate class as the single client interfacing with multiple servers.

There is a close temporal relation between the containing class and its components. Objects created from the Airplane class will have the same lifetime as their components (we are ignoring the time it takes constructors to create the objects and the destructors to delete them). This will be different if the data members are referencing other classes. There is then a much weaker temporal coupling between the containing objects and its components. Booch refers to this relation as containment by reference [BOO93, p. 129].

Aggregation should be used whenever we can implement the has-a or whole-part decomposition. This represents a layering of objects in a hierarchy, and provides a high degree of modularity. Even though C++ does not have constructs to create this structure (as it does for inheritance), it is relatively easy to decompose a system as an aggregation.

As was the case with inheritance hierarchies, we should resist the temptation to create deep layers of contained components. The constructor/destructor problem of multiple objects is also present for aggregation, even though we don't have to debug obscure polymorphic relations.

Some designs may be created by combining inheritance and aggregation. Again, keep the hierarchies shallow for the first few projects. Debugging deep hierarchies, which include both inheritance and aggregation, can be an interesting experience!

19.6 USING RELATIONSHIP

The "using" relationship between classes is neither inheritance (is-a) nor aggregation (has-a). One object will be using another object of a different class via a communication mechanism. This mechanism can be a direct call to a member function or a reference to an object of another, unrelated class.

The using relation can be viewed as a client/server mechanism with the class using the other classes as servers. A "using" relationship between classes and objects means that a reference is made to a class or object that is outside the current abstraction. An example of this relationship is the following ATM class, which is using an outside Account class:

```
extern class Account;
...
Account userAccount (...);
...

class ATM {
  ...
  float Balance (const char* accountNo);
  void Print (receipt& r);
  ...
};

...
float ATM::Balance (const char* accountNo) {
  ...
  return userAccount.GetBalance (accountNo);// using
}
```

In this example, the ATM class is the client and the Account class is the server. An Account object is not a component of the ATM class, nor is it a specialization. An ATM object simply communicates with an Account object without containing it and without having a parent-child relationship with it.

The using relationship is the most general of the three possible class/object relations. As a general design guideline, this paradigm should be used after we attempt to create a hierarchical relationship of inheritance and aggregation.

19.7 CONSTRUCTORS

When an instance of a class is created, a constructor is invoked to prepare the object and set up the class members. The design of a constructor seems, at first, to be straightforward, but there are a number of important design and implementation issues to be aware of.

When we transition classes as design entities to programming entities, constructors will have to be added to the class interface. These member functions are related to implementation issues rather than design issues of the abstractions to be implemented as C++ classes.

One of the important implementation issues is what type of constructors should be included for a particular class. We will discuss the following basic types of constructors: "ordinary" constructor, default constructor, copy constructor, initialization constructor, and assignment operator. A class can include a number of constructors as member functions, and any combination of the four types may be required for a given class.

The invocation of one constructor may result in the invocation of a series of constructors when derived classes are used, and the order of the invocations becomes an important run-time issue.

19.7.1 Ordinary Constructor

This constructor creates a new instance of the class and sets the data members to the values provided in the declaration. Here is an example of a class that can be used in the creation of complex numbers:

```
class Complex {
public:
  Complex (double, double); // ordinary constructor
  ~Complex ();              // destructor
  //...other member functions
private:
  double real;
  double imag;

};

...
Complex C1 (2.0, 5.0); // using ordinary constructor
```

The "ordinary" constructor given here must be used in assigning specific values to the data members. A number of other ("non-ordinary") constructors may have to be provided for special cases, as discussed below. If, for example, we tried to declare an object such as

```
Complex C2; // what constructor?
```

the compiler would complain that it "cannot find a match for *Complex::Complex()*," and we would have to provide a special default constructor if this is a valid declaration.

19.7.2 Default Constructor

A default constructor is a constructor that requires no arguments; the argument list is either empty, or all the arguments have default values assigned to them:

```
class Complex {
public:
  Complex () {real = 0; imag = 0;}
                              // default constructor
  ~Complex ();                // destructor
  //...other member functions
private:
  double real;
  double imag;
};
```

If we now declare an object as

```
Complex C3; // invokes default constructor
```

the compiler will create the object C3 with both the real and imaginary parts set to zero, as provided by the inline default constructor.

A default constructor is used to initialize an array of objects of its class. It is also used to create a copy of an object passed as an argument via call-by-value.

19.7.3 Initialization Constructor

If we want to take control of how an object should be initialized upon its creation, we must provide one or more initialization constructors. A *const* object, for example, must include an initial value. If none is supplied with the object declaration, then a default constructor must exist to provide the required initialization.

An initialization constructor is invoked to provide values for the data members associated with a new object:

```
ClassX Y (objectZ);
        // create new object Y and initialize with
        // objectZ
```

Initialization constructors may provide initialization of only a portion of the new object with values that do not represent an entire object of the same type as the new object (see copy constructor below):

```
class String {
public:
  String (const char*);// initialization constructor
  String ();
  ~String ();
private:
  char* string;
  int length;
};
```

The parameter passed to this initialization constructor is a pointer to an ordinary string, i.e., the parameter has a different type than instances of the constructor's class. This constructor can be implemented as follows:

```
#include <string.h>
#include <assert.h>
#include "string.h"

String::String (const char* str) {
                        // copy str to new string
  length = strlen (str);
  string = new char [len + 1]);
                        // rather than string = str
  assert (string =! 0);

  strcpy (string, str);
              // copy chars to the new string
}
```

Note that we first find the length of the string (str) we are copying from, then create a new string of that length, check if storage was allocated, and, finally, copy each character from the initialization string. We do not simply copy the address of the initialization string (*string = str*). This would be unsafe, since the longevity of the initialization string is unknown.

An initialization constructor is used to provide values of data members for new objects. This is sometimes referred to as bitwise or deep copy, as opposed to the memberwise or shallow copy used with copy constructors.

We distinguish between the initialization constructors used for new objects, and an assignment used to provide new values to the data members of existing objects.

19.7.4 Copy Constructor

A copy constructor is used to create a new object and initialize that object with the values of another object of the same class. A default copy constructor is created by the compiler if we have not supplied a copy constructor as one of the class member functions. A copy constructor is of the form *X::X (const X&)*, where *X* is the class name:

```
class Complex {
public:
  Complex (double, double); // ordinary constructor
  Complex (const Complex&); // copy constructor
  ~Complex ();              // destructor
  ...
private:
  double real;
  double imag;

};
```

If a copy constructor is not declared for the class, the compiler will create one for us. This default copy constructor will be called automatically when objects of the class are passed by value to a function. The temporary objects that are created will be destroyed when the function returns:

```
double func (Complex);
            // func prototype; arg passed by value
...
Complex C2 (5.0, 10.0);//ordinary constructor for C2
double  D1 = func (C2); // pass a copy of C2
```

The function *func()* will be passed a copy of C2 with a call to

```
Complex::Complex (const Complex&);
                // create a temp object
```

The temporary object is set to the value of C2, using the copy constructor. Upon return from func(), the temporary copy is destroyed with a call to the destructor *~Complex()*.

A default copy constructor created by the compiler will automatically provide member-wise copy. This is usually sufficient if the entire state of an object is contained within that object. Any time we are designing classes that involve pointers to storage allocated during run-time, we may have to provide our own copy constructor. Consider the following *String* class:

```
// File: string.h
class String {
public:
  String (const char* sPtr = 0);
                           // default constructor
  ~String () {delete [] str;}
private:
  char* str;

};

// File: string.cpp
String::String (const char* sPtr) {
  if (sPtr) {
    str = new char [strlen (sPtr) + 1];
                    // allocate storage
    strcpy (str, sPtr);  // copy chars into str
  {
  else { // empty string
    str = new char [1];
    *str = '\0';
  }
}

...
String Str1 ("String1");
                 // use class default constructor
String Str2 ("String2");
...
Str2 = Str1; // potential problem here
```

Chapter 19 • Implementing Object-Oriented Features in C++

The class default constructor in *String* will copy the actual strings furnished as arguments into *Str1.str* and *Str2.str*, respectively. The result of the creation of the two objects is shown in Figure 19-1. Each *str* data member is pointing to its associated string that is located somewhere in memory.

After the assignment of *Str1* to *Str2*, the result is as shown in Figure 19-2. Both the two data members are now pointing to the first string, and the second string is dangling, thus creating a memory leak. Since we did not provide an assignment operator, the compiler created code for a default assignment operator which performs a member-wise copy, accounting for the memory leak. In addition, if any of the two string pointers were deleted, the string would also be deleted, and the remaining pointer would be invalid. The inclusion of an assignment operator is discussed below.

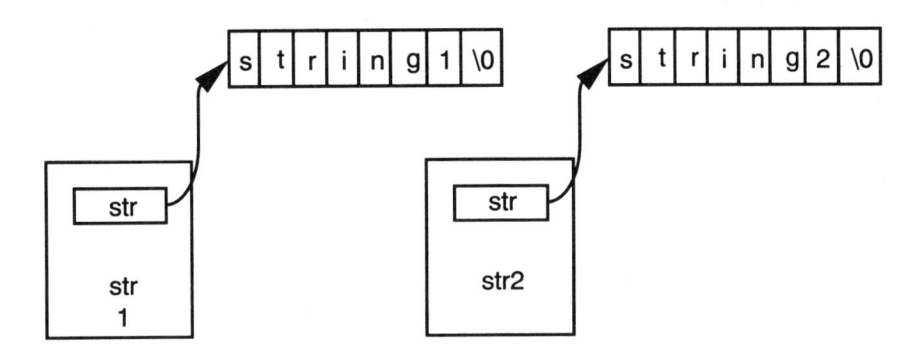

Figure 19-1. Separate string objects

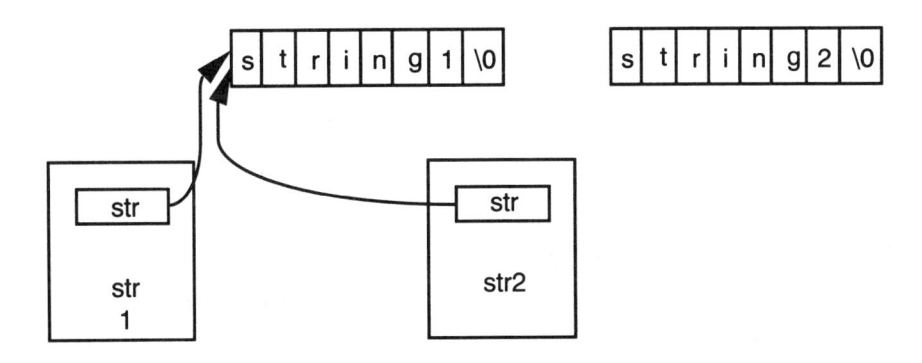

Figure 19-2. Result of member-wise copy

There is yet another copy constructor to be concerned with. We could declare a new object *Str2* and want it initialized with the value of an existing object *Str1*:

```
String Str1 ("String1");
                // use class default constructor
...
String Str2 (Str1); // use copy constructor
```

Again, a default copy constructor employing member-wise copy will be called if we do not provide our own. Here is a suggestion for such a copy constructor:

```
// File: string.h
class String {
public:
  String (const char* sPtr = 0);
                // default constructor
  String (const String&);
  ~String () {delete [] str;}
private:
  char* str;
};

// File: string.cpp
...
String::String (const String& sObj) {
  str = new char [strlen (sObj.str) + 1];
                // allocate storage
  strcpy (str, sObj.str);   // copy chars into str
}
```

For this constructor, we are using the string length of the furnished object to determine the length of the new object. Each character from the existing object is copied into the new object.

19.7.5 Assignment Operator

An assignment operator is used to change the value of an existing object; no new object is created:

```
T = Z; // value of existing object T changed
       // to that of object Z
```

The assignment is performed by the *operator=()* function, not by a constructor. If member-wise assignment is not acceptable, we must provide our own operator as a member function. To prevent the kind of problem illustrated in Figure 19-2, we can include an assignment operator as follows:

```
// File: string.h
class String {
public:
  String (const char* sPtr = 0);
                            // default constructor
  String& String::operator= (const String&);
  ~String () {delete [] str;}
private:
  char* str;
};

// File: string.cpp
...
String& String::operator= (const String& sObj) {
  if (this == &sObj)
    return *this;   // self-assignment
  strcpy (str, sObj.str); // copy actual chars
  return *this;
}
```

The assignment operator provided as a member function will now perform a character-wise copy, rather than a member-wise copy of only the pointer addresses.

The complete set of suggested constructors and the assignment operator discussed above and included as member functions is summerized as follows:

```
// File: string.h
class String {
public:
  String (const char* sPtr = 0);//default constructor
  String (const char*);
                    // initialization constructor
```

```
    String (const String&);        // copy constructor
    String& operator= (const String&);
                                   // assignment operator
    ~String () {delete [] str;}    // destructor
  private:
    char* str;

};
```

An assignment operator is similar in functionality to a copy constructor, but there are some major differences [MUR93, p. 31]:

- An assignment operator may return a value.
- An object may be assigned to itself.
- Every invocation of an assignment operator changes the existing values of the object. Resources held by the previous state of the object may have to be released.

19.7.6 Constructor Invocation

The invocation of constructors becomes extremely important for a class structure that includes derived classes. When we create an object of a derived class, the constructors of the parent classes are invoked before the constructor of the derived class. To illustrate this order, assume that we have a base class WinObj, and a high-level Window class that all the applications are expected to derive from (only a skeleton is shown here):

```
// File: winobj.h
#include <windows.h>

class WinObj {
public:
  WinObj() {}
                            // abstract (empty) constructor
  virtual ~WinObj() {}      // virtual destructor
  virtual void Error (....);
                            // Display an error message
  virtual void Warning (....);
                            // Display a warning message
```

```
  virtual int  Message (...); // Display a message box
};


// File: window.h
#include "winobj.h"

class Window: public WinObj {
public:
  Window ();          // constructor
  ~Window ();         // destructor
  friend LONG CALLBACK AppWinProc (....);
                                // callback function

  HWND hwnd;          // window handle
  Window * HScrollBar;
  Window * VScrollBar;

protected:
  static FARPROC Handler;

  void Create (....);    // create a window

  void Move (....);      // move the window
  BOOL Show (....);      // show or hide the window
  int GetText (....);    // get window text
  int SetText (....);    // set window text

  virtual int   MessageLoop (); // get messages
  virtual LONG  MessageProc (....);
                           // handle message events
  virtual LPSTR Register (....);
                           // register a window
  virtual BOOL  InitMenu (....);// initialize menu
  virtual BOOL  QueryClose (); // close window
  virtual BOOL  Size (....);
  virtual BOOL  Char(....);
  virtual BOOL  KeyDown (....);
  ...
};
```

```
// File: window.cpp
#include "window.h"
  ...
Window::Window() {
  hwnd=0;
  HScrollBar = NULL;
  VScrollBar = NULL;
  Handler = MakeProcInstance
              ((FARPROC)AppWinProc, ....);
  ...
}
```

The unfamiliar looking types used for data members and member function return types are unique to PC Windows implementations, and are specified in *Windows.h* (see [PET92]). The base class *WinObj* includes an empty constructor, a virtual destructor, and general error and warning functions.

The high-level *Window* class includes a data member to identify a particular window, *hwnd*, a constructor and destructor, and a number of member functions for the creation and manipulation of windows. We can now derive an application window class:

```
// File: appwin.h
#include "window.h"

class AppWindow : public Window {
public:
  AppWindow(....);  // constructor

private:
  int Height; // window height
  int Width;  // window width

  LPSTR Register(....);   // register window
  BOOL  Paint();          // paint the window
  BOOL  Size(....);       // set the window size
};

// File: appwin.cpp
#include "appwin.h"
```

```
MyWin::MyWin(....)
{
  Create(....); // create a window
}
  ...
```

The class *AppWindow* includes a constructor, data members for the window height and width, and member functions to register a window, paint the window, and set the size of a window.

Since the *AppWindow* class is derived from the Window class, when an object of type *AppWindow* is declared, the *Window* constructor is invoked before the *AppWindow* constructor. The constructor in *WinObj* is empty and will not be invoked. The Window constructor sets up initial values for global data members and creates a handler for the callback function. The *AppWindow* constructor calls *Window::Create* to create a window for the new application.

The invocation of constructors is an important issue and may have a direct bearing on run-time performance. Objects may be created needlessly, depending on how we declare objects, pass objects as parameters to functions, and return objects as value results or references. These performance issues are discussed further in section 19.12.

19.8 DESTRUCTORS

Destructors provide a complementary function to constructors: They destroy class objects that are no longer used by our program. A destructor is a special user-defined member function that takes no arguments, has no return type, and cannot be overloaded. A class destructor has the same name as the class it is contained in, and is prefaced with a "tilda."

In general, constructors for derived objects are invoked after the constructors of their respective parents have been called. Similarly, constructors for aggregate objects are invoked after the constructors for their components have been called.

Destructors can be invoked in three different situations:

- An object goes out of scope.
- The operator *delete* is applied to a class object pointer.
- The destructor is called directly by our program.

Here is an example of a destructor for String objects:

```
class String {
public:
  // ...
 ~String () {delete [] string;} // destructor
                                // see [ELL90, p.64]
private:
  int length;
  char* string;
};
```

The data member *string* was allocated using *new*, and is explicitly deleted. Note the use of the square brackets to make sure all the characters are deleted; not just the pointer to the character array.

The destructor is invoked when the *String* object goes out of scope. Storage for the data member length is deallocated automatically and does not require any special handling.

The operator *delete* can be invoked directly, and can be part of a debugging strategy [LIP91, p. 285]:

```
#include <iostream.h>

String::~String () {
#ifdef DEBUG
  cout << "~String () "
       << length << " " << string << endl;
#endif
  delete [] string;
}
```

If the DEBUG flag is set, the values of the two data members are sent to standard output before the *string* is deleted. We can thus perform "last rites" before an object is destroyed.

A destructor is not invoked automatically for a pointer to a class object that exits scope. These cases require an explicit call to *delete*, which will invoke the default destructor:

```
#include "String.h"
```

```
String string1 ("Hello");

void func () {
  String* pstr = &string1;
                  // don't want destructor for pstr
  String* pp = new String ("World");
                            // need destructor here
  // ...
  delete pp; / default destructor for pp
}
```

The value of *pp* cannot be used outside of this function, and the associated object should be destroyed prior to exiting. This is performed with the call to *delete*. We do not use the square brackets here, since *pp* is not an array. The call to *delete* invokes the destructor for the *String* object created dynamically inside *func()*. If pp is a null pointer, the destructor is not invoked. A good design guideline is to always check the allocation of dynamic objects using *assert()*.

19.9 POLYMORPHISM

The term polymorphism ("multiple forms") refers to the characteristic that objects can exist at run-time as instances of different classes that are derived from the same base class. C++ implements polymorphism as a run-time feature of an inheritance hierarchy. Member functions have both static and dynamic types associated with them, and the dynamic type reference may change during execution.

The concept of polymorphism can be demonstrated by declaring a base class *Shape* and a number of derived classes for shapes such as circle, square, triangle, etc.:

```
class Angle { ... };

class Shape {   // abstract class
public:
  virtual void Draw () = 0; // pure virtual function
  virtual void Erase ( );
  virtual void Rotate (Angle a);
```

```cpp
    virtual void Move (int x, int y);
    virtual void Error (char* msg);
private:
    int x;
    int y;
};


class Circle: public Shape {
public:
    Circle (double x0, double y0, double r);
    void Draw ();
    void Move ();
    int Radius ();
private:
    int r;
};


class Square: public Shape {
public:
    Square (int x, int y, int side);
    void Draw ();
    int Side ();
    void Rotate ();
private:
    int side;
    Angle angle;
};


class Triangle: public Shape {
public:
    Triangle (int x0,    int y0,
              int side1, int side2, Angle alpha);
    void Draw ();
    void Rotate ();
    void Move ();
    int Side (int s); // return side1 or side2
```

```
      double Angle ();
              // return angle between side1 and side2
  private:
    int s1;
    int s2;
    Angle alpha;
};
```

The base class *Shape* is an abstract class by virtue of the pure virtual function *Draw()*. This function must be declared and defined in all derived classes. Instances cannot be created from an abstract class, only from derived classes. (The purpose and use of abstract classes and pure virtual function are discussed in the next chapter.)

The polymorphic feature of C++ is accessed by declaring instances of the derived classes and invoking their member functions via pointers. The compiler has created instructions for dynamic binding, and polymorphism is automatically invoked during run-time. We could, for example, create a derived class for drawing several different shapes:

```
class DrawObject: public Shape {
public:
  DrawObject ();
  void Draw ();
private:
  Shape* list;
  int nDrawObjects;
};

void DrawObject::Draw () {
  int i;
  Shape* ps;

  for (i = 0; i < nDrawObjects; i++)
  {
    ps = list [i]; // get next shape
    ps->Draw ();
        // bind Draw() to the current Shape object
  }
}
```

Let's assume that we have created a list of three *Shape* objects, as shown in Figure 19-3. The dynamic binding of *Draw()* with these three different objects will cause the polymorphic effect of using the correct drawing routine associated with each object.

Polymorphism is a powerful reuse feature of C++. We can add any number of new shapes to the Shape hierarchy listed above, for example, without changing any of the existing code. Without inheritance and polymorphism, the equivalent functionality would have to be implemented with a set of switch statements (case statements). Dynamic binding doesn't come entirely free, since there is a certain amount of run-time overhead associated with polymorphism. The advantage of code reuse, however, by far favors the use of inheritance and being able to take advantage of the coding techniques (using pointers to member functions) associated with dynamic binding.

19.10 EXCEPTION HANDLING

Exception handling can be implemented as a software fault tolerance mechanism with a wider scope than simply detecting and reporting errors. C++ has constructs to support the declaration, raising, and handling of exceptions. It also has the necessary semantic rules to effect an orderly propagation of exceptions from their point of being raised to their point of being handled.

The general design guideline from Chapter 13 is to implement exception handling for the following software fault tolerance categories:

1. **Anticipated Exceptional Conditions.** This is where a (rare) condition over a long execution time may eventually result in an overflow exception, e.g., we can use an exception handler to re-initialize a set of handlers.
2. **Protection of Server Software.** Used to protect a software server from erroneous or inconsistent input data.
3. **Reporting of Hardware Failures.** Used to detect when a hardware device fails.
4. **Reporting of Unanticipated Errors (Bugs).** Used to detect and report bugs.

With the emergence of C++ compilation and run-time systems that support the specified exception handling syntax and semantics, this design and programming paradigm should be taken seriously. Specific details of the C++ programming aspects of exception handling are discussed in detail in Chapter 21.

```
          list        ┌──────────┐
          ─────────▶  │ Triangle │
                      ├──────────┤
                      │  Circle  │
                      ├──────────┤
                      │  Square  │
                      └──────────┘
```

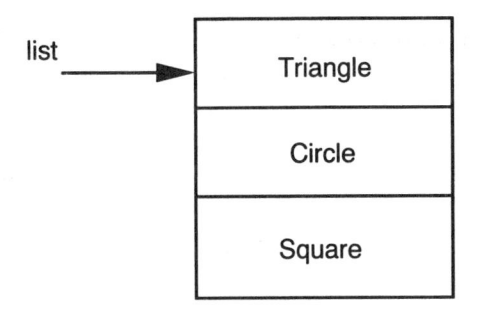

Figure 19-3. List of shapes to be drawn

19.11 TEMPLATES

Another dimension of reuse can be accomplished with parameterized types that can be instantiated with different types at compile time. This is usually referred to as *genericity* and is implemented with *parameterized* or *generic* classes. The generic class is created as a template with formal parameters, and instances of the class are created by providing the corresponding actual parameters. This concept offers the ultimate in reusability, since the same class can be used with any number of types without resorting to inheritance relations of superclasses and subclasses.

The use of C++ templates falls in the same category as the use of exception handling. Until recently, templates were only supported with macros or special syntax implemented by individual vendors of C++ development systems. Current development systems now support both the syntax and semantics specified in [ELL90] and [STR91], and should no longer be ignored.

Templates can make a significant contribution to reuse, and are used to create reusable classes and member functions by specifying generic, formal types. The templates are instantiated by furnishing the required types as actual parameters.

Important design decisions must be made regarding whether to use an inheritance hierarchy or create templates. General guidelines for deciding between these two paradigms can be summarized as follows:

- *Templates.* Use templates when the operations used to manipulate objects are not dependent on the objects themselves. For example, a swap function is only dependent on the type of objects to be swapped, and not on the objects themselves.

- *Inheritance.* Use inheritance for a true is-a relationship, and when child objects require different operations than the parent objects. Different *Shape* objects, for example, do not differ only by type; their behavior are different, depending on a particular shape. Rectangles and polygons can be rotated, but it does not make sense to rotate a circle.

Here is an example of a (simplified) generic stack to illustrate the use of templates:

```
template <class TYPE>
class Stack {
public:
  void reset();
  void push (TYPE);
  TYPE pop();
  TYPE topOf();
private:
  TYPE *stptr;
  int top;
  int length;
};
```

The parameterized type for the generic Stack class is TYPE, and we can now declare stacks of different types:

```
Stack<int> intStack;            // stack of integers
Stack<float> floatStack;        // stack of floats
Stack<complex> complexStack;
                                // stack of complex numbers
Stack<char> charStack;          // stack of characters
```

The generic class represents a higher level of abstraction than the ADT described earlier. It supports reusability directly since a multitude of instantiations can be made by simply varying the type or value of the actual parameters without rewriting the class for each type. The structure of a generic class is significantly simpler than the class hierarchies used with inheritance relations.

19.12 PERFORMANCE ISSUES

The creation of classes produces a layered hierarchy that has an effect on both compilation time and run-time performance. The associated performance issues should be carefully considered, even though future applications will be running on platforms with "screamer" processors, such as the Alpha, Pentium and PowerPC.

Compilation time is affected by the inclusion of inline functions in a class declaration using header files. This inclusion prevents a clear separation of the declaration (specification) and the implementation (definition). If a change is made to an inline function in a header file, every file using that header file must be recompiled. If we move the implementation of the inline functions to the class implementation, only the files depending on the implementation file need to be recompiled.

The primary sources of the run-time overhead associated with C++ classes are caused by the creation and destruction of instances from constructors and destructors and from the multi level calls that are made as a user calls a member function. The use of constructors and destructors is a necessary property of using C++ to implement object-oriented programming features and cannot be avoided.

Care should be exercised to pass objects by reference whenever possible and, similarly, to return objects by reference rather than by value.

The calling mechanism in C++ compilation systems is as efficient as for C compilation systems. If we have an application (e.g., a real-time application) where the multiple calls could become a problem, the use of inline functions can be expanded. Ordinarily, we tend to only use inline functions for short routines that will be called a limited number of times. Significant code increases of the executable image may result if larger routines, and routines that are called repeatedly are made inline. A trade-off must be established between reduced number of function calls versus increased executable code amounts.

19.13 REUSABILITY ISSUES

Reusability can take place at different levels and in many forms. At the lowest level we can, for example, reuse existing code within a member function via cut and paste and add new functionality to that function. Many GUI products, e.g., Windows and X/Motif, employ reuse in this fashion.

At a higher level we can reuse existing functions in libraries that are linked with our application code. Examples of this include *printf()* and *strcpy()* functions from the C libraries, and the *CreateWindow()* and *BeginPaint()* from the Windows API (Applications Programming Interface) libraries.

The next level of reuse for C++ programs is the importation of the type of individual classes we have discussed above. The highest level is where we include an entire layer between our application and the underlying run-time mechanism (including the operating system). Such a layer has been implemented as the Microsoft Foundation Classes (MFC) [BAR93] and Borland's ObjectWindows Library (OWL) [BAR94]. For the remaining part of this chapter, we will discuss reusability issues for individually designed C++ classes.

The reusability of a class may be enhanced if we include inverse (or complementary) functions to the ones already identified. Typical pairwise functions that include an inverse are add/delete, hide/show, and paint/clear. By adding an inverse to make a pair of related functions, we provide a better interface for the clients. The function we add during the initial implementation may have to be added anyway after a client informs us that the function is required. The drawback to the additional functions is more coding and testing, but it is usually worth the extra effort.

One of the most important reuse features of C++ is the direct support for inheritance. A careful design of base classes with regard to user visibility and virtual functions can provide significant reuse of classes and class libraries. It is important to realize that this type of reuse doesn't come for free. Significant planning and management is required to provide users with the services they will want to reuse. Documentation, retrieval, and ease of use are some of the important features for a successful reuse strategy.

19.14 SUMMARY

Design entities transitioned to programming entities are primarily implemented with the C++ class constructs. Class attributes are implemented as data members, and operations as member functions. Some attributes are collections of data elements and can be implemented using structs.

The constructor/destructor mechanism provides for automatic allocation and deallocation of class objects. Several different constructors may have to be developed for a given class:

Chapter 19 • Implementing Object-Oriented Features in C++

- ordinary constructor
- default constructor
- initialization constructor
- copy constructor
- assignment operator

Data member objects have their constructors invoked before the constructor for the containing class. Constructors for class objects are invoked in the lexical order in which the objects are declared in the class specification. Destructors are invoked in the reverse order.

Memberwise copy can be used for initialization of an existing object. This may represent a problem (shallow copy), and bitwise (deep copy) may be required if the persistence of the initialization objects is not the same as the newly created objects.

Inheritance and polymorphism provide a powerful mechanism for code reuse. Other reuse strategies include the use of templates.

Exception handling is an important part of software fault tolerance, and is now supported by major C++ development systems.

20

Class Construction in C++

One of the most important object-oriented features of C++ as a programming language is the direct support of classes and class instances, i.e., objects. This feature provides a great opportunity for developing reusable and extendible software for a wide variety of applications.

The primary concern of this chapter is to offer guidelines for the creation of proper C++ classes. By "proper" in this context, we mean efficient, easy to understand, easy to use, includes the right level of abstraction, and highly reusable.

The objective of this chapter is to describe how and when to use the various access control mechanisms for C++ class construction. This includes the creation of class interfaces for client access, as well as access for the creation of derived classes.

20.1 PUBLIC

A C++ class has a default access control of private, i.e., all the class members specified in the class interface are hidden from potential clients. This is the exact opposite to structs, where the default is public, i.e., all data elements and member functions specified in a struct are visible to potential clients.

A C++ class without any visible class members is not viable for creating reusable software elements, there has to be some access to the class members.

C++ has the keyword *public* to provide a code segment with access to member functions. In the following example, clients of the class Message have access to all of the member functions listed in the code segment between the keywords *public* and *private*. If there are any data members that we wish to make available, they are also placed in this segment. All of the data elements in the struct *date* are visible to client programs:

```cpp
// File: message.h
struct date {
  int month;
  int day;
  int year;
};

class Message {
public:
  Message (...);    // constructor
  ~Message ();      // destructor
  void Send (...);     // send message
  void Retrieve (...); // retrieve message
  void Delete (...);   // delete message from buffer
  ...
private:
  date* timeTag;  // time tag
  char* source;   // sender
  char* dest;     // receiver
  char* text;     // message text
};
```

The use of the public interface should be limited to the member functions that are required to manipulate and provide information about the instances created from the class. Any member functions used to merely assist the other member functions should be hidden and not made available to clients.

The implementations of the visible member functions are hidden from the interface, and are usually placed in a separate source file. (See section 20.9, Program Organization, below.)

20.2 PRIVATE

C++ provides for information hiding via the default private access, as well as with the keyword private to override a previously visible segment. Information hiding is an important element of encapsulation and should be used extensively in class construction. In the class that follows, all of the data members are hidden in the private segment:

```
class Message {
public:
  Message (...);     // constructor
  ~Message ();       // destructor
  void Send (...);      // send message
  void Retrieve (...); // retrieve message
  void Delete (...);    // delete message from buffer
  ...
private:
  date* timeTag; // time tag
  char* source;  // sender
  char* dest;    // receiver
  char* text;    // message text
};
```

Note that if the keyword *private* had not been included, all of the data members would have been visible, and thus provided no information hiding for the data. As a general guideline, all class attributes implemented as data members should be hidden. Only special design decisions would allow a data member to be placed in the public segment.

20.3 PROTECTED

The primary concern for the creation of a visible client interface and data hiding is the reuse of classes by client software. Different concerns are involved when we consider reuse of a base class by a derived class in an inheritance hierarchy.

C++ provides the keyword *protected* to lessen the level of information hiding to allow anticipated derived classes access to the private data members of the base class. Clients of the base class can still only access the public data members; the protected segment only affects the derived classes.

To prepare a base class for potential derivation by inherited classes, we preface the hidden segment with the *protected* keyword:

```
class Message {
public:
  Message (...);  // constructor
  ~Message ();    // destructor
  void Send (...);    // send message
  void Retrieve (...); // retrieve message
  void Delete (...);   // delete message from buffer
  ...
protected:
  date* timeTag; // time tag
  char* source;  // sender
  char* dest;    // receiver
  char* text;    // message text
};
```

All of the data members in the protected segment are visible to member functions of the derived classes, but not to clients of the base class:

```
class LocalMessage : public Message {
                        // public derivation
public:                  // protected data is visible
  // unique member functions here
private:
  // unique data members here
};
```

This example is a *public* derivation from the base class. The derived class inherits all the members of the base class, but the derived class has access privilege only to the public and protected members of the base class.

Derived classes can also be created using *private* derivation:

```
class ExternalMessage : private Message {
                            // private derivation
public:
  // unique member functions here
```

```
    private:
      // unique data members here
    };
```

In this case, the public and protected members of the base class become private in the derived class. They can be accessed by members of the derived class, but not by external programs using the derived class:

```
    int main {
      LocalMessage     locMsg;
      ExternalMessage extMsg;
      ...
      locMsg.Send(); // ok, public derivation
      extMsg.Send(); // error, private derivation
```

With the rarely used *protected* derivation, protected and public members of the base class become protected in the derived class. Member functions of the derived class can call member functions in the protected base class.

In most cases with a true is-a relation, we use public derivation. Private derivation can be used to hide a class implementation. In most of those cases, however, private derivation can be replaced by aggregation.

A protected segment should only be used for intended and expected derivation. We should never place members in a protected segment just because we are not sure if the class will be used for derivation. Someone could circumvent the intended information hiding by creating an unexpected derived class.

20.4 FRIEND FUNCTIONS

Information hiding has been stressed as one of the most important OT paradigms throughout this book. There are instances, however, when the level of information hiding will have to be relaxed in order to provide access to hidden data members.

The relaxation of data hiding is provided in C++ by the *friend* keyword. A friend function has access to all private and protected data members. A friend is a non-member function of a class that is given access to the private and protected members of the class. A friend can be an individual non-member function, a member function of another class, or an entire class.

A general area for allowing access to private or protected data members is the creation of operators that manipulate concrete data types. Since a friend function is a non-member of a class, its declaration can be placed anywhere in the class specification and is not affected by the public, private, or protected segments. As a convention, friend declarations should be placed just after the class header [LIP91, p. 240]:

```
#include <iostream.h>
class Screen {
  friend istream& operator>>(istream&, Screen&);
                              // "using" relation
                              // of Screen object
  friend ostream& operator<<(ostream&, Screen&);
public:
  void home (); // position cursor at "home"
  char get (); // return cursor pointer
  char get (int, int);  // return screen pointer
  void move (int, int); // move cursor to (x, y)
  virtual void dumpImage (); // dump image of screen
  . . .
protected:
  short height,  width;
  char  *cursor, *screen;
};
```

The operators *istream* and *ostream* can now be implemented to access the protected data members of *Screen* objects for I/O.

Another example of the use of a friend function is when we provide a non-member function the access privilege to change a specific value, e.g., a buffer size in an object:

```
#include <iostream.h>
class Object {
  friend void changeValue (Object &);
                            // non-member function
public:
  Object () {bufSize = 256;} // constructor
  void print ();
private:
  int bufSize;
};
```

```
void Object::print () {
 cout << "\tbufSize = " << bufSize;
}

void changeValue (Object& someObject) {
                            // "using" class Object
  someObject.bufSize = 1024;
                    // access to private bufsize
}

int main () {
  Object myObject; // invokes default constructor
  changeValue (myObject); // call friend function
  myObject.print (); // print result
  return 0;
}
```

In both of these examples, the non-member function has a "using" relationship with the objects with which it is a friend, i.e., it is merely referencing these objects without an is-a or has-a relationship.

20.5 FRIEND CLASSES

An entire class can also be declared a friend of a class. In this case, all the member functions of the friend class have access to both the public and non-public members of the class in which the friend declaration is made:

```
class List; // forward reference
class LinkedList {
  friend class List;
              // all member functions of list can
              // access the private data members
              // of LinkedList
private:
  LinkedList *next;  // pointer to next element
  LinkedList *prev;  // pointer to previous element
};
```

```
class List {
public:
  ...
  void add (LinkedList *p) { // add to head of list
    p->prev = NULL;
    p->next = head;
    head = p;
  }
private:
  LinkedList *head;
};
```

In this case, the *add()* function needs access to the private data members of a LinkedList object to add a new node. Again, we note the "using" relationship between the classes List and LinkedList.

If a function needs to manipulate objects of two different classes, that function can be made friend to both classes, or it can be made a member function of one class and friend of the other. Here is an example of a non-member function being made a friend of both classes:

```
class Window; // forward declaration
class Screen {
  friend Boolean Compare (Screen&, Window&);
public:
  // ...
private:
  // ...
};

class Window {
  friend Boolean Compare (Screen&, Window&);
public:
  // ...
private:
  // ...
};

// Compare is implemented as a non-member function
```

Here is an example where the function manipulating objects of two different classes is declared a member of one class and a friend to the other:

```
class Window; // forward declaration
class Screen {
public:
  Screen& Copy (Window&);
                // member function of Screen
  // ...
private:
  // ...
};

class Window {
  friend Screen& Screen::Copy (Window&);
                // friend of Window
public:
  // ...
private:
  // ...
};

Screen& Screen::Copy (Window& win) {
                // "using" Window
  // ...
}
```

The use of friends is a design alternative for implementing "using" relationships between classes. If friends start to proliferate the design, however, it may be a sign that information hiding has been seriously violated. Since the granting of friend status relaxes the level of information hiding, it should only be allowed where necessary.

20.6 VIRTUAL MEMBER FUNCTIONS

Virtual member functions allow us to redefine general operations specified in the base class to more specialized operations in the derived classes. Any function prefaced by the virtual keyword in the base class can be overridden with a specialized implementation in a derived class:

```cpp
class Message {
public:
  Message (...);                  // constructor
  virtual ~Message ();            // destructor
  virtual void Send (...);        // send message
  virtual void Retrieve (...);    // retrieve message
  virtual void Delete (...);
                  // delete message from buffer
  ...
protected:
  date* timeTag;  // time tag
  char* source;   // sender
  char* dest;     // receiver
  char* text;     // message text
};

class LocalMessage : public Message {
                // public derivation
public:
  LocalMessage ();      // constructor
  ~LocalMessage ();     // destructor
  void Send (...);      // specialized Send
  void Retrieve (...);  // specialized Retrieve
  void Delete (...);    // specialized Delete
  // unique member functions here
private:
  // unique data members here
};
```

Note the use of the virtual destructor in the class specification for Message. If any of the class member functions are declared virtual, the destructor should be declared virtual. This is necessary for an orderly invocation of destructors for objects created via inheritance. Constructors are not declared virtual, since the semantics of the invocation order automatically selects the correct constructor.

Non-virtual functions that are redeclared in a derived class hide the corresponding operation in the base class. This could cause a potential problem if we wanted to access the hidden operation with an object derived from the base class. If the hiding was not intended, the base class will have to be changed by declaring the hidden function as virtual in the base class.

20.7 ABSTRACT BASE CLASSES

A virtual member function that is succeeded by "= 0" after its declaration is called a pure virtual function. Its purpose is to provide a specification of a common operation for all derived classes. These classes must include their own implementation of the pure virtual function. There is no definition of a pure virtual function in the base class, and it is expected that every implementation will be different for each derived class.

A class that includes a pure virtual function is referred to as an *abstract* base class. Instances cannot be declared from an abstract class. Here is an example of an abstract base class:

```
class Shape {
public:
  virtual void Display () = 0; // pure virtual f'n
  virtual void Error (char* msg);
  // ...
protected:
  double x;
  double y;
};

class Square : public Shape {
public:
  Square ();  // constructor
  ~Square (); // destructor
  void Display () { // specialized implementation }
  // ...
private:
  // ...
};
```

The base class *Shape* is an abstract class by virtue of the pure virtual function *Display()*. Instances cannot be created from the *Shape* class, only from the derived class *Square*. The abstract class contains all the common operations that can be used by the derived classes. Pure virtual functions provide an interface to derived classes, but no implementation. Even though all the classes derived from *Shape* will have a *Display()* function, every implementation will be different.

20.8 STATIC MEMBERS

C programmers use the keyword *static* in a non-class context to create persistent data objects inside a function, and to force file scope for a function to prevent name clashes. C++ has additional semantics for the use of static in a class context.

- To provide a single data member shared between all objects declared as instances of a given class. Static data members obey the public, protected, and private access rules. This can be considered an implementation of "shared" variables with information hiding (at the class level). The name of the data element is not entered into the global name space, thus preventing name clash.
- To make certain a member function can only access static data members, similar to the use of const. Static member functions can only be used on static data members and are not associated with any instances of their class.

Here is an example of the use of static members in a class context [LIP91, p. 247]:

```
// File: Invest.h

class Invest {
  friend compareCost (Invest&, Invest*);
                              // access to private
public:
  Invest( int, char* );
  ~Invest();
  double monthlyMaint();
  static void raiseCost(double incr);// can only
                              // access
                              // costPerShare
  static double getCost();

private:
  static double costPerShare; // single copy only;
                   // only need to make 1 update
  int    shares;
  char*  owner;
};
```

Each instance of *Invest* can access the static data member *costPerShare* via the static member functions *raiseCost()* and *getCost()*. This is the only data member these two functions can access. They cannot access *shares* or *owner*, since these two data members have not been declared static.

The class member function can be implemented, and the static data member can be accessed as follows:

```cpp
// File: Invest.cpp

#include "Invest.h"
#include <string.h>

double Invest::costPerShare = 19.99;
                              // no object declared,
                              // init at file scope
Invest::Invest( int shr, char* name ) {
   shares = shr;
   owner = new char [strlen (name) + 1];
   strcpy (owner, name);
}

void Invest::raiseCost (double incr) {
   costPerShare += incr;
}

double Invest::monthlyMaint() {
   return (costPerShare * shares);
                              // multiplication op
}

int compareCost (Invest& unit1, Invest* unit2) {
                                        // friend
  double account1, account2;
  account1 = Invest::costPerShare * unit1.shares;
                                       // class scope
  account2 = Invest::costPerShare * unit2->shares;
  // ... make the comparison
}
```

Note that the static data member is accessed directly without an association with an object. It could also be accessed by referencing any object that belongs to the class.

The feature of static members in a class context adds an important aspect of information hiding of "global" data. This can be used, for example, to manage a set of resources that would otherwise be globally visible to any program that could include the file containing the global declarations.

20.9 PROGRAM ORGANIZATION

C++ programmers have the ability to implement a level of information hiding by using separate specification and definition files. This must be done by convention, however, since it is not enforced by the compiler. The separation of specification and implementation files can support an incremental development strategy. It can also minimize the amount of recompilation necessary when changes are required.

Class declarations should be kept in header files. These are C++ source files that provide an interface to other program units. They should have an extension of ".h" or ".hpp" (or whatever else may be required by a particular C++ development system).

Class definitions are kept in C++ source files and the preferred file extension is ".cpp" or "cp." If a particular development system demands something different, that will have to be adhered to. Many C++ programs will link to C code, which usually has a ".c" extension for source files. Having different source extension files for C and C++ code makes it easier to manage large projects.

The use of automatic inlining should be carefully monitored. Unrestricted use of this feature will usually lead to significant recompilation of entire systems when changes are made to the automatic inline functions in the header file. A better approach is to place the functions to be inlined in separate source files and declare those functions explicitly as inline.

Multiple inclusions of the same header files can be avoided by the use of compiler directives such as *#ifndef* and *#define*.

```
// File: message.h

#ifndef _MSGTYPES_H
#define _MSGTYPES_H 1
```

```
#include "msgtypes.h"
#endif _MSGTYPES_H

struct date {
  int month;
  int day;
  int year;
};

class Message {
public:
  Message (...);    // constructor
  ~Message ();      // destructor
  void Send (...);     // send message
  void Retrieve (...); // retrieve message
  void Delete (...);   // delete message from buffer
    ...
private:
  date* timeTag; // time tag
  char* source;  // sender
  char* dest;    // receiver
  char* text;    // message text
};
```

A program unit needing the elements in the *msgtypes.h* file will check the value of the header definition to determine if the header file has already been included.

For consistency and readability, large header files should be organized with the interfaces at increasing levels of information hiding:

```
class Message {
  friend void func ();
public:
  Message (...);    // constructor
  ~Message ();      // destructor
  void Send (...);     // send message
  void Retrieve (...); // retrieve message
  void Delete (...);   // delete message from buffer
    ...
```

```
    protected:
      // ...
    private:
      date* timeTag; // time tag
      char* source;  // sender
      char* dest;    // receiver
      char* text;    // message text
};
```

This provides for a minimum scan by someone who is only interested in the visible parts of the interface, and should be made part of the project programming guidelines.

20.10 SUMMARY

The proper level of access is controlled in C++ programs with the use of public, protected, and private class interface segments. The level of information hiding can be relaxed by creating friend functions and classes.

Member functions to be overridden in derived classes are declared virtual in the base class. A base class intended for inheritance should have a virtual destructor. Constructors are not virtual.

An abstract base class can be specified to provide a common interface to derived classes. Pure virtual member functions must be defined in the derived classes. Instances cannot be created from abstract classes.

Static members can be used to create "shared" data elements with information hiding at the class level.

C++ programs should be structured with separate specification and definition files. This can support incremental development and can minimize recompilation when changes are required.

21

Exception Handling in C++

We noted in Chapters 13 and 17 how we can design for a level of software fault tolerance by including an exception handling strategy to provide a common mechanism for handling run-time exceptional conditions. The following categories of exceptions will cover most of the situations arising from expected and unexpected run-time conditions:

- anticipated exceptional conditions
- protection of server software
- reporting of hardware failures
- reporting of unanticipated errors (bugs)

The general strategy for use of exception handling is determined during the design phase. The objectives of this chapter are to describe how we implement our exception handling strategy using the available language features of C++ to:

- declare exceptions
- raise exceptions
- handle exceptions
- propagate exceptions

21.1 DECLARING EXCEPTIONS

Exceptions are treated as objects and are declared with specific names in the class specification:

```
class MathLib {
public:
  // ...
  class OutofRange { }; // exception class
  class Overflow  { };  // exception class
  class InvalidData {   // exception class with data
                        //    elements
  public:
    int    index; // data elements associated
    double value; // with InvalidData
  };
private
  // ...
};
```

The exception declarations are nested within a class for which they will provide exceptions to the outer class member functions. An exception class can be empty as shown for *OutofRange* and *Overflow*, or it can include data elements as shown for *InvalidData*. The data elements are used to provide details about a particular exception.

A client of the class *MathLib* should carefully note the exceptions, and prepare to handle those exceptions within the code that uses *MathLib*. Exceptions listed in the class interface will not be handled within that class; they will be propagated to the clients of the class.

Since an exception is an object, it can be of any type, and does not have to be specified as a class. We can, for example, arrange a set of exceptions as a family of related exceptions in an enumerated type [STR91, p. 302]:

```
enum MathException {OutofRange, Overflow, Underflow,
                    Zerodivide};
```

Related exceptions can also be declared with an inheritance hierarchy:

```
class MathException { };
```

```
class OutofRange : public MathException { };
class Overflow   : public MathException { };
class Underflow  : public MathException { };
class Zerodivide : public MathException { };
```

All of the inheritance rules that apply to instances of ordinary classes also apply to exceptions.

A function *throw* list can be specified using a suffix to a function declarator:

```
// exceptions of type int and double raised:
  void fException () throw (int, double);

// no exceptions raised:
  void fNoException () throw ();
```

Exceptions are declared by type in the throw list following a normal function declaration. If the throw list is empty, no exceptions can be thrown by that function. There is only a limited amount of type checking performed for a throw list, and its use is primarily for documentation purposes.

21.2 RAISING EXCEPTIONS

A C++ exception is raised with a *throw* expression anywhere an executable statement is allowed. This can be in a main program or at the lowest level of a calling tree.

In the following class, the exception *NoConnection* is declared in the public segment of the interface, and is raised in the member function *SendMessage()*:

```
// File Message.h
class Message {
public:
  Message (...);   // constructor
  ~Message ();     // destructor
  void SendMessage (const char*); // send message
  void Retrieve (...);   // retrieve message
  void Delete (...);     // delete message from buffer
  class NoConnection { }; // exception raised in
                          //   SendMessage
```

```cpp
private:
  date* timeTag; // time tag
  char* source;  // sender
  char* dest;    // receiver
  char* text;    // message text
};

void Message::SendMessage (const char* msg) {
  // ...
  if (getConnection ())
    Send (msg);
  else
    throw NoConnection; // raise exception
  // will not return here if exception is thrown
}
```

After the exception is raised, the run-time system starts looking for an exception handler that matches the thrown exception. For the case above, the client program using the class Message will have to provide the handler. Note that after the exception is handled, the program control will not return to the statement immediately following the throw statement. Program control will continue after the handler or block of handlers (see below).

Exceptions can also be raised with parameters and data values. Here is a slightly different version of the *NoConnection* exception declaration:

```cpp
class Message {
public:
  // ...
  void SendMessage (const char*); // send message
  class NoConnection { // exception class
  public:
    NoConnection (const char*); // constructor
    char* msg;   // data member
  };
private:
  // ...
};
```

```cpp
void Message::SendMessage (const char* msg) {
  // ...
  if (getConnection ())
    Send (msg);
  else
    throw NoConnection (msg); // raise exception
  // will not return here if exception is thrown
}
```

In this case, we have included the message to be sent as a parameter to the exception *NoConnection*. A constructor was added to the exception declaration to allow for the passing of the message as a parameter.

Returning to the class *MathLib* defined above in the previous section:

```cpp
class MathLib {
public:
  // ...
  class OutofRange { }; // empty class
  class Overflow { };   // empty class
  class InvalidData {
  public:
    InvalidData (int i, double x)
                     {index=i; value=x;}
    int    index; // data elements associated
    double value; // with InvalidData
  };
private
  // ...
};

double mathFunc (int k, int n, double x) {
  // ...
  throw InvalidData (n, x);
}
```

In this case, we are raising an exception and include parameters that correspond to the two data members. A handler that catches this exception can interpret the data members and, perhaps, correct the erroneous values or print a report. We will now look at how the exceptions are handled.

21.3 HANDLING EXCEPTIONS

C++ exceptions are processed in exception handlers via a *catch* statement. The context for a handler immediately follows a *try* block, i.e., the set of statements where an exception can be raised.

```cpp
#include "Message.h"
// ...
int main () {

  Message localMsg;
  // ...
  try {
    // ...
    localMsg.SendMessage ("ack1");
    // ...
  }
  catch (Message::NoConnection) {
    cout << "NoConnection exception in SendMessage"
         << endl;
  }
  catch (...) { // unknown exception"
    cout << "Unknown exception captured in main()"
         << endl;
  }
  return 0;
}
```

The exception handler (catch block) is placed after the try block, and will handle any exception raised as a result of executing *SendMessage()* or any lower functions in its calling hierarchy. In this case, we are catching the exception *NoConnection* without any parameters or data members attached.

Any number of exception handlers can be placed after a *try* block. The location of a handler is extremely important, as the run-time system searches in lexical order for a match between an exception thrown and a suitable handler. Control is given to the handler of the first match. After that handler has completed its execution, control is given to the statement following all of the handlers, i.e., any handlers that follow are skipped.

In the example above, we added a handler to catch unknown exceptions (*catch (...)*). This must be placed after all the exception handlers for named exceptions. If we had placed the handler for an unknown exception first, this would "match" any one of the named exceptions raised, and none of the named exceptions would be handled.

In the following example, we are catching an exception that is passed as an object:

```
#include "Message.h"
// ...
int main () {

  Message localMsg;
  // ...
  try {
    // ...
    localMsg.SendMessage ("ack1");
    // ...
  }
  catch (NoConnection& nConn) {
    cout << "NoConnection exception in SendMessage:"
         << nConn.msg << endl;
  }
  return 0;
}
```

By throwing the exception as an object, we gain access to the data member msgs which gets printed out. This provides additional information about why the exception was raised and can shed light on a resolution to the problem.

The creation of exception classes follows the exact same semantics as other classes. Exception classes can thus be derived from base exception classes. Don't get carried away with this capability for your first few projects, however. Attempt to keep the exception declarations simple. An intricate hierarchy of exceptions could be just as difficult to debug as the application itself. The strength of an exception handling strategy is to quickly gain insight into a problem and to provide a certain level of fault tolerance.

21.4 PROPAGATION OF EXCEPTIONS

The exception handling used in C++ is considered *non-resumptive* or *frame-based*. Separate code segments are used to handle an exception that is raised anywhere within the scope of a handler. After the handler has completed its executable instructions, program control is not returned to the statement immediately following the point at which the exception was raised.

If the run-time system does not find a matching handler following the *try* block where the exception was raised, a handler is sought in the next enclosing block up the calling chain. The stack is unwound and destructors are called as this process is continued.

As soon as a matching handler is found, program control is transferred to that handler. When the handler has completed its execution, control is transferred to a location following that handler, regardless of how high up in the calling tree the match was found. Control will not be returned back down the calling tree to the point where the exception was raised.

If no matching handler is found, control is transferred to the function *terminate()*. This function will abort the program.

21.5 EXCEPTION CATEGORIES

Our design guidelines for exception handling suggested preparing handlers for four categories of exceptions. An example for each of these categories follows.

1. **Anticipated Exceptional Conditions.** This is where a (rare) condition over a long execution time may eventually result in an overflow exception, e.g., we can use an exception handler to re-initialize a handle:

   ```
   long getSeqNumber () {
     // ...
     try {
       seqNumber++;
     }
     catch (...) {
       seqNumber = 0; // re-initialize
     }
     return seqNumber;
   }
   ```

2. **Protection of Server Software.** Used to protect a software server from erroneous or inconsistent input data:

```
class MathLib {
public:
  class OutofRange { };
  // ...
  int math1 (int);
  // ...
private:
  // ...
};

MathLib::math1 (int i) {
  if (i < 0) // check for erroneous input data
    throw OutofRange ();//caller handles exception
  // normal processing
}
```

3. **Reporting of Hardware Failures.** Used to detect when a hardware device fails to respond:

```
...
{
  // ...
  hwOutBuf = 0;
  hwInBuf  = input; // expect device to respond by
                    // putting data in hwOutBuf
  // ...
  for (int i = maxRetries; i > 0; i--) {
                    // polling loop
    if (hwOutBuf)
      return hwOutBuf;
  }
  throw deviceXFault; // device X did not respond
                      // within maxRetries
}
```

4. **Reporting of Unanticipated Errors (Bugs).** Used to detect and report bugs:

```
void func (int x, double y) {
  try {
    // normal processing here
  }
  catch (...) { // unexpected exception (bug)
    cerr << "bug detected in func() "
         << x << y << endl;
    throw; // re-raise exception
  }
}
```

The positioning of the exception handler depends on the exception category we are implementing. In the first case, the handler is placed immediately following the try block. Normal processing continues after the re-initialization of the sequence number.

In the second category, the exception *OutofRange* is declared in the class specification. This is an indication to the client of this class that the exception could be raised in one or more of the class member functions. It is up to the client software to handle this exception, and no handler is placed inside the function *math1()*, which raises the exception.

The detection of a hardware fault in the third case is the cause of raising the deviceXFault exception. No handler is provided, since this function can only detect the fault and not correct it.

In the last category, the run-time system or another of our functions is raising an unknown exception. The entire function is covered by a *try* block during debugging. By placing a handler for an unknown exception at the end of the function, we can catch any unknown exception that is raised during the execution of *func()*. After the bug is reported, the exception is re-raised, supposedly to be handled at a higher level. We could also choose to end the program right here by calling *abort()* or *terminate()*.

Note that re-raising the exception for the bug detected in the last case makes the run-time system look for a handler outside the function *func()*, and continues up the calling tree. The handler inside *func()* is not entered recursively, thus avoiding an infinite loop.

21.6 EXCEPTION HANDLING IN C++ LIBRARIES

It is recommended that exception handling of the second category be included for all C++ libraries. This provides for protection of the server software and a uniform exception handling mechanism that the client software can respond to.

All exceptions raised within class member functions and exported to the callers should be shown in the class specification. The client software using these class libraries should include the necessary exception handlers, and expect to handle the exceptional conditions.

A disadvantage of this approach is the potential non-portability of the software. All of the C++ compiler vendors have not yet implemented the exception handling mechanism, or they have a non-standard version. Software using the recommended exception handling strategy may execute fine in one environment, but not in another.

Another disadvantage is the additional code and the run-time execution overhead associated with exceptions.

A more subtle, but no less important, disadvantage is the introduction of non-local program flow [CAR94] and the potential loss of resources:

```
void f() {
  Widget* w = new Widget;
  g (); // exception could be raised from here
  delete w;
}
```

If an exception is raised in *g()* or in any function it may call, the destructor for the object *w* will not be called. Any widget resource that is ordinarily freed when *w* exits the scope of *f()*, will now not be freed, thus causing memory and resource leaks. Lack of resources is sometimes more important than memory for windows-oriented programs. The simplest solution to this problem is to include a try block for the statements that may raise an exception, and a local handler [CAR94]:

```
void f() {
  Widget* w = new Widget;
  try {
    g (); // exception could be raised from here
  }
```

```
    catch (...) {
      delete w;
      throw; // re-raise exception
    }
    delete w; // normal case
}
```

The problem with potential loss of resources does not apply to local objects allocated statically. C++ guarantees that destructors for local variables are invoked when the call stack is unwound. This avoids the problem associated with objects allocated using the operator *new*.

Despite the potential disadvantages, an exception handling mechanism of the second category should be used for all class libraries. More and more compiler vendors will have efficient compilation and run-time systems to support this important software fault tolerance strategy.

21.7 SUMMARY

The exception handling mechanism implemented for C++ is non-resumptive, separate code blocks are required for handling exceptions, and program control is not returned to the statement following the point at which an exception is raised.

C++ exceptions are types and are declared as nested classes. These classes can be empty, without any implementation, or they can include member functions and data members.

An exception is raised with a *throw* statement for named and unnamed exceptions. The latter is used to re-raise an exception within a handler.

Exception handlers are created with the *catch()* statement for named and unnamed exceptions. The lexical order of multiple exception handlers determines the matching order of named exceptions. A handler for an unnamed exception must be the last of multiple handlers.

Exceptions are propagated up to the next enclosing block in the calling hierarchy. This unwinds the stack, and the appropriate destructors are called.

C++ libraries should include exceptions that are propagated to the client programs for fault tolerance. These exceptions are declared in the visible class interface.

22

Developing a Windows C++ Library

The objective of this chapter is to show how we can apply some of the concepts of the earlier chapters to the design and programming of a C++ library that can be used by Windows applications. This is not intended to be an exhaustive treatment of C++ Windows programming techniques. The focus will be on the software development process for a C++ class library structure for Windows applications. The primary emphasis will be on how we can design, organize, and build C++ classes for Windows programs; less emphasis will be placed on the detailed C++ programming aspects.

The term "Windows library" means a collection of C++ classes that can collectively support the development of Windows applications. One of the evolving development approaches for Windows applications is the use of vendor-supplied foundation class libraries.

Some of the material presented in this chapter assumes some knowledge of programming Microsoft Windows or similar GUI using C. If you need to brush up on this material, excellent texts describing the details of Windows programming include [PET92], [NOR92], and [YAO94].

22.1 DOMAIN ANALYSIS

The general problem domain for our C++ class library is a collection of applications that can run under MS Windows on PCs. The versions of Windows we are targeting are Windows 3.1 and 4.0, and the PCs must be powered by at least an Intel 80386 processor. The programs that will use the C++ library include Single Document Interface (SDI) and Multiple Document Interface (MDI) applications, e.g., multiple Word documents can be open simultaneously.

The problem domain is well understood and documented by the Application Programmers Interface (API) access for applications written in C. This interface consists of approximately 1,000 documented C functions that support the creation of menus, control buttons, dialog boxes, coloring, and memory management.

The problem with the Windows API is the large number of functions required to prepare an application, and the procedural design without any kind of encapsulation. Windows applications consist of a number of real-world objects that can be encapsulated, e.g., windows, dialog boxes, and buttons, and a C++ class library can be constructed to hide many of the complex details that are necessary when using the API.

There are no standard C++ classes available for Windows applications. The only standard C++ class library is the *iostream* library, which is included with any C++ development environment that is compatible with AT&T's C++ version 3.0. This library only includes I/O functions, and does not support either Windows or X/Motif applications. Some of the vendors that supply C++ development systems have C++ Windows foundation libraries, e.g., Borland's ObjectWindows Library (OWL) and the Microsoft Foundation Classes (MFC).

Since we are creating a new C++ library, reusable components are restricted to what is available in the API. These are all the C functions that can be called from the C++ implementations. How much of this should be utilized, and whether or not the API should be hidden entirely to the applications programmer, is postponed to the software analysis phase.

The key abstractions to be captured as real-world classes and objects are created during the software requirements analysis phase. This is not considered a large system development, but a small, software-intensive effort that can be accomplished by a small team of developers. Analysis and design phases are still required before the implementation should start.

The products of this phase include, as a minimum, the following:

- *Reusable Software.* The only reusable software for this project includes the API C interface, and existing Windows C legacy code. The entire C++ library will be developed from scratch.
- *Build Plan.* This includes the Windows features to be included in the various versions.

- *List of In-House Experts.* This list includes staff members with expertise in Windows programming, C++ class construction, or both.

Since this is a relatively small project, the development of real-world entities is deferred until the software requirements phase.

22.2 SYSTEM DESIGN

In this case, we are not analyzing an application, but a graphical user interface (GUI). There are no system requirements to allocate between hardware and software. The entire C++ library will be compiled and loaded on a single machine without a distributed environment. The hardware analysis is reduced to finding a motherboard, bus interface, processor, memory, and peripherals that will be an efficient host for the GUI. Any of the modern PCs with at least an Intel 80386 running at 30 MHz, 16-bit ISA bus, at least 8 MB of RAM, and a 250 MB hard drive will suffice as a platform for the type of Windows 3.1 applications we are targeting. The exact resources required for Windows 4.0 are not yet known, but will most likely require more RAM: 16 MB should be sufficient.

22.3 SOFTWARE REQUIREMENT ANALYSIS (OOA)

A Windows C++ class library may hide access to all of the API C functions, or it may only encapsulate a portion of the API and give the applications programmers access to the API for the functions that are not provided. The latter course was taken here. This allows for an incremental development of the library with additional features made available in future versions. New applications can then use the added features, whereas the old applications can still use the API functions that were not available in older versions.

The software requirements for the programming interface can be stated in terms of a number of development goals [DIL92, p. 7]:

1. **Full Windows Functionality.** It is preferable that all of the API functions that developers can access directly be included in the class library we provide. If we don't provide the equivalent of these functions, the developers will simply avoid using our library and access the API directly. As an overall strategy, however, we choose to perform an incremental development by adding functionality to each new version.

2. **Maintain Windows Look and Feel.** We should strive to maintain familiar Windows names and concepts. This will make it easier for developers already familiar with the Windows API to understand our implementation and interfaces.

3. **Performance.** The class libraries we provide must not incur severe run-time overhead, and should only be a "thin" interface between Windows and the applications using our libraries.

4. **Escape Mechanism.** If a client of the class libraries needs direct access to the Windows API, this escape route should be made available. It is conceivable that we have not provided every Windows function that a client may want to use. This is also consistent with our incremental development approach: some of the required features will simply not be available in the early versions.

A view of the MS Windows environment is shown in the system diagram in Figure 22-1 (see [MIC92] for more detailed information about the system features). Windows applications run as non-preemptive, cooperative multi-tasking programs. The primary control feature of a Windows program is the message loop. Each application message loop retrieves input messages from its queue and dispatches them to the appropriate windows. The Windows operating system (OS) lets an application complete its set of messages before the next scheduling event takes place. The Windows OS includes default processing for several sets of messages. An application only needs to handle messages that are unique to that application; the rest of the messages are passed on to Windows for default processing.

22.3.1 Creating Real-World Classes and Objects

This development does not lend itself to the use of scenarios, since we are providing a programming interface to satisfy a client/server view, not an interface for external system users. There is no way to determine in advance all the different applications that will use the server interface. We thus use the functional classification model (rather than the interface, entity, and control model) for determining real-world classes and objects.

To get a better feel for the type of objects that will exist in a typical Windows application, the Windows Notepad application is shown in Figure 22-2. The primary parts of this figure include the main window, the client window (where we can create source code in this case), pull-down menus, minimize and maximize buttons, and horizontal and vertical scrollbars.

Chapter 22 • Developing a Windows C++ Library

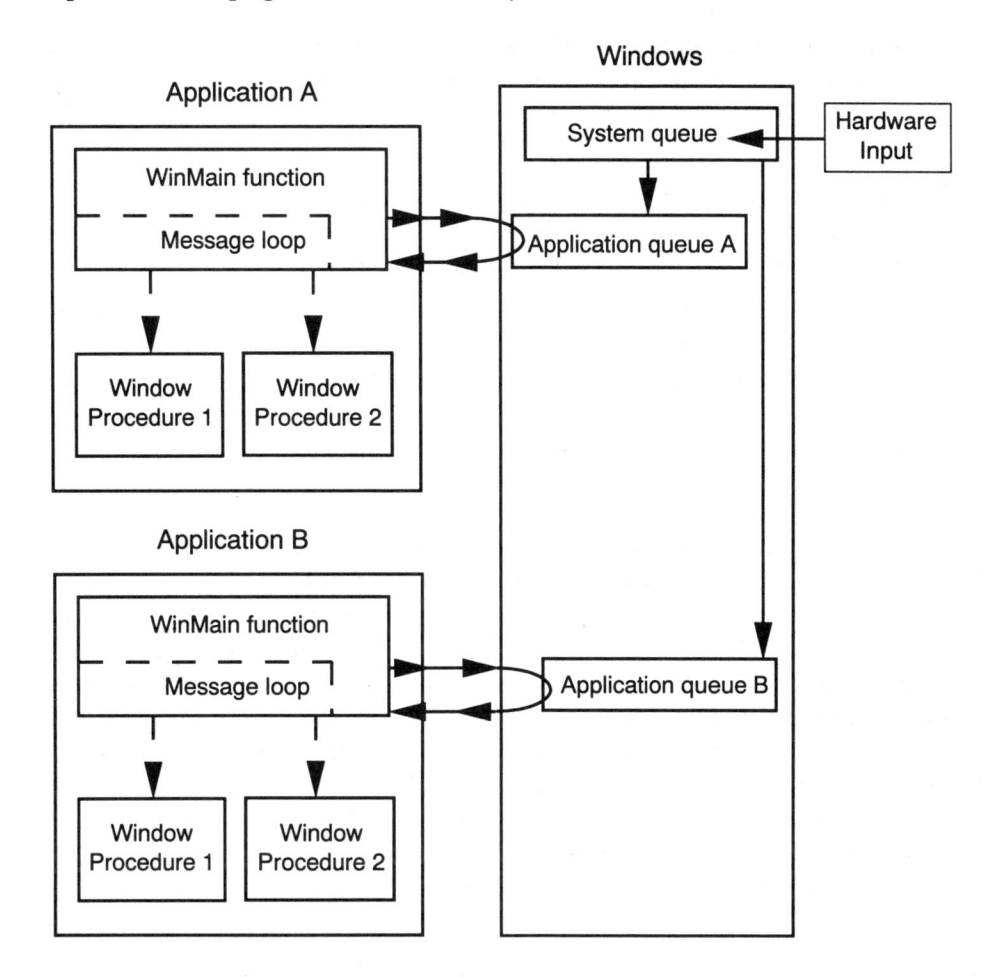

Figure 22-1. MS Windows system diagram

Other elements of a typical Windows application include dialog boxes that prompt a user for information. Dialog boxes include controls such as list boxes, buttons, and edit boxes. An example of a dialog box for opening files in a Windows application is shown in Figure 22-3.

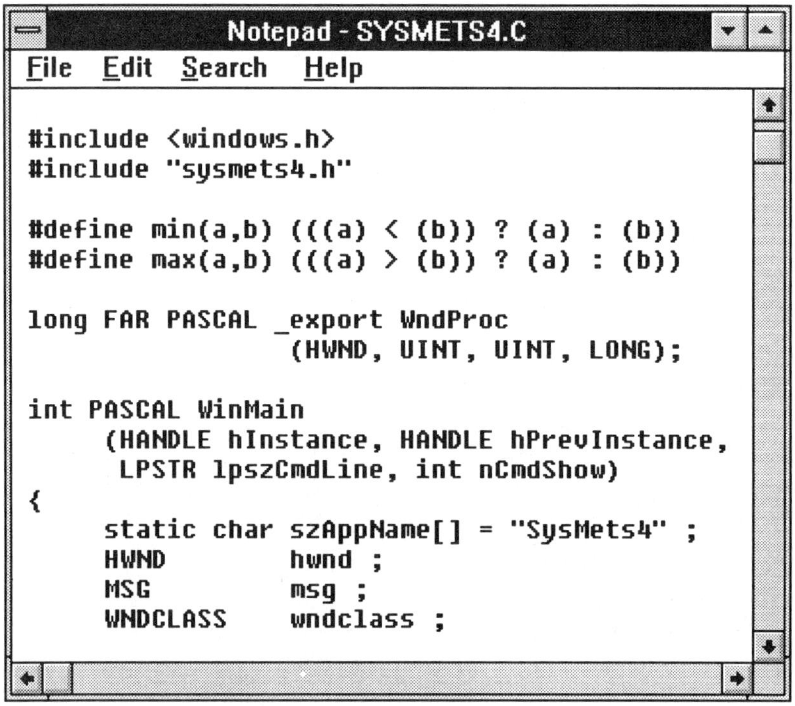

Figure 22-2. A Windows application

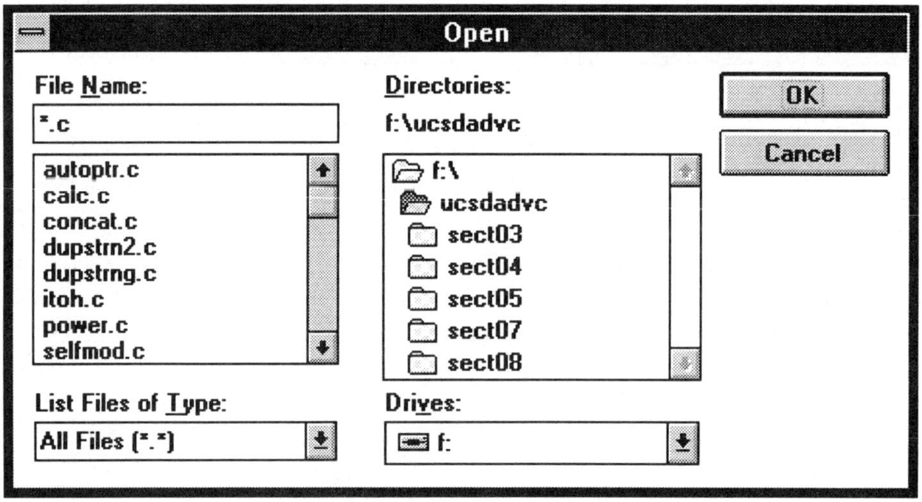

Figure 22-3. Windows Notepad open dialog box

By applying our domain expertise to Windows applications, the primary objects to be represented as key abstractions can be put in three main categories: Window abstractions, Graphics Device Interface (GDI) draw abstractions, and GDI device information abstractions. Real-world entities that can be modeled as window abstractions include:

- *Main Window.* The entire window used by an application, including the caption, scroll bars, and the client window.
- *Client Window.* The portion of the main window that is available to the users of the application.
- *Menus.* This includes the standard system menu, main menus, pop-up menus, and tear-off menus.
- *Multiple Document Interface (MDI).* Some applications allow multiple documents to be open simultaneously. The MDI is used to arrange the multiple documents on the desktop, e.g., as cascaded or tiled layouts.
- *Dialog Boxes.* Dialog boxes are used to provide information to the users and to allow them to furnish and change information used by the application. Dialog boxes usually come in two versions: modal (a user has to respond to the dialog box before processing will continue), and modeless (a user can go outside the dialog box without responding to any of the queries first).
- *Controls.* Controls include edit controls, list boxes, scrollbars, and buttons.

Based on these abstractions, we can create the initial windows class hierarchy shown in Figure 22-4. This hierarchy is anchored by the class WinObject. This is a "metaclass" used as the root of the hierarchy. The preface "W" is used to designate abstractions relating to window objects. The term "Object" in the class name WinObject signifies an "instance" of a fictitious metaclass (since C++ doesn't have metaclasses). All classes that are related to window abstractions will have "W" as their initial character in their class names.

The initial structure shown in Figure 22-4 implies inheritance relations. This hierarchy needs to be scrutinized to determine the correct relationships between the classes, i.e., inheritance, aggregation, and using.

Real-world entities that can be modeled as GDI draw abstractions include:

- brushes
- pens
- fonts
- curves

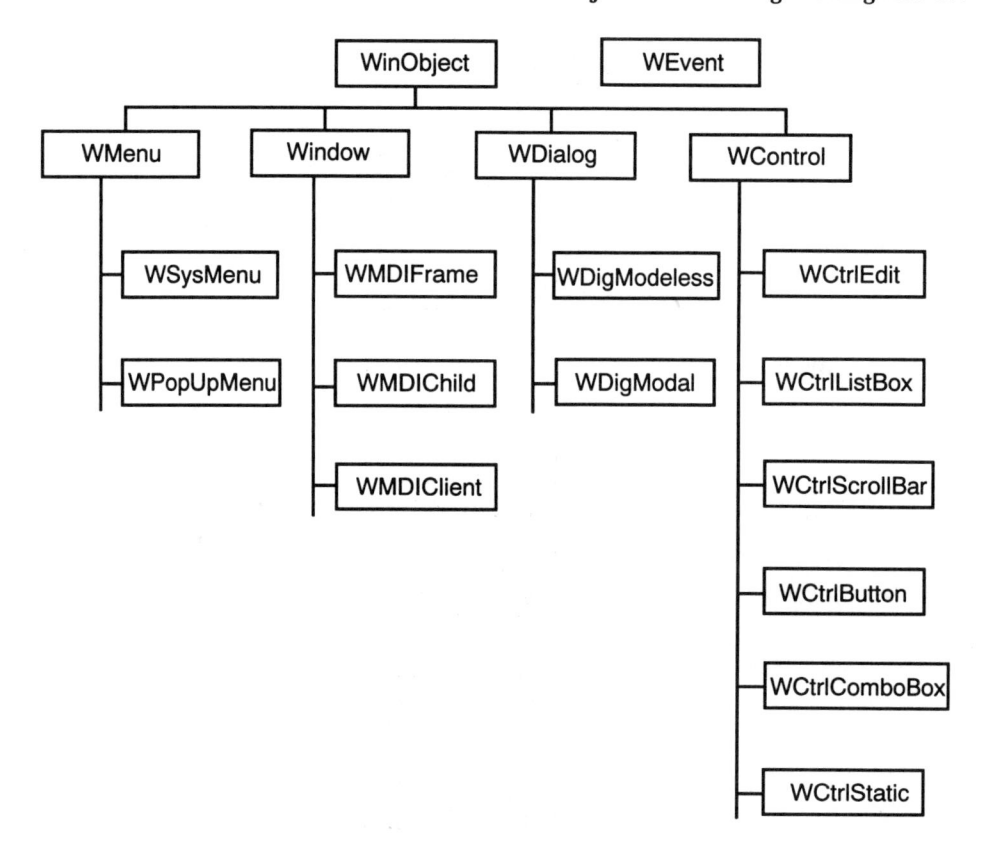

```
                    WinObject              WEvent
         ┌─────────────┼──────────┬──────────────┐
       WMenu        Window     WDialog        WControl
         │            │           │              │
    ┌ WSysMenu    ┌ WMDIFrame  ┌ WDlgModeless  ┌ WCtrlEdit
    │             │            │               │
    └ WPopUpMenu  ├ WMDIChild  └ WDlgModal     ├ WCtrlListBox
                  │                            │
                  └ WMDIClient                 ├ WCtrlScrollBar
                                               │
                                               ├ WCtrlButton
                                               │
                                               ├ WCtrlComboBox
                                               │
                                               └ WCtrlStatic
```

Figure 22-4. Initial window class hierarchy

- icons
- lines
- regions,
- palettes

Based on these abstractions, we can construct the initial class hierarchy shown in Figure 22-5. The leading characters for GDI drawing object classes are "GDr," to distinguish them from the window classes.

Real-world entities that can be modeled as GDI device information abstractions include:

- display screens
- hard copy devices

Chapter 22 • Developing a Windows C++ Library

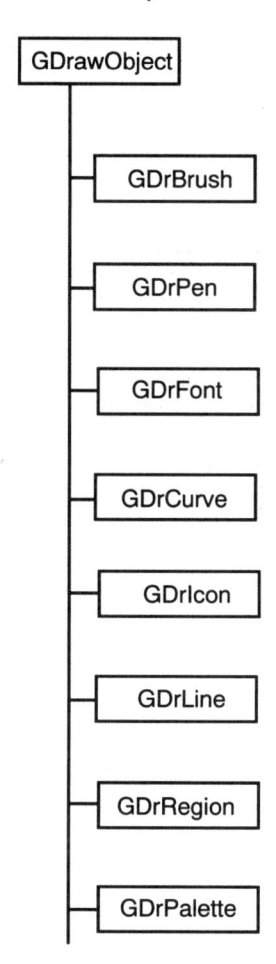

```
GDrawObject
    ├── GDrBrush
    ├── GDrPen
    ├── GDrFont
    ├── GDrCurve
    ├── GDrIcon
    ├── GDrLine
    ├── GDrRegion
    └── GDrPalette
```

Figure 22-5. Initial GDI draw objects

- device contexts
- bitmaps
- metafiles (used to store a collection of executable instructions)

The initial hierarchy for GDI device information objects is shown in Figure 22-6. The class names in this category are prefaced with "G" or "GDev" to make them uniquely different from the GDI draw classes.

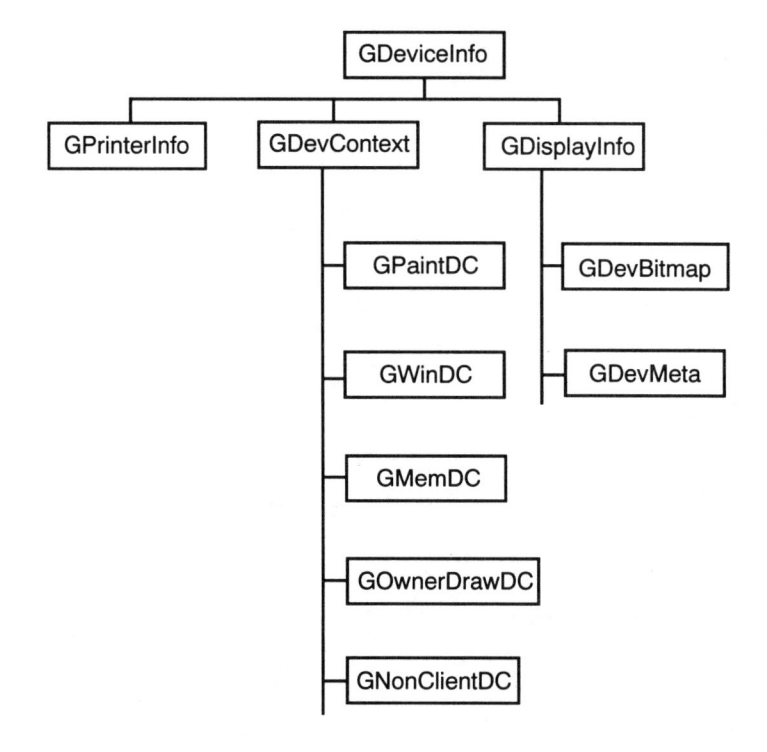

```
                    ┌─────────────┐
                    │ GDeviceInfo │
                    └──────┬──────┘
          ┌────────────────┼────────────────┐
   ┌──────┴──────┐  ┌──────┴──────┐  ┌──────┴──────┐
   │ GPrinterInfo│  │ GDevContext │  │ GDisplayInfo│
   └─────────────┘  └──────┬──────┘  └──────┬──────┘
                           ├─ GPaintDC      ├─ GDevBitmap
                           ├─ GWinDC        └─ GDevMeta
                           ├─ GMemDC
                           ├─ GOwnerDrawDC
                           └─ GNonClientDC
```

Figure 22-6. Initial GDI device information objects

The class hierarchies shown in Figures 22-4, 22-5, and 22-6 are anchored by separate base classes. This could have been modeled as a giant, monolithic class with a single base class. We prefer the separate base class approach for an incremental development strategy. This provides for loose coupling between the three primary class families and will minimize recompilation during the development phase. This topic will be discussed further in Section 22.5.

After the initial class hierarchies have been established, each class is scrutinized to determine the set of associated operations and attributes. We determine the operations first, using the "contract" model.

22.3.2 Client/Server Class Model Using CRC Cards

In Chapter 4, we described the OT concept of a "contract" interface as it applied to the use of classes. The users of a class are the clients, and the class itself represents the server. The server interface presents the contract for client access to class attributes and operations. The primary access mechanism is via C++ member functions. The attributes are implemented as data members and are usually hidden from the clients.

The first step in creating a class library is to anticipate the client programs that will be using the library and the type of operations these clients will require. To help us analyze the classes and their interfaces, we will use the CRC card mechanism. Rather than show actual "cards," we will create the equivalent tables for the appropriate class-responsibilities-collaborations information for each class.

Since the term "handle" will show up in several of the operations descriptions, a brief explanation of this term is in order (for more details see [NOR92]). A handle is an identifier of a certain object, e.g., a window or a device context. A handle is used by the application as a reference number; only the internal Windows system knows anything about the actual object associated with the handle. Each window in the application has a unique handle. Other handles are used for device contexts associated with graphics output; graphics objects such as pens, brushes, and fonts; and for menus, icons, and cursors.

Starting with the hierarchy shown in Figure 22-4, we can create the following CRC card (without the collaborators) for the Window class:

- Class Name: Window

    Responsibilities:

        get window handle (for existing window)

        get window handle (window may not exist)

        get window from handle

        register window class

        create window

        show window

        update window

        handle messages

        destroy window

        . . .

        get window information

        set window information

These responsibilities represent encapsulations of one or more API functions that C Windows applications would normally be using.

Additional CRC cards can be developed for each of the classes shown in Figures 22-4, 22-5, and 22-6.

22.4 DESIGNING THE INTERFACES (OOD)

The overall design goals for our Windows development effort can be summarized as follows:

- *Reusability*. The class library must be highly reusable for a large selection of Windows applications. This is supported with a complete set of operations for the advertised features.
- *Efficiency*. The features available from the library must be implemented without significant extra overhead compared to the same applications using the API directly. The use of *inline* functions can eliminate most of the overhead associated with additional function calls.
- *Maintenance*. Windows applications using our library must be easy to maintain and extend. The library structure should not be too deep or convoluted in terms of class relationships. Multiple inheritance should only be used where there is a clear is-a relation to more than one class.
- *Ease of Use*. There must be a one-to-one relationship between the encapsulated API functionalities in the library and the corresponding API functions they replace. This is best supported by making the library features well documented, and by providing the proper level of information hiding. The file structure must be organized to allow incremental compilation.

The client/server relation is fundamental to the design of C++ class libraries. Each library will include a class hierarchy that can be accessed by client programs and/or extended by derivation to lower-level classes. Different design decisions must be made for the two sets of interfaces.

The OOA classes determined during the software requirements analysis phase are transitioned to OOD entities with the initial hierarchical structure.

The CRC cards developed during the OOA activity are used to determine the appropriate attributes associated with each class. The proper class relationships can be determined by focusing on the class collaborations. Each class interface must be carefully designed with respect to encapsulation and data hiding to provide a suitable server interface.

Chapter 22 • Developing a Windows C++ Library

Since the CRC card mechanism focuses on the operations to the detriment of the data elements, a special effort must be expended to determine suitable attributes.

Once the initial set of attributes has been determined, each attribute must be analyzed to ascertain whether it is a single data element or a collection of related items.

Great care must be taken to determine whether an attribute should be global or local. There is a significant semantic difference between local and global data items for an object-oriented implementation. A global data structure declared within a class is shared by all instances created from that class. A local data structure, however, is associated with each instance declared from that class.

Some of the attributes associated with the Window class include (we are using the names of the corresponding structures documented in the Microsoft SDK (Software Development Kit [MIC92]):

- CREATESTRUCT (defines initialization parameters passed to the window procedure of an application)—WCreateStruct.
- MDICREATESTRUCT (information about the class title, owner, location, and size of multiple document interface (MDI) child window)—WMDICreateStruct.
- PAINTSTRUCT (information about how to paint the client area of a window owned by the application)—WPaintStruct.
- POINT (defines x- and y-coordinates of a point)—WPoint.
- RECT (defines the coordinates of the upper-left and lower-right edges of a rectangle)—WRect.
- TEXTMETRIC (basic information about character fonts)—WTextMetric.
- WNDCLASS (contains window classification data used to register a window regarding style, icon, menus, background color, etc.)—WinCategory (a Window "class" is different from a C++ class).
- Window handle (handle that uniquely identifies a window)—hwnd.

The attributes listed in uppercase (from the SDK) represent collections of data elements. The corresponding C++ library name for window objects is listed at the end of each attribute description, e.g., WCreateStruct is our C++ name for API's CREATESTRUCT.

Whether the attributes should be implemented as C++ classes or structs is deferred to the OOP phase. Design decisions regarding local attributes (i.e., separate data elements for each object) versus global data elements shared by all instances of a class, should be determined during the OOD activity.

Some of the collaborators and their relationships with the WinObject class include the following classes (and, perhaps, structs):

- WEvent (using)
- WMenu (inheritance)
- Window (inheritance)
- WDialog (inheritance)
- WControl (inheritance)
- WCreateStruct (aggregate)
- WMDICreateStruct (aggregate)
- WCreateStruct (aggregate)
- WPaintStruct (aggregate)
- WPoint (aggregate)
- WRect (aggregate)
- WTextMetric (aggregate)
- WinCategory (aggregate)
- hwnd (data member using HWND type from Windows.h)

Objects created from WCreateStruct and WTextMetric should be global, i.e., there is only one instance of each of these shared between window objects. Each window will have a unique handle, however, and hwnd is not shared. Similar design decisions must be made for each attribute. This may not be completed until the OOP phase, since we may not be able to determine the proper use of all attributes during the OOD phase.

Having determined the structure and interfaces of the classes, they can now be implemented with C++ constructs. This is usually not a one-way transitioning from design to implementation. Significant iteration will most likely take place between these two phases before the C++ implementation is completed.

22.5 IMPLEMENTING THE CLASSES (OOP)

This is the last phase of the software development process and includes the actual coding using C++ constructs.

The classes, operations, attributes, and collaborations determined during the OOD phase are transitioned to the OOP phase as C++ classes, member functions, and data members. The attributes will now have to be closely examined to determine if they should be implemented as simple data members, C++ classes, or structs. The collaborations are used to determine the proper class interfaces, including the possibility of relaxing the level of information hiding.

The class user interfaces are created using the proper access level of *public*, *private*, and *friend* visibility constructs. The class *inheritance* interface is created using the appropriate *protected* and *private* visibility constructs, and virtual base member functions for the derivation of unique member functions in child classes.

22.5.1 Encapsulations

To demonstrate many of the design and implementation paradigms discussed earlier, we will create skeleton C++ code for a portion of the *WinObject* class interface contained in *WinObject.h*. The focus in this section is on the creation of proper user interfaces. For clarity, we have omitted the usual use of compiler directives to prevent multiple inclusions of header files.

```
// WEvent.h - header file for event message class

class WEvent {
public:
  WEvent (....);
  ~WEvent ();
  HWND wHandle ();//get handle for object with focus
  WPoint cursorPos ();// get cursor pos at last msg
  WORD wCmnd (); // return wParam
  ...
private:
  WORD message; // complete message
  LONG lParam;  // long part of message
  WORD wParam;  // short part of message
  LONG returnCode;
  ...
};
```

The *WEvent* class encapsulates the handling of message events. A message is contained in the *lParam* and *wParam* data members. We chose to make it a class, but could have used a struct as well. This will make it easier to modify the class if we decide later that it should function as a base class; structs cannot be used for inheritance. This class will be used by the various window objects to handle message events.

We next focus on the structure of the header file for the *WinObject* base class:

```
// WinObject.h - header file for window base
//                object file

struct WRect {
  int left;
  int top;
  int right;
  int bottom;
};

struct WPoint {
  int x;
  int y;
};

struct WCreateStruct {
  WNDCLASS wndclass; // used to register window
  HMENU hMenu; // menu handle for new window
  HWND hwndParent; // owner of new window
  WRect pos; // positioning and size of new window
  LONG style; // style of new window
  LPCSTR lpszName; // window name
  DWORD dwExStyle; // extended style for window
};

class WinObject {
public:
  WinObject (....); // constructor
  virtual ~WinObject (); // destructor
  HWND getHwnd (); // get window handle
  virtual BOOL createWindow ();
```

```
                                  // create window object
    virtual void destroyWindow ();
                                  // destroy win object
    static WCreateStruct createParams; // aggregate
    static TEXTMETRIC textMetric;      // aggregate
    ...
  protected:
    HWND hwnd;
    virtual LONG msgProc (WEvent& evt);  // using
    LONG defaultMsgProc (WEvent& evt);   // using
    BOOL dispatchEvent (WEvent& evt);    // using

    friend LONG FAR PASCAL WWndProc
                       (HWND, WORD, WORD, LONG);
    friend BOOL FAR PASCAL WDlgProc
                       (HWND, WORD, WORD, LONG);
    ...
};
```

Encapsulations included in the *WinObject* header are the structs WRect for a rectangular window area, WPoint for an (x, y) coordinate point, and WCreateStruct for the registering and handling of a new window. The latter is a combination of the SDK WNDCLASS structure and miscellaneous other data elements. Each of these structures represents a collection of related data elements without any associated operations. There are also no inheritance relations associated with any of these encapsulations. They were thus implemented as simple structs rather than as classes.

The primary encapsulation in this header file is the *WinObject* class. This is the base class for the windows-related subclasses *WMenu*, *Window*, *WDialog*, and *WControl*. Only some of the class members have been included in the skeleton code sample. We now look at the design decisions we have made regarding user and inheritance interfaces.

22.5.2 User Interfaces

Visible operations in the *WinObject* specification include a constructor and destructor, as well as various functions for getting the handle to the window, and creating and destroying windows. We may have to provide additional constructors for a complete and efficient implementation. The completeness refers to our design goal of a high degree of reusability and ease of use. An appropriate set of constructors will ensure an efficient implementation that prevents needless copying of objects passed as function arguments.

The two objects *createStruct* and *textMetric* are two of the primary data structures used by Windows programs and have been left visible. The overhead associated with attempting to hide these two structures and to provide necessary access functions for every one of their data elements is not considered a worth while trade-off. These two data structures represent aggregate relations with instances of *WinObject*. They are made static because they are shared by all instances created from a particular category of *WinObject*.

The data member *hwnd*, representing a window handle, is local and hidden. Each window object gets a unique handle.

Member functions for handling message processing are hidden from other objects. Messages are handled by the main window processing functions, however, and these must have access to the hidden functions. This is accomplished by granting *friend* status to *WWndProc()* and *WDlgProc()*, two of the main windows application functions.

A using relationship is formed between instances of *WinObject* and *WEvent* objects, as the latter are passed by reference to the message processing functions.

22.5.3 Inheritance Interfaces

The second set of interfaces provides proper access and derivation for child classes. The primary emphasis for this type of interface is the use of *protected* to allow derived classes access to private members in the base class. The use of virtual base member functions is required to allow the derived member functions to override the base member functions.

We have followed the general design guideline of making destructors virtual [MEY92, p. 44]. This provides for an orderly succession of destructor calls up the inheritance tree, starting with the most derived class. Other virtual functions include the creation and destruction of individual window objects.

It is anticipated that message processing may have to be performed differently from what is provided in the base class. We are allowing derived classes to access the hidden members in the *protected* segment, and they will implement their own *msgProc()* function as a virtual function.

22.5.4 File Structure

An important part of the implementation is the determination of the file structure for the C++ code. The following file organization is recommended [HEI94]:

- *Application Files.* These are unique to an application and are produced by the users of our C++ class library. They will have file extensions of ".h" and ".cpp."
- *Specification Files.* These are contained in ".h" files and represent the class interfaces that the client software will use. An extensive use of *inline* functions, and implementations in general, should be avoided to prevent massive recompilations when changes are required. Information hiding must be carefully traded off against required access by "friends."
- *Implementation Files.* These are the implementations of the class member functions and are kept in separate ".cpp" files. They are typically linked with the application files to produce an executable image. They may also be used to create dynamic link libraries.

Associated with this type of a file structure is a versioning mechanism to provide for an orderly release of versions that represent different levels of features and capabilities. Files that are delivered for use in formal product versions must have been thoroughly evaluated and tested and placed under configuration control.

22.6 SUMMARY

In this chapter, we have used several of the design and implementation paradigms discussed in earlier chapters to suggest how we can create a Windows class library. The library is constructed using separate class families related by relatively shallow inheritance, rather than a huge, monolithic structure with a deep inheritance structure.

Reusability is supported by supplying a complete set of operations and by anticipating an inheritance hierarchy. A balanced level of information hiding is provided via a judicious use of the *public, private, protected,* and *friend* access mechanisms.

Appendix A

Moving from C to C++

Most organizations moving to C++ have already been developing applications using C as their programming language. The transition from C to C++ is a natural path to take advantage of OT paradigms and the associated higher level of software reusability. How to best accomplish this transition is far from obvious, however, and considerable planning is required. Although C++ is a superset of C, the OT paradigms are sufficiently different from traditional, procedural programming, and a significant amount of training will be required for the entire development staff.

The focus of this appendix is to point out the main differences between C and C++ syntax and semantics, and how these differences may affect the design and implementation of large systems development.

The primary difference between C and C++ is the degree of emphasis placed on types and structure [STR91, p. 7]. C++ implements strong typing with compiler checking of the number of function parameters and parameter types, and a requirement that prototypes be included. Parameter checking is now also included in ANSI C, but prototypes are not required.

As applications have become more complex and feature laden, the programs to implement them have grown larger. This has placed a larger emphasis on how big programs can be structured, and how we can take advantage of exiting code for reuse. The most important C++ feature for taking advantage of reuse is the class construct and the associated inheritance hierarchy with run-time binding for implementation of polymorphism. Another important reuse feature is the use of templates for multi-type functions and classes.

One area of importance for moving an entire software development team from C to C++ has to do with potential organizational changes that must be made.

A.1 ANSI C AND C++

C++ is sometimes considered a bigger and better C. The C++ syntax is a natural extension of C with object-oriented features added. ANSI C has adopted many of the C++ syntax features, and this provides a straightforward migration path from C to C++.

A.1.1 NEW KEYWORDS

Several new keywords have been incorporated with C++, and these must be avoided as variable or function names in C code that will be reused in a C++ application. The new keywords include:

- *catch* — keyword to handle (catch) an exception
- *class* — keyword to declare a class, and to define templates
- *delete* — operator used to deallocate objects; replaces *free()*
- *friend* — keyword to specify friend function or class
- *inline* — keyword to specify an inline function
- *new* — operator used for dynamic allocation; replaces *malloc()* and *calloc()*
- *operator* — keyword to specify overloaded operator
- *private* — keyword to delineate hidden class access
- *protected* — keyword to delineate hidden class access for users, but allows access for derived class members
- *public* — keyword to delineate visible class access
- *template* — keyword for creating function and class templates
- *this* — keyword to designate current object
- *throw* — keyword to raise an exception
- *try* — keyword to define scope for raising and catching exceptions
- *virtual* — keyword to specify function that can be overridde in derived classes

A.1.2 Declaration of Variables

Variables can be declared anywhere in a program before they are referenced.

They do not have to be declared at the top of a block.

This feature should be used with caution. It is not recommended to place variable declarations within if statements, for example, since this could greatly complicate debugging.

A.1.3 Type Checking

The type checking in C++ is more rigid than in C. This provides some differences worth noting [LIP91, p. 586]:

- *Use of Undeclared Function.* This is illegal in C++, but permitted in C:

    ```
    int main () {
      // ...
      printf (x); // C: int printf ();
                  // C++: illegal, printf() not declared
      return 0;
    }
    ```

- *Failure to Return a Value in a Function.* A C++ function declared with a type for returning a value must return a value of that type. This is allowed in C.
- *Void Pointer Assignment.* The assignment of a type *void** to a pointer of another type must be done with an explicit cast in C++. It is done implicitly in C.
- *Initialization of String Constants.* Space for the terminating null character must be provided for in C++ when string constants are initialized. C allows the missing null character:

    ```
    int main () {
      // ...
      char ch [5] = "hello"; // ok in C
                             // error in C++
      // ...
      return 0;
    }
    char ch [] = "hello";
                // preferred; ok in both C and C++
    ```

A.2 FUNCTION PROTOTYPES

A function prototype specification must be declared before a function can be invoked. This allows the compiler to perform parameter checking of function calls.

A function prototype must be included for all external functions including a type specifier for each argument:

```
extern max (const int*, int);  // required in C++
extern max ();                 // legal in C
```

If C legacy code is to be used with a new C++ development, all extern declarations will have to be changed to conform to the C++ style.

Functions in C can be specified without a parameter list. In C++, a function specification without an argument list means that there cannot be any arguments in calls to that function. C functions with intended arguments will have to be changed to include the list.

A.3 FUNCTION PARAMETERS

Formal function parameters in C++ can be assigned default values:

```
int Power (int n, int k = 2); // defaults to square

Power (256); // 256 squared
```

The parameters given defaults need not be specified when the function is called. Parameters with default values must be at the end of the parameter list:

```
void func1 (int i =3, int j);  // illegal
void func2 (int i, int j = 0, int k = 0);  // ok
void func3 (int i = 2, int j, int k = 0);  // illegal
```

A.4 CALL-BY-REFERENCE PARAMETERS

A frequent source of error for novice C programmers is the call-by-value parameter passing mechanism. The infamous swap (x, y) function has been used extensively to demonstrate the potential problem for unsuspecting C programmers:

```
void swap (int x, int y) { // C/C++ call-by-value
  int temp = y;
  y = x;
  x = temp;
}
// ...
swap (i, j); // i and j not swapped
```

Call-by-reference is simulated in C by using pointer types for the formal parameters in the prototype declaration. This permits the function implementation to access the values passed as actual parameters:

```
void swap (int* x, int* y) {
                          // C/C++ pointer notation
  int temp = *y;
  *y = *x;
  *x = temp;
}
// ...
swap (&i, &j); // i and j swapped ok
```

C++ supports call-by-reference directly via reference parameters. This simplifies the implementation in the function body, and provides call-by-value syntax:

```
void Swap (int& x, int& y); // C++ call-by-reference
  int temp = y;
  y = x;
  x = temp;
}
// ...
swap (i, j); // i and j swapped ok
```

The use of reference notation is also recommended when passing large objects as parameters to functions. This will avoid the overhead of creating and copying the objects passed inside the function.

A.5 VARIABLE NUMBER OF PARAMETERS

C++ supports a variable number of function parameters via a special syntax:

```
int printf (const char* ctrlString, ...);
```

The three dots ("ellipse") signify to the compiler that this function can be invoked with a variable number of parameters. This feature should only be used in special cases, since the compiler relaxes the normal type checking performed on parameter lists.

A.6 FUNCTION OVERLOADING AND TYPE SAFE LINKAGE

Functions in C++ can be overloaded by having different member functions in the same class with the same name. This means that the overloaded functions have the same name, but different signatures, i.e., different parameter lists.

Function overloading provides for better name management and makes obsolete the necessity in C for concocting different names for the same functionality with different parameter types.

Different functions can be recognized by the run-time system because the compiler attaches symbolic names to the overloaded functions depending on their signatures. This is usually referred to as *name mangling*. As long as the function calls made are unambiguous with regard to the number and types of the parameters, the run-time system can determine the correct function invocation.

An example of function overloading is the following:

```
int    max (int, int);
double max (double, double);
```

The encoding of the function name with the return type and parameter types is referred to as type safe linkage: An erroneous function declaration will be detected by the linker, and eliminates a common type of errors associated with C programs.

A drawback to the type safe linkage is that if we want to call C functions from C++ programs, the C functions must be identified with a different linkage mechanism. This is usually done by using the extern "C" compiler directive:

```
extern "C" Cfunction (args);
```

The C++ compiler will then not perform name mangling on the C function, and the function will link correctly with the rest of the C++ functions.

Note the difference between overloading and overriding: Function overloading refers to having two or more functions within a class with the same name, but with different signatures. Overriding refers to the implementation in a derived class of a virtual function declared in a base class. The corresponding functions have the same name and the same signature.

A.7 THE *CONST* TYPE MODIFIER

The *const* type modifier is used in C++ to provide read-only protection for variables and function parameters. Class member functions that do not modify the data members they access can be declared const. This prevents these members from accessing non-const data members. This is also used to prevent parameters passed by reference to be modified:

```
void copy (const char* source, char* dest);
```

A.8 CLASSES AND STRUCTS

C uses structs extensively for the creation of data structures. The OT equivalent construct in C++ is a class which encapsulates a data structure and the operations that act on instances declared from the class type. C-type structs can also be used in C++, including the declaration of operations within a struct. All data members of a struct are public by default, and inheritance is not allowed.

The predominant encapsulation mechanism for C++ application is the class. A struct can be used to encapsulate a collection of related data elements that are used by other classes. For example, a Windows application may want to create a struct that combines data elements to register and create a Windows class:

```
struct WCreateStruct {
  WNDCLASS wndclass; // used to register window
```

```
    HMENU    hMenu; // menu handle for new window
    HWND     hwndParent; // owner of new window
    WRect    pos;//positioning and size of new window
    LONG     style; // style of new window
    LPCSTR   lpszName; // window name
    DWORD    dwExStyle; // extended style for window
};
```

This type can be used by the object(s) that register and create the original window. Operations on the window object are all included in the classes that encapsulate the window.

Note the difference in syntax between C and C++ structs: The name following the struct keyword in C++ signifies the name of a type, and objects of this type can be declared using the same syntax as we use for the predefined types :

```
WCreateStruct newWindow; // declare object newWindow
```

A.9 I/O LIBRARIES

Any C++ development system includes a special I/O library, just as C has the *stdio* library. The I/O library in included as the header file *iostream.h* and provides services for a number of I/O operations, for example:

```
#include <iostream.h>
#include <string.h>

int main () {
  // ...
  cout << "Hello World\n"; // standard output
  // ...
  cout << "The length of 'Hello World' is:\t"
       << strlen ("Hello World") << endl;//length=11
  // ...
  cout << "The size of 'Hello World' is:\t"
       << sizeof ("Hello World") << endl;//length=12
  // ...
  return 0;
}
```

The insertion operators (<<) and extraction operators (>>) can be concatenated and simplify the I/O functions:

```
#include <iostream.h>

int main() {
  int x, y;

    cout << "Please enter two integers: " << endl;
    cin >> x >> y; // Left-to-right association
    cout << "Values read are: < " << x << ", "
        << y << " >" << endl;
    return 0;
}
```

The C++ I/O library functions and operators are preferred over the equivalent C functions. Functions available in *stdio.h* should only be used in special cases.

A.10 INLINE FUNCTIONS

Function in C++ can be declared *inline* to prevent run-time overhead of multiple function calls. This provides the benefits of C macros with compile time checking of parameters. Overuse of inlining may, however, cause an excessive amount of code expansion and, possibly, recompilation when class specifications are modified. Here are some examples:

```
// File: localMath.h
// Prototypes (function declarations)

inline int abs (int i);
inline int min (int v1, int v2);
int gcd (int v1, int v2); // not an inline candidate
```

Functions declared inline should be simple, with just a few program statements. They should only be called a limited number of times and should not be recursive.

Member functions declared with a definition in the class specification are automatically considered inline by the compiler:

```
class Rect {
public:
  Rect ();
  ~Rect ();
  int left () {return x;}
  int right () {return x + width;}
  int top () {return y;}
  int bottom () {return y + height;}
private:
  int x, y;
  int width, height;
};
```

A.11 FUNCTIONS *NEW* AND *DELETE*

C programmers typically use *malloc()* and *free()* to create and destroy objects created from the heap. This should not be done in C++ programs. The equivalent C++ functions are the operators *new* and *delete*. The reason why these two functions must be used is that they invoke the appropriate constructors and destructors, respectively. The functions *malloc()* and *free()* are accessible to C++ programs via the ANSI Standard libraries, but instances of classes will then not be created and destroyed properly.

A.12 ORGANIZATIONAL ISSUES

The primary impact on the development organization will be the determination of who will be the class providers, and who will be the class users.

The creation of classes and class libraries should be performed by the C++ experts who fully understand the construction and semantics of constructors, destructors, inheritance hierarchies, and polymorphism. These experts should also understand the differences between the class relationships of aggregation, inheritance, and using.

The application programmers do not need to have the detailed knowledge that it takes to create class libraries. They will merely access the class interfaces for their applications.

Scheduling can become an organizational issue if analysis and design have not been practiced on prior projects. Significant time and effort must be devoted to these two development phases before any C++ programming can start. This can skew previously used schedules towards a front-loading for analysis and design by a few experts. The programmers will be hired or engaged after the analysis and design phases are sufficiently complete.

Some managers may have to be "educated" with the fact that they will not see any code produced as soon as they would like to, or are used to seeing.

A significant training budget will have to be allocated to allow sufficient training in OT and the use of C++. Another budget item should be the planning and management of a reuse facility.

A.13 STRATEGY FOR ADOPTING C++

A move from C to C++ should be carefully planned and managed. There is usually a significant amount of legacy C code that can be reused in new C++ developments and should not simply be discarded. The move should be made in stages, not all at once. Few organizations can afford to stop their current software productions and resurface with a brand new product totally written in C++. Here are some recommendations for affecting the move:

- *Training.* The key to using C++ properly and efficiently is training. It has been estimated that it takes between six and twelve months of intensive training and hands-on experience for designers and programmers to become proficient in design and programming with C++. Training is required for OOD/OOP as well as for the language features of C++. When training funds are authorized, an emphasis should be placed on the training of in-house trainers. Key individuals should be earmarked to continue the training of staff personnel and to provide a mentor function for less experienced designers and programmers. It is extremely important that the C++ training be hands-on, preferably using the same development system that will be used for product development.
- *Analysis and Design.* A significant effort should be placed on analyzing and planning future products, and to designing them with reuse in mind. This is especially important for the creation of problem domain C++ class libraries. Another important factor is how existing legacy C code can be used in future C++ products.

- *Gradual Implementations.* The move to C++ should be implemented gradually. The initial effort should be placed on using C++ syntax in C programs. The next phase can be to start using classes instead of structs as encapsulations. An ongoing effort should be to prepare class libraries for reuse. The final phase is where the implementation is focused on a client/server strategy of reusing classes from the available libraries. Some of the libraries have been developed in-house, others have been obtained from vendors.

Appendix B

C++ Coding Guidelines

The primary purpose of adopting a set of coding guidelines is to improve code reliability, readability and ease of understanding, and portability. Reliability is improved by adhering to the rules suggesting ways to avoid unsafe coding traps, e.g., the use of macros. Readability and ease of understanding is obtained by maintaining uniform coding standards for all the software developed for a large project. Portability is improved by planning for multi-platform use and avoiding machine dependent features. Any necessary machine dependencies should, of course, be carefully documented.

These guidelines can be used as a basis for code reviews. Reviewers can evaluate C++ program units against the suggested guidelines and determine if they pass the organization's quality standards.

The guidelines that follow represent a compendium of various recommendations made in previous chapters, and some suggestions from other sources. This appendix should be considered a baseline for a "living" document, i.e., additional guidelines should be added as lessons are learned with each new project implementation.

B.1 DESIGN OF ADTS

The design of an ADT should reflect an appropriate encapsulation and an adequate interface for access by clients. The following checklist can be used to evaluate the design of an ADT:

- *Encapsulation.* The encapsulation should represent a single abstraction.
- *Structure.* The client interface and functional specification should be separate from the implementation.
- *Public Interface.* Access should be limited to the member functions necessary to manipulate objects of the class. Data members should be hidden.
- *Member Functions.* A complete set of member functions should be available, and should include functions of the following categories (see Chapter 17):
  - *Manager Functions.* These member functions include management of initialization, assignment, type conversion, and memory management. Constructors and destructors are included in this category.
  - *Implementor Functions.* Functions in this category manipulate the objects created from the class and represent a portion of the "contract" interface for the class.
  - *Helping Functions.* Functions in this category perform auxiliary tasks needed by the other member functions. In their strict support role, they are usually hidden and not available to clients of the class.
  - *Access Functions.* Since our designs are heavily based on encapsulation and information hiding, we create access functions to provide information about the hidden data members. This set of functions constitutes the other part of the contract interface to clients of the class.

B.2 USE OF CLASSES AND STRUCTS

If we create classes to replace the functionality of existing structs, the size of the new class instances should correspond to the size and elements in the associated struct [DIL92, p. 13]. This will allow us to use older code and cast between the old structs and the new class instances. For Windows applications, for example, if we create a class dealing with points in a window, the structure should correspond to the POINT structure already available in *windows.h*:

```
class WPoint {
public:
  WPoint (...);
```

```
    set (...);
  private:
    int x;
    int y;
    // other member functions here
};
```

The declaration from *windows.h* includes:

```
typedef struct tagPOINT {
  int x;
  int y;
} POINT;
```

A Windows application can now be using types from both the API and the custom class library by appropriate casting:

```
WPoint pt; // from custom library
...
ScreenToClient (hwnd, (POINT)&pt);//cast 'pt' to API
POINT type
...
```

The size of the custom object 'pt' is exactly the same size as any API object of type *POINT*; the additional member functions declared in the class *WPoint* do not affect the size of the object declared as an instance of the class *WPoint*. The casting from the custom object to an API object will use the correct data structure inside the API function *ScreenTOClient ()*.

B.3 CLASS INTERFACES

Place interface segments in the same order in all class specifications:

```
class X {
// friend functions and classes here
public:
  // public members here
```

```
protected:
  // protected members here
private:
  // private members here
};
```

A consistent order makes it easier to read large class specifications. This particular order starts with the list of friend classes and functions and follows with class interface visible to a client. Class users don't have to scan any further to determine the class members they can use.

Avoid the use of protected data members except as required for an inheritance hierarchy. Clever users can create a derived class to circumvent the intended information hiding.

B.4 VIRTUAL FUNCTIONS

An initial design guideline is to make all member functions in the base class virtual while the hierarchy is being developed. This will allow these member functions to be overridden in the derived classes. If it is decided that some of the member functions in the base class should not be overridden in the derived classes, the virtual description is removed before the class is released for reuse.

Member functions that are unique to a derived class should not be overridden from a base member function, but should be added to the derived class with a unique name. This will preclude the creation of artificial polymorphism that is likely to become confusing during testing and debugging.

A base class X should have a virtual destructor whenever:

- X has at least one derived class Y
- Y's destructor behaves differently from X's destructor
- an instance of Y may be deleted via a pointer or reference to an instance of X

These rules will provide for an orderly destruction of objects in an inheritance hierarchy. If the destructor in the base class is not made virtual, destructors in the derived classes may not destroy instances of the derived classes properly.

B.5 INHERITANCE

Inheritance hierarchies should be developed using public inheritance to provide users of the derived class access to the public and protected members of the base class.

Private inheritance should only be used when the inheritance is an implementation detail. Users of the derived class have no access to the public and protected members of the base class.

Inheritance should never be used just because it may be convenient to "derive" properties from an existing class and thus save a little coding. Inheritance should only be used for a true is-a relationship. Private inheritance should be avoided except when we have to override a base member function that is required for the implementation of the derived class.

Multiple inheritance should be avoided on the first few projects, until the development staff fully understands the invocation order of constructors, and the effects of polymorphism. When multiple inheritance is used, a derived class should be based on true is-a relationships of all the base classes used.

A protected segment should only be used for intended and expected derivation. We should never place members in a protected segment just because we are not sure if the class will be used for derivation. Someone could circumvent the intended information hiding by creating an unexpected derived class.

B.6 PUBLIC VERSUS PRIVATE DERIVATION

In most cases with a true is-a relationship, we use public derivation. Private derivation can be used to hide a class implementation. In most of those cases, however, private derivation can be replaced by aggregation.

B.7 DYNAMIC ALLOCATION

A good design guideline is to always check the allocation of dynamic objects using *assert()*.

B.8 USE OF FRIENDS

The use of friends is a design alternative for implementing "using" relationships between classes. If friends start to proliferate the design, however, it may be a sign that information hiding has been seriously violated. Since the granting of friend status relaxes the level of information hiding, it should only be allowed where necessary.

B.9 INLINE FUNCTIONS

Functions declared inline should be simple, with just a few program statements. They should only be called a limited number of times, and should not be recursive.

Member functions declared with a definition in the class specification are automatically considered inline by the compiler. Great caution must be exercised in the use of automatic inline functions, since any change in an inline implementation will result in recompilation of that interface and all application programs accessing the interface.

B.10 MIXING C AND C++ FUNCTIONS

C linking conventions should be used when a C++ program accesses C library functions [STR91, p. 120]:

```
extern "C" char* strcpy (char*, const char*);
```

A set of functions can be declared as follows:

```
extern "C" {
  char* strcpy (char*, const char*);
  int strcmp (const char*, const char*);
  int strlen (const char*);
  // ...
}
```

This can also be used to create a standard C++ header from a standard C header:

Appendix B • C++ Coding Guidelines

```
extern "C" {
#include <string.h>
}
```

An alternative solution is to use conditional compiler directives to specify the linking conventions for C or C++ programs:

```
#ifdef __cplusplus
extern "C" {
#endif

  char* strcpy (char*, const char*);
  int strcmp (const char*, const char*);
  int strlen (const char*);
  // ...
#ifdef __cplusplus
}
#endif
```

The value of *__cplusplus* is used to determine whether this is a C or C++ program. The *extern* "C" constructs are edited out for C programs.

The use of the *extern* "C" directive only specifies a linkage convention; it does not turn off the strong type checking performed by the C++ compiler.

B.11 PARAMETER PASSING

Use the *const* modifier for all function parameters passed by reference or as pointers that should not be modified:

```
void func (const classA& param);
extern "C" {
  char* strcpy (char*, const char*);
  int strcmp (const char*, const char*);
  int strlen (const char*);
  // ...
}
```

A large object is passed to a function via call-by-reference to avoid the overhead of constructing a local object and copying members to it. Any such object passed should be prefaced by *const* if it should not be modified inside the function. This also applies to any string function that is used to copy, compare, access, etc. Any of the string parameters not to be modified should be prefaced by the *const* modifier.

If this convention is used consistently throughout a large program, we use the compiler to detect inconsistencies, rather than discovering bugs during the testing phase. A good compiler will detect most attempts to modify *const* data.

The use of *const* parameters must be planned during the design phase. Any attempt to retrofit a large existing C++ program with const parameters will most likely be frustrating, because of the *const* restrictions.

B.12 USE OF MACROS

Macros are important elements of C programs. In C++, they should not be used, unless there is a compelling reason to use them. Macros are commonly used in C programs to define global constants. These constants should be declared with a constant type specification in C++:

```
#define BUFSIZE 256 // C macro
const int BUFSIZE = 256; // C++
```

B.13 EXCEPTION HANDLING

Exception handling should be a part of the design and will provide a measure of software fault tolerance. This is not just for error handling, but for exceptional conditions that fall into the following four categories:

1. **Anticipated Exceptional Conditions.** This is where a (rare) condition over a long execution time may eventually result in an overflow exception., e.g., we can use an exception handler to re-initialize a set of handlers.

2. **Protection of Server Software.** Used to protect a software server from erroneous or inconsistent input data.

3. **Reporting of Hardware Failures.** Used to detect when a hardware device fails.

4. **Reporting of Unanticipated Errors (Bugs).** Used to detect and report bugs.

The C++ language mechanism for exception handling should be used throughout, rather than typical C methods of error exits and the use of *setjmp* and *longjmp*. Details of declaring, raising, and handling exceptions are covered in Chapter 21.

Appendix C

Object Technology Glossary

This appendix provides an alphabetical list of the terms and concepts used in the previous chapters and appendices.

- *Abstract Class.* A base class containing at least one pure virtual function. Instances cannot be created from an abstract class.
- *Abstract Data Type (ADT).* An encapsulation of a key abstraction. Includes operations and attributes necessary to manipulate instances of the type. Implemented as C++ class or struct.
- *Abstraction.* High-level description of an entity or concept, leaving out essential details.
- *Active Object.* Object which has its own process. The process must be active (recognized by the operating system) during the object's existence.
- *Actual Parameter.* A value provided as a parameter in a function call.
- *ADT.* See *Abstract Data Type.*
- *Aggregation.* A decomposition of classes that satisfies the has-a or whole-part paradigm. An object is composed of subobjects of other types.
- *Analysis Phase.* The analysis and specification of a set of problem domain requirements.
- *Application.* A software program that provides a set of specified features or functionalities for use on a particular platform.
- *Architecture.* The structure of hardware and/or software components in

a computer system. Includes interfaces between the components and how they communicate.

- *Argument.* A value provided in the call of an operation. See *Actual Parameter* and *Formal Parameter.*
- *Association.* Relationships between instances of types.
- *Asynchronous Message.* Message sent by a client who does not wait for delivery or a reply.
- *Attribute.* Data element associated with an instance of a class.
- *Base Class.* Class from which other classes can be derived. Anchor of an inheritance hierarchy.
- *Binding.* The association of a name with an object. Bindings are performed at compile time (static binding) or run-time (dynamic binding).
- *Call-by-Reference.* Actual parameters refer to objects in a call to an operation. These objects can be modified inside the operation.
- *Call-by-Value.* Actual parameters are passed as values in a call to an operation. These values are copied inside the operation, and their associated objects cannot be modified.
- *Cardinality.* The number of objects related in an association.
- *Class.* An encapsulation mechanism used to implement abstract and concrete data types.
- *Class Attribute.* An attribute that is common to all instances of the class. Implemented with the *static* keyword in C++. Also referred to as a class variable.
- *Class-Based.* Method or programming language that supports ADTs, where the ADT is a type or a class.
- *Class Hierarchy.* A layering of classes related by inheritance or aggregation.
- *Class Member.* An operation or attribute specified for a class.
- *Client.* A program entity that requests a service.
- *Collaborator.* A client class in a client/server relationship between two classes. Used in CRC cards.
- *Composition.* See *Aggregation.*
- *Concrete Class.* Class from which instances can be created.
- *Constructor.* A special operation called to create an instance of a class. Each class may have multiple, special-purpose constructors.

- *Container Class.* Class whose instances are collections of other objects.
- *Contract.* The set of services provided in the specification of a server and made available to clients.
- *Data Member.* Attribute of a C++ class.
- *Decomposition.* An application of the divide-and-conquer paradigm to divide a complex entity into smaller, manageable entities.
- *Derived Class* The creation of a new class from one or more base classes, with the addition of specialized attributes and operations to the new class.
- *Design.* The act of creating a structure or architecture from which a system can be implemented.
- *Destructor.* A special operation called to destroy an instance of a class.
- *Dynamic Binding.* The association of a name with an object at run-time. Basis for implementation of polymorphism.
- *Encapsulation.* Abstraction of a data entity that includes a set of operations for manipulating instances of an implemented type. Specified with a separate interface and a body part that hides implementation details.
- *Event.* An action that may affect the state of an object. An event will usually invoke an operation associated with the behavior of an object.
- *Formal Parameter.* The specification of a local argument type and name in an argument list. The value of the formal parameter is replaced by the corresponding actual parameter when the operation is called.
- *Framework.* A set of classes that provides services for a particular problem domain, e.g., the Microsoft Foundation Class (MFC) library or Borland Object Windows Library (OWL) for Windows applications.
- *Friend.* A class or function given access to hidden class members of another class.
- *Genericity.* The use of templates to create identical program entities that only differ by types.
- *Handle.* A value (usually an integer) that uniquely identifies an object, e.g., a window.
- *Inheritance.* The mechanism of inheriting attributes and operations from a set of generalized base classes, with the opportunity to add specialized members to the deriving class.
- *Inline Operation.* An operation that is replaced by its implementation to save the overhead of a function call.
- *Instance.* The creation of an object from its class.

- *Instance Variable.* An attribute that is associated with a specific instance of a class.
- *Instantiation.* The creation of an instance of a class. Objects are created and initialized via class constructors.
- *Interface.* The set of services listed in the class specification that is available to clients. See *Contract.*
- *Iterator.* A program entity that can access all the objects in a collection or list.
- *Mapping.* Rules for transitioning analysis and design entities from one phase to another.
- *Member Function.* A C++ operation specified in the class interface.
- *Message.* An element of information used to communicate between two objects. Also used to describe the invocation of an operation to affect the behavior of another object.
- *Meta-Class.* A top-level class considered an object and used to anchor an inheritance hierarchy.
- *Method.* An operation associated with a class. A member function in C++.
- *Mixins.* Abstract classes used to specify a common interface for a number of subclasses.
- *Model.* A textual and/or graphical representation of an abstract problem domain concept or requirement.
- *Module.* A collection of programming entities that constitutes a software solution to a portion of an application.
- *Multiple Inheritance.* An inheritance mechanism that allows a derived class to inherit from two or more base classes.
- *Multiplicity.* See *Cardinality.*
- *Object.* An instance of a class that has a unique identifier, a set of attributes, and a set of operations.
- *Object-Based.* A programming language or mechanism that supports the creation of objects, but not inheritance. Ada is an object-based programming language.
- *Object-Oriented.* A method or programming language that supports encapsulation and information hiding, the creation of classes, inheritance, and objects.
- *Object State.* The unique set of values associated with an object.
- *Operation.* A service specified in a class interface that can be requested

by a client. An operation can include a set of C++ member functions, some of which are hidden from the clients.

- *Overloaded Operations.* Operations specified in a class interface that have the same name but different signatures.
- *Overloaded Operators.* Redefinitions of operators normally used for built-in types to be used with user-defined types, e.g., vector multiplication.
- *Overriding.* A language mechanism that allows the redefinition of base class operations in subclasses.
- *Passive Object.* An object that only responds to requests from other objects. It does not contain its own process (see Active Object).
- *Persistent Object.* An object that exists until it is explicitly deleted. Non-persistent objects are usually destroyed automatically when they exit their scope.
- *Polymorphic Operation.* An operation implemented by two or more member functions.
- *Polymorphism.* Run-time selection of a member function associated with an object. Client requests for member functions without specifying an object are automatically translated to the correct invocation.
- *Problem Domain.* The general set of requirements that describes a particular system to be implemented as an application.
- *Relation.* An association or mapping between classes or objects.
- *Request.* The invocation of a specific operation by name. Clients issue requests for the visible operations specified in the class interfaces.
- *Responsibilities.* A set of related operations that constitutes a contract for the class. They are specified in the class interface.
- *Server.* A program entity that responds to a service request from a client.
- *Signature.* The name and list of parameter types for an operation. The return type is not part of the signature.
- *Single Inheritance.* A mechanism that allows a derived class to only inherit from a single class.
- *State Transition.* The result of an event or activity that changes an object from one state to another.
- *Static Binding.* The association of an operation with an object at compilation time. See *Dynamic Binding*.
- *Strong Typing.* Language feature that provides for checking of consistent use of object types, and the declaration and invocation of operations.

- *Subclass.* A class derived from a base class.
- *Superclass.* A base class from which a subclass inherits its attributes and operations.
- *Synchronous Message.* Message sent by a client who waits for delivery and, possibly, a reply.
- *Using Relation.* Relation of a client that refers to or issues a request to a server. The client and server are not related by inheritance or aggregation.
- *Virtual Member Function.* A C++ member function for which dynamic binding will automatically be applied.
- *Visibility.* The level of access to the members specified in a class interface allowed by clients making requests. Data members are usually hidden from clients.

References

ABB83 Abbott, R.J., Program Design by Informal English Description, *Communications of the ACM*, Volume 26, Number 11, November 1983.

ACC93a Advanced Concepts Center, Martin Marietta, Object-Modeling Technique: Object-Oriented Analysis, Course Notes, Volumes 1 and 2, April 1993.

ACC93b Advanced Concepts Center, Martin Marietta, Object-Modeling Technique: Object-Oriented Design, Course Notes, Volumes 1 and 2, April 1993.

ARJ93 Arjomandi, E., and O'Farrell, W., Active objects in C++: how far can we stretch the library approach?, IBM Canada Laboratory Technical Report, TR-74,116,1993.

ARJ94 Arjomandi, E., et al., Concurrency Support for C++: An Overview, *C++ Report*, January 1994, p. 44.

BAR93 Barkakati, N., and Hipson, P.D., *Visual C++ Developer's Guide*, Sams Publishing, Carmel, IN, 1993.

BAR94 Barkakati, N., *Borland C++ 4 Developer's Guide*, Sams Publishing, Carmel, IN, 1994.

BAR93 Bar-David, T., Concepts of Object-Oriented Programming, Object World Conference, San Francisco, June 15, 1993.

BEN82 Ben-Ari, M., *Principles of Concurrent Programming*, Prentice-Hall In-

	ternational, Englewood Cliffs, NJ, 1982.
BER93	Berard, E.V., *Essays on Object-Oriented Software Engineering*, Volume I, Prentice Hall, 1993.
BOO86	Booch, G., Object-Oriented Development, in *IEEE Transactions on Software Engineering*, Volume SE-12, Number 2, February 1986.
BOO87	Booch, G., *Software Engineering with Ada*, Second Edition, Benjamin/Cummings, 1987.
BOO91	Booch, G., *Object-Oriented Design with Applications*, Benjamin/Cummings, 1991.
BOO93	Booch, G., *Object-Oriented Analysis and Design with Applications*, Second Edition, Benjamin/Cummings, 1993.
CAR77	Carey, R., and Bendick, M., The Control of a Software Test Process, *Proceedings COMPSAC 77*, pp. 327-333.
CAR94	Carroll, M., and Ellis, M., Error Handling in C++ Library Code, *C++ Report*, May 1994, p. 43.
CHA93	Champeaux D. de, et al., *Object-Oriented System Development*, Addison-Wesley, 1993.
CHE76	Chen, P., The Entity-Relationship Model — Toward a Unified View of Data, *ACM Trans. on Database Systems*, Volume 1, Number 1, 1976.
CLA93	Clamage, S.D., Debugging C++, Object World Conference, San Francisco, June 17, 1993.
COA90	Coad, P., and Yourdon, E., *Object-Oriented Analysis*, Yourdon Press, 1990.
COA91	Coad, P., and Yourdon, E., *Object-Oriented Analysis*, 2nd Edition, Yourdon Press, 1991.
COA91a	Coad, P., and Yourdon, E., *Object-Oriented Design*, Yourdon Press, 1991.
COP92	Copelien, J.O., *Advanced C++*, Addison-Wesley, Reading, MA, 1992.
DAH70	Dahl, O., et al., *Simula 67 Common Base Language*, S-22, Norwegian Computing Center, Oslo, Norway, 1970.
DAN86	Dannenberg, R.B., Arctic: Functional Programming for Real-Time

References

Systems, *Proceedings Hawaii International Conference on System Sciences,* IEEE Computer Society Press, 1986, pp. 216-226.

DDC94   C++ RTOS, DDC-I, Inc., 410 N. 44th Street, Phoenix, AZ, 85008, (602) 275-7172.

DEM79   DeMarco, T., *Structured Analysis and System Specification,* Prentice Hall, Englewood Cliffs, NJ, 1979.

DEU88   M.S. Deutsch, Focusing Real-Time Systems Analysis on User Operations, *IEEE Software,* September 1988, pp. 39-50.

DEU91   Deutsch, M.S., and Nielsen, K.W., User Scenarios as the Basis for System Architecture and Design, *Proceedings 13th International Conference on Software Engineering,* Austin Texas, May 13-16, 1991.

DIJ68   Dijkstra, E.W., Co-operating Sequential Processes, in *Programming Languages,* F. Genuys, Ed., Academic Press, New York, NY, 1968.

DIL92   DiLascia, P., *Windows++, Writing Reusable Windows Code in C++,* Addison-Wesley, Reading, MA, 1992.

DOD88   Military Standard for Defense System Software Development, *DOD-STD-2167A,* 29 February 1988.

ELL90   Ellis, M.A., and Stroustrup, B., *The Annotated C++ Reference Manual,* Addison-Wesley, Reading, MA, 1990.

ENC88   Encore Parallel Threads Manual, Encore Computer Corporation 724-06210, May 1988.

FAI93   Faison, T., Object-Oriented State Machines, *Software Development,* September 1993, p. 37.

FIC92   Fichman, R.G., and Kemerer, C.F., Object-Oriented and Conventional Analysis and Design Methodologies, *IEEE Computer,* October 1992, p.22.

FIE85   Field, A., *International Air Traffic Control,* Pergamon Press, Oxford, England, 1985.

FIR93   Firesmith, D.G., *Object-Oriented Requirements Analysis and Logical Design,* John Wiley, New York, NY, 1993.

FOR85   Ford, G. and Wiener, R., *Modula-2: A Software Development Approach,* John Wiley & Sons, New York, 1985.

GEH84   Gehani, N., *Ada Concurrent Programming,* Prentice-Hall, Englewood

Cliffs, NJ, 1984.

GEH88a Gehani, N.H., and Roome, W.D., Concurrent C++: concurrent programming with class(es), *Software Practices and Experience* (18) 12, 1988, p.1157

GEH88b Gehani, N.H.,*C: An Advanced Introduction*, Computer Science Press, Rockville, MD, 1988.

GIB90 Gibbs, S. et al., Class Management for Software Communities, *Comm. ACM*, September, 1990, p. 90.

GOL83 Goldberg, A., and Robson, D., *Smalltalk-80: The Language and Its Implementation*, Addison-Wesley, Reading, MA, 1983.

GOM84 Gomaa, H., A Software Design Method for Real-Time Systems, *Comm. ACM* Volume 27, Number 9, September, 1984.

GRA93 Graham, I., *Object-Oriented Methods*, Addison-Wesley, Reading, MA, 1993.

GRI92 Grimshaw, A.S., Easy-to-use object-oriented parallel processing with Mentat, Technical Report No. CS-92-32, Department of Computer Science, University of Virginia, Charlottesville, VA.

HAN90 Hanson, T.L., *The C++ Answer Book*, Addison-Wesley, Reading, MA, 1990.

HAR87 Harel, D., State Charts: A Visual Formalism for Complex Systems, *Science of Computer Programming*, Vol. 8, North-Holland, Amsterdam, 1987.

HAT87 Hatley, D.J., and Pirbhai, I.A., *Strategies for Real-Time System Specification*, Dorset House, New York, NY, 1987.

HEI94 Heintze, S., Mastering the C++ Construction Zone, *Software Development*, February 1994, p. 45.

HIN94 Hines, K., and Sanders, B., Communications Systems Design with Object Oriented Analysis/Recursive Design, *Object Magazine*, March-April, 1994.

HOA74 Hoare, C.A.R., Monitors: An Operating System Structuring Concept, *Comm. ACM*, Volume 17, Number 10, October 1974.

ISH92 Ishikawa, Y., et al., An Object-Oriented Real-Time Programming Language, *IEEE Computer*, October 1992, p.66.

References

JAC92	Jacobson, Ivar., et al., *Object-Oriented Software Engineering: A Use Case Driven Approach*, Addison-Wesley, Workingham, England, 1992.
JOR90	Jordan, D., Implementation Benefits of C++ Language Mechanisms, *Comm. of ACM*, September, 1990, pp. 61-64.
KAF90	Kafura, D., and Lee, K.H., ACT++: Building a Concurrent C++ with Actors, *Journal of Object-Oriented Programming*, May/June 1990, p.25.
KAL93	Kale, L.V., and Krishnan, S., CHARM++: a portable concurrent object-oriented system based on C++, OOPSLA'93, 1993.
KOE90	Koenig, A., and Stroustrup, B, Exception Handling for C++, *Journal of Object-Oriented Programming*, July/August 1990, p.16.
KOR90	Korson, Understanding Object-Oriented: A Unifying Paradigm, *Comm. ACM* Volume 33, Number 9, September, 1990.
LAN93	Lang, N., Shlaer-Mellor Object-Oriented Analysis Rules, *Software Engineering Notes*, ACM Press, Vol. 18, No. 1, January 1993.
LEE93	Lee, M.M., Case Study: Comparative Assessment of Methods, Object World, San Francisco, June 16, 1993.
LIP91	Lippman, S., *C++ Primer*, Second Edition, Addison-Wesley, Reading, MA, 1991.
LIS86	Liskov, B. and Guttag, J., *Abstraction and Specification in Program Development*, The MIT Press, Cambridge, MA, 1986.
MCM84	McMenamin, S.M. and Palmer, J.F., *Essential Systems Analysis*, Yourdon Press, NY, 1984.
MEL93	Mellor, S.J., The Shlaer-Mellor Method, Presentation at Hughes Aircraft Company Object-Week, El Segundo, CA, April 13, 1993.
MEY88	Meyer, B., *Object-oriented Software Construction*, Prentice Hall, New York, 1988.
MEY92	Meyers, S., *Effective C++*, Addison-Wesley, Reading, MA, 1992.
MIC92	*Microsoft Windows 3.1 Programmer's Reference, Volume 3*, Microsoft Press, Redman, WA, 1992.
MIL87	Mills, H., Box Structured Information Systems, *IBM Systems Journal*, Vol. 26, No. 4, 1987, pp. 395-413.
MON93	Monarchi, D.E., and Puhr, G.I., A Research Topology for Object-

Oriented Analysis and Design, *CACM*, September 1993, p. 35.

MUR93   Murray, R.B., *C++ Strategies and Tactics*, Addison-Wesley, Reading, MA, 1993.

NIE88   Nielsen, K.W. and Shumate, K.C., *Designing Large Real-Time Systems with Ada*, McGraw-Hill, New York, 1988.

NIE90   Nielsen, K.W., *Ada in Distributed Real-Time Systems*, McGraw-Hill, New York, NY, 1990.

NIE92   Nielsen, K.W., *Object-Oriented Design with Ada*, Bantam Books, New York, NY, 1992.

NOL90   Nolan, M.S., *Fundamentals of Air Traffic Control*, Wadsworth, Belmont, CA, 1990.

NOR92   Norton, P., and Yao, P.L., *Windows 3.1 Power Programming Techniques*, Second Edition, Bantam Books, New York, NY, 1992.

ODE92   Odell, J., and Martin, J., *Object-Oriented Analysis and Design*, Prentice Hall, 1992.

PAG80   Page-Jones, M., *The Practical Guide to Structured Systems Design*, Yourdon Press, New York, NY, 1980.

PAR72a   Parnas, D.L., On the Criteria To Be Used in Decomposing Systems Into Modules, *Comm. ACM* Volume 15, Number 12, December, 1972.

PAR72b   Parnas, D.L., A Technique for Software Module Specification with Examples, *Comm. ACM* Volume 15, Number 5, May, 1972.

PER90   Perry, D.E., and Kaiser, G.E., Adequate Testing and Object-Oriented Programming, *Journal of Object-Oriented Programming*, January/February '1990, p. 13.

PET92   Petzold, C., *Programming Windows 3.1*, Third Edition, Microsoft Press, Redmond, WA, 1992.

POR93   Porter, A., *C++ Programming for Windows*, Osborne, Berkeley, CA, 1993.

RAC94   Racko, R., Inside Inheritance, *Software Development*, May 1994, pp. 79-83.

RUM91   Rumbaugh, J. et al., *Object-Oriented Modeling and Design*, Prentice Hall, 1991.

References

SEL90	Seliger, R., Extending C++ to support remote procedure call, concurrency, exception handling, and garbage collection, Proceeding of 1990 USENIX C++ Conference, 241-264, 1990.
SHL88	Shlaer, S., and Mellor, S., *Object Lifecycles: Modeling the World in Data*, Yourdon Press, 1988.
SHL90	Shlaer, S., and Mellor, S., Recursive Design, *Computer Language*, March, 1990.
SHL92	Shlaer, S., and Mellor, S., *Object Lifecycles: Modeling the World in States*, Yourdon Press, 1992.
SHL93	Shlaer, S., et al., *Shlaer-Mellor Method*, 1993, Project Technology, Inc., 2560 Ninth Street, Suite 214, Berkeley, CA, 94710
SHO87	Shopiro, J.E., Extending the C++ Task System for Real-Time Control, *Proceedings of the USENIX C++ Workshop*, Santa Fe: USENIX Association Publishers, November 1987.
SHU92	Shumate, K. and Keller, M., *Software Specification and Design: A Disciplined Approach for Real-Time Systems*, John Wiley, New York, NY, 1992.
STE94	Steele, R.D., and Backes, P.G., Ada and Real-Time Robotics: Lessons Learned, *Computer*, April 1994, p. 49.
STR91	Stroustrup, B., *The C++ Programming Language*, Second Edition, Addison-Wesley, Reading, MA, 1991.
STR93	Stroustrup, B., Library Design Using C++, *C++ Report*, June 1993, p. 14.
SUN86	Remote Procedure Call Protocol Specification, Remote Procedure Call Programming Guide, and External Data Representation Protocol Specification, Sun Micro Systems, Mountain View, CA, 1986.
TOP94	Topper, A., Which OOA/D method is best?, *Object Magazine*, May 1994, p. 74.
UNI94	UnixWorld's *Open Computing*, page 20, February 1994.
WAR85	Ward, P.T., and Mellor, S.J., *Structured Development for Real-Time Systems*, Volumes 1-3, Yourdon Press, New York, NY, 1985.
WEG87	Wegner, P., The Object-Oriented Classification Paradigm, in *Research Directions in Object-Oriented Programming*, p. 479, eds. B.

Shriver and P. Wegner, The MIT Press, Cambridge, MA, 1987.

WIR90 Wirfs-Brock, R., et al., *Designing Object-Oriented Software*, Prentice Hall, Englewood Cliffs, NJ, 1992.

YAO94 Yao, P., *Borland C++ 4.0 Programming for Windows*, Random House, New York, NY, 1994.

YOU79 Yourdon, E., and Constantine, L.L., *Structured Design*, Prentice-Hall, Englewood Cliffs, NJ, 1979.

Index

A

Abbott 39
ABC++ 315
abstract base class 365
abstract class 347
abstract data type 44, 321
abstract objects 174
abstraction 41
abstraction by specification 43
access functions. 269
access operations 62
access to hidden data members 359
accounting system 16
ACT++ 311
actors 119, 180
actual parameters 349
Ada 19, 25, 281
Ada packages 101, 114
ADFDs 111
adopting OT methods 158
ADTs 44, 322
agents 119
aggregation 64, 123, 154, 194, 268, 274, 300, 329
air traffic control system 16, 24, 141, 236

algorithmic decomposition 7
analysis entity 8
analysis model 94, 193
analysis products 17
ANSI C 403
aperiodic task 128
API 384
apparent concurrency 17, 255
application domain 111
AppWindow 343
architectural domain 111
architecture context diagram 212
architecture diagrams 33
architecture dictionary 218
architecture interconnect specification 218
architecture modules 212, 218, 220
architecture templates 222
assignment operator 338
associating scenarios, objects, and subsystems 230
associations 67, 76
asynchronous
    communication 153
    functions 257
    mechanism 312
ATM application 40, 74, 141

attribute layer 126
attributes 56, 121, 242
automated teller machines 40
automatic inlining 368
automatic transitioning 33
auxiliary support functions 62

B

background processes 257
base object class 304
behavior axis 190
benefits of OT methods 132
binding 50
bitwise copy 334
black boxes 15, 174
blocks 99
Booch 39, 45
Booch method 104
Booch'93 104, 129
Borland C++ 277
bridge 111
broadcast 260
browsers 48, 133, 308
bug 265
"build" plan 14, 176
build structure 186
built-in types 44, 322
busy wait 267

C

C 25, 281
C++ 19, 39, 281
    class library 161, 233
    classes 101
    frameworks 306
    libraries 381
    real-time libraries 309
C++ Designer 103, 154
C++ RTOS library 309
C++ Task Library 309, 314
Cadre's TeamWork 119
call-by-reference 407

call-by-value 406
canned scenarios 20
canonical form 322
cardinalities 67, 104
CASE tools 8, 32, 137
catch block 376
catch statement 376
categories of exceptions 378
change units 98
character-wise copy 339
CHARM++ 311
checklists 175, 202
class 40, 59
    architecture 299
    categories 61, 156, 172, 174
    construction 355
    description 172
    design 294
    diagram 105, 114
    evaluations 268
    hierarchy 269
    interface 242, 297
    libraries 303
    model 74
    providers 293, 412
    structure 295
    structure chart 114
    users 293, 412
    variables 60, 70
class-based 282
class/object icon 122
classification 171
classification by association 108
client 58
    view 268
    window 389
client/server relation 44
client/server technology 37
client/server view 45
close temporal relation 330
cluster 18
clustering 113, 121, 126
Coad-Yourdon 122, 129

Index

coarse-grained objects 171
coding guidelines 415
cohesion 31, 128
collaborations 45, 119
collaboration graph 121
collection of data elements 324
commercial products 170, 174
common modules 137
communication 153
communication protocols 259
compilation units 51
complementary operations 268, 352
complete data hiding 294
complete set of operations 296
complex attribute 242
complexity of the class hierarchy 304
component testing 276
components 64
composition 64
computational class 61, 156
concrete data types 285, 322
concurrency
    model 13, 17, 234
    requirements 128
    support 311
Concurrent C 312
Concurrent C++ 312
concurrent elements 101
configurable components 15
configuration control 308
configuration item 16, 211
configuring step 221
connectionless communication 260
const
    modifier 421
    object 333
    type modifier 409
constant type specification 422
constructors 320, 331
consumer 153, 313
containing class 330
containment by reference 330
context diagram 141

contract 45, 51, 120, 392
control interrupts 101
control objects 95, 157, 191, 193, 196
controls 389
convoluted structures 286
cooperative multi-tasking programs 386
coordinator task 128
copy constructor 335, 338
coroutines 83
cost estimate 139
cost factors 207
coupling 29, 31, 42, 128
CRC cards 45, 108, 119, 393
creating classes 60, 293
creation of scenarios 239
critical data 128
critical section 253
critical time limits 257
customers 5
customer's views 14
cyclic process 109
    dependencies 267

D

dangling pointer 337
data abstraction 31, 43
data abstraction classes 61, 157
Data Acquisition Subsystem 218
data dictionary 121
data element 46
data flow diagram 7, 23
data hiding 262
    relaxed 294
data integrity 259
data modeling 61
data objects 42
data structures 293, 323
data-intensive applications 24, 222
deadlock 253
DEBUG flag 344
debugging phase 48, 276
declarations 368

decomposition 7, 40
deep copy 334
default constructor 333
default copy constructor 335
defensive programming practice 265
definition for an object 55
dependency diagram 113
derived classes 63
derived requirements 174, 192, 237
design
    artifacts 29
    evaluation 18, 118, 266
    goals 288
    icon 77, 145
    model 94
    of an ADT 415
    paradigms 12
    reviews 19, 298
    trade-offs 304
destructor 320, 343
    virtual 400
detailed design 295
Deutsch 181
development
    category 174
    process 3, 12
    time 7
device drivers 256
device interface class 61, 156
DFD 7, 23, 33, 199
dialog boxes 389
    modal 389
    modeless 389
distributed architecture 17, 82, 150
distributed system 210, 259
documentation 308
documenting scenarios 185
DoD protocol 261
domain
    analysis 14, 94, 165, 168
    chart 111
    expertise 389
    object model 94

dynamic 50
    behavior 33, 78
    binding 348
    events 253
dynamic models 12, 74, 88
    object model 78, 146
    late binding 50

E

Eiffel 39, 281
empty constructor 342
encapsulated entities 29
encapsulated object 29, 42, 262
encapsulation 41, 283
entity objects 95, 157, 191, 193, 195
entity relationship diagram 24
entity-driven 29
EPT/C++ 315
ERDs 24,
    33, 61, 111, 139, 157, 199, 236
error handling 264
error handling strategy 305
Ethernet 168
evaluation criteria 173
event analysis 186
event flows 114
event trace diagram 79, 147
exception
    declarations 372
    handlers 374, 376
        positioning of 380
exception handling 264, 302, 348, 371
    categories 265, 378
    strategy 377
    raising 373
exceptional conditions 284
executive 110
existing software 175
explicit casts 306
explicit concurrency 311
Extended C++ 312
extendible systems 210
extern "C" directive 421

Index

external system class 61, 156
extraction operators 411

F

fault tolerance 264, 284, 302, 348
feedback 18
file structure 274, 400
Firesmith 129
flag 46
Flight Management System 212
formal design reviews 266
formal parameters 349
Fortran 25
foundation classes 72, 294
FoxPro 14
frame-based 378
frameworks 72
friend 359
    classes and functions 113, 295
    of a class 361
    status 363, 400
function
    overloading 277, 408
    parameters 406, 408
    prototype 406
function-driven 29
functional
    approach 8
    classification 156
    cohesion 257
    coupling of objects 230
    decomposition 7
    models 88, 153

G

GDI 389
GDI device information 389
GDI draw abstractions 389
Gen-Spec 123
generalization 64
generic class 53, 349
genericity 52, 349

GFE 174
global data 368
good class 297
goto mechanism 302
Government Furnished Equipment 174
Graphical User Interface 41
Graphics Device Interface 389
GUI 41
guidelines 138
    for creating objects 199
    for partitioning 211
Guttag 32

H

hacking 5, 28, 206
handle 393
hardware architecture 227
    diagram 91
hardware nodes 82, 150
hardware-intensive systems 108
Harel 181
has-a 64, 268, 274
Hatley-Pirbhai 212, 216, 234
header file 51, 368
helping functions 269
heterogeneous
    container class 70
    hardware environment 216
    processors 259
heuristics 90
hidden data 42, 44
hierarchical decomposition 63
high cohesion 51
high level of reuse 308
high-level abstractions 175
homogeneous container 70
hwnd 342
hybrid strategy 274

I

identification of classes and objects

108, 156, 171
identification of objects 202
implementation domains 111
implementation phase 20, 273
implementor functions 269
implementor operations 62
implicit concurrency 311
in-house
    experts 14, 168
    product 174
    trainers 413
incremental development
    14, 51, 93, 142, 186, 285, 385
informal design review 267
information axis 190
information hiding 32, 42
information model 236
inheritance 30, 46, 154, 350, 419
    diagram 113
    relationship 299
    structure 269
initialization constructors 333
inline functions 351
inlining 411
insertion operators 411
instance 40
instance connections 124
instance variables 60
integration testing 276
inter-processor transfers 216
interaction diagrams 101
interconnected scenarios 181
interface objects 95,
    157, 191, 193, 194
interprocess communication 260
interprocess communication (IPC)
    mechanism 216, 260, 261
interrupts 128, 255
inverse functions 352
invocation
    of constructors 340
    of destructors 364
IPC 216, 260, 261

is–a 47, 268, 269
iterator 321

J

Jacobson 171, 191
Jacobson's OOSE 129, 141

K

key abstractions 12, 60, 389
kind-of 47
kitchen sink 270

L

LAN 82
language dependence 34, 139
language features 305
large systems 159
late binding 50
layered abstractions 12
layering of objects 330
legacy code 285
lessons learned 290
level of encapsulation 262
levels of information hiding 369
library of tasking primitives 314
Line Replaceable Units 209
link 58
linkage mechanism 285
Liskov 32, 39
Lisp 281
liveness property 253
loose coupling 44, 51
LRUs 209

M

Macintoshes 168
macros 422
maintenance 7, 41, 132
manager operations 62, 268
managing class libraries 308
MDI 384, 389

Index

Mealy notation 98
mean time between failures (MTBF) 265
medium-size system 159
member-wise copy 336
membership 64
memory leaks 337, 381
Mentat 311
mentor function 413
mentoring 205
menus 389
message
    abstraction 298
    class 326
message description document 220
message loop used by Windows 296, 386
message passing
    45, 153, 251, 258, 259, 283
metaclass 60, 70, 304
Microsoft Foundation Classes (MFC) 72, 295
Microsoft Visual C++ 277
mixin class 70
mixing structured and OT methods 136
modeling tools 74
models 12
modular 6
modular programming 31, 274
modularity 51
module 51, 90
    boundaries 90
monitor 257
    process 267
monolithic class 392
moving to C++ 403, 414
multi-threaded C++ programs 309
multicast communication 260
multiple design reviews 189
Multiple Document Interface 384, 389
multiple inheritance 46, 269
multiplicity 67, 88
multiprocessing 46
multiprocessing model 258
multitasking system 315
mutual exclusion 252, 267

N

name mangling 277, 408
new keywords 404
Nielsen 181
node 215
non-preemptable 255
non-preemptive 109, 386
non-resumptive 378
notation 154
noun phrase 8
number of processes 267

O

object 40
    classification 174
    communication diagram 114
    decomposition 77, 144
    diagram 106
    evaluation 176
    icons 76, 104
    layer 122
    model 74, 87
Object Modeling Technique 68, 75
object technology 37
object-based 282
object-oriented 282
    computing 39
    concepts 40
    decomposition 7
    design 39
    programming 32, 39
    techniques 6
object-orientedness 282
Objective Solutions' ObjectiveAnalyst 119
ObjectiveAnalyst 119
Objectory 93, 103, 192

ObjectWindows Library (OWL 2.0) 72, 295
OCM 119
OMT 87, 129
OMT notation 194
OMTool 103, 154
OOA 17
    classes 394
    products 288
OOA/RD 110, 129
OOD
    activity 262
    entities 394
    phase 19, 92
OODLE 113
OODTool 129
OOP 32, 274
    phase 396
OOSE 93, 129, 141
Open System Interconnect (OSI) 261
operational concepts 20, 207
operations 45, 56, 174
operator delete 344
operators istream and ostream 360
operators new and delete 412
ordinary constructor 332
organizational changes 403
orthogonal 136
OSI model 261
OT seminars 9
outside vendor 294
overflow exception 265
overloading 409
overriding 409

P

packaging 52
    of a reusable class library 308
pairwise functions 352
paradigm shift 30
parameter passing 45
parameterized class 53, 349
parameterized types 52, 349

partitioning 15, 111, 210
    activity 210
partitions 211
passed by value 335
Patient Monitoring Computer 224, 234
Pentium 168
performance issues 351
periodic 128
periodic function 257
persistent data 24
physical node 82, 221
Picking the "right" method 138
PMC 224
PNs 221
point to point 260
polling 267
polymorphism 30, 48, 284, 345
portability 287
PowerPC 168
preemptive 109, 255
presentation axis 190
priorities 128
private access 357
private derivation 358
private inheritance 328
problem domain 137
problems 133
procedural abstraction 41
procedural decomposition 7
procedural programming 30
process 18
    abstraction 18, 83, 253
    architecture 16
    diagram 108
    interactions 267
    selection rules 18, 256
    structure chart 83, 102, 151
    structuring 17
processing element (PE) 255
producer 153, 313
product line 160, 166, 211
product orientation 169
productivity 29, 131

Index

productivity gains 133
programming activity 274
programming paradigms 30
Prolog 281
proper classes 293
protected access 357, 358
protecting server software 266
prototypes 135
prototyping 14, 20, 207
public access 356
public inheritance 328
pure abstractions 73
pure virtual function 347, 365

Q

quality control 308
Quicken 14

R

rapid prototyping 7
Rational 110
re-raising the exception 380
real concurrency 255
real-time aspects 128
real-time structured design 151
real-time systems
    16, 26, 46, 102, 139, 284
real-world classes 157
real-world entities 12, 132
real-world names 173
real-world objects 7
recompilation 305, 368
recursive design 110
recycling machine 94, 185
reference counting 71
reference notation 407
relations 24
Remote Procedure Call 195
renumbering 224
resource leaks 381
responsibilities 45, 119
responsibility 45

responsibility-driven design 119
retrieval 352
return on investments 134
reusability 6, 40, 42, 52, 53, 196, 351
reusability in-the-large 14, 71, 132,
    159, 167
reusabilty - portability 287
reusable
    classes and member functions 349
    code 264
    components 169, 215, 233
    software 5
reuse 32, 166
    facility 413
    repository 159
    strategy 135, 159
"right" OT method 137
risk 158, 204
    areas 134
    reduction plan 14, 175
role class 61, 156
roles 199
Rose 103, 110
RPC 195, 261
RTC++ 315
RTSA 234
RTSD 151
rule-based development 32, 140
run-time
    efficiency 304
    overhead 128, 267
    penalties 303
    performance 343, 351

S

SA/SD 23, 28, 33
safety properties 252
scenario 180
    model 94
    analysis 183
    approach 180
    driven 93, 141, 189
    sequence diagram 186

schedulable entities 151
scheduling 413
screen objects 360
script diagrams 107
SDI 384
seamless transition 206
selection of classes 202
selection of processes 119
semaphores 102
separate base class 392
separate specification and implementation 283
sequencing of events 78
server 58
service
    chart 126
    domains 111, 118
    layer 126
    packages 98
SES's ObjectBench 119
shallow copy 335
Shape objects 348
shared data 45, 251, 259, 267
shared memory 283
Shlaer-Mellor method 110, 129, 140
Shumate-Keller 234
signals 153, 283
signatures 408
Simula 39, 281
single abstraction 44
single base class 392
Single Document Interface 384
single-thread program 250
singly-linked list 324
small systems 160
Smalltalk 39, 281
software
    certification 133
    configuration items 215
    design 16
    design document 19
    drivers 20
    fault tolerance 371

    product 4
    product line 5
    requirements analysis 239
    requirements specification 240
source files 51, 368
specialization 64, 327
SRS 240
standard notation 33
startup costs 206
starvation 253
state transition diagram 26, 80
states 56
static
    binding 50
    data members 366
    keyword 60, 70
    member functions 366
    model 33, 74, 75, 145
    references 49
    view 144
STD 26, 33, 80
stimulus-response 186
stopping criteria 32, 118, 140, 198
storage and retrieval system 176
strong cohesion 44
strong typing 283
Stroustrup 30
structs 323
StructSoft's TurboCASE 119
structure chart 25, 33
structured design 6, 30, 39
structured techniques 6
stubs 20
subclasses 46
subject layer 126
subsystems 15, 82, 121, 167, 198
    boundaries 90
    model 94
suitable data members 290
Sun/Unix workstations 168
SunPro WorkShop 277
superclasses 46
swap (x, y) function 407

Index

synchronization 85, 119
    mechanisms 153
    transactions 312, 313
system
    analysis 108
    architecture 90
    context diagram 212
    design 15, 209
    design document 16, 219
    design model 82, 150
    interaction diagrams 107
    requirements document 5
    requirements specification 15, 174, 209
    specification document 167
    view 141

T

task
    coordination 129
    object 314
    selection rules 128
tasking libraries 19
tasking model 19
TCP/IP communication 168, 261
TeamWork 119
templates 53, 274, 283, 349
temporal cohesion 257
test effort 275
test scripts 276
thread analysis 183
throw expression 373
throw list 373
time slice 128
time-critical, embedded system 222
time-ordered events 88
time-slicing 255
top-level DFD 141
total correctness 253
traceability 132, 188
traceability matrix 224, 247
train-the-trainers 138
training 138, 413

transactions 312
transient data 24
transition 289
    from analysis to design 287
transitioning 92, 126, 319
    activity 250
    between analysis and design 290
    from design 273
    guidelines 141
transparency 260
true concurrency 17
try block 376
TurboCASE 119
type checking 405
type of constructors 332
type safe linkage 408

U

unexpected derived class 359
unified notation 88
unifying notation 73
unnecessary exceptions 270
upgrades 288
use case model 180
use case driven 93
user interface class 61, 156
user-defined types 43, 321
users 180
using relationship 69, 289, 301, 330, 361

V

vague classes 202
variable number of parameters 408
vector abstraction 322
verb phrase 8
virtual
    destructor 342, 364, 418
    function 400
    machine 253
    member functions 327, 363
    nodes 211

specifier 50
visible operations 242
volatility 168

W

Ward-Mellor 234
whole-part paradigm 64, 123, 127
Window abstractions 389
window class 342
Windows 14, 342
    applications 3
    class 324
    for default processing 386
    library 383
    Notepad application 386
    programming 383
Windows.h 342
Wirfs-Brock 119
Word 14

X

XDR 195